The Financial History of the Bank for International Settlements

The Bank for International Settlements (BIS), founded in 1930, works as the "Bank for Central Banks." The BIS is an international forum where central bankers and officials gather to cope with international financial issues, and a bank which invests the funds of the member countries. This book is a historical study on the BIS, from its foundation to the 1970s. Using archival sources of the BIS and financial institutions of the member countries, this book aims to clarify how the BIS faced the challenges of contemporary international financial systems.

The book deals with following subjects: Why and how was the BIS founded? How did the BIS cope with the Great Depression in the 1930s? Was the BIS responsible for the looted gold incident during World War II? After the dissolution sentence at the Bretton Woods Conference in 1944, how did the BIS survive? How did the BIS act during the dollar crisis in the 1960s and the 1970s? A thorough analysis of the balance sheets supports the archival investigation on the above issues.

The BIS has been, and is still an institution which proposes an "alternative view": crisis manager under the Great Depression of the 1930s, peace feeler during World War II, market friendly bank in the golden age of the Keynesian interventionism, and crisis fighter during the recent world financial turmoil. Harmonizing the methodology of economic history, international finances and history of economic thoughts, the book traces the past events to the current world economy under financial crisis.

Kazuhiko Yago, Professor at Waseda University, Japan, works on banking history. He published a book on French public sector financial institution, revising his doctoral dissertation "L'épargne populaire comme fonds de placement public: Caisse des dépôts et consignations (1919–1939)" which he defended at Université Paris X in 1996.

Routledge studies in the modern world economy

The Financial History of the Bank for International Settlements

Kazuhiko Yago

Routledge
Taylor & Francis Group

LONDON AND NEW YORK

First published 2013
by Routledge
2 Park Square, Milton Park, Abingdon, Oxfordshire OX14 4RN

Simultaneously published in the USA and Canada
by Routledge
711 Third Avenue, New York, NY 10017

First issued in paperback 2015

Routledge is an imprint of the Taylor & Francis Group, an informa business

British Library Cataloguing in Publication Data
A catalogue record for this book is available from the British Library

Library of Congress Cataloging in Publication Data
Yago, Kazuhiko.
The financial history of the Bank for International Settlements /
Kazuhiko Yago.
    p. cm. – (Routledge studies in the modern world economy ; 111)
    Includes bibliographical references and index.
    1. Bank for International Settlements–History. 2. International finance–
    History. 3. Banks and banking, Central–History. I. Title.
    HG3881.5.B38Y34 2012
    332.1'5509–dc23   2012028006

ISBN 13: 978-0-415-70589-9 (pbk)
ISBN 13: 978-0-415-63524-0 (hbk)

Typeset in Times New Roman
by Wearset Ltd, Boldon, Tyne and Wear

The author acknowledges the Suntory Foundation for its financial support donated to the publication.

Contents

Figures

Tables

Foreword

Basel: a medieval city at the crossroads of civilization and ideas, where the Rhine originating in the Alps transforms into its vibrant middle course. This city, where Erasmus and Nietzsche stood on the university lectern and Hesse set his sights on the world of literature, also is known for the clarity of its church bells. As twilight gradually blackens the current of the Rhine, the sound of the bells ringing at the Münster and the St. Elizabeth Church rises into the European sky.

The primary subject of this book is the history of the Bank for International Settlements (BIS),[1] headquartered here in Basel.

The BIS is an international institution, founded in 1930 with the goal of resolving the reparations problems that arose following World War I. To date, it has functioned as a "forum" for the coordination and drafting of each country's financial policies. At the same time, as a joint-stock bank the BIS also takes deposits and makes investments. In this book, based on primary materials in the possession of the BIS and affiliated institutions, we will attempt to delineate the history of the BIS, starting with its founding in 1930, from an independent perspective. The focus of this study will be on the BIS's responses during the various epochs of prewar and postwar international financial history. The main topics of this book are the administration of German reparations, responding to global financial crises, design of postwar international currency systems, policy advice on settlement within the European region, contributions to European currency markets, responses to crises in the US dollar and the British pound and to the system of floating exchange rates, the origin of international bank supervision, and business expansion into Asia.

Let's review here the history of related studies. While until now historical studies of the BIS have been widespread in a number of areas[2] – such as its relation to the Nazis during World War II – there have been no studies for a long while that have provided an overview of the entire history of the BIS. In the early period of the BIS's history, first-rate reportage by contemporary journalists was published,[3] and the BIS itself published commemorative works,[4] but these did not address their subjects as historical studies. In addition, in the period of the BIS's founding a number of studies were published[5] including Paolo Baffi's detailed retrospective study,[6] and James Baker has attempted a theoretical approach to the contemporary BIS.[7] Each of these works has covered the BIS over a limited period of time. While BIS officials assembled an excellent brief history in 1999, it is merely an introduction.[8]

However, in 2005 *Central Bank Cooperation at the Bank for International Settlements, 1930–1973*, by editorial adviser Professor Gianni Toniolo, and Piet Clement, head of library, archives and research support at the BIS, was published.[9] This achievement by Toniolo and Clement is a voluminous book of more than 600 pages, putting to full use the internal materials of the BIS and truly is worthy of being called an official history. Some important studies followed Toniolo's work, focusing on central-bank cooperation.[10]

But why, and how, will we address the BIS in light of the above? Let's elaborate on the motives for this study, from the following four perspectives.

1 The BIS as a "venue" for cooperation between central banks

More than anything else, the BIS was a "venue" for central-bank cooperation. Toniolo's official history too expresses the role of the BIS straightforwardly as an institution that provided "valuable services in international banking and research" while serving also as a "meeting place."[11] Here, for the time being central-bank cooperation refers to cooperative relations for official and unofficial policy coordination by the central banks of each country in the running of international currency and financial systems in international markets. To provide support for these cooperative relations, the BIS has arranged meetings for central-bank governors, in which the governors of the central banks of leading nations gather in Basel for exchange of opinion and policy coordination. In addition, the BIS also has performed the important role of tracing in detail the currency and financial conditions of each country and serving as an accumulation point for information between central banks. But how has the BIS functioned as such a "venue"? That is the first perspective addressed in this book.

From this perspective, a variety of groups of problems becomes apparent. One of these is the issue of just what a central bank is to begin with.[12] Another is the major theme in international currency and financial history of how central banks have cooperated with each other since the establishment of the international gold standard in the nineteenth century.[13] The theme of why central banks cooperate with each other, or in what situations such cooperation takes place, also has been a subject of recent lively debate in domains such as international political economy and game theory. On this point, "costs" of creation and maintenance of international currency "regimes" such as the IMF are seen to be the standard for review. Perhaps the finest example of such debate in recent years is the debate between Barry Eichengreen and Marc Flandreau on central-bank cooperation.[14]

Even when restricting the subject to relations with the BIS, questions such as the following can be asked. How is the central-bank cooperation described above possible at the BIS? How do official and unofficial cooperative relations such as those of the IMF, the Group of Ten (G10), summits between the leaders of leading nations, or the Group of Seven (G7) differ from those coordinated by the BIS? Or, how "efficient" or "inefficient" has the BIS been among the various "venues"? Toniolo's official history too treats this issue of the evaluation of central-bank cooperation within the history of the BIS as the most important focal point.

In this book, we will attempt to meet face-to-face the research current described above concerning central-bank cooperation. However, this book will not attempt to use this or that indicator to measure the "success or failure" or the "efficiency" of cooperative relations on the BIS stage. While we recognize the importance of such a debate, what this book will attempt to address is the issue of "interconnectedness," concerning under what conditions central banks cooperate at the BIS and what kinds of subsequent conditions result from such cooperation. Now let's look at this approach in greater detail.

The BIS is a joint-stock company in which the governors of the central banks of leading nations serve as directors and each country's central bank is a shareholder. For this reason, final decision-making authority in the BIS is held by the central banks, and to this extent it could be said that the BIS is an organization subordinate to central-bank policies. However, a full-time secretariat is responsible for day-to-day BIS operations. This secretariat occasionally obtains information overwhelming that of the central banks and executes authority beyond the intentions of the countries. Put another way, while it represents the authority grounded in the currency sovereignty of each country, the BIS also is in an international void beyond the sovereignty of each country. A look at central-bank cooperation in the BIS from this perspective brings into relief the point in dispute of whether this has been active cooperation by the central banks themselves or the table has been set by something else – such as the Monetary and Economic Department that plays a central role in BIS theoretical activities. The actuality of a "venue" for central-bank cooperation has been that of a special stage mixing together the "actors" and the "stagehands" in the shadows. In this book, when addressing the issue of central-bank cooperation we will also attempt to isolate the "interconnectedness" that mixes the actors and coordinators of "cooperation," focusing on movements in the BIS Monetary and Economic Department in particular.

2 The BIS as a "bank"

At the same time as it promotes cooperation between central banks, the BIS also seeks to earn profits as a joint-stock bank and as a commercial bank. The Banking Department is in charge of the BIS's activities as a commercial bank. This two-sidedness of the BIS as both a "venue" for central-bank cooperation and a "business" on its own is a unique characteristic not seen in the IMF or the World Bank, both of which were founded later. In this book, as a second perspective for an unobstructed view of the history of the BIS, we will focus on the BIS as a bank, making clear the various phases of its collection of deposits and investment of funds and its distribution of net earnings.

This perspective concerns the following issue domains. The BIS collects deposits and invests them. The counterparties in these activities (i.e., depositors and borrowers) are the central banks of countries and other institutions both large and small. On this point, naturally interest is paid on deposits and loans. But does this interest satisfy the intents of depositors and borrowers? Furthermore, has no conflict of interest arisen with the central banks, who were shareholders at the same time, in decisions on these interest rates? As a bank, the BIS must tackle such issues in which it comes face-to-face with the normal course of events at a bank.

However, as an international institution the BIS also has come face-to-face with issues different than those faced by ordinary banks. Simply put, these issues involve gold. When international markets are in a phase risking a move toward contraction, such as the Great Depression or the postwar sterling crisis, BIS depositors – in other words, the central banks – withdraw their deposits. However, each country converts these withdrawn deposits into gold and, moreover, deposits it (as earmarks) in reliable institutions such as the BIS. Such earmarks deposited with the BIS are under the administration of the BIS although they do not show up on its financial statements. In this way, BIS deposits and earmarks have become an accumulation point for safe-haven currency in the event of a crisis in the international currency system.

The distribution of earnings is also important. As a joint-stock company, the BIS needs to distribute earnings to its shareholders, the central banks. At the same time, as a "venue" for cooperation between central banks it also needs to contribute to the stability of the international currency system. For this reason, the distribution of BIS profits involves various struggles between its motives as a profit-earning company and as an international public agency securing funding for the purpose of central-bank cooperation.

In this book, we will ask some basic questions about banking operations, through consideration of BIS financial statements. These include from where the BIS originally accepted deposits, where it invested these, how much income it earned and how it disposed of this income. While it is essential to rely on such an approach when attempting to address the actual state of BIS operations, the authors make several attempts to extend this approach beyond the history of management of a single bank. This is the historical method known as organizational history. A brief description follows.

Game theory and comparative institutional analysis have contributed to the research on central-bank cooperation seen above. However, historical research on management of a single organization, such as the BIS banking operations studied here, has again attracted attention as the historical research method known as organizational history, beginning in France in recent years. We say "again" because organizational history was a current in management history that first began in the 1970s, centered on Alfred Chandler and Louis Galambos, and the organizational history being conducted chiefly in France today is an extension of this 1970s research current.[15] However, while the past theories of Chandler and Galambos focused on large enterprises and bureaucratic organizations, current revived organizational history attaches importance to more flexible internal and external "networks."[16] Its scope too has expanded to the domains of mentality and business culture instead of just narrowly defined rationality and pursuit of short-term profit.[17]

Returning to the current subject of the BIS as a "bank," from an organizational history approach we can identify the following issues. How, and from where, did the ebbs and flows of the banking business impact BIS management? How did the ups and downs in the BIS as a "bank" affect cooperation between central banks? Of importance are the functions of the organization and network distributing management resources and the BIS business culture in which these are contained.

3 The history of twentieth-century economic thought: neoliberalism and Wicksellian economic thought

The third viewpoint of this book concerns economic thought. The BIS has continued its activities over a relatively long period of time, from the prewar through the postwar periods, and today it can be counted – along with organizations such as the International Red Cross and the International Labor Organization (ILO) – among the international institutions with the longest traditions. Thanks to this tradition, and to the tradition of strong ties with not just governments and central banks but also the private-sector banking world – the BIS has formed massive networks with contemporary economists and financial practitioners. The BIS was a major point of intersection between ideas on currency and credit in the twentieth century.

For example, Per Jacobsson, the first head of its monetary and economic department, was one of the central theorists in international finance through the 1960s and he was the starting point of a network linking others including Knut Wicksell and John Maynard Keynes. In addition, the talent that each country sent to the BIS as representatives or staff included theorists and practitioners in their prime at that time or in the near future. Examples included Henry Strakosch from Great Britain, Charles Kindleberger of the United States and Karl Blessing of Germany. In the documents left behind from their day-to-day duties can be read points of dispute surpassing discussions of policy narrowly defined, covering currency and credit theory and further spreading to the broader subjects of capitalism and contemporary society. In this way, the BIS had a presence as a major crossroads at which various economic ideas representative of the twentieth century blended together and diverged.

On this point, the economic ideas focused on in this book as having impacted the BIS are neoliberalism and Wicksellian economic thought. We will review each of these briefly here.

The former ideology, neoliberalism, is a current of thought in liberalism born in Europe upon reflection on twentieth-century liberalism. As is well-known, its scope is quite broad. It calls to mind the neoliberalism that began in Britain at the turn of the century, the new liberalism that attempted to move liberalism in the exact opposite direction and the *neolibéralisme* that appeared in France at the end of the 1930s. Broadly defined, neoliberalism also can be said to include the Austrian school of economists and the German *Ordo-Liberalismus*, which showed a complex relation to these schools of thought. In this way, although it included numerous branches and variants, neoliberalism had a major impact on the postwar world.[18] Generally speaking, neoliberalism is understood to link the economic theories and thought of Friedrich von Hayek, Lionel Robbins and Milton Friedman. But in tracing the historical roots of this school of thought – on subjects such as the roles of national government and responses to labor and social issues – it should be seen as a current including a broader range of ideas. It is this "broadly defined" neoliberalism that impacted the BIS.

The other school of thought, Wicksellian economic thought, is an ideology and policy theory based on the monetary economic analysis and dynamic dise-quilibrium economics of Knut Wicksell, a Swedish economist active from the nineteenth through the twentieth centuries.[19] While nineteenth-century econom-ics was unable for a long time to break free from the spell of the "Veil of Money," within such economics it was Wicksell who explicitly positioned within this structure the concept of monetary equilibrium as distinct from real equilibrium. While Wicksell's theory would later be continued and further developed by Keynes into his theory of liquidity preference, Wicksell himself was close to Eugen von Böhm-Bawerk, and his theory contained aspects that were connected to the neoliberalism of the Austrian school.

Leaving the theoretical structures of each economic school of thought to the main text, what should be emphasized here is the fact that these economic ideas deeply permeated among those responsible for BIS policy, and that the set of eco-nomic ideas known as "neoliberalism" and "Wicksellian" economic thought differ subtly from the conflict generally spoken of as between "market" and "govern-ment" or between "market fundamentalism" and "Keynesianism." While grounded in these currents of economic thought that can be said to have been born in Europe, the central bank personnel gathered at the BIS and BIS officials squared off against the Nazism and socialism that swept the prewar world and the thought and theories of the American Keynesians based at the IMF in the postwar period.

The period from the founding of the BIS (1930) through the mid-1970s, for which primary materials are available for viewing, makes up the less than 50 years of BIS history covered in this book and accounts for less than one-half of the twentieth century. The champions of economic ideas that prepared their own individual responses to the issues of the twentieth century continue to live within the BIS. The author attempts to depict the way this history of the BIS goes back to before its founding and has a certain continuity.

4 The history of the BIS as a "story of individuals"

Until now, we have discussed the three perspectives of central-bank cooperation, bank management and economic thought. The fourth perspective posited by this book should, in a sense, be positioned higher than the above perspectives. In brief, this is the history of the people who gathered at the BIS.

While they were specially chosen as persons of exceptional talent from each of their countries, occasionally they were excluded from the policy mainstream of their central banks. In the policy proposal documents left behind by these "non-mainstream elites," strong criticism of political powers including those of their own countries and alternative ideas clearly ahead of their times stand out. Furthermore, perusal of primary materials such as their journals and letters seems to show slices of their lives, which were not necessarily happy ones. The first general manager, Pierre Quesnay, who met with an untimely death; Leon Fraser, who came from the American banking world and rose to the position of BIS president in the prewar period but would criticize the Bretton Woods Accord after the war; Milton Gilbert, the second head of the Monetary and Economic Department, an American who continued to criticize thoroughly his country's postwar dollar policies – these BIS officials, behind the scenes of the spectacle of international finance, continued to communicate their own unique messages while also mixing with contemporary economic thought.

How should their personal histories be connected to the history of the BIS? On this point the author keeps in mind the practice of prosopography, an inheritor of the French tradition of corroborative history. This involves throwing into relief the characteristics of a specific historical "situation," such as "those responsible for the network" that formed at the BIS, instead of simply investigating the work histories and family lines of various individuals. Prosopography is a method that also is linked to that of organizational history touched on above, focusing on the points of what personal aptitudes are, or are not, welcomed by the organization. From this perspective, this book looks in particular at the group of top management on the operational side of the BIS – its general managers and members of management at the level of department heads, such as the heads of the Monetary and Economic Department and the heads of the Banking Department.

Indeed, this book will not attempt to calculate some average value through statistical analysis of their histories and the organizations from which they came. Isn't the truly important thing the human image, without fitting it into this or that methodology? We will look at the thoughts, actions and unachieved plans of these BIS personnel, as they coordinated cooperation between central banks, looked closely at financial markets in each country, or exchanged private letters with contemporary economic idealists. The final goal of this book is to construct a unified BIS history combining a variety of methodological perspectives, in particular telling the story of the twentieth century personified by the people of the BIS.

This book takes the structure of a complete history from the perspective described above. Chapter 1 examines the issues surrounding the establishment of the BIS, while Chapter 2 looks at the depression of the 1930s and Chapter 3 the World War II period. Chapter 4 examines the process, during the postwar recovery period, of rehabilitation of the BIS, which at one point was pronounced ready for liquidation, and Chapter 5 addresses the background of the international regulatory structure proposed in response to the sudden rise in Eurocurrency markets.

The bells are ringing. Now, let's visit twentieth-century Europe.

Abbreviations

BIS	Bank for International Settlements
CDC	Caisse des Dépôts et Consignations
ECA	Economic Cooperation Administration
EEC	European Economic Community
EMA	European Monetary Agreement
EPU	European Payments Union
FRB	Federal Reserve Board
FRBNY	Federal Reserve Bank of New York Archives
NARA	United States National Archives and Records Administration
OECD	Organization for Economic Co-operation and Development
OEEC	Organization for European Economic Cooperation
ROA	Return on assets
ROE	Return on equity
WP3	Working Party 3

1 The founding of the Bank for International Settlements

A "commercial bank," or a "bank for central banks"?

In 1929, representatives of the great powers of the time gathered in the famous Southern German health resort town of Baden-Baden. The purpose of this meeting was to decide on the statutes of the BIS and begin its banking operations. The BIS founding committee, generally known as the Baden-Baden Committee, was made up of representatives of the central banks and governments of Great Britain and France, the primary winners of World War I; Germany, which had suffered a crushing defeat in that war; and Belgium, Italy, the United States and Japan. In this meeting, complicated and inscrutable diplomatic negotiations would unfold. On October 23, in the midst of this conference, the New York Stock Exchange crashed. At the Baden-Baden Committee, it was a female typist accompanying the US delegation who first responded to this news of the outbreak of panic.[1] This was the true moment of inception of the BIS, as the focus of international policies and economics began to move from the issue of reparations and war bonds to a global panic.

The main subject of this chapter is the history of the birth of the BIS, starting with the negotiations at Baden-Baden and continuing through a number of trials. In general, the background of the founding of the BIS is understood as follows. After World War I, the interests between the allies were complicated as at the two extremes France took a hard line on demanding reparations from Germany, while the United States, against a backdrop of direct investment in Germany, adopted a position somewhat more amenable to appeasement. To break free from these circumstances, the Dawes Plan was approved first, under which reparations were paid over time. However, Germany fell behind in payment of reparations due to domestic inflation and changes in the international situation. The Young Plan was proposed to remedy this situation thoroughly. The core of this plan was the securitization of claims on reparations from Germany. If the Young Plan were to be realized, there would be a need for a bank to issue and underwrite such securities. The BIS was founded in 1930 as the bank for that purpose.

However, behind this founding of the BIS are some lesser known points of dispute. While the BIS was established as an institution to address the reparations problem as described above, its operations – above and beyond the intentions of the countries that took part in its founding – later would spread to cover a very broad scope. In addition, in the founding of the BIS it was argued that it should be linked to plans for reforming the international currency and financial systems as a whole instead of just problems with reparations. What's more, participants in this controversy included not just the authorities of the leading nations but also members of a new stream in economics, such as John Maynard Keynes, and the power of the left-wing labor movement of the time. The goal of this chapter is to elucidate these points of dispute based on primary materials.

Below, Section 1 will consider the controversies surrounding the founding of the BIS in connection with plans for reforming the international currency and financial systems as a whole following World War I. Section 2 will examine the direct background of the founding of the BIS – that is, its connection with the issue of German reparations. Section 3 will take a look at the design of the new system after the decision was made to establish the BIS along the process of the establishment its statutes. Section 4 will scrutinize the statutes and the BIS's structure. Here, the author's intent is to discern the starting point at which the BIS grew into an "international bank" instead of just an "institution for handling reparations." Section 5 will elucidate the actual conditions of the BIS's business, through scrutiny of BIS financial statements. Section 6 concludes.

1   Various reform plans: central-bank cooperation and a "financial utopia"

Following World War I, each country adopted a gold exchange standard and strived to economize on gold reserves to address bonds balances that had swelled during the war. Some countries even were forced to review prewar par values. Internationally as well, there was an even greater need for cooperation between nations to achieve stability in exchange rates than in the past.

A variety of reform plans was announced to achieve this new postwar reality. The various proposals that would bear fruit in the founding of the BIS were born from the flow of these debates on reforming the international currency and financial systems. The focal point of debate was cooperation between central banks as a means of international collaboration.

Central-bank cooperation in theory and practice

How did central-bank cooperation start? Looking solely at the period following World War I – and according to the words of BIS officials of the time themselves – it began with provision of credit between central banks to stabilize currencies in the 1920s. According to Roger Auboin, who propounds this view, this experience bore fruit in Article 3 of the BIS statutes, which called on the BIS to "promote the co-operation of central banks."[2] According to another BIS official, the central issues in postwar international finance were the problem of German reparations and the management of the gold exchange standard, and central-bank cooperation began in order to address this issue.[3]

However, what should be noted here is the fact that a debate on further creation of a common currency and an international bank developed from the above practice of central-bank cooperation – or even well in advance of such cooperation. Here too, observations by BIS officials shows that in 1913, during World War I, Guillaume Otswald advocated an international *"grammor"* for gold transactions, and in 1914 Faithfull Begg proposed the accumulation of each country's metal reserves in the leading financial centers. In 1922, Montagu Norman, the governor of the Bank of England, argued for convening international conferences of central banks, and in 1927 Pierre Quesnay, head of the Banque de France's Economic Research Institute, and Harry Siepmann of the Bank of England proposed the establishment of an "Association of European Central Banks [*Association des Banques Centrales de l'Europe*]."[4] This last proposal, for an "Association of European Central Banks," in particular is very close to the concept of the BIS that would materialize three years later, and its advocate Quesnay would become the first BIS general manager.

Proposals such as those calling for monetary union, along with the establishment of the League of Nations, strongly reflect the idealism that appeared after the end of World War I. It is highly interesting that these plans, also referred to as "financial utopianism," appeared at the same time as the debate on cooperation between central banks. However, the ultimate objective of each of these plans was the stabilization of exchange rates, which were in confusion following the war. Put another way, the main goal was the stabilization of the framework for international settlement, while the provision of credit was restricted to transactions between central banks.

The plans of the socialists and radicals: Blum, Auriol and Mendès-France

However, the reform plans that led to the founding of the BIS included another – not very well-known – utopian plan. This was a plan for reforming the international currency system advocated by the socialists and radicals, and by the French left and center.

The left-wing plan was proposed by Léon Blum and Vincent Auriol. As is well known, these two were the leaders of the Popular Front that took the government of France in 1936, and were politicians in the Socialist Party that rose to power in post World War II France as well.[5]

Blum and Auriol saw the international currency issues following World War I not only to consist of the reparations problem and disorder in exchange rates, but also to be linked to issues of domestic recovery from the destruction of the war. For this reason, together with the commercialization of German reparation payments and the rectification of international disparities, they advocated the establishment of an international financial institution for reconstruction purposes. French socialists, including Blum, were opposed to demanding excessive reparations from Germany in the 1921 Conference of London and, in solidarity with German social democrats including Rudolf Hilferding, called for cooler negotiations on reparations and Europe-wide postwar reconstruction. Having read articles of the time critical of demanding reparations from Germany, such as

Keynes' *Economic Consequences of the Peace*, Blum also advocated a policy of respecting "the various normal conditions of production in all related countries."[6] The bulk of this proposal was formalized in a socialist and labor-movement conference held in Amsterdam in 1922 and can be said also to have affected the decision of the Genoa Conference held that same year. Blum wrote, "Amsterdam, that is swift payment of reparations," "Reparations under Amsterdam, that is an attempt to maximize payment through payment in kind and in labor, and to reduce payment of funds accordingly," and "Amsterdam, that is payment covered by a broad-ranging trust in which all nations take part, without intervention of international finance [*finance cosmopolite*]."[7] Furthermore, in connection with the BIS, the important parts of this proposal were realized in the Young Committee's meeting in Paris, described below. In this Blum–Auriol proposal can be seen the plan for reforms under which an international bank in charge of international settlement also would, at the same time, provide credit – not just to stabilize exchange rates but also for large-scale projects such as postwar reconstruction.

Another BIS-related utopian theory was proposed by the radicals. This was the argument by Pierre Mendès-France, who at the time of the BIS's founding was distinguishing himself as a young intellectual and politician, for a "United States of Europe." As is well-known, Mendès-France was a politician drawing on the currents of the French moderate left and Christian democrats, who would become a leading figure in French politics, for example leading the way to a ceasefire in Indochina as prime minister after World War II.

In 1930, the year the BIS was founded, Mendès-France published a pamphlet entitled "*La Banque Internationale.*" As used here, "*La Banque Internationale*" referred to the BIS, and this pamphlet summarized the controversies about the BIS and argued for an ideal form for the BIS. The pamphlet's subtitle was *Contribution à l'étude du problème des Etats-Unis d'Europe* [A contribution to the study of the issue of the United States of Europe], clearly indicating the author's belief that the BIS should aim toward the formation of such a "United States of Europe." It declared the need to "build a new, a rational, organized, harmonious Europe."[8] In this context, Mendès-France expressed the difficulties of the Baden-Baden Committee in the following aphorism: "The organization they attempted to establish was nothing other than the federal bank of a federation that did not yet exist."[9] Specifically speaking, the BIS as a "federal bank," as imagined here, is an organization akin to that of the Federal Reserve Board (FRB) of the United States of America. This was the argument that the BIS should be planned as a "venue for cooperation between central banks" to avoid the apprehension that would develop among part of public opinion as described below that the BIS would become the "world's central bank." This Mendès-France idea of setting up the BIS as a "bank for the United States of Europe," while different in flavor from the left-wing ideas of Blum and Auriol seen above, anticipated the BIS of the future, which was to take shape as a "European institution."

It is interesting that the BIS as the "bank of the United States of Europe" was imagined in Mendès-France's plan as an institution that would proactively create and provide credit: "The BIS will issue a '*monnaie d'écritures*' [ledger currency], since it will function as a settlement agency through current accounts, clearing of bills, and checks and transfers." "As stated in Article 22 paragraph d of the Statutes, the BIS is to 'make advances to or borrow from central banks against gold, bills of exchange and other short-term obligations of prime liquidity or other approved securities'." "The BIS also needs to carry out supervision to ensure that each country's central bank does not waste credit."[10] Indeed, these interpretations were not unique to Mendès-France but were made public by the BIS authority after the statutes were finalized. However, it is worth paying attention to this argument emphasizing the course of action of setting out to provide international credit, greatly exceeding the initial framework of an "institution for handling the reparations problem," from before the BIS began operation. As described below, BIS officials too developed at the time arguments largely overlapping with this Mendès-France plan to provide credit. It also seems important that on the point of the provision of credit, Mendès-France's utopian vision of a "bank of the United States of Europe" employs a logical structure similar to that of Blum and Auriol's socialist plan outlined above. The ideas of the French left and center were not just utopian visions but also firmly affected the actual conditions of the time.

2 The negotiation in establishment of the BIS: behind closed doors and public opinion

Negotiations on establishing the BIS began in January 1929. At this time, a specialist committee on the problem of German reparations met in a Paris hotel to deliberate on a new proposal known as the Young Plan. This specialist committee put together a proposal including the establishment of a new bank, the BIS, and this proposal bore fruit in the form of the Hague Convention, signed in August 1929. In response to the Hague Convention, in October 1929 design of the system of the new bank began in Baden-Baden. The so-called Baden-Baden Committee, officially entitled the "Organization Committee of the Bank for International Settlements," put the finishing touches on the draft BIS Statutes, and in January 1930 the convention establishing the BIS, including these draft Statutes, was signed. Thus established, the BIS began operation in May 1930 in Basel.

Below, while tracing the path of these negotiations, we also will consider movements in public opinion over the same times: the opinions presented in the media of the time such as economic journals and newspapers bring up important points of dispute in looking at the later developments at the BIS.

The start of the Young Committee's Paris meeting

First, let's take a look at the Young Committee's Paris meeting, where the founding of the BIS was first proposed. When this meeting was convened in 1929, two proposals had already been made concerning the handling of the reparations problems. One of these was from Emile Francqui of the National Bank of Belgium, the other from Hjalmar Schacht of the Reichsbank of Germany. Each of these proposals advocated the establishment of an institution to distribute credit internationally in connection with the reparations problems.[11]

It was on March 4, 1929 that the idea of establishing an international institution first appeared in the Paris meeting. At that time, there was unity behind the idea of establishing such an institution. The proposal to establish an international institution was made by four attendees: US representatives Walter Stewart and Randolph Burgess together with German representative Schacht and French representative Quesnay, both mentioned above.[12] However, when deliberations began two days later, the idea of establishing an international institution covered in these proposals was the target of severe criticism. At the March 6 meeting, the point of whether handling the reparations problems required an international institution in the first place was debated. While Sir Josiah Stamp of the Bank of England first agreed with the proposal to establish a new bank, Alberto Pirelli of the Bank of Italy was opposed to the idea. The reason for this opposition was the fact that while the establishment of a new institution required cooperation between central banks, this had already become a "large, difficult problem." Kengo Mori, sent to the meeting from Japan's Ministry of Finance, also called for caution, adopting a point of view close to that of Pirelli. However, Schacht from the Reichsbank and US representative John Pierpont Morgan rallied back from this opposition. They insisted that it was impossible to separate the resolution of reparations problems from the establishment of an international institution.[13] In the end, it was Stamp from the Bank of England who took leadership of the day's discussions, backed by "theories and plans which had developed at the Bank of England." This was also an idea – an institution for easy settlement of currency trades – with a focus on "improvements in the working of the gold standard."[14] However, at the same time Schacht, who backed up the arguments supporting the establishment of a new bank, as described below supported Stamp from a somewhat different point of view.

Two days later on March 8, committee chairman Young, who chaired the Paris meeting, pointed to three possibilities concerning the form of the new international institution. These were (1) as a "trustee" for payment of reparations in kind, (2) as a "central institution for countries' banks of issue," and (3) as a "trustee organization." While the wording was somewhat vague, the content of this Young Plan positioned the new bank as a trustee for the reparations problem – and as a passive institution for that purpose only. In response, even Pirelli of the Bank of Italy, who had led the vanguard of earlier opposition, reluctantly decided to support this proposal, noting,

> I feel like somebody who has been too late to leave the ball and as a result is unable to choose the umbrella he prefers. In my case, I do not have the option of choosing the argument I prefer.[15]

As a result, the consensus reached at this time was to create the new bank as a trustee. Two days later on March 10, this agreement was announced as the statement of the Young Committee. The committee itself positioned this statement as "a purely tentative proposal for the organisation of a new International Bank" and stated, concerning the new bank, that it would function as a "trustee" while at the same time serving as "an essential intermediary between all existing central and issuing banks" for the purposes of underwriting and sale of securities related to payment of German reparations. It also declared that the new bank would "receive both clearing and investment deposits" and serve as "a reservoir of foreign exchange."[16]

When viewed in terms of the process of negotiations to this point, this statement was quite commonplace. However, the statement aroused suspicion in – according to the prominent contemporary economics journalist Paul Einzig – "a section of public opinion." It was said that the Young Committee, "having arrived at a deadlock upon the task for which it was summoned" had been "trying to save appearances by producing an agreement on a side issue."[17] But from where did these suspicions arise? Next let's take a look at the kind of public opinion that was formed in parallel to the negotiations behind closed doors toward the establishment of the BIS.

A change in public opinion: wariness of a super bank

For now, we will take a look at how the debate in the Young Committee, including the proposed establishment of the BIS, was received in typical economics journalism in France, the United States and Britain.

Narrowly speaking, the earliest response appeared in the French economics journal *L'Economiste Français.* This article, appearing six days after the Young Committee's statement and written by the journal's editor-in-chief André Liesse, was skeptical about the roles of the new bank. Citing as an example the credit operations related to delivery of reparations in kind touched upon in the Young Committee's statement, Liesse argued that the new bank proposed by the committee "is likely to become a super-bank, which the statement refers in order to negate it." Liesse also said that this bank "should be treated with caution, to ensure it does not become an axis of excessively close cooperation."[18]

Similar skepticism appeared in the United States as well. An article in the *Commercial and Financial Chronicle*, a weekly economics and finance journal published in New York, warned that the proposed new bank was "to promote an era of ease through artificial means and by resort to inflationary measures" This article was headlined, "The proposed International Bank – the Federal Reserve should not participate."[19] The next week's issue of this same journal criticized the participation of the FRB's representative Burgess, mentioned above, in negotiations from the stage of planning the establishment of the BIS, arguing passionately that "why should the Federal Reserve give paramount consideration to things abroad, when the situation is so critical at home?"[20]

But not all public opinion was skeptical of the BIS. The traditional British financial journal the *Banker* took a clear moderate position on the statement's proposal. An anonymous article in the *Banker* criticized both extremes on the

Young Committee's statement. It called these extremes "idealists" on one hand, who wanted to build a "League of Nations Bank," and "nationalists" on the other, who would make no realistic attempt to address the reparations problem. The article also envisioned a situation in which each nation's central bank would become a branch of an international bank and argued that even in such a case the new bank would not be a "superbank."[21] This issue of the *Banker* also featured Joseph Caillaux, a leading French politician of the time who also had served as finance minister, who wrote of the Young Committee's statement that the activities of the proposed new bank "will have a wider range than those of a mere connecting link between the banks of issue," and that such operations should be restricted to the range of issues of debt between member nations, as what could be called a "Bank of Europe."[22]

A turning point in the Paris meeting: the BIS capital and shareholder composition

While public opinion was seething on the subject of the Young Committee's statement, the next phase came into view in the Paris meeting. A new dispute began in the meeting on the subject of the nature of the new bank that should be created. The dispute began on the point of how to structure the capital and shareholders of the new bank. This dispute began to spread to the inflationary nature of the "super-bank" feared in the journalism described above, and this would bring the Paris meeting to a major turning point. Let's look at this course of events, which is not addressed in traditional research on the subject, as it developed over time.

The dispute began March 11, 1929. The fuse was lit by Schacht of the Reichsbank, who, while accepting the main point of the Young Committee's statement – that the new institution would be a trustee in connection with the reparations problem – argued the following concerning the issue of the capital structure of the new bank: "I have no intention to insist upon the credit-generation system [of the 'new bank'] from the start. However, I would like this to remain a possibility for the future."[23] In the statement, the fact that the new institution, intended as a "trustee," would be responsible for "generating credit" – as was warned of in public opinion – is a major turning point. At the same time, Schacht argued the following four points concerning the sources of funding for the new bank: (1) sale of equity shares in the new bank to the public with restrictions; (2) acceptance of deposits from each country's central bank; (3) payment of German reparations; and (4) transfer of the profits of the new bank.[24]

This Schacht proposal faced immediate opposition. Emile Moreau, the governor of the Banque de France, criticized the Schacht proposal as an impediment to the independence of each country's central bank. Regarding the credit operations argued for by Schacht, Moreau argued that there was a need for limits on the "risk of inflation" in light of the statutes of each nation's bank of issue. He also pointed to the public offering of shares in the new bank in the Schacht proposal as a problem. Governor Stamp of the Bank of England also touched on the issue of public offering of shares, articulating the concern that once shares were offered for sale to the public the new bank would be required to guarantee dividends. In the end, at this time the Schacht proposal was defeated in the Young Committee.[25] Issues concerning the capital of the new bank would be later deliberated on in a working group led by Lord Revelstoke.

Two days later, on March 13, the process of deliberations in the Revelstoke working group was brought to the Young Committee. Its findings were that the new bank should have capital of $100 million, only countries' banks of issue responding to the offering of shares would take part in bank decision-making, and the impact of each country's government would be eliminated. This proposal was approved by the committee and later bore fruit in the form of the BIS Statutes.[26] In this process of deliberations in the Young Committee, Schacht's argument – that shares should be sold to the public and the new bank should have a credit-generating function – was defeated, and the BIS was envisioned as a venue for "cooperation between central banks," with only central banks participating in management and governmental pressure eliminated.

After addressing these issues of the new bank, the Young Committee began discussion of the pending problem of payment of reparations. Later negotiations became very difficult, and in the middle of negotiations on April 19 Lord Revelstoke unfortunately died suddenly. Final agreement was reached on April 23, and the agreement announced on June 7 came to be known as the Young Plan.[27] Looking back in later years on the process of negotiating the Young Plan, Charles Addis said that the British hoped the Young Plan would create the BIS to reduce the amount of German reparations. In the end, the level of reduction in reparations was limited, and "the hopes founded on the Dawes and Young Plans are melted into air – into thin air; only the BIS remains."[28]

This Young Plan described the new bank that would become the BIS as follows: This "institution with banking functions" would have two clearly differentiated functions. The first would be its "essential or obligatory functions" for transfer of reparations, while the second would be its "auxiliary or permissive functions" in credit and deposit-taking operations. These credit and deposit-taking operations should be noted here. As described above, these operations proposed by Schacht had been rejected in March in the deliberations of the Young Committee. However, they had been restored, albeit as "auxiliary or permissive," in the plan announced in April. While there are a number of explanations for how this occurred, none of them has been successfully backed by documentary materials. However, as the contemporary Einzig noted, "no clear distinction" was possible between these two functions.[29] The starting point of the BIS, which though begun as a bank to handle the reparations problem later saw these "auxiliary or permissive operations" grow into its main lines of operations, was within the process of these Young Committee negotiations held behind closed doors.

Public opinion following the announcement of the Young Plan: criticism of "banking functions" and "managed currency"

Once the Young Plan was announced in June 1929, the world of journalism was filled with voices criticizing the new bank. The British *Banker's Magazine* described the new bank proposed by the Young Plan as a "super central bank" and expressed the apprehension that it "might in any way impair the pre-eminence which was hitherto enjoyed by London as the banking and financial centre of the world."[30] Another British journal, the *Banker*, also sounded the alarm about the expansion of the operations of the new bank, stating that even if the Young Plan attempted to restrict the operations of the new bank, "in practice it is likely to outgrow these restrictions." The same journal also stated that "one of the principal tasks of the new bank will be to become an international clearing house for gold."[31]

While these British publications warned of expansion of the domain of the new bank's operations, the tone of the argument in France was more complicated. The journal *L'Economiste Français* said that while the new bank initially had been thought of as a bank solely for the purpose of payment of reparations, soon after it was likely to become "*la banque centrale du globe.*" It also speculated that the business of buying and selling bonds, which was approved for this bank in the Young Plan, was adopted due to the impact of "deceptive theories of managed currency."[32]

The above British and French journalism had in common the forecast that the new bank – at this time, the name "Bank for International Settlements" already had taken hold – likely would not just handle reparations but embark on diverse credit operations as well. If not over the short term, this projection would prove accurate over the long term.

Indeed, concerning the international interests leading the way to establishment of the new bank, the journalistic debate did not venture beyond speculation. The British *Banker's Magazine* was suspicious of French and German "financial power."[33] In contrast, *L'Economiste Français* insisted on the impact of the US representatives, backed by New York bankers.[34] These observations, which could even be referred to as international "conspiracy" theories, developed against the backdrop of international relations following the end of World War I. On the other hand, the ideas of the forces behind the "financial utopianism" discussed above in Section 1 do not appear to have been on the radar screen of this financial journalism.

Later, negotiations on the establishment of the BIS would at last reach the final phase. As described above, the Young Plan discussed here was signed on August 31, 1929 as the Hague Convention. On October 3 of the same year, representatives of the seven countries that would found the new bank (Great Britain, France, Germany, Belgium, Italy, the United States and Japan) would meet in Baden-Baden as the "Organization Committee of the BIS." This committee was chaired by Jackson Reynolds, the president of the First National Bank of New York. Next, let's take a look at this Baden-Baden meeting, in which deliberations took place in the midst of the Depression.

3 Designing the BIS system: the Baden-Baden meeting

The Baden-Baden meeting featured an exchange of opinions among represent-atives of nations in attendance on the draft BIS Statutes that already had been prepared in the Young Committee. Japan's eligibility to participate was also a subject of concern (See Chapter 2). Here, we will look at the developments in this meeting focusing on points of dispute that would have major impacts on the form the BIS later would take: how Treasury bills should be traded, the currency of accounting and the location of the headquarters.

Article 22 of the draft BIS Statutes: BIS trading in Treasury bills

We will begin with a look at the issue of BIS trading in Treasury bills. This debate began October 17, 1929. Article 22 of the draft statutes prepared by the Young Committee permitted the BIS to purchase Treasury bills issued by each national government. Another draft Statue, Article 26, prohibited lending to national governments. Since the purchase of Treasury bills constitutes an "indi-rect form of lending," some uncertainty was apparent about Article 22 in the Baden-Baden meeting. The debate was led by British representative Sir Charles Layton and French representative Clément Moret, the governor of the Banque de France. Moret expressed the opinion that government securities should be pro-hibited in principle (with purchases from the foreign bond accounts of central banks as an exception), due to factors including concerns that private banks would bring Treasury bills to the BIS disguised as demands for rediscounting of bills.[35]

In response, British representative Charles Addis stated that since the BIS would be led by a powerful board of directors, the concerns pointed to by Moret could be eliminated. In contrast to Moret and Layton, Addis insisted that the Statutes should state clearly that the BIS was authorized to trade in Treasury bills.[36]

In response to Addis' opposition, Moret argued that the Treasury bills handled by the BIS should be restricted to "discounted eligible bills for which rediscount-ing is permitted by each central bank." Layton replied that while Moret's stand-ard on rediscounting was a necessary condition, it was not a sufficient one, since Article 26 (f) of the draft Statutes prohibited the purchase of rediscounted bills. Moret accepted the voices of caution of Layton and others, and Belgian repre-sentative Louis Franck too argued that abuse of government securities could lead to inflation, and it was not differentiated whether each country's government securities had sufficient value or whether their value was "less than that of British or US treasuries." As a result, the debate ended with Layton calling for it to be put off until a later date. In the end, Layton summarized the issue as one of differentiating "Treasury bills constituting lending to government" and "Treas-ury bills functioning as a means of trading in financial markets."[37]

While the underlying tone was the "anti-inflationary" one represented by the arguments of Layton and Moret (warnings about inflation, differentiation of

Treasury bills by the issuing government), the drift of the argument in the Baden-Baden meeting was one of seeking out a course of action on how much deviation from that tone would be acceptable as proposed by Addis and, in doing so, on how to differentiate Treasury bills by government. Perhaps the proposal described above made by Schacht at the Paris meeting of the Young Committee – participation in credit generation – should be said to have been revisited with slight variation in this Baden-Baden meeting as well.

The BIS statutes later finalized at the Baden-Baden meeting would permit the handling of Treasury bills on the condition that they be "short-term obligations of Governments which are currently marketable."[38] Dulles, who wrote the most systematic contemporary treatise on the BIS, lauded this decision as the fruit of "a majority agreed very quickly to eliminate rapid expansion of purchasing power as far as possible."[39] Jacobsson too – at the time an economist working at the League of Nations and later BIS economic adviser and head of the Monetary and Economic Department – welcomed this decision, stating that "from what one hears about the current negotiations at Baden-Baden, it would appear that the present intention is to limit the Bank's activities so that it can do business only through central banks."[40] In contrast, the journalist Einzig saw the permitting of handling of Treasury bills under these conditions as "one of the interesting departures of the statutes from the Young Plan" and saw this as the end of the preceding "anti-inflationary" argument.[41]

Accounting currency and headquarters location

After the issue of Treasury bills was shelved for a while at the Baden-Baden meeting, the debate began on the accounting currency. Put simply, this was the issue of which currency to use to denominate the financial statements of the new bank, the BIS. The argument was triggered by French representative Quesnay. Quesnay advocated the new bank employing as its accounting unit a new currency unit called a "*grammor*." This would be a basket of currencies employing a fixed amount of gold ("*or*" in French) as a unit. This proposal was made to the meeting on October 22, but it was quickly rejected and the Swiss franc was adopted as the BIS accounting unit.[42]

Although Quesnay's proposal of a "*grammor*" was not realized, it gave a unique color to the process of the establishment of the BIS. This linked the founding of the BIS to financial utopian ideas that surpassed the dynamics of the pragmatic politics that pushed for the establishment of the BIS. In fact, Jacques Rueff, a senior official in the French finance ministry at the time, evaluated this idea as follows one year after the Baden-Baden meeting, in 1930. He said that through the settlement of gold between countries the BIS was able to shrink the gap between gold export and import points and, ultimately, to bring about a single, fixed gold parity. This gold parity itself was a "*grammor*."[43] When the IMF was started 15 years after Quesnay's proposal, Keynes, who took part in planning its establishment, advocated the creation of a new accounting unit. While in the end it was not adopted, this unit was called the "bancor." This unit too would refer to the value of gold. It may be valuable to look at how the current of "financial utopianism," from the reform plans during World War I described above in Section 1 through Quesnay to Keynes, had in common advocacy of the "*grammor*" and "bancor" units based on a gold standard – even when examining the historical nature of the BIS.

After the decision was made to employ the Swiss franc as the accounting currency, what remained was the issue of where to locate the BIS headquarters. Initial candidate cities proposed at the Baden-Baden meeting were London, Berlin, Paris, Brussels, Amsterdam, Geneva, Zurich and Berne. Representatives of countries in attendance clashed over the choice, bemoaning "London hegemony" and "French–German plotting." While as of October 1929 the British representative had not yet given up on the idea of attracting the BIS headquarters to London, after receiving this information the governor of the Banque de France sent official instructions to the French representatives to "strongly oppose any proposal to select London," to "extol the proposal of Brussels," and, "if that was unsuccessful, to agree to a Swiss city: Basel, Lausanne, Geneva, or Zurich in order of preference."[44] At the end of negotiations, the choice of a city in Switzerland, a neutral nation, remained standing. However, Geneva was rejected since it was the site of the headquarters of the League of Nations and independence from the league was considered an important issue, Zurich due to too strong a German influence, and Berne due to the pronounced influence of the Swiss federal government. As a result, the proposal of Basel, a city in close proximity to the French and German border, far from the center of politics, and well known as a transportation hub, rose to the top.[45]

As seen from the above description, what all participants in the Baden-Baden meeting agreed upon concerning the location of the new bank's headquarters was the point of view that the new bank required "independence." Consideration of securing a distance not just from the government of each country but also from the League of Nations would serve the interests of each country.[46] In this can be seen the starting point of the tradition of the BIS as a forum of central banks, which would continue into the future.

Contemporary journalism – including journalists who had made arguments strongly critical of the BIS – was uniformly favorable toward this choice of Basel out of consideration for "independence." The *Banker* said that this decision was "fairly satisfactory from a British point of view."[47] *L'Economiste Français* too recalled the following year that "this was an excellent choice."[48]

The issue of choosing a headquarters location would lead to a byproduct concerning the BIS. This was the issue of "branches." In fact, when the prospects worsened for the idea of locating the BIS headquarters in London, the British representatives to the Baden-Baden meeting brought up the possibility in consultation on the Statutes that the BIS could establish branch offices. The French representatives, led by Clément Moret, were strongly opposed to this idea. Moret's argument in the consultations officially was that it was not a good idea to set up branches because doing so could "lead to suspicions" that the BIS was going to compete with private banks. However, within the French delegation it was thought that the intention of the British delegation was if the headquarters would not be located in London, to have a branch established there, and then once this branch had obtained overwhelming importance, to have the branch upgraded to a headquarters as part of procedures to amend the Statutes.[49]

Regardless of whether or not this observation was correct, it is interesting that the principle that the BIS would not establish branches did emerge from British–French antagonism during the Baden-Baden meeting. This principle would be revised for the first time when the BIS established a representative office in Hong Kong much later, at the end of the twentieth century.

In this way, the Baden-Baden meeting drew to a close. While leaving some leeway for the handling of Treasury bills, the Statutes adopted abandoned Quesnay's utopian ideas and established the BIS in Basel, stressing the independence of the new bank. But how did contemporary public opinion react to the Statutes finalized in this way, and to the BIS depicted therein?

The argument on the statutes: BIS critics and their antagonists in public opinion

Contemporary journalism began criticizing the BIS as soon as the Baden-Baden meeting began – without waiting for a formal report. Two weeks after the meeting's start, *L'Economiste Français* repeated its claim that the argument to expand the domain of the BIS's operations was led by advocates of managed currency.[50] Even French politician Caillaux, who had taken a moderate position in the pages of the *Banker* in the past, became anti-BIS in August 1929[51] and from then on did not hesitate to call the BIS a "super-bank."[52]

But what kind of stand did this journalism take after the statutes were announced? Let's examine this question using the example of the *Banker*, which commented point-by-point on the BIS statutes.

In its December 1929 issue, an anonymous writer on the *Banker* critiqued the text of the announced statutes in detail. This article criticized the operations that the BIS should conduct, listed under Article 4 of the statutes, as of "No explicit provision ... for a possible inclusion of inter-Allied Debt." It argued that Article 20, which covered the board of directors' right of veto, would deter the actual exercise thereof. It concluded that Article 22, which touched on reciprocal operations between the BIS and each central bank, had a "striking feature." Its criticism was unsparing on Article 24, which it called "an attempt to interfere with the automatic character of international gold movements" that was a "fatal mistake." Finally, this article criticized Article 26 as a "mistake to prescribe a minimum gold reserve" and argued that the BIS was pursuing a "commercial banking model."[53]

In fact, this article in the *Banker* criticized the Statutes from two different points of view. One of these was the criticism that the BIS would be an intervening institution ranked higher than each country's central bank – in other words, a "central bank to each country's central bank" The other was the criticism that even though entrusted with a mission in international affairs, the BIS was expanding to the domain of the operations of ordinary banks – becoming a "commercial bank." Even if they did contain some mistakes in the details, these critiques can be said to reflect precisely the contradiction from the planning stages of the establishment of the BIS – whether it would be a bank for reparations or would also conduct credit operations. It could even be said that the dual nature of the BIS, as both a "central bank" and a "commercial bank," offered a good indication as to the nature of the BIS in the future.

What other kinds of critiques were leveled once the Statutes had been announced? Let's take a look at the critiques of Gustav Cassel, a famous economist at the time, and Einzig, who has made numerous appearances above.

Cassel's comment is conspicuous among criticisms of the BIS "central bank" function. Noting that "the cooperation between chief banks is already extremely close," Cassel argued, with BIS credit operations in mind, that "The idea that the Bank [the BIS] can avoid disagreeable discount policies by having resort to foreign credits is an extremely treacherous one."[54]

On the other hand, Einzig, while seeing the BIS "central bank" function as problematic, was led to a different conclusion than Cassel. Einzig's argument was that each country's central bank acts in accordance with its own national interest. The fact that the official discount rates of Britain, the United States and France were cut in a coordinated manner was because doing so served the interests of these three nations. As such, he argued that it was lamentable that the BIS needed to begin its operations amid a spirit of competition in which the interests of each nation struggle with each other.[55]

Cassel claimed that central-bank cooperation was "sufficient," while Einzig described it as "insufficient." This contradiction can be seen to symbolize the unstable relations between central banks at that time. Amid such instability, the BIS began operation steeped in criticism that was a mixture of both expectations and uncertainty.

But how did the BIS respond to such criticism? The first response to the criticism that raged following the announcement of the statutes was an anonymous essay published in the leading French economics journal *Revue d'Economie Politique*.[56] Later research confirmed that the author of this anonymous essay was Quesnay, the first BIS general manager.[57] For this reason, the anonymous essay can be seen as the unofficially announced opinion of the promoters of establishment of the BIS.

This essay first insisted that the BIS was an organization similar to the Federal Reserve System of the United States. While recognizing that there were "partial grounds" for the criticism that the operations prescribed in the BIS statutes exceeded the framework decided on by the Young Committee, the essay stated that the BIS would employ these functions for payment of reparations and foreign-exchange settlement. The essay also touched on gold settlement conducted by the BIS, arguing that changes in the gold point would be restrained through concentration of gold transactions in the BIS. It also spoke of the logic that due to this stabilization of the gold point there would be no need to create a new currency unit. It also said that BIS gold settlement would neutralize the effects of international gold movements on domestic markets, together with the interest-rate policies and open-market policies of each country.

The anonymous essay also spoke of the point of dispute that had shaken up the Young Committee and the Baden-Baden meeting – BIS credit operations. The BIS would provide credit. This "was an operation to a sufficient degree explicitly foreseen in the specialists' plan [the Young Plan]." The abuse of these credit operations would mean that the structure of the board of directors and the executive sections would be a "guarantee of security." While arguments differ on whether the Young Plan "explicitly" called for BIS credit operations, it is interesting that this essay expressed frankly the course of action the BIS was aiming for at the time.

A further point that should be given attention is the fact that the author of the anonymous essay described the ideas of concentration of "gold transactions at the BIS" and "restraining changes in the gold point" as based on the theories of Feliks Mlynarski, the deputy governor of the Bank of Poland.[58] Actually, in *Gold and Central Banks* (1929) Mlynarski advocated a move to implementing these ideas with the Financial Committee of the League of Nations as the base,[59] and in the later work *Credit and Peace, a Way Out of the Crisis* (1933) spoke of central-bank reforms, including relaxation of issuing monopolies and issue by multiple banks.[60] Together with contemporary French economist Charles Rist, Mlynarski contributed an essay to the special issue of the *Revue d'Economie Politique* on currency issues.[61] Rist was a leader among liberal economists of the day, and Mlynarski's study too drew a distinction between the gold exchange standard advocated by Keynes and others and a view toward overcoming panics within the gold standard and market functions. Incidentally, two other writers who contributed to the same special issue of this journal in addition to Rist and Mlynarski were authors using the unusual pen names of "Elver" and "***." The actual users of these pen names will ring a bell among people familiar with BIS documents. "Elver" was in fact Jacobsson, BIS economic adviser and head of the Monetary and Economic Department, who will appear in the next chapter of this book, and *** was Quesnay, the first BIS general manager, mentioned above. To this special issue, Jacobsson, aka Elver, contributed an essay titled "*Le contrôle des devises et le maintien normal de l'étalon-or*" introducing the results of the new BIS in gold settlement and developing the argument that a return to the economic liberalism and free trade in products, services and capital from before the Great War is a necessary precondition for the recovery of the ordinary functions of the gold standard. From these authors one can see the position of BIS core management – the group of theorists and practitioners referred to as "neoliberals" from the point of view of this book – linked to Rist and Mlynarski.

The operations that the new BIS aimed to conduct – participation in gold settlement, cooperation with domestic policy in each country, provision of credit – already were established policies allowing no room for criticism when the convention establishing the BIS was signed in February 1930 in the Hague. After the charter was signed, in April 1930 Addis – the British representative at the Baden-Baden meeting who had insisted that the BIS handle Treasury bills – had the following to say: "The development of Reparation was the occasion rather than the cause of its inception [of the BIS]"; "We shall find that sufficient freedom of action has been preserved for all normal banking purposes" Addis continues, citing an example, that the BIS "may not issue notes, but it can buy and sell and ear-mark gold."[62] The broad domain of operations permitted in the statutes truly was what Addis desired.

Addis' conclusion was that such BIS statutes expressed "financial utopianism." Contemporary leaders of the BIS stated that the current of "financial utopianism" – the ideas spoken of among socialists since before the Young Committee and the "*grammor*" proposal from Quesnay that did not see the light of day – truly was expressed in the BIS statutes. The idea of a BIS that sought to embark on a broad range of credit operations instead of functioning solely as a bank for addressing the reparations problem was viewed as an extension of the course of "financial utopianism."

4 The BIS statutes and structure

As mentioned above, the various BIS-related systems were decided on in the "Hague Convention," consisting more precisely of the convention respecting the following two documents: the "Convention respecting the Bank for International Settlements" and the "Statutes of the Bank for International Settlements." Each of these was concluded on January 20, 1930.

"The Convention respecting the Bank for International Settlements"

The former document, the "Convention respecting the Bank for International Settlements," was signed by representatives of the governments of Germany, Belgium, France, the United Kingdom, Italy and Japan constituting one party to the convention, and the representative of the Swiss federal government as the other party. This convention stipulated that the Swiss government would exempt the BIS, to be established in Basel, Switzerland, from taxes and other public charges. It is notable that the "Constituent Charter of the Bank for International Settlements," which constitutes part of this convention, stipulated guarantees for BIS deposits etc. In fact, Article 10 states,

> The Bank, its property and assets and all deposits and other funds entrusted to it shall be immune in time of peace and in time of war from any measure such as expropriation, requisition, seizure, confiscation, prohibition or restriction of gold or currency export or import, and any other similar measures.[63]

This provision would likely become a problem during World War II.

The Statutes of the Bank for International Settlements

The BIS statutes are made up of seven chapters and 60 articles.

Chapter I, "Name, Seat and Objects," covers the name of the BIS (Article 1) and its headquarters location in Basel (Article 2), and Article 3 describes its object as follows.

> The objects of the Bank are: to promote the co-operation of central banks and to provide additional facilities for international financial operations; and to act as trustee or agent in regard to international financial settlements entrusted to it under agreements with the parties concerned.

The concerns with this Article are the content of "co-operation of central banks" and the scope of the "additional facilities" added to this. Since the business objectives of the BIS were expressed vaguely in this way, it would take part in a wide range of businesses. Another point that should be focused on is the use of the expressions "trustee" and "agent." Later, when the BIS took part in the design of the international financial system, which of these roles – "trustee" or "agent" – the BIS was acting as would become a subject of debate both inside and outside the bank.

Incidentally, looking back on the flow of establishment of the BIS statutes beginning in the Baden-Baden Conference in later years, the French finance ministry offered the frank opinion that the fact that Article 3 of the statutes gives higher priority to central-bank cooperation than to handling reparations problems was "a remarkable change of front."[64]

In Chapter II, "Capital," Article 5 stipulates the BIS's nominal capital at 500 million Swiss francs, divided into "200,000 shares of equal gold nominal value." It states that "the nominal value of each share also be expressed on the face of each share in terms both of Swiss francs and of the currency of the country in which it is issued, converted at the gold mint parity."

This nominal capital would be subscribed to by the nations' central banks[65] (Article 6). However, in Japan and the United States, instead of the central bank, groups of private banks[66] would handle subscription (Article 6). This was because participation by the Japanese and American central banks in the joint-stock company of the BIS would violate the statutes of each central bank.

The statutes state that for the unissued component of nominal capital the board "shall arrange for the subscription" (Article 7) within two years after establishment of the BIS. It states that this unissued component will be provided to "central banks or other banks" of countries not participating in the establishment of the BIS, and the amount subscribed to by these newly participating countries would be decided by a two-thirds majority of the board (Article 7). At the same time, conditions were applied to newly participating banks. They must be "countries interested in Reparations" or "countries whose currencies, in the opinion of the Board, satisfy the practical requirements of the gold or gold exchange standard."[67] As mentioned below, these complex conditions were prescribed in consideration of Japan, which at the time of the decision-making process on the statutes had not returned to the gold standard. In addition, the statutes state that newly participating countries must not own more than 8,000 shares. They also state that only 25 percent of the face value of shares shall be paid upon subscription (Article 8). Any increase or decrease in capital would be decided on in the general meeting, after proposal by the board, and each of these would require a two-thirds majority decision (Article 9). Shares would be endorsed and any transfer of shares would take effect upon its recording with the BIS. Transfer of shares would be severely restricted: "The Bank shall not transfer shares without the prior consent of the central banks, or the institution acting in lieu of a central bank, by or through whom the shares in question were issued" (Article 13).

As is made clear from this introduction to the statutes, the BIS was established as a joint-stock company. But how would this joint-stock company be governed? Article 15 of the statutes states,

> The ownership of shares of the Bank carries no right of voting or representation at the General Meeting. The right of representation and of voting, in proportion to the number of shares subscribed in each country, may be exercised by the central bank of that country or by its nominee.

Thus, practically speaking, decision-making by participating countries' central banks is provided for. Based on this assumption, participating countries' central banks or groups of banks are permitted to issue subscribed BIS shares to the general public (Article 16) and, with the approval of the board, to issue bonds with these shares serving as reserves (Article 17). However, concerning Article 16, the BIS shares initially sold to the public gradually were repurchased, so that all shares were held by the central banks of participating countries.

Chapter III, "Powers of the Bank," is an important section establishing the scope of the BIS's operations. First, at the start of the chapter, Article 20 stipulates the following: "The operations of the Bank shall be in conformity with the monetary policy of the central banks of the countries concerned." Next, the statutes stipulate matters such as the provision of an opportunity to dissent for central banks concerned when any BIS "financial operation" is carried out in a given market or currency, and that funds invested by the BIS where no such dissent has been lodged may be withdrawn from a market without the consent of the relevant central bank. These stipulations concern the BIS's commercial banking operations – performed by the Banking Department. The dispute between the Bank of Japan and the BIS, discussed below, began with this provision of the statutes.

Article 21 states that BIS business and operations "shall only be carried out in currencies which in the opinion of the Board satisfy the practical requirements of the gold or the gold exchange standard." This provision was in response to the membership conditions (Article 7) seen above.

Article 22 lists ten operations that the BIS "may in particular" carry out,[68] along with three that it "may also" carry out.[69] Also, the following operations are noted as those that the BIS may conduct by entering into special agreements with central banks: (1) holding earmarked gold transferred on the order of central banks; (2) opening transfer accounts for central banks at the BIS; and (3) taking other measures as deemed advisable by the board (Article 24). Deposit-taking and other banking operations are to be conducted through each central bank, and direct transactions with private-sector firms were limited to cases in which "the central bank of that country does not object" (Articles 21, 23).[70]

Article 25 lists six prohibited activities. These are (1) issuing notes payable at sight to bearer; (2) "accepting" bills of exchange; (3) making advances to governments; (4) opening current accounts in the names of governments; (5) acquiring a predominant interest in any business concern; and (6)

> except so far as is necessary for the conduct of its own business, remain(ing) the owner of real property for any longer period than is required in order to realize to proper advantage such real property as may come into the possession of the Bank in satisfaction of claims due to it.

Comparison of this negative list to the positive list in Article 22 brings some interesting characteristics to the surface. While the BIS is permitted to discount notes, it is not permitted to issue or accept them. While it may open accounts for central banks, it may not open accounts for governments. While it may hold gold, it should avoid holding real estate as much as possible. These can be said to represent a system carefully designed to maintain the function of a "bank's bank" like the Bank of England while also seeking to earn a profit as a joint-stock bank.

The ideas behind this design also are shown in Article 26, which covers the liquidity of BIS assets. Article 26 states that "The Bank shall be administered with particular regard to maintaining its liquidity," listing as liquid assets for this purpose

> bank-notes, checks payable on sight drawn on first-class banks, claims in course of collection, deposits at sight or at short notice in first-class banks, and prime bills of exchange of not more than ninety days' usance, of a kind usually accepted for rediscount by central banks.

Chapter IV, "Management," and Chapter V, "General Meetings," will be discussed later.

Chapter VI, "Accounts and Profits," establishes the form of the BIS's financial statements as a joint-stock company and its distribution of profits. Its fiscal year would start April 1 and end March 31 (Article 50), the board would be required to report to the annual general meeting on its financial statements (Article 51), and auditing would be required (Article 52). Next, Article 53 covers distribution of profits. In summary, first a legal reserve fund would be deducted from net profits (what ordinarily would be referred to as gross profit), with the remainder applied to dividends paid to shareholders. Up to 6 percent of paid-in capital could be applied to dividends, with the portion in excess of this percentage in principle transferred to the general reserve fund. What this principle of dividends as 6 percent of paid-in capital stipulated in Article 53 of the statutes would mean in reality is likely to become a point of dispute.

The final chapter, Chapter VII "General Provisions" enumerates some important matters related to the application of the statutes.

Article 55 addresses liquidation requirements: "The Bank may not be liquidated except by a three-fourths majority of the General Meeting. It shall not in any case be liquidated before it has discharged all the obligations which it has assumed under the Plan." This Article 55 was the grounds for dispute immediately after World War II, when the BIS faced the threat of liquidation, as will be described later.

Article 56 stipulates how any dispute between the BIS and a central bank, financial institution, etc. would be handled. It provides that any dispute would be referred for final decision to the tribunal provided for in Article 2 of the Convention respecting the Bank for International Settlements mentioned above. As will be discussed later, this provision was nearly implemented in the dispute between the Bank of Japan and the BIS.

Article 58 is an important passage that defines the terms used in the statutes. In particular, Paragraph 1 of that Article is worthy of attention for its definition of "central bank," reproduced below.

> Central bank means the bank in any country to which has been entrusted the duty of regulating the volume of currency and credit in that country; or, where a banking system has been so entrusted, the bank forming part of such system which is situated and operating in the principal financial market of that country.

This definition can only refer to a "bank's bank" modeled on the Bank of England – more precisely, modeled on the image of the Bank of England envisioned by its governor, Norman. As seen in the next chapter, the use of this definition in the statutes would later cause an unexpectedly large stir.

In addition, this Article 58 also defines the meanings of "Governor of a central bank" and a "two-thirds majority of the Board."

Articles 59 and 60 cover amendment of the statutes.

The BIS structure

The structure of the BIS is first prescribed in Chapter IV, "Management," and Chapter V, "General Meetings," of the statutes. However, significant revisions were made to the statutes later, greatly modifying the BIS's structure. These changes were not merely technical adjustments but reflected a development in the nature of the BIS itself – both officially expressed and not. On this point, let's proceed below with a study of this structure addressing the statutes at the time the BIS was established through subsequent changes.

Decision-making body: the board

Article 27 in Chapter IV stipulates that the "the administration of the Bank shall be vested in the Board," and Article 28 prescribes the following structure of the board.

1   Ex officio directors: the incumbent governors of the central banks of Germany, Belgium, France, Great Britain, Italy, Japan and the United States.
2   Appointed directors: directors appointed by governors as their alternates if the governors themselves are unable to be present.
3   One director appointed by each central-bank governor: these directors shall be "seven persons representative of finance, industry or commerce, appointed one each by the Governors of the central banks,... of the same nationality as the Governor who appoint them."
4   During the period of payment of reparations, if they so desire the governors of the Banque de France and the Reichsbank may appoint "two persons of French and German nationality respectively, representative of industry or commerce."

As a result of these provisions, at the time of the BIS's founding, the board was made up of the following nationalities: three directors each from France and Germany and two each from Belgium, Britain, Italy, Japan and the United States. Under the clauses above, France and Germany each sent the governors of their central banks as ex officio directors under clause (1), directors such as deputy governors of their central banks appointed under clause (3), and representatives of private banks under clause (4). Belgium, Britain and Italy sent the governors of their central banks as ex officio directors and each appointed one additional director.

Japan and the United States each sent appointed directors and appointed one more person. In the case of Japan, Tetsusaburo Tanaka, director of the Bank of Japan's London agency, was the appointed director, accompanied by Daisuke Nohara, manager of the London branch of Yokohama Specie Bank. The case of the United States was a bit complicated one. Originally, the United States neither signed nor ratified the Constituent Charter of the Bank for International Settlements (Hague Convention). Also, as a joint-stock bank the BIS issued shares of stock upon its founding, with each country contributing stock proceeds as allocated in the convention. However, in the case of the United States it was not the FRB but a private banking association, including J.P. Morgan, that invested in the BIS. The direct cause of these actions was the 1929 statement by US Secretary of State Henry Stimson that Federal Reserve System staff were prohibited from becoming BIS members.[71] It appears that behind this declaration by Stimson was a political decision to avoid a commitment on the European reparations problem. In this way, in the BIS the United States chose a unique position regarding decision-making, in which although it was a nation with members on the founding board the FRB would not dispatch directors (either ex officio or appointed) to the BIS board.

With the exception of the change made when Japan withdrew from the BIS after World War II, the structure of the BIS board has remained unchanged since its founding. The current BIS statutes (revised July 8, 1975) guarantee ex officio directorships for the six board member countries other than Japan from the time of the bank's founding. Each of these ex officio director nations appoints one person "representative of finance, industry or commerce,... of the same nationality as the Governor who appoints him." In the current BIS, in addition to the 12 ex officio directors from the above six nations, the board includes

> not more than nine persons to be elected by the Board by a two-thirds majority from among the Governors of the central banks of countries in which shares have been subscribed but of which the central bank does not delegate ex officio Directors to the Board.
>
> (Article 27, Paragraph 3 of the current statutes)

These directors, referred to ordinarily as "elected directors," serve renewable three-year terms. In 1994, the countries sending such elected directors to the board were Canada, Japan, the Netherlands, Sweden and Switzerland, and in 2006 China, Mexico and the European Central Bank were added to their ranks.

Now let's return to the founding statutes. Article 29 establishes procedures for filling vacancies and Article 30 establishes the requirement that directors must be resident in Europe or in a position to attend meetings of the board regularly. Article 31 is important; "No person shall be appointed or hold office as a Director who is a member or an official of a Government, or is a member of a legislative body, unless he is the Governor of a central bank." This stipulation is the most straightforward expression of the BIS's characteristic as a "bank for central banks." This stipulation is observed unchanged – except for the amendment that a member of a legislative body may be not just the current governor but also "a former Governor" of a central bank – in Article 30 of the current statutes.[72]

Another important stipulation in the founding statutes is that of Article 39, concerning the chairman of the board. It states, "the Board shall elect from among its members a Chairman and one or more Vice-Chairmen," and "the Chairman of the Board shall be President of the Bank." However, only the first three chairmen in the pre-World War II period – Gates McGarrah, Leon Fraser and L.J.A. Trip, in that order – served as both chairman and president. During World War II and later, either the chairman and president were different individuals or one of these positions remained vacant. The chairman and president again was the same person, as prescribed in the statutes, beginning in 1948 with the sixth chairman, Maurice Frère.

Parenthetically, a large number of Americans served as BIS chairmen of the board and presidents. From the time of the committee on establishment of the BIS, which prepared the way for the bank's founding, there were concerns about a clash of interests between European nations regarding the issue of reparations for World War I. It was expected that representatives of the United States, as non-European members, would play coordinating roles by serving as committee representatives. While from the American side the Department of the Treasury and the Department of State in particular were reluctant to accept this role, compromise was reached with the Federal Reserve Bank, which asked to dispatch staff. Under this compromise, although (1) the chairman of the Federal Reserve Bank of New York would not be a member of the founding committee, and (2) the Federal Reserve Bank of New York staff would not be prevented from participation. In this way, Jackson Reynolds, a director of the bank, became the first chairman of the BIS founding committee. Later, the principle declared by Stimson mentioned above was withdrawn, and former bank chairman McGarrah was named the first BIS chairman of the board and president, and then in 1935 Fraser, an American who had been counsel for the agent general for reparation payments, was named the second BIS chairman of the board and president. While the third and fourth presidents were Dutch, the American Thomas McKittrick, a former banker, was appointed the fifth president.[73]

Executive bodies: the general manager and three departments

Article 41 of the statutes prescribes appointment by the board of a general manager recommended by the president, as chief executive officer. This general manager would be "responsible to the President of the Bank for the operations of the Bank" and would be "the chief of its operating staff," and he or she could take part in recommendation of heads of departments and any others, as noted in the provision "The Heads of Departments, and any other officers of similar rank, shall be appointed by the Board on the proposal of the General Manager." Many successive general managers have been French.

Article 42 of the statutes stipulates that "the departmental organization of the Bank shall be approved by the board." In accordance with this provision, at the time of the establishment of the BIS, its organization consisted of three departments: the Secretary General, the Banking Department and the Central Banking Department.[74] The Secretary General was in charge of general operations for the BIS's departmental organization overall, while the Banking Department handled operations related to enactment of the Young Plan, such as payment of reparations. Lastly, as will be seen in the next chapter, the Central Banking Department was reorganized in 1932 into the Monetary and Economic Department, which would handle policy advice and theoretical activities concerning currency and finance in general. The process of reorganization of these departments and the power relations between them are likely to be important points of reference in looking at the history of the BIS.

General meetings

Chapter V of the statutes, entitled "General Meetings," consists of provisions concerning general shareholders' meetings of the bank. Authorized to attend general meetings of the bank are "nominees of the central banks or other financial institutions referred to in Article 15" (Article 46). This corresponds to the right of representation under Article 15 looked at above – the fact that individual shareholders have no right of representation. Also, voting rights in a general meeting would be distributed "in proportion to the number of shares subscribed in the country of each institution represented at the meeting" (Article 46). Thus, while the board of directors applies the principle of one person, one vote, the general meeting employs a system of voting rights proportional to share ownership.

From the above consideration of its statutes and structure, it can be seen that at the time of its founding the BIS, while at first glance extolling a rigid structure, in practical terms was envisioning a very flexible organization.

In fact, a look at the structure of the board shows a complex allocation of seats, reflecting the intricate international negotiations on the issue of reparations. Distribution of shares too gave a heavier weight to the seven founding nations and a lighter weight to countries joining later. These distributions – as evidenced by Japan's inability to recover the position it had as an ex officio board member state at the time the BIS was founded following its withdrawal from and later rejoinment of the BIS – would prove not easy to change.

However, under the BIS structure efforts such as restructuring of the executive bodies could be conducted at the initiative of the general manager. In these areas, room remained for the intervention of official and unofficial negotiations on international currency matters, outside the constraints of the statutes. The appointments to the positions of BIS president and general manager demonstrate this exquisite balance resulting from "behind-the-scenes maneuvering."

5 Bank operations and distribution of profits

This section addresses the business activities of the BIS. As shown in the examination of the statutes in the previous section, the BIS was established as a joint-stock bank that would invest deposits and distribute profits to shareholders, at the same time it was an international institution handling the reparations problem. Based on this main point of its founding, the BIS developed its own business activities of a type not seen in other international institutions such as the later established IMF. The subject of this section is tracing this nature through financial statements and related materials. Hereinafter in this book, the end of each chapter will be devoted to this business analysis, looking at trends in banking operations and profits during each period. In this chapter, we will examine the BIS' financial statements from the time of its founding.

Structure of financial statements (1): collection of deposits

First let's check the structure of the financial statements. Here, we will look at the balance sheet and the profit and loss account for the year in which the BIS was founded, fiscal 1930 (the period of 10.5 months from May 17, 1930 through

March 31, 1931).[75] The BIS financial statements as referred to here represent the main operations of the BIS itself – chiefly the acceptance of deposits and the generation of credit. Also, according to the provisions of the statutes, during this period BIS financial statements were denominated in Gold Swiss francs (*franc suisse-or*). Gold Swiss francs are an accounting unit calculated at intervals from the exchange rate between the Swiss franc and other currencies and the price of gold.[76]

Table 1.1 depicts the balance sheet for this fiscal year. Under liabilities is booked the roughly 103 million Gold Swiss francs of paid-up capital from the countries involved in the founding of the BIS. This corresponds to 25 percent of the BIS's total of 165,000 shares issued and outstanding (412.75 million Gold Swiss francs). This amount accounts for 5.4 percent of total liabilities. The next item is long-term deposits. Included within these long-term deposits, the annuity trust account represents the deposits paid into the BIS by countries holding claims on German reparations, under the trust agreement of the Young Plan (the Hague Convention).[77] The deposits of these nations began with the 226,178,400 Gold Swiss francs paid into the BIS by the Reparations Office when the BIS opened. Each country deposited with the BIS an amount corresponding to the amount of German reparations received from the Reparations Office (partially consumed by costs such as those of delivery of reparations in kind).[78] Moreover, German government deposits and a French government guarantee fund are booked under this item as well. Each of these is an interest-free deposit or fund. These long-term deposits in total account for 15.9 percent of total liabilities.

The next liabilities account item is short-term and sight deposits. This includes the own accounts opened by each country's central bank (as a whole, 42.7 percent of total liabilities) and trust accounts opened by these central banks with funds from their countries' finance ministries and others (as a whole, 34.4 percent of total liabilities). These short-term and sight deposits alone account for more than 75 percent of total liabilities, an indication that from its early stage the BIS had the nature of a commercial bank taking short-term deposits.

At issue here are the maturity and currency composition of these deposits. Regarding maturity, at the end of fiscal 1931, deposits maturing in "not exceeding three months" accounted for the largest percentage of deposits (Table 1.1). As for currencies, the US dollar accounted for 71 percent of the deposits, followed by the Reichsmark (11 percent), the pound sterling (9 percent), the French franc (3 percent), the Dutch florin (3 percent), and the Swiss franc (2 percent).[79] The BIS annual report, while referring happily to the way this variety of deposit currencies shows the "steady growth of the volume of funds at the disposition of the Bank," also notes that "certain of the Governmental Treasuries which maintain deposits through their central banks have accumulated with the Bank the sums necessary to meet their so-called outpayments abroad."[80] According to the BIS annual report, collection of these deposits at the international agency of the BIS "has led to the organization of a clearing of inter-governmental payments" and that conversion between currencies through transactions in internal BIS accounts had "eliminated numerous conversions from one currency to

Table 1.1 BIS balance sheet, fiscal year 1930 (as of March 31, 1931, in Gold Swiss francs)

Assets	Amount	%
Cash	7,238,738.52	0.4
Sight funds at interest	186,281,460.50	9.8
Rediscountable bills and acceptances (at cost)	609,527,654.50	24.8
Commercial bills and bankers' acceptances	*471,424,314.83*	
Treasury bills	*138,103,339.67*	7.3
Time funds at interest	863,481,719.87	44.7
Not exceeding 3 months	*850,694,058.69*	
Between 3 and 6 months	*12,787,661.18*	0.7
Sundry bills and investments	222,652,358.14	
Maturing within 1 year	*184,781,880.60*	9.7
Over 1 year	*37,870,477.54*	2.0
Other assets	11,966,981.38	0.6
Total	1,901,148,912.91	100.0

Liabilities	Amount	%
Capital		
Authorised 200,000 shares 500,000,000.00		
Issued 165,100 shares of which 25 percent paid up 412,750,000.00	103,187,500.00	5.4
Long term deposits	301,190,561.96	
Annuity trust account	*154,873,960.00*	8.2
German government deposit	*77,436,980.00*	4.1
French government guarantee fund	*68,879,621.96*	3.6
Short term and sight deposits		
Central banks for their own account:	811,806,576.40	
Between 3 and 6 months	*5,700,262.50*	0.3
Not exceeding 3 months	*495,126,691.51*	26.0
Sight	*310,979,622.39*	16.4
Central banks for the account of others:	653,174,903.62	
Between 3 and 6 months	*5,253,989.44*	0.3
Not exceeding 3 months	*355,730,774.08*	18.7
Sight	*292,190,140.10*	15.4
Other depositors:	14,021,420.39	
Not exceeding 3 months	*13,793,737.30*	0.7
Sight	*227,683.09*	0.0
Miscellaneous items	6,581,428.57	0.3
Surplus (profit for the period from May 17, 1930 to March 31, 1931)	11,186,521.97	0.6
Total	1,901,148,912.91	100.0

Source: *BIS First Annual Report* (1931), annex IV.

another, operations which, if they occurred through the ordinary markets, would only have unnecessarily troubled the exchanges."[81] As seen in the next chapter, such experience in international deposit-taking and settlement operations may have led to the BIS offering its own opinions on policy.

Structure of financial statements (2): investment of funds

Under assets, as with an ordinary bank the first items booked are ones with high liquidity, such as cash and sight funds at interest. The next item is rediscountable bills and acceptances. Commercial bills and bankers' acceptances, included in this item, account for 24.8 percent of total assets. Concerning these commercial bills (discount bills) and bankers' acceptances, the BIS annual report says, "With a view to aiding the development of business affairs," the BIS has "progressively increased the volume of its commercial bills."[82] Next come Treasury bills, accounting for 7.3 percent of all assets. While at the time the BIS opened, Treasury bills accounted for 33.4 percent of all assets, as the banking business grew these came to make up a minor item after less than one year.[83]

After these items related to notes and bills comes time funds at interest: representing funds that, as if in answer to the provision of Article 20 of the statutes – "The operations of the Bank shall be in conformity with the monetary policy of the central banks of the countries concerned" – the BIS, through the mediation of each country's central bank, lent to profitable investments in each country. The majority of time funds at interest consisted of loans with terms "not exceeding three months," and the balance of these short-term loans accounted for 44.7 percent of total assets. As seen in the next chapter, against the background of its performance with these short-term loans the BIS would advocate a policy of medium-term credit securitization during times of panic.

The final item under assets is sundry bills and investments. This includes the sub-items of those with one year or less to maturity and those with more than one year to maturity. As of June 10, 1930, immediately after the BIS started operation, a breakdown of investments under this item by country shows that Germany accounted for 97 percent of the total of 67,883,635.31 Gold Swiss francs in long-term investments and the United States for the remaining 3 percent. A look at specific investments shows that the three investments in Germany were in imperial German postal securities (*Reichspostschatzanweisungen*) and gold-backed securities from Rentenbank bearing 8 percent interest (*Goldpfandbriefe Hypothekar Schuldscheine der Rentenbank Kreditanstalt*), while the four investments in the United States were in private-sector corporate bonds (Louisville and Nashville (4 percent), Chicago Rock Island and Pacific (4.5 percent), Southern Pacific Equipment (4.5 percent), and Great North General (7 percent)).[84] Thus, at the start of BIS operation its long-term investments were mostly in Germany.

Speaking of the start of BIS operation, the above investments were made by investing in their localities funds paid in by each central bank as capital and deposits. Nevertheless, the Banking Department right after the BIS started operation converted $5 million of the initial investment amount to Reichsmark and allocated it to operations for the payment of German reparations in-kind and invested 7,708,500 Yugoslavian belga in the markets in Italy, London and New York. The main reason for the latter operation is said to have been that of enabling the bank to "obtain experience of exchange operations as soon as the necessary contacts have been made with the foreign centres notably London, Berlin and New York."[85] One month after it began operation, in the meeting of the BIS board of directors held June 16, 1930, the decision was made that "the Bank should not make investments with maturities exceeding two years." For this reason, bonds the BIS had purchased prior to that point with maturities of more than two years were sold, and the proceeds channeled to short-term investments. At that time, regarding BIS accounts deposited in each nation the board of directors also demanded each country's central bank to provide "the best time-deposit interest-rate terms available to us [the BIS] in each currency of denomination" and instructed that investments be made in each country in accordance with the responses to this demand.[86] While investment policies were confused, they appear to have been very firm. Table 1.2 shows the above investments arranged by maturity and currency. A look at the weights of initial investments when the BIS started operation, converted into Swiss francs, shows that on average 43.7 percent were denominated in Reichsmarks, 23.4 percent in pounds and 21.9 percent in dollars. From these figures, the importance of Germany stands out.

But what kinds of yields did these investments enjoy? In May 1930, yields of "6.08–7.20 percent" for long-term bonds and mortgage bonds with maturities of less than one year were reported in German markets, and yields of "approximately 4.5 percent" in American markets. In German markets, even short-term bonds were said to enjoy "yields of 6.08 percent" which was "comparable with long term investment."[87] Thus investment conditions when the BIS began operation – despite the fact that this was right after the crash of the New York Stock Exchange – appear to have been strong, chiefly in European bond markets.

Under the Hague Convention, funds invested were divided into: Account A, enjoying tax exemption from the governments of countries invested in; and Account B, to which ordinary taxes applied. At the time it started, the BIS transferred some notes it discounted in the Berlin market from Account A to Account B, taxable by the German government, and transferred the corresponding amount in cash Reichsmarks to Account A for the Reichsbank, to draw funds in connection with delivery of reparations in kind from the German government.[88]

Immediately after its founding, the BIS, which had only accepted long-term funds in connection with reparations, began within one year following the start of operations to accept short-term funds from each national government and central bank and invested these funds chiefly in short-term loans. In this way, the BIS in its early stages had begun the move toward super-bank status, although it had been established as an "institution to handle the reparations problem."

Table 1.2 Analysis of assets as at June 10, 1930 (%, in 1,000 Swiss francs at par)

Currencies	Cash	Money employed	Acceptances	Treasury bills	Other short term investments	Long term investments	Total
Dollar	31.1		40.5	18.6		3.0	21.9
Belgian franc	1.0	5.7	1.9				1.0
Pound	11.8	31.6	2.2	51.7			23.4
French franc	0.6		6.1	2.8			3.2
Reichsmark	53.0		41.0	26.9	100.0	97.0	43.7
Florin	0.2		1.7				0.6
Lire	0.3	40.5					2.5
Yen	0.9		6.6				2.3
Swedish krone	0.2	9.1					0.4
Swiss franc	0.7	13.1					0.8
Unknown	0.2						0.2
	100.0	100.0	100.0	100.0	100.0	100.0	100.0

Source: Yokohama Specie Bank Archives, the second period (mf04/w3/69) "Analysis of Assets as at June 10, 1930".

Profit and loss, and distribution of profits: the presence of hidden reserves

But how much did the BIS earn from these investments? The calculation of such profits conceals an important issue. In fact, the prewar BIS profit and loss account featured "hidden" ledgers, and there was an important difference between the publicly released figures and the actual "hidden" figures. This difference was transferred to accounts that BIS officials themselves referred to as "hidden reserves." Let's look at this development in the profit and loss account of the bank's founding fiscal year – in both public and hidden figures.

First of all, let's look at the method of calculating operating income in the true, hidden ledgers[89] (Table 1.3). The BIS shows gross revenue at the end of this fiscal year in Gold Swiss francs. Deducting from this figure interest allowed and costs of administration gives the net balance.

Next, specific profits and losses are subtracted from this net balance. The resulting item is called transfers from specific reserves and adjustments. In the prewar period, this covered three items: payment of taxes to the canton of Basel (fiscal 1932–1933), foreign-exchange profits from transactions in notes with repurchase agreements (fiscal 1933–1934), and interest earnings from loans to the national bank of Hungary (the four fiscal years beginning with fiscal 1935–1936). During the war, the following two items were booked to this account: payment of federal income tax resulting from transfer of deposits to the United States (fiscal 1939–1940) and receipt of Belgian Treasury bills in dollars (the four fiscal years beginning with fiscal 1941–1942).[90]

In BIS profit and loss accounting – the true hidden ledgers – the total after adjusting this net balance for various expenses was adjusted as exchange differences. As seen in Table 1.2, in fiscal 1930 (the ten-month accounts for the bank's founding fiscal year) these exchange differences showed differences of roughly 200,000 Gold Swiss francs. The amount resulting after deducting these exchange differences is the net profit or the net balance published, which equals the total amount available for allocation.

Over the period from the founding of the BIS through fiscal 1946, the above process was booked to the nonpublic ledger.

But what did the public profit and loss account look like? Let's take a look at the profit and loss account for the year of the bank's founding. In this fiscal year, the following three "techniques" were employed (Table 1.2).

The first of these is the manipulation of the profits figures on which the calculation of profit is based. According to the true profit calculation – the hidden ledgers – in fiscal 1930 the BIS earned gross revenue (before exchange adjustments) of 43,325,000 Gold Swiss francs. However, this gross revenue is not shown on the public ledgers. Instead, net income of 12,940,008 Gold Swiss francs, "from the use of the Bank's capital and the deposits entrusted to it" is reported, with the proviso that this figure represents the amount "after necessary allowance for contingencies." On the public ledgers, fee revenues and remittance fees are added to this figure, resulting in a gross profit of 15,143,395.88 Gold Swiss francs.

Table 1.3 BIS profit and loss account fiscal year 1930, published and unpublished versions, in Gold Swiss francs

Published account

Net income		12,940,008.00
Commissions earned		2,202,360.18
Transfer fees		1,027.70
Gross profit		15,143,395.88
Expenses relating to preliminary organization and installation	(−)	733,310.46
Provision for indemnities to and repatriation of staff	(−)	400,000.00
Costs of administration	(−)	2,823,563.45
Board of directors – fees and travelling expenses		*226,157.67*
Managing board and staff – salaries and travelling expenses		*2,081,095.75*
Rent, insurance, heating, light and water		*200,038.12*
Consumable office supplies, etc.		*121,242.78*
Telephone, telegraph and postage		*117,355.81*
Miscellaneous		*77,673.32*
Expenditure		3,956,873.91
Net profit		11,186,521.97

Unpublished account

Gross revenue		43,325,000.00
Interest allowed	(−)	25,182,000.00
Costs of administration	(−)	3,557,000.00
Net balance		14,586,000.00
"Hidden reserves" account		
Exchange differences		202,000.00
Provision for exchange and other losses		3,000,000.00
Administration account		400,000.00
Net balance published		11,186,000.00

Source: BIS Historical Archives, file 7.5, 1/2, "Disposal of the Surplus on the Profit and Loss Account, 1949–50", March 28, 1950; *BIS First Annual Report*.

Note
The total of the published and unpublished accounts do not correspond for the latter account rounds up the figure by 1,000 SF.

Comparison of this public gross profit with actual profit calculation shows the following points. As seen above, the actual hidden ledger subtracts interest allowed from gross revenue. In fiscal 1930, this difference totaled 18,143,000 Gold Swiss francs. This amount is greater than the publicly released gross profit by exactly three million Gold Swiss francs. In other words, in this fiscal year the BIS first pooled to hidden reserves three million Gold Swiss francs from the amount resulting from subtracting interest allowed from gross revenue on the hidden ledgers and announced the resulting figure of just over 15,143,000 Gold Swiss francs as gross profit. In the hidden reserves account on the hidden ledgers – called allocations to undisclosed reserves on the ledger – this three million Gold Swiss francs is categorized as provision for exchange and other losses.

The second "technique" concerns calculation of expenses. In the public calculation of profit, the expenditure items relating to preliminary organization and installation, and costs of administration, are totaled to derive the expenditure figure of 3,956,873.91 Gold Swiss francs, resulting in the final net profit figure of 11,186,521.97 Gold Swiss francs when these expenditures are deducted from gross profit above. However, on the hidden ledgers only the corresponding operating expenses of 3,557,000 are booked. That is, actual expenditures were 400,000 Gold Swiss francs less than the publicly released amount. Regarding this difference, on the public accounts a figure of exactly 400,000 Gold Swiss francs was booked as provision for indemnities to and repatriation of staff, while on the hidden ledgers this amount was booked to the administration account under allocations to undisclosed reserves. Thus, while on the public ledger this was booked to provision for indemnities to and repatriation of staff, on the hidden ledgers it was pooled as reserves.

The third manipulation involved the booking of gains on foreign exchange. As touched on above, the figure for exchange differences was not released. In fiscal 1930, 202,000 Gold Swiss francs in gains on foreign exchange arose, and this amount was pooled to hidden reserves.

In the end, the net profit figure was in agreement between the public and hidden ledgers, at 11,186,521.97 Gold Swiss francs.[91] What happened was that pooling to hidden reserves had taken place in the process of deriving this figure. As for fiscal 1930, the amount of hidden reserves was 32.2 percent of net profit. Put another way, if this pooling to hidden reserves had not taken place, the amount of BIS profit appropriated at the end of this fiscal year would have been about 1.3 times the publicly released figure. As seen in the following chapter, this ratio would rise markedly in the first half of the 1930s. To this degree, the BIS reduced dividends and accumulated hidden reserves.

But whose intent was it to build up these hidden reserves? According to an internal BIS document that studied this issue after the war, the policy of pooling funds to hidden reserves was "the position adopted by the Board of Directors in 1930." This internal document recognizes this laying away of hidden reserves as "current practice, at least among banks" and states that it is not prohibited by the BIS statutes.[92] If this was the intent of the board of directors, then it must have been based on the opinion of the central-bank representatives from the founding

Table 1.4 BIS profit and loss appropriation account, fiscal year 1930 (in Gold Swiss francs)

Net profit	11,186,521.97	Legal reserve fund 5% of net profit	559,326.10	French govt. guarantee fund	**452,593.31**
		Dividend at the rate of 6% per annum on paid-up capital	5,156,250.00	German govt. non-interest-bearing deposit	**581,440.63**
		Remainder(A)	*5,470,945.87*	Creditor govt. minimum deposits	**1,154,344.41**
		Dividend reserve fund 20% of (A)	1,094,189.17		
		Remainder(B)	*4,376,756.70*		
		General reserve fund 50% of (B)	2,188,378.35		
		Remainder	*2,188,378.35*		

Source: BIS Historical Archives, file 7.5, 1/2, "Disposal of the Surplus on the Profit and Loss Account, 1949–50", March 28, 1950; *BIS First Annual Report.*

nations. As such, they gave a higher priority to first strengthening the business foundation of the new bank, the BIS, than to dividends paid to the central banks as shareholders.

The document does not say much about the purpose of establishing these hidden reserves. It probably would be appropriate to assume that in fiscal 1930 these reserves were accumulated against exchange-rate fluctuations, in response to the outbreak of a global panic. In fact, the monthly business report distributed to the board of directors in November 1930 – naturally, a confidential internal document – touched on foreign-exchange risk, advocating "forming an 'exchange reserve' fund from part of the Bank's operating income," in a "manner similar to that of each central bank."[93] As seen in the following chapter, the purpose of establishing these reserves would repeatedly be based on different perspectives over time, in connection with dividend policies.

Unappropriated profit in fiscal 1930, finalized through the above process, was distributed as shown in Table 1.4. Each item represents pooling to reserves and distribution of dividends in accordance with the provisions of Article 53 of the BIS statutes (see Section 4 of this chapter). This balance was distributed to the French government's reparation fund, the German government's non-interest-bearing deposits and the deposit accounts of each government. Of these, on the balance sheet for the following year, fiscal 1931, the French and German funds and deposits would be included under long-term deposits on the credit side, and similarly the deposits of each government would be included in central bank trust accounts under short-term deposits.

6 Conclusion

To be a commercial bank or to be a bank for central banks? This question, asked at the time of the BIS's founding, was likely to become a fundamental issue regarding the BIS in later times.

As a "bank for central banks," the BIS was established as a venue for cooperation between central banks, in terms of both the ideas behind its founding and the substance of its system. Seen at first as a "bank for handling the reparations problem," the BIS transformed rapidly into a "forum" for international finance, over the short period from the planning stage through its founding. From the start, this transformation was not easy. The official history by Toniolo points out that at this time the BIS had two meanings: "national allegiances and even rivalries" and "friendliness and a collaborative climate" among practitioners of individual member nations.[94]

At the same time, the face of the BIS as a "bank for handling the reparations problem" developed into the commercial banking function performed by the Banking Department. Over a short space of time following the BIS's founding, the core of its assets shifted from long-term to short-term funds, and early signs of its gold-settlement function appeared as well. In addition, the BIS was strengthening its own business foundation and starting to build hidden reserves at the time it first began operation. The board, the core of the BIS's decision-making function, bundled experienced European central-bank governors with chairmen and presidents from the United States. The central organization gathered together a budding elite in the three departments of the Central Banking Department (later to become the Monetary and Economic Department), the Banking Department, and the Secretary General, under the leadership of General Manager Quesnay.

Also, two major currents in European economic thought – "financial utopianism" and neoliberalism – were involved in the design of the BIS system and in the bank's founding. The debates surrounding the BIS at the time of its founding – whether to see the new bank as a "super-bank" and whether to approve "managed currency" – created a stir in the press, among a variety of participants ranging from leading figures in the worlds of politics and finance to financial journalists, and from left-wing advocates to BIS officials. Despite the differences in individual goals, these debates can be seen to embody the will to rebuild a Europe weary from the Great War and the reparations problem. This idealism would continue in the operations and organization of the BIS.

History is made up of the voices of the dead. In the history of the BIS too, many now-deceased figures, both famous and unknown, come to the surface.

Among those who strived to found the BIS, it is perhaps Addis whose varied life is of the greatest interest. Addis played a very important role throughout the BIS from the planning stage through several years following its founding. Born to a pastor's family, he had spent a long time in China. He was fluent in Chinese and rose to the position of senior manager of the London branch of the Hongkong and Shanghai Bank. Following World War I, he was very active in international finance, serving as a director of the Reichsbank while under control of the allies until 1924, when its independence was restored. Addis's connection to the BIS was a continuation of this career. It is said that it was Addis who contrived to have the Americans McGarrah and Fraser serve as chairman and president, right before the BIS began operation.[95] World War I shook up the elite class structure in each country, so that even persons lacking in terms of academic history could rise to key positions in central banks and international finance provided they had the "requisite ability." Addis was a child of these times.

After the BIS began operation, Addis served as a key person issuing reports, from positions such as chairman, in various in-house committees on currency and credit. At the Bank of England, in Addis's home country, in-depth discussions on BIS operations were held between the governor of the Bank of England, Norman, and Addis and other aides. Addis was in a position to reflect their intentions in BIS policy. However, Addis and Norman had a difference of opinion, on which they were "far from agreeing."[96] At the time, the "new elite" was attempting to prove its own importance by daring to challenge the views of the previous generation of elites, such as central-bank governors. The glimpse of Addis seen here likely is one aspect of this "new elite."

In 1932, Addis, who had recorded the profound impression that the first annual general meeting of the BIS (1931) had been "a unique and historic occasion,"[97] resigned from the BIS and returned to Britain. It was raining on the day of his resignation, when Addis disappeared into the streets of Basel while listening to "flattering speeches by Moret, Luther, Beneduce and McGarrah."[98] At the time, the Mukden Incident had already broken out, and Addis was anxious about the future prospects for relations between Japan and China, as exemplified by his attempt to gain information about Japan through Daisuke Nohara of the Yokohama Specie Bank. Until his death in December 1945, Addis spent most of the rest of his life in China, devoting himself to relations between East Asia and the British Empire.[99]

2 The Bank for International Settlements and central banks during the 1930s

Another anti-depression measure

Paris, April 17, 1931: Inside a financial institution standing next to the Gare d'Orsay railway station along the banks of the Seine are arrayed the faces of the governor of the Banque de France and senior officials of the French finance ministry. This is the head office of the Caisse des Dépôts et Consignations (CDC), a quasi-official financial institution that accepts French postal savings and savings bank accounts and invests them in government bonds and other investments. At 9:30 a.m., a meeting of the audit committee, the highest decision-making body in this institution, began. At the start of the meeting, Clément Moret, the governor of the Banque de France, began making a proposal concerning the provision of medium-term credit to foreign countries. This proposal consisted of international cooperation to supply medium-term funds to European markets, which had begun to feel the effects of the Depression, with French banks and the CDC together playing a role. In response to this proposal, the CDC decided to take part in the unique business domain of medium-term credit.[1] However, light should be shed beyond that. Even down to the details of its wording, the proposal made in this meeting by the governor of the Banque de France was in accord with the plan prepared at the BIS months earlier.

During the Depression, the BIS had arranged for financial services to be provided by financial institutions – which were called to cooperate by the central banks of their own countries – using means that were revolutionary in the context of the relevant countries to supply funds to overseas markets. In a situation in which the era of globalization that had begun at the end of the nineteenth century was about to end with the Depression, the BIS made efforts toward inter-central-bank cooperation. How did this cooperation start, and what consequences did it bring about? These are the subjects of this chapter.

Section 1 will consider the circumstances in which the Monetary and Economic Department was set up as the BIS organizational response to the Depression. Section 2 will look at the plan – important parts of which were implemented – developed by the BIS to rebuild the international financial markets shaken by the Depression, with the Monetary and Economic Department serving as a base. Sections 3 and 4 will discuss the relations between the BIS and the central banks of individual countries during this period, using the Banque de France and the Bank of Japan as examples. Section 5 will look at BIS banking operations and distribution of profits, which were hit directly by the Depression. Section 6 concludes.

1 Establishment of the Monetary and Economic Department: the appearance of Jacobsson

As the effects of the Depression spread in Europe, reparations payments themselves came to a standstill, and the Hoover Moratorium on June 20, 1931 announced a freeze on reparations payments under the Young Plan. The BIS was shocked at these circumstances. This was because leaving reparations payments unfinished would mean the loss of the basis for the business of the BIS itself, whose objective was the economic resolution of the reparations problem.

However, at the same time the disorder in international markets that had resulted from the Depression also afforded an opportunity to the BIS, which had called for cooperation among central banks. In fact, as the situation intensified in each country's markets governments and financial authorities inclined toward unilateral policies, with this trend peaking with the collapse of the World Monetary and Economic Conference in London in 1933, but at the same time major central banks aimed for independence from government and financial authorities and worked independently toward international cooperation.[2] It was the BIS that served as the venue or forum for such cooperation.

The BIS established a new section to address this situation, with the shock of the Depression on the one hand and demands for international cooperation on the other. This section was the Monetary and Economic Department, examined in this section, and Per Jacobsson was appointed its first head.

Structural reforms: the Monetary and Economic Department

The organization that had been called the Central Banking Department when the BIS was founded was renamed the Monetary and Economic Department in 1931. While the process through which this renaming took place has not been confirmed, there is no doubt that the revisions to payment of reparations spurred by the Hoover Moratorium were behind it. Now let's look at the state of operations of this Monetary and Economic Department, using a currently available document as a clue.

The document we will refer to here is an anonymous memo submitted to Johan Beyen, the then-vice-president of the BIS, in 1935 – three years after the new department's establishment.[3] Titled "Reorganization of the Monetary and Economic Department," this memo mentions that the department's chain of command at that time (1935) was separated into two. One was a line going up from Secretary General Raffaele Pilotti to General Manager Quesnay, while the other was a line from Head of the Monetary and Economic Department Jacobsson to President Fraser. According to this memo, Pilotti and Jacobsson each had their own secretaries and staff and did not work together very well.

A look at staffing and assignments shows that while research staff were assigned to specific individual subjects – such as gold, budgeting and public debt, international balance of payments, external short-term obligations and central banks – no country-specific research had been conducted.

The memo suggests that such circumstances should be improved and proposed reorganization, even providing organizational charts. The author of this memo wrote that "before considering the immediate re-organization of the department it is useful to consider what we might hope the club side of the BIS should develop into after a number of years."

This reorganization proposal is highly interesting from both the aspect that it mentioned the ideals of the time and that it expressed the actual circumstances of the time. The proposal for reorganization first advocated unification of the chain of command of the Monetary and Economic Department to the President-Jacobsson line. Then, it suggested full-time staff be assigned by subject. The memo identified research subjects as central banks, banking systems, short-term external position, gold production and distribution, international balance of payments, prices, and budgeting and public debt and so on. It also advocated that human resources from each country – "young men from central banks" – assigned should be sent to the BIS to carry out continuous research on each country and that statistical and graphical sections should be made separately from these research sections.

From these observations, it appears that the situation in the Monetary and Economic Department at the time was one in which a small number of staff was busy with everything from subject-specific research through graphing and had no time at all for country-specific research. How this department was strengthened thereafter to become a presence rivaling other departments, especially the Banking Department, would appear to be an important point in looking to the subsequent history of the BIS.

Jacobsson was the first head of this Monetary and Economic Department and worked vigorously, for example writing a massive volume of memos and authoring singlehandedly most of the important parts of the BIS annual report. Next, let's consider Jacobsson the man and his ideas.

Jacobsson: the man and his ideas

Born in 1894 as the son of veterinarian in the small city of Tanum in western Sweden, Jacobsson was the eldest of three siblings. After completing primary and middle school in Uddevala, near Tanum, he entered Uppsala University in 1912. There he studied statistics, economics and then law.

His younger years at Uppsala University contributed greatly to the formation of Jacobsson's thinking. While the economist David Davidson was at Uppsala University at the time, it was Knut Wicksell, then holding the position of assistant professor at Lund University, who had a greater impact on Jacobsson. Wicksell was born in 1851 and gave lectures at Uppsala University and Jacobsson said that he was strongly impressed by Wicksell's theory of financial panics. Also, in 1917 Jacobsson took part, together with Wicksell, Cassel and Eli Heckscher, in setting up the Economics Club, as one of its founding members. This

Economics Club later invited Keynes to speak. Subsequently, after returning to the university following military service during World War I, Jacobsson also chaired the reformist student organization Verdandi before graduating in 1919 and going to Stockholm. There he wrote economics pieces for Swedish and foreign journals while changing jobs several times, including serving as a temporary employee of the Swedish Ministry of Finance.[4]

In 1920, on Cassel's recommendation, he was transferred temporarily to the League of Nations, going to London to work in the secretariat for the Brussels Conference. The Brussels Conference, intended to discuss a post-World War I international fiscal and financial framework, would see the airing of opinions from representatives of each country's central bank and financial authorities. Here Jacobsson joined a subcommittee led by Lord Layton, working on preparation of research reports on the financial situation of each League of Nations member state. Later appointed editor of *The Economist*, Lord Layton also took part in the founding of the BIS (see Chapter 1).[5] Jean Monnet, who later became known as the "Father of Europe," also was with the League of Nations at the time, and Jacobsson developed a close friendship with him.

Two years later Jacobsson, who after the Brussels Conference had transferred to the League of Nations headquarters in Geneva, took part in the Genoa Conference as well. As seen in Chapter 1, prior to the Genoa Conference Blum and Auriol of the French Socialist Party had announced their plan for international settlements, also known as "financial utopianism," part of which had an impact on the Genoa Conference. However, Jacobsson, a participant at the time, was opposed to the socialists' proposal. Seeing the post-World War I inflation as an issue of gold buying power, he criticized the recovery plan proposed by Blum and others at the Genoa Conference. This recovery plan argued for rebuilding the postwar economy from the perspectives of economic growth and increasing the share of labor. In later years Jacobsson talked about this plan that "it is only natural that the financiers at Genoa should have been obsessed by the fear of the scarcity of gold," but "in 1923 and 1924 the situation changed."[6] Thus, even before the founding of the BIS, beginning as early as the time around the Genoa Conference, there was divergence apparent between the socialists' plan, which also had an impact on the founding of the BIS, and the ideas of Jacobsson, who later became the theoretical leader of the BIS.

Following the Genoa Conference, Jacobsson worked at the League of Nations Financial Committee and then in 1928 returned to his motherland of Sweden to take the public position of secretary general of the Economic Defense Committee. During this period, Jacobsson also devoted his energies to recommending other Swedes to the League of Nations, sending Swedes including Gunnar Myrdal and Bertil Ohlin to the League of Nations or related institutions. Later, Jacobsson resigned from his public position in July 1930 and joined Kreuger and Toll – a match manufacturer and one of Sweden's largest businesses – as economic advisor.

He left Kreuger and Toll in September 1931 to become head of the BIS's newly established Monetary and Economic Department. The departure of the

British pound from the gold standard one week after he had taken the position of BIS department head made Jacobsson's start a turbulent one.

What was the background of Jacobsson being invited to the BIS? Actually, matters are not clear on this point. According to a biography by Jacobsson's daughter Erin Juker-Fleetwood (née Jacobsson), when Jacobsson began working at Kreuger and Toll the company was involved in accounting fraud and bribery, and manager Ivar Kreuger, fearing that sooner or later Jacobsson would detect the fraud, frequently pushed him to travel overseas on business. It is not hard to imagine that Jacobsson, forming an international personal network through these business trips, would come to dislike working for Kreuger and Toll and try to switch to the BIS. But why he chose the BIS remains a mystery.[7]

Leaving aside inquiries concerning his appointment as head of the BIS Monetary and Economic Department, the important point is the aspect of Jacobsson as a theorist and economic thinker.

As outlined above, Jacobsson was close to the Swedish school of economics, in which Wicksell played a central role. He also was well-versed in Keynesian theory, which had been in the limelight during the Depression. In this independent position Jacobsson, from the standpoint of a financial practitioner, maintained a lifelong stance closer to that of Wicksell. For example, he criticized Keynes' *General Theory*, arguing the point of view that structurally it was preconditioned on the status of a strong creditor nation such as Great Britain or the United States, which to some extent did not have to take into consideration the amount of international balance-of-payments deficit, while most other nations, especially the smaller nations of Europe, needed to consider the international balance of payments and trust in their currencies. From this point on, Jacobsson later rejected total demand control involving public expenditures and extolled sound currencies and free markets.

But what kind of doctrine was this Wicksellian theory to which Jacobsson was devoted? Wicksell's doctrine has been the subject of outstanding research from the standpoint of economics.[8] Here, instead of delving into it in detail, we will quote Wicksell's own reminiscences as reported by Jacobsson himself. Jacobsson says he heard the following when meeting with Wicksell in "1918 or 1919."

> When reading the standard works on political economy, he [Wicksell] had suddenly been struck by the fact that in one part of these books– the section dealing with the question of price-formation and distribution – there were long explanations of the set of factors (supply of real capital, etc.) by which interest rates are determined in this sphere, while in another section there were equally long explanations of the different set of factors (gold movements, etc.) by which interest rates are determined in the money and capital markets; but that in spite of this there was hardly ever any attempt made to establish a link between the two sets of phenomena which had thus been described separately in different parts of these standard works.[9]

It can be said that this flash of inspiration was the moment at which Wicksellian theory was born, which later became known as monetary equilibrium analysis. The issue is how this theory was received by Jacobsson. While Jacobsson's analysis of Wicksellian theory appears to extend to a highly detailed level, regarding the relationship between real interest rates and market interest rates, especially the cumulative process that begins with differences between the two, he focused more on cumulative processes leading to inflation and did not give much attention to the converse relationship to deflation. "It is only to a very limited extent that Wicksell admits that a lowering of the market rate may lower the 'real' rate." From this argument one can see germ of the policy theory that should be called Jacobssonian theory, which reached a compromise between the neoliberalism discussed below and Wicksellian theory.

Another important characteristic of Jacobsson's economic thought is his unique focus on gold. Beginning with his appointment as head of the BIS Monetary and Economic Department, Jacobsson followed statistics on gold mining with great interest, seeing the supply of monetary gold as an important variable in the international economy. On the other hand, highly familiar with a type of very simple quantity theory of money, his point of view was that at some times gold production should be enhanced for the purposes of economic recovery. However, Jacobsson's point of view on gold was the other side of his extolling of sound currencies and free markets, and on this point a strange kind of accordance with the "financial utopian" plans mentioned in Chapter 1 can be seen – arguments for gold settlement using a unit such as the "*grammor.*"

It was at the World Monetary and Economic Conference of 1933 held in London that these economic thoughts of Jacobsson were expressed officially for the first time on the stage of international currency diplomacy. As is well known, this London conference attempted policy coordination among participating countries to effect a recovery from the Depression. However, it was driven to collapse with the withdrawal of the Roosevelt administration of the United States, which was advancing its New Deal policies. As chair of the preparatory committee for the London conference, Jacobsson had planned to bring up, together with Frederick Phillips, Charles Rist and John Williams, the policies of lowering prices in countries sticking to the gold standard and expanding credit in countries devaluing par value. While they were not realized as a result of the US withdrawal, these draft policies incorporated Jacobsson's own individual point of view – especially the subtle positioning toward Keynesian theory. At this time, concerned about rising prices and wages in the United States, Jacobsson was critical of the New Deal policies. At the same time, he regarded highly the arguments in Keynes' *General Theory* that "real wages and the volume of output are uniquely correlated" and that "in general, an increase in employment can only occur to the accompaniment of a decline in the rate of real wages," making clear his position extolling an increase in "real wages" rater than an increase in "wages" in general – that is, an increase in real wages through a decrease in the level of prices.

This thinking of Jacobsson on policy – differing subtly from Keynesianism, which was becoming the prevailing current at the time – was likely to have a considerable impact on the international financial system from the prewar through the postwar periods, through theoretical activities including the authoring of the BIS annual report.

The BIS in the early period and neoliberalism

Jacobsson's economic thought, especially about its relationship with Wicksellian economic thought, is as outlined above. However, in looking at the economic thinking of Jacobsson and the BIS, there is one more point that should be referred to: neoliberalism. There are various definitions of neoliberalism, and its exponents are diverse as well. Perhaps this diversity itself, which differs from other schools of thought such as Marxism in which various factions or schools compete for the status of orthodoxy, is a characteristic of neoliberalism. In this book, the theoretical position of neoliberalism is understood as follows, conforming to the definitions of the movement itself appearing at that time: that is, neoliberalism (1) extols market mechanisms, respecting price postulates, (2) accepts state intervention to ensure the functioning of markets, (3) sees balanced budgets and price stability as important, (4) takes social issues into consideration and opposes various types of monopolies. These points of view, which differ subtly from so-called market fundamentalism, were given concrete form in the prewar neoliberalism movements – such as the Lippmann Symposium held in Paris, the International Research Center for the Renovation of Liberalism Reforms (*Centre international d'études pour la rénovation du libéralisme*), and the Mont Pèlerin Society, founded in 1947 drawing on these currents.

As for the movement's connections to the BIS, the second BIS general manager, Roger Auboin, and its first head of the Banking Department, Marcel van Zeeland, attended the Lippmann Symposium, and as seen above Jacobsson, the head of the Monetary and Economic Department, interacted closely with members of the Mont Pèlerin Society. In theoretical research, Jacobsson regarded highly Fritz Machlup, Wilhelm Röpke, Walter Eucken and Heckscher, mentioned above, and he exchanged occasional private letters with these men. They were either members of the Mont Pèlerin Society or those surrounding it.

But what is the logic behind the monetary and credit theories of neoliberalism? Above all, neoliberalism advocates free and fair competition and avoidance of inflation. For this reason, it aimed to restrict the issuance of banknotes through high ratios of gold reserves. Good examples are opinions advocating fully reserved currency through a reserve ratio of 100 percent and currency-unit ideas such as commodity-reserve currency.[10] However, as the neoliberals themselves have pointed out, such simple monetary theory did not evolve into credit theory and was weak on banking-system theory.[11]

Rather, neoliberal monetary and credit theory are characterized by their having brought up the issue of conditions necessary to ensure the functioning of currency as a fair yardstick of markets. For example, Jacques Rueff, a leading

French neoliberal, advocated the "absoluteness of the laws of economics," stating that "an economic system cannot remain in existence without equilibrium conditions" and arguing that such equilibrium is realized through the pricing mechanism. What is important about Rueff's theory is the point that regarding this pricing mechanism it accepts "intervention working on the causes of prices." For example, while maintaining the argument that the post-World War II international currency system had an urgent need for market reconstruction through such means as the restoration of convertibility, Rueff also accepted the reconstruction of fixed exchange rates by the IMF as an unavoidable measure and acknowledged that there was room for "effective planning for purposes of international exchange."[12] We will revisit Rueff's theory in Chapter 5.

At the same time, the neoliberals saw the automatic regulating function of the classical gold standard as already having been lost in the twentieth century.[13] They then advanced to the point of argument of how to secure currency stability if this automatic regulating function could not be relied upon. On this point, there was an apparent difference of opinion within neoliberalism. On one side was Milton Friedman's well-known argument for control of the money supply – a theory that later developed into monetarism. On the other side were those, like Lionel Robbins, who rejected Say's Law and adopted a position almost identical to that of their old rival John Maynard Keynes. Between these two extremes were arrayed a variety of views on full employment and public investment.[14] Even Friedrich von Hayek, the leader of neoliberalism, suggested the need for a degree of participation by the state, noting that currency and monetary policies were "preconditions of competitive discipline."[15] In this way, neoliberalism – while there were important differences within the movement – kept some distance from the nineteenth-century laissez-faire, developing monetary and credit theory aiming to avoid inflation and balance budgets based on state involvement. Their ideal was someplace between the two extremes of the "jungle," governed by naked competition, and the "jail," restricted by controls and plans.[16]

However, the expansion of neoliberal monetary and credit theory beyond policy theory for a single nation to the international domain involves some peculiar contractions. Is the ideal form of international markets a jungle or a jail? Should future neoliberal governments approve of or oppose international liberalization? Should the forces of deregulation in the domestic economy welcome or reject free trade or entry of foreign capital? In fact, Robbins, mentioned above, identified the discovery of an automatic stabilizer functioning for the whole system as an unresolved issue for liberalism to address in the future.[17] While on the other hand Maurice Allais argued that it would be a major error to fail to recognize that liberalism has an international perspective, the reality of this international system theory was a federalism oriented toward a loose system of governance, distinct from supranational sovereignty, and the subject of debate too appears to have been limited to Europe.[18] Regarding such federalism, while Hayek in 1939 identified "financial policy" together with colonial policy as a category of policy likely to remain in existence even under federation, he too was opposed to supranational systems of governance.[19] It would appear that in the international domain, especially the international currency domain, in the absence of supranational authority there would be no authority to rival state power and that the conditions of achieving equilibrium too naturally would differ from domestic conditions.

No documentation has been found of these neoliberals having contributed directly to BIS policy decision-making. Rather, it is conceivable that their impact on the BIS was at more of an indirect level. But even if indirect, the impact of the theorists respected by top BIS management such as Roger Auboin, van Zeeland, or Jacobsson should not be underestimated. Jacobsson in particular cited Hayek and Robbins in his journal articles and speeches, and after World War II he spoke of their neoliberal theories frequently to counter Keynes and the Keynesians. The actual policies adopted by the BIS too show the impact of neoliberalism – in complex ways, as described in this book.

The point at issue is the relationship between Wicksellian economic thought and neoliberalism within the economic thought of Jacobsson in particular. In this book, we will study this point historically – that is, along the practical manifestations of BIS theory and policy. As one venue for such study, here we will verify the BIS response to the Depression. Needless to say, Keynesianism emerged as a major current of thought regarding the causes of and countermeasures to the Depression and various planning ideas and design policies were put into practice. The theme of the following section concerns the standpoints of neoliberalism, which was said to be on the defensive, and Wicksellian economic thought, which appeared to have been overcome by Keynesianism, within BIS theory and policy in the context of the Depression.

2 International regulation and provision of credit: in the context of the Depression

As the Depression deepened, the BIS began lively theoretical activities. The first results of these activities to appear were the concepts of international regulation and settlement.

The starting point of working out the concepts seen below was the first BIS annual general meeting.[20] The BIS, which had begun operation in May 1930, opened the first annual general meeting as required under its statutes on May 19, 1931. In the process of preparing for this general meeting, the BIS authorities planned to discuss the various issues relating to central banks not in the general meeting itself, but in the form of a working group. That is, they intended to form two groups – one on credit and one on currencies – with subcommittees set up under each and panels that participants in the general meeting could attend. The BIS authorities established the following subcommittees based on the recognition that "discussions on broad subjects by a large assembly not only tend to lead nowhere, but may indeed do more harm than good unless they are carefully organised and directed into proper channels."

Credit group (names in parentheses indicate lead presenters):

1   The BIS and the markets in each country (BIS Head of Banking Department Ernst Hülse)
2   Credit creation (Swiss National Bank Governor Gottlieb Bachmann)
3   Interest rates (Swedish central bank Riksbank Governor Ivar Rooth)

Currency group (names in parentheses indicate lead presenters):

1   The BIS and foreign-exchange issues (BIS General Manager Quesnay)
2   Convertibility of currency (Czech National Bank Governor V. Pospisil)
3   Foreign reserves (De Nederlandsche Bank Governor G. Vissering)

As can be seen from the above, central-bank governors from BIS member states – smaller ones at that – were appointed as presenters in the second and third sub-committees under each group, while BIS General Manager Quesnay and Head of the Banking Department Hülse were assigned to the first subcommittee in each group. The presenters in the first subcommittees in particular planned to hold meetings on the first day of the general meeting to open the discussions "with the appropriate statements of the BIS's position, requirements, experiences and aims under each subject." The role of the BIS secretary general pulling the strings was already shown in such way of managing the meeting. Below, we will look at the main content of discussions in this meeting.

Regulation and settlement concepts

The study of these concepts began in the second subcommittee under the credit group. Let's look at the content of these discussions, based on the report from Swiss National Bank Governor Bachmann, coordinator of deliberations in that subcommittee.[21]

According to Bachmann's report, the "bank of issue" – note that this does not refer to "central bank" – in each country began to use new policy methods around World War I. These were the methods of trading in foreign-exchange markets and trading government bonds on the open market to manage the total amount of domestic credit. Needless to say, the functions and status of banks of issue are determined by the structure of and changes in the domestic economy, and therefore these vary by each nation. However, it should be noted that each country began to employ unprecedented means of credit adjustment.

Based on this recognition, Bachmann recommended the policy of stimulating trading in gold and foreign exchange between each country's bank of issue and the BIS, to coordinate policies of each country so that they would not conflict with each other.

The concept incorporated into this Bachmann report was realized when an international financial crisis broke out in Europe in 1931. The BIS had provided emergency financing to central banks of countries caught up in the financial crisis by forming syndicate groups with central banks of other countries – the Hungarian National Bank, the Austrian National Bank, the Reichsbank of

Germany and National Bank of Yugoslavia. The total amount of financing reached roughly $1 billion. It is said that this amount corresponded to one-tenth of the total balance of international short-term obligations as of the beginning of 1931.[22]

The scale and effectiveness of this support were evaluated in many ways at the time, and in today's historical studies as well.[23] However, such formation of syndicates among central banks, while each country was oriented toward economic recovery of its own and as a result the fiscal authorities had considerable influence on central banks, can be considered to have been very important. Also, every country paid back these loans in their entirety. This was an important precondition – a successful example of complete repayment of loans – of central-bank cooperation conducted under unprecedented circumstances.

It was Jacobsson, the head of the Monetary and Economic Department, who extended Bachmann's recommendation further to the planning of international regulations. In February 1935, Jacobsson wrote a long memorandum entitled, "Memorandum on the Tasks of Central Banks." Its content was to require the private banks in each country to reserve a certain amount of deposits with their countries' central bank accounts and restrict foreign-reserve ratios at each central bank.[24]

It should be noted here that the BIS began to claim the authority to carry out supranational regulation, or to present international standards and demand conformity to them. In this way, the international regulations that became an important role of the BIS in later times first appeared in the theoretical activities of the Monetary and Economic Department during the Depression.

Securing liquidity of mid-term credit

In the 1930s the BIS was acting in response to the international financial crisis as described above – especially to the financial panic in Europe. Primarily, this was a response to the settlement crisis – foreign-currency loans to central banks. However, the BIS had prepared plans concerned with each country's countermeasures against the economic downturn, not just responses in the area of settlement. These were the plans for securing liquidity of mid-term credit.

These plans had their origin in the third board meeting in July 1930, soon after the BIS had begun operation. This board meeting set up a committee to study "the possibility to establish a procedure which enables to transform short-term funds into mid-term funds."[25] This "procedure" referred to mid-term credit, known at the time as "*pensions de crédits.*"

But why was there a need to plan such "mid-term" credit in the first place? The Banking Department, which stood on the front lines of BIS funds management, reported bluntly on the circumstances of the time: "What most debtor nations need at this time is capital, not short-term deposits – at the very least, mid-term funds."[26] Taking into consideration factors such as the stability of the banking business and the guarantees by central banks called for in the Statutes, it was difficult to expand business operations beyond short-term deposits.

However, new demand had appeared in Europe, where the shockwaves of the Depression had begun to appear. Based on this recognition of the circumstances, in October 1930 a committee on mid-term credit was formed, to consider the issues above.[27] Central figures in this committee were members from Britain and North America, such as Bank of England representative Harry Siepmann and US representative Oliver Sprague.

The committee indicated the following recognition of the situation: "There are appropriate means for provision of short-term credit alone. However, no similar means have been organized for mid-term credit."; "On the other hand, it cannot be denied that the volume of short-term funds is abundant." This document led to a memo by the governor of the Banque de France, touched on at the start of this chapter. Here the committee was thinking about world trade, which had contracted with the deepening of the Depression – particularly export industries. According to the committee's definition at the time, "mid-term" meant the period of three months to one year.[28]

The mechanism for mediation of these short-term funds to mid-term credit was at issue. First of all, the committee referred to a plan to set up a new credit-providing agency. However, it rejected the creation of a new agency, stating that "our proposal is limited by what the BIS can do under its current structure." The committee also referred to direct acceptance by each country's central bank of mid-term bills for discounting, but it rejected this idea too, because "in most cases, central-bank statutes prohibit discounting of bills with maturities of 90 days or longer."[29]

So what should be done? The answer was "discounting not of the currency for which each country's central bank is responsible, but using foreign-exchange." The central banks held abundant foreign reserves. The committee suggested that central banks invest these foreign reserves to secure liquidity of mid-term credit in countries other than their own. To secure this liquidity of credit, the BIS would "contribute to this object a part of its paid-up capital and its perpetual deposits, of 100–150 Swiss francs, for example." These perpetual deposits must refer to the long-term deposits to which each country's central bank paid in. Also, it would be a special-purpose financial institution in each country, rather than its central bank, that would be in charge of this provision of mid-term credit.[30]

In response to the report from this committee, each country on its own began the establishment of specialized financial institutions to handle this mid-term credit, without waiting for the details of the policy to be finalized. The secretary general was requested to study each country's responses and send the statutes of these financial institutions to the BIS.[31] At the end of the year, consultations between the BIS and each central bank showed progress, and it was reported to the board of directors that "practical results are expected in the near future."[32] At the sixth BIS board meeting in December 1930, the mid-term credit operations were approved.

How did actual operations progress? First, in February and March 1931, right after the operations were approved, the above committee on middle-term credits met again to finalize the details of the operations. In this meeting, the maturity of "up to 12 months" was extended to "five years." This revision was the result of the argument that "one of the objectives of the BIS under the Young proposal is to assist in the recovery of international trade."[33] In March 1931, President McGarrah himself contributed an essay to a US business journal publicizing the BIS mid-term credit business.[34] Demands for mid-term credit later delivered to the BIS were mainly investments in central Europe especially those concerning transportation such as railways and shipbuilding.[35]

Furthermore, the BIS also provided capital to establish companies in Amsterdam and Basel to handle mid-term mortgage credit.[36] The proposal to establish these companies was discussed in the meeting of the BIS board of directors in February 1931, where the committee on middle-term credits mentioned above was preparing to submit its report. The Bank of England governor, Norman, who had submitted a draft proposal for discussion, indicated his recognition that

> in view of the serious crisis which the world is now facing and for which there appears no immediate remedy of an ordinary character, it is suggested that the time has arrived when extraordinary measures should be adopted to meet the situation and to help to re-establish confidence.

The outline of this plan, as seen in a confidential memo from the board of directors meeting, is as follows:[37]

1   Establish an international corporation.
2   For fiscal reasons, headquarter the company in Switzerland or the Netherlands, with paid-in capital in Swiss francs or Dutch guilders.
3   Set its nominal capital to no less than the equivalent of £25 million sterling, with paid-in capital at 10 percent of this amount.
4   Issue public bonds by the company up to three times the amount of nominal capital and lend the funds to foreign national and local governments, mortgage credit institutions, port committees, and railway and public-service businesses.
5   Issue the company's bonds in France and the United States, and let them be listed in Switzerland and the Netherlands as well, though trading in Great Britain to be conducted only within a severely restricted range.
6   Management of the company to be conducted by an international board of directors.
7   Consider lending "on a purely business basis."

Norman's idea was to attempt an international redistribution of funds through establishing an independent "international corporation" separate from the mid-term credit operations in which the BIS took part. The plan to establish a headquarters in Switzerland or the Netherlands and issue bonds in France and the United States can be understood to reflect the recognition of market conditions during the middle of the Depression in 1931 – the expectation that the United

States would overcome the Depression quickly and gold-bloc countries would hold their own.

Still, the Banque de France said it had "some reservations" concerning this Norman plan. In February 1931, immediately before the plan was decided on by the BIS board of directors, Governor Moreau of the Banque de France sent a letter to President McGarrah of the BIS that, while in sympathy with the plan Norman proposed that month, he would restrain the plan in the following manner. During exchange of opinions between French private-sector banks and the Banque de France, it became apparent that a number of private-sector banks were about to start up on the Paris market operations similar to those in the Norman's plan. The letter stated, "Highly interesting operations toward currency stabilization, promotion of agriculture, and improvement of communication means between European nations are being prepared in the Paris markets." He also pointed out that Article 22 of the BIS Statutes prohibited the BIS from purchasing equities and therefore "cannot help hesitating to admit the BIS to get judiciously involved with the institutions where BIS may not acquire their capital" by institutions that cannot take part in capital participation.[38] This reflects the fact that to France, which unlike other countries had been spared the impact of the Depression, the plans of Norman and the BIS would be an impediment to advancing its plans to make Paris an international financial center.[39]

The process of deliberation from Norman's plan through actual establishment of the companies is unclear. Tracing developments from the board of directors meeting in which the plan was proposed, in the end these companies were unsuccessful, and before long they were liquidated. However, the fact that the BIS had broken out from the narrowly defined framework of being a settlement bank and begun making operations to provide and secure the liquidity of mid-term credit through operating its own subsidiaries was an epochal development.

Acceptance of gold deposits

Another business planned and implemented during the Depression along with securing liquidity of mid-term credit was the acceptance of gold deposits. While the BIS had accepted earmarked gold since the time of its founding, the gold deposits referred to here were gold deposits accepted from each central bank to deposit accounts, as a main business of the BIS. This was an important business that would have an even more significant impact on future generations than did mid-term credit. Now let's look at the course through which this business was established.

In 1930, the BIS did not admit acceptance of gold deposits. While at the time it received inquiries from a number of central banks concerning gold deposits, the board of directors did not clarify its attitude, stating that "before accepting gold the BIS should investigate the conditions for earmarking gold to central banks."[40] Later, in November 1932, it became clear – in the form of a response to an inquiry from the Yugoslav national bank – that the BIS would accept gold deposits.[41] Since the BIS balance sheet shows gold deposits beginning with the

1933 fiscal year, it appears that actual acceptance of gold began soon after this response. An outline of this business is as follows:

1   The BIS accepts gold in bare metal, coined money and other forms to the account of each central bank.
2   Since the BIS did not possess its own vaults, the depositing central bank (A) places the gold in a BIS account at a central bank in another country (B).
3   The central bank at which the gold actually is deposited (B) accepts this gold as a deposit of earmarked gold in the name of the BIS.
4   The BIS opens a guarantee account (*compte de garde*) for central bank (A) in a BIS account.
5   The above *compte de garde* account is subject to the protections under Article 10 of the BIS statutes.
6   Central bank (A) is permitted to sell or transfer the gold to the central bank (B) at which it is earmarked, to convert it to foreign currency, or to sell or transfer it to other institutions.
7   When converting the gold to foreign currency, if the currency requested by central bank (A) is the currency of the country of central bank (B), the BIS would promptly execute the conversion in its own name. If the requested currency was a currency other than that of the country of central bank (B), the BIS would obtain the requested foreign currency by lending the gold at an interest rate higher than the deposit interest rate.[42]

This was a fairly broad-ranging business. According to this description, if for example a European central bank deposited its own gold bare metal with the BIS and that bare metal was earmarked at the Federal Reserve Bank of New York, if it was necessary to convert the gold to dollars then the dollars would be credited to the central bank's *compte de garde* account immediately through a BIS operation. However, an important point about the design of this business is the fact that in the end the conversion to dollars would take place "through lending of gold" – that is, in the end the gold would return to the original position.

The fact that the BIS, which had been cautious about gold deposits at first, expanded the business to this extent is related to the final point above. The BIS explained that since its aim was to "arrest the liquidation of the gold exchange standard" it needed to "prevent a further conversion of exchange into gold, or alternatively to facilitate a reconversion of gold into exchange," and that the gold deposits truly were a system intended for this purpose.[43] Still, it is said that "skepticism was displayed" about the usefulness of these gold deposits.[44] As seen in Section 5 of this chapter, actual gold deposits, which started at 28 million Swiss francs in fiscal 1933, decreased during the 1930s.

In connection with the gold deposits, another interesting plan from the Depression years is van Zeeland's plan for gold-secured lending. This plan, developed by van Zeeland, then a young member of the Banking Department, based on an inquiry from the Austrian National Bank, brought about severe discord both inside and outside that department. An outline of the course of these developments follows.

In September 1933, when the gold deposit system started, the Austrian National Bank made a proposal to the BIS to the effect that it would like to allocate the proceeds from Austrian foreign bonds issued in France and Italy to repayment of gold borrowed from the BIS. In response to this proposal to repay gold loans in foreign currency, van Zeeland showed a positive approach and came up with the further idea of lending against gold deposits.[45]

However, this plan led to a rare internal dispute involving BIS legal advisor Felix Weiser and Marcel van Zeeland, who at the time was on temporary assignment in the Banking Department. In criticizing the plan, Weiser told the following anecdote: Suppose a homemaker borrowed one pound of coffee from a neighbor homemaker to serve to a sudden guest. However, the homemaker borrowing the coffee already had one pound of coffee at home. "Is this not sheer nonsense?"[46] Van Zeeland responded: Suppose the homemaker lived in Basel, and while she does have a pound of coffee, it was at her summer house in Arlesheim. At the same time, the homemaker from whom she borrowed the coffee also had a summer house in Arlesheim, with no coffee in it. This plan is like the first homemaker borrowing the coffee she lacks in Basel and repaying it to her neighbor later in Arlesheim.[47] Weiser shot back: "this would clearly be a spot sale of currencies and a purchase of forward gold"; "There is of course nothing legally or logically impossible in such a transaction, but I understand that our Board is opposed to the BIS making such transactions."[48]

While this plan appears to have fizzled out in the end, it was realized as option transactions in gold operations in the postwar years. While overall it sided with the voices of caution, in handling gold the BIS during the Depression had by chance come to grips with innovations in financial techniques: swaps and gold and foreign-exchange options.

Depression countermeasures and the banking business

The above plans from Bachmann, Jacobsson and van Zeeland did in part take concrete shape, and regardless of the success or failure of such efforts the BIS did contribute to addressing the Depression at that time. Incidentally, another point that must be touched on here is the relation between these plans and the proper businesses of the BIS. Even in the middle of the Depression the BIS did not cease being a "reparations bank," and its governance structure too was one of a joint-stock company distributing its earnings to its shareholders (i.e., the central banks). Thus, the BIS proposed and implemented countermeasures against the Depression as a player in the markets itself, not simply a think tank.

But if that is the case, with what kind of unique logic did the BIS as a bank address the Depression? Put another way, how did the Banking Department view the countermeasures led by the Monetary and Economic Department? This question, which penetrates to the heart of the BIS, is another important point in question addressed by this book. Below, we will attempt an examination of this point, focusing on internal BIS documents from the Depression era – confidential internal memos on banking operations submitted to the board of directors.

In each monthly BIS board of directors meeting, a confidential report entitled *"Rapport sur les opérations de la Banque"* was distributed. While over the years this report would become standardized, at the time the BIS began operations "special reports" often were attached. These special reports covered matters such as an overview of BIS funds management, examples of failed investments and examples of differences of opinion between central banks and the BIS. These special reports, which sometimes took the form of massive essays, are colored with passionate writing style and grand claims, communicating the enthusiasm of the BIS during its youthful years. Let's take a look at a report distributed in May 1931.[49]

This report considers actual examples of difficulties in investing in each country's markets, from verification of monthly performance of BIS investments. Its conclusion addresses in a youthful manner the argument over what are the goals of the BIS to begin with. According to this report, the BIS is a public-interest organization (*"organisme d'intérêt public"*). As such, the BIS "strives to eliminate imperfections in the current currency system instead of trying to profit from them." Based on this objective, BIS investment consisted of two types: administrative investments and active investments. Here, active investments refers to using more effective methods not just to satisfy public needs but also to provide indicative intervention to each country. Specifically, this is the concept of placing time deposits with the central bank in each country and investing funds in rediscounting of superior-grade notes in each country or backing central banks' open-market operations. This ideal, however, encountered various difficulties. "Some countries lack financial markets in which money markets can be used to generate sound notes or trade in notes on a daily basis." As a joint-stock company, the BIS needed to consider the soundness of its investments. Under such circumstances, such difficulties justified the argument that the BIS should "invest funds over the short term in the form of deposits."

However – and from this point the relation to the banking business becomes apparent – even if funds are deposited with central banks "most central banks do not pay interest on deposits." Conceivable responses to these circumstances were the methods of opening funds-management accounts in which the funds were managed in proprietary accounts with central banks or depositing with private-sector banks in each country instead of central banks. Even so, adjustments still would need to be made with each country to avoid risk. The BIS's lofty ideal of protecting the gold standard through breaking out of the Depression (embodied in the Monetary and Economic Department) was, at the same time, not freed from the motive of securing returns on investment (the intention of the Banking Department). Put another way, the BIS's ideas on reforming the financial system were restricted by the banking business's framework of earning returns on investment. This point can be described as a unique characteristic of the BIS and one that differs from the principles behind the design of the IMF and other postwar institutions not subject to such restriction.

3 The BIS and France: central-bank cooperation strategies

In concluding the prewar BIS history, let's return to the viewpoint of central-bank cooperation which is the theme of this book. The nature of the relationship formed between BIS authorities and individual central banks and fiscal authorities is the issue to be looked at in the following sections.

For reasons of data and space available (and naturally those of limits on the author's ability as well), it is impossible to look at all of the central banks. Therefore, in this chapter Section 3 will focus on France and Section 4 will focus on Japan. It goes without saying that France, along with Germany, played one of the greatest roles in the founding of the BIS and was one of the leading actors in the BIS, filling key BIS posts including successive general managers.

The French Ministry of Finance and the Banque de France: their strategies

When looking at the relations between the BIS and individual countries, perhaps the first issue that arises is the relationship in each country between the government and the Ministry of Finance and the central bank. France was no exception. Let's examine this point first, going back to the time of the BIS's founding.

French foreign relations and domestic affairs following World War I developed along the axis of the reparations issue. Backed by domestic public opinion, the French government always maintained a hard-line stance in international negotiations on the issue of German reparations, while domestically it attempted to achieve a domestic recovery through special budgeting of what were called "*dépenses recouvrables*" under a policy on the premise that Germany would pay the reparations. While this fiscal path sooner or later reached a dead end, at the time of the founding of the BIS in 1930 this line was maintained, supported as well by domestic economic conditions.[50]

Against this background, the French government and Ministry of Finance – as touched on in Chapter 1 – were wary of the BIS inclining toward being a "club of central banks" and insisted that the main goal of the organization be the handling of the reparations issue. This policy appeared in the form of a demand to the Banque de France. The French Ministry of Finance confirmed that it would consult with the governor of the Banque de France in advance concerning important BIS-related matters. The Banque de France responded to this demand and the *Mouvement Général des Fonds* in the Ministry of Finance, a major decision making department of the ministry, consulted in advance with the governor of the Banque de France on important matters such as BIS staffing – even during the period when those had been matters subject to decision by central banks exclusively under the BIS Statutes.[51]

On the other hand, the Banque de France welcomed the BIS as a "club of central banks" with its governor visiting Basel frequently and deeply involved in BIS management. The appointment of Quesnay, who had been head of the Banque de France's economic research bureau, as the first BIS general manager also deepened connections between the bank and the BIS.[52] However, the Banque de France responded carefully to the proposals for the settlement business made successively by the newly established BIS. While the BIS administration directed that the capital proceeds paid by each country be invested in the markets of each country in its early days, in autumn 1930 they demanded measures including rediscounting of the funds invested in such markets to other foreign banks – what the Banque de France called *remobilisation des dépôts*, or remobilization of deposits – in order to invest such funds more profitably. The Banque de France rejected this demand on the grounds of restrictions under domestic French law. According to a careful study by the Banque de France, it regarded the BIS's demands as leading to the creation of international credit and judged this series of new proposals as "involving more drawbacks than benefits" and "premature."[53]

The Ministry of Finance focused on the reparations issue and the Banque de France, while welcoming central-bank cooperation, saw maintenance of the domestic financial system as the most important issue – this was the relationship between the government and the central bank in France concerning the BIS. While the same form of relationship could be seen in other countries to a greater or lesser extent, in the case of France it showed the following highly unique characteristics.

First, even when payment of reparations was suspended under the Hoover Moratorium, France's interest in the reparations issue showed no signs of weakening. A symbolic incident occurred in 1934. At that time, in response to the Hoover Moratorium, Schacht of the Reichsbank began reviewing Young Plan bonds. Since Germany's foreign reserves had decreased as a result of the Depression, Schacht argued for adjustments by the claimant nations regarding whether Germany's limited foreign funds should be allocated to payment of reparations or to payment of interest on bonds by German firms. The strategy of Schacht and the Reichsbank was to create "disagreement among claimant nations" by dividing Britain and France, which placed importance on carrying out the Young Plan, from Switzerland and the Netherlands, which gave priority to redemption of bonds since they were owed relatively little in reparations and had highly developed private markets.[54]

France responded to the situation with its overseas diplomatic establishments, the Ministry of Finance and the Banque de France acting in unison, moving to ensure maintenance of the conditions of reparations payment.[55] Specifically, at the same time when the French consulate in Basel ascertained information on a secret meeting of private claim holders convened by Schacht and conveyed it to the French Ministry of Foreign Affairs and the Ministry of Finance, the Banque de France made a similar analysis of information brought by BIS President Fraser. In collection of this information, the French Ministry of Finance and Ministry of Foreign Affairs took charge of putting pressure through diplomatic channels and the Banque de France took charge of laying the groundwork through the BIS and private-sector banks. After all, this movement turned out to be in vain and the payment of interest on Young bonds was suspended completely beginning July 1, 1934.[56] However, the process of these negotiations shows that on the issue of reparations the responses of the French government and central bank – despite their differences in degrees of enthusiasm regarding the BIS – were in step with each other. It also is worth noting that during these processes BIS General Manager Quesnay – despite being in a position of executive responsibility in an international agency – had provided information and given guidance by telephone on negotiation strategies in accordance with French interests.[57]

Second, the Banque de France deployed its own information activities, developing unofficial routes of communication with the BIS. This started with a written proposal from a Banque de France employee dispatched to the BIS.[58] In July 1930, just after the BIS began operation, this proposal offered the following advice to the Banque, from the standpoint that the Banque de France had the "right and duty" to "be well-informed of all operations planned by the BIS" and "have a direct impact on BIS policies": (1) Two liaisons should be appointed from the economic research bureau of the Banque de France, with one stationed in Basel and the other standing by in Paris. (2) The liaison stationed in Basel should obtain information on "all letters" to be sent from the BIS to the Banque de France, before they were issued. When the liaison had determined that such information was related to policies in general or to monetary policies, he or she should notify the Banque de France's economic research bureau. (3) Prior to each BIS board meeting, the liaison stationed in Basel should collect "information from various points of view concerning the agenda of the meeting" and notify the Banque de France "by telephone or letter." Also, the liaison should report to the Banque de France on information concerning ordinary BIS investment operations. (4) The liaison in Paris should collect letters to be sent to the BIS from the Banque de France in the economic research bureau.

> If numerous different sections were involved in these matters, it would be impossible to avoid the situation in which it is unclear who is responsible for them, forcing the governor to ask around among multiple cooperating parties to obtain information.

Summarizing the above structure, the person making this proposal identified staff members in the economic research bureau named Guérin and Michel Mitzakis as the liaisons. In addition, this person also had notified BIS General Manger Quesnay about the prior inspection of letters outlined under proposal (2) above and obtained his approval. While the process through which these proposals were studied is unclear, the proposal appears to have been implemented, as in 1931 the Banque de France received a detailed note from the Economic Research Bureau staff member Mitzakis.[59] While no materials are available backing either of the viewpoints that this communication structure was maintained continuously later or was used only at the time the BIS was founded and withdrawn later, the process described above does indicate the Banque de France's posture of devotedly pursuing collection of information at the BIS.

A dispute between the BIS and France: the gold clause

This dispute started in 1933 when the United States abandoned the gold stand-ard. As a result of the US withdrawal from the gold standard, countries which deposited dollars with the BIS suffered substantial losses. France especially had deposited dollars with the BIS as guarantee fund. France demanded the BIS make up for these losses, which showed the characteristic of France as a leading nation in international affairs with significant influence on the BIS. While the BIS attempted to respond with an amicable settlement in which it would pay only 10 percent of the losses to the French government, France refused to accept this offer and in the end brought the case to the court of arbitration as stipulated in Article 56 of the BIS Statutes. Wallenburg was designated arbitrator in the court. France argued that the BIS was at fault for failure to withdraw the dollar deposits prior to the US decision on devaluation of the dollar and that it should refund France for the amount of the dollar deposits converted at the previous par value.[60]

In 1935, the arbitrator Wallenburg rendered an award which ordered the BIS to pay 15 percent of France's losses. The BIS expressed its satisfaction with this decision, which was similar in content to its original settlement proposal, saying that it was a matter of "mutual congratulation."

What is important here is the way the arbitration award under the BIS statutes approached the relation between the BIS and each central bank in connection with the breakdown of the gold standard and the logical framework behind the award. Below, we will take a look at the main points of Wallenburg's award.

1   It was impossible to anticipate a future devaluation of the dollar from Presi-dent Roosevelt's inaugural address (March 5, 1933).
2   When Roosevelt had asked the US Congress for authority to devalue the dollar on April 20, the BIS should have withdrawn dollar deposits as part of its fiduciary duty of a good manager. The BIS was at fault for having delayed such action.
3   While, beginning April 14 the BIS had questioned the French government, both orally and in writing, concerning the handling of dollar deposits, France did not reply until July 3.
4   For these reasons, the French government should be paid the amount of damages identified from average dollar exchange rates and other factors for the period for which the BIS appears to be at fault, namely the five-day period beginning April 20.

While the available materials do not make explicitly clear the reasons for deter-mining that the period for which the BIS had been at fault was a five-day period, it is possible to infer from the context that the BIS actually withdrew the dollar deposits five days later.

As regards this arbitration award, Jean Tannery, who had attended the BIS board meetings as the governor of the Banque de France, stated that France placed a high value on "the fact that the arbitrator recognized the validity of the gold clause" after making introductory remarks that France gave more importance to "matters of principle" than to "matters of calculation." While this "gold clause" appears to refer to an agreement similar to the guarantees of gold value demanded of each central bank by the BIS, no such provisions existed either in the BIS Statutes or between individual countries. In fact, following this statement by Tannery, the British representative Niemeyer said the following on a visit to the office of Japan's representative Hisaakira Kano: "Tannery's statement today on the gold clause and other matters was completely off track. I have no idea why he linked the matter with the gold clause." Kano explained that Tannery probably intended to say "France had to endure this disadvantageous arbitration award because of the lack of the gold clause."[61]

From the perspectives of the international situation at the time and France's traditional foreign-affairs strategies, it is possible to explain to some extent France's attitude of pursuing its own national interest through sending spy like employees to the BIS and liaising with the French general manger. Even so, France was forced into a dispute with the BIS on the matter of a drop in the gold value of its own BIS deposits as a result of the Depression. This dispute ended in dissatisfaction to France. BIS organizational and financial management during the Depression was carried out through the accumulation of similar interactions with individual countries.

4 The BIS and Japan: prewar relations

As one of the BIS founding nations, before World War II Japan had two seats on the board (the head of the Bank of Japan's London branch and a representative of the Yokohama Specie Bank). After World War II, Japan withdrew from the board in 1945 and then released its shares in the BIS in 1951 under the San Francisco Peace Treaty. This section will focus on the prewar period.

Negotiations on the establishment of the BIS and Japan's representatives

Japan sent high-level representatives from the government and the Bank of Japan to the series of conferences on the establishment of the BIS. Kengo Mori (former overseas resident finance secretary in the Ministry of Finance) and Takashi Aoki (head of the Nagoya branch of the Bank of Japan and former London representative office head) took part in the Young Committee's meeting in Paris (March 1929). The first Hague Convention (August 1929) was attended by Mineichiro Adachi (ambassador to France), Shozo Nagai (ambassador to Belgium), and Koki Hirota (ambassador to the Netherlands) from the Ministry of Foreign Affairs, and by Tetsusaburo Tanaka (London representative office head) from the Bank of Japan and Saburo Sonoda (Hamburg branch head) from the Yokohama Specie Bank. Of these, Tanaka from the Bank of Japan and Sonoda from the Yokohama Specie Bank also attended the Baden-Baden Committee meetings

(October–November 1929).[62] As is clear from this lineup, Japan's interactions with the BIS took the form of management by the Ministry of Finance and the Ministry of Foreign Affairs of all matters related to negotiations on reparations, while in regular relations the Bank of Japan, in particular the head of the London representative office, served as an important contact, aided by a European branch head from the Yokohama Specie Bank. Perhaps this reflects prewar Japan's external financial state, in which it had established its own unique system of specie holdings abroad.[63]

Now, as negotiations on the establishment of the BIS took shape from the Hague Convention to the Baden-Baden Committee, a number of issues rose to the surface concerning Japan's membership in the BIS.[64]

The first of these was the issue of who in Japan would hold BIS shares.[65] While in other countries the central banks held BIS shares in their own account, in Japan ownership of shares by the Central Bank would violate Articles 11 and 12 of the Bank of Japan Act. For this reason, a syndicate of 14 banks was formed, led by the Industrial Bank of Japan.[66] As seen above, the United States employed similar handling.

Second, it also was pointed out that attendance of the governor of the Bank of Japan at BIS board meetings violated Article 18 of the Bank of Japan Act. This is the reason why representatives such as the head of the Bank of Japan's London representative office, not the governor, attended these meetings, which were attended by other countries' central-bank governors. In addition, it would be impossible to attend the monthly meetings for geographical reasons to begin with.

The third issue was even more important: This was the fact that Japan had not returned to the gold standard at the time the Baden-Baden Committee met. While the initial draft of the BIS Statutes obliged participating countries to work toward currency stability, in the first Hague Convention this was revised to grant greater latitude, as requested by Japan. This is why the expressions employed in the BIS statutes as seen in Chapter 1 were so indirect.

In the end, through the Baden-Baden Committee negotiations Japan secured seats on the BIS board but did not participate proactively in the formation of policies such as the design of Depression-era restrictions. While the two Japanese representative board members appear to have left a deep impression on the governors from each country and on BIS executives including Jacobsson, their actual voice and influence appear to have been limited.[67]

Regarding position levels within the BIS, while the great Western powers scrambled for the distribution of nationalities among BIS positions, Japan secured the post of manager of the foreign-exchange section of the Banking Department, sending a succession of personnel from the European branches of the Yokohama Specie Bank to this position.[68] Japan's control of this post later proved to be highly significant in Japan's maneuvers to end the war on the BIS stage.

A dispute between the BIS and Japan: issues related to the resumption of prohibition of gold exports

In looking at the relations between the BIS and Japan in the 1930s, one's attention is drawn to the response of the BIS when Japan ventured to resume prohibition of gold exports. From minor differences, a dispute arose between Japan and the BIS on this issue. A look at the course of this dispute's development provides a glimpse at the unique forms of behavior of the BIS Banking Department at the time. Below, we will confirm the process of this dispute and its key points.

When the BIS began operation on May 20, 1930, each country paid the price of its shares in the institution, denominated in each country's own currency. Of these funds, the BIS deposited the amount paid by Japan in yen in a BIS account at the Bank of Japan, instructing the Bank of Japan to invest these funds in 90-day government securities, bankers' acceptances, or commercial papers.[69] Accepting these instructions, the Bank of Japan deposited with the Yokohama Specie Bank 3,870,000 yen of the 3,870,967.74 yen paid, and the Yokohama Specie Bank invested these funds in first-class paper in the Osaka clearinghouse, at a discount rate of 3⅝ percent.[70]

In August 1930, the BIS requested additional payment for shares, which was handled in the same manner as the above funds: as of the end of September 1930 the BIS had invested a total of 7,870,000 yen in Japan through its account at the Bank of Japan.[71]

However, since it was in the midst of the Depression, the discount rate on commercial paper in the Osaka market fell, reaching the level of 2½ percent on May 19, 1931. In response to these circumstances, the BIS Banking Department first requested a reduction in Yokohama Specie Bank fees and announced that if this request was denied it would withdraw part of its investment. Finally no change was made in the fees, and 4,660,000 yen was transferred at the end of October 1931 from the account in the Bank of Japan to that of the Federal Reserve Bank of New York.[72]

It was around this point that the dispute began. In September 1931, in the middle of the Depression, the BIS requested member countries' central banks to guarantee the gold value of the investments made by the BIS in each country. In response to this request, the Bank of Japan sent a telegram to Tetsusaburo Tanaka, the head of the Bank of Japan London branch and also appointed a BIS director, expressing the Bank of Japan's opposition to the BIS's notion that such guarantees of gold value were obligations of member nations under the BIS Statutes.[73] Tanaka did not act on the matter for this reason. However, the BIS understood this response to mean that

> the Governor of the Bank of Japan explained the monetary situation on his market, which he described as satisfactory, and indicated in addition that gold might be freely consigned in support of the yen exchange; he did not, however, give the precise undertaking which we had in mind.[74]

While the Bank of Japan did not make its posture clear, on November 10, 1931 the BIS inquired by telephone to the London branch of the Yokohama Specie Bank, requesting guarantee of gold value or other substitute measures. The BIS also gave notice that it would transfer the deposits to the United States if this request was rejected. Neither the Bank of Japan nor the Yokohama Specie Bank responded to this notice.[75]

One month later, on December 12, 1931, the BIS, perceiving that Japan's withdrawal from the gold standard was near, attempted to convert its yen deposits to dollars. Although that day was a Saturday: "Unfortunately, when the exchange operation was attempted, the yen quotation in New York had already depreciated some 15 per cent, so that it was decided to postpone discussion of the operation until the following Monday, December 14th."[76] However, on the following day, Sunday, December 13, the government of Japan announced the resumption of prohibition of gold exports.

At the start of the week on Monday, December 14, the astonished BIS sent an urgent telegram to the Bank of Japan demanding guarantee of gold value or equivalent rediscounting.[77] The Bank of Japan's response to this demand – according to the *Bank of Japan One Hundred-Year History* – was that such operations were impossible because the Bank of Japan and the BIS had not concluded any agreement on rediscounting.[78] However, it is said that the BIS took this response – according to materials in BIS files on the Japanese market – as leaving room for the interpretation that the Bank of Japan could not rediscount "at present."[79]

From this developed the dispute on the damages suffered by the BIS, and eventually the BIS even lodged a complaint against Japan at the court of arbitration as seen in the above case involving France. As advised by Tetsusaburo Tanaka the Bank of Japan, which saw the situation as grave, agreed to compensation through splitting the damages equally between the BIS and the Bank of Japan. In this aspect of the situation, Tanaka laid the groundwork for the BIS bringing up the compromise proposal of splitting equally the compensation for damages.[80] On this matter, Governor Fraser stated,

> as we have claims against certain other central banks for losses arising out of depreciated currencies, it seemed to us that if we took the initiative of formally proposing, as the BIS itself, a 50–50 settlement, this would form a precedent in other cases.

Fraser thus concluded to leave "a little in the dark the origin of the proposal."[81]

In reviewing this dispute, what stands out is the posture of the BIS, especially the Banking Department, in demanding guarantee of gold value in the process of the breakdown of the reconstructed gold standard. In its interactions with the Bank of Japan and the Yokohama Specie Bank, it should be said that behind this situation lay a difference between the BIS, which despite minor technical errors attempted as its main course of action to preserve the gold standard, and individual central banks, which had been forced to abandon the gold standard. At the same time, from the final conclusion of the dispute – the somewhat vague equal splitting of damages – the aspect of the BIS as a "club" stands out, as it attempted to maintain cooperative relations between central banks through somehow controlling the complications of the situation. Also, in comparison with the case of France seen above – while with regard to the BIS the positions of "defendant" and "plaintiff" were reversed – the amicability of Japan stands out. In comparison with the said case of France lodging a claim with the court of arbitration demanding compensation of the entire amount, while the BIS was satisfied with the award which ordered to pay 15 percent of the amount, the case of Japan, which refused the case to be ruled in the court of arbitration and agreed to pay 50 percent of the disputed amount though the grounds for calculation of damages was ambiguous, indeed showed a Japanese-style handling of the situation.

At all events, after this there was no major dispute between Japan and the BIS through the 1930s. The situation began to change again after World War II.

5 The banking business and distribution of profits

This section reviews the financial statements for the period from the fiscal years 1931 (ended March 31, 1932) through 1938 (ended March 31, 1939). This period corresponds to its second through ninth year from the establishment of the BIS.

It goes without saying that the BIS business environment during this period was a tough one because of the Depression. However, with regards to the BIS, unlike an ordinary bank, the impact of the Depression did not lead to a mere business crisis: when each country withdrew from the gold standard, its central bank withdrew deposits at the BIS and deposited gold in bars instead; as global trade contracted and foreign-exchange markets began to malfunction, each country settled foreign exchange through the BIS. In this way, although BIS business activities were forced to contract overall during the Depression, they showed unexpected vitality in this unique field. The subject of this section is to trace these developments from the financial statements.

Trends in the financial statements (1): collection of deposits

First, let's look at the trends in total amounts on the balance sheet (Figure 2.1). The total balance sheet amount, which had exceeded 1.9 billion Gold Swiss francs at the end of the fiscal year in which the BIS was founded, fell to 1,126 million Gold Swiss francs by the end of 1931, one year later. During the period covered in this section, this total balance sheet amount for fiscal 1931 had never been surpassed and overall the amounts showed a decreasing trend, though they did show minor increases and decreases. In the prewar period, the total amount recorded the highest in the fiscal year of the founding of the BIS, while the record low came in fiscal 1938 (approximately 600 million Gold Swiss francs).[82] Thus, as seen from such total amount on the balance sheet, the size of the BIS's business contracted by roughly one-half over the period from its founding until just before World War II.

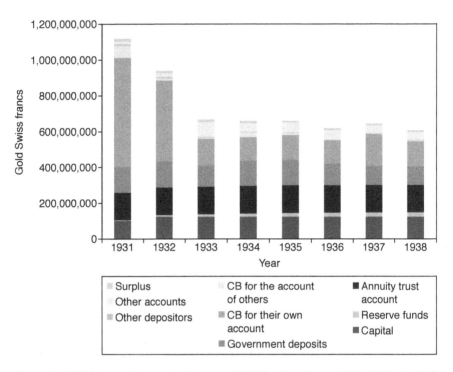

Figure 2.1 BIS balance sheet: major items on liabilities (fiscal years 1931–1938), in Gold Swiss francs (source: *BIS Second–Ninth Annual Reports*).

Next, let's look at the trends in accounts on the liabilities side (credits) of the balance sheet. As a result of additional payment by the seven founding board member nations for 26,400 shares in fiscal 1933, paid-in capital totaled 125 million Gold Swiss francs.[83] This amount remained unchanged, through the World War II period. It goes without saying that as the total amount of the balance sheet decreased the ratio of paid-in capital to total liabilities increased, rising to more than 20 percent in fiscal 1938.

Long-term deposits, which consist of three reparations-related accounts such as annuity trust accounts, remained almost unchanged during this period. The ratio of this account to total liabilities also increased along with the decrease in the total amount of the balance sheet. This ratio, which had been 15.9 percent in the BIS founding year, rose to 42.1 percent in 1938. In this way, as the maturities of accumulated BIS deposits lengthened and current assets decreased, restraint on asset management increased as outlined below. The actual state of these long-term deposits is said to be reserves entrusted to the BIS by the central banks of Central and Eastern European nations which were newly established during the period between the world wars.[84] The BIS advocated cooperation between central banks and during this period central banks were established one after another by nation-states formed after World War I. Since these new central banks lacked the capacity to manage gold reserves by themselves, they hold reserves as deposits with the BIS (as either central banks' own accounts or reparations-related annuity trust accounts).

On the other hand, short-term and sight deposits decreased continuously from fiscal 1931 through fiscal 1933. While some accounts did or did not decrease considerably depending on the fiscal year, each of these is characterized by the withdrawal of deposits and other funds due to incidents occurring during the Depression era – the announcement of the Hoover Moratorium and the withdrawal of leading currencies from the gold standard. First of all, in response to the announcement of the Hoover Moratorium in July 1931 each country's finance ministry withdrew funds that had been placed at the BIS. According to the BIS annual report, the amount of finance ministry-related funds withdrawn totaled 332 million Gold Swiss francs from June 1931 through March 1932. The report explained that this was because of their own budgetary deficits, or for financing deliveries in kind from Germany which had been ordered prior to the inception of the Hoover Moratorium.[85] Next, when the British pound was withdrawn from the gold standard in September 1931 "the Bank's balance-sheet precipitately fell by 331 million Swiss francs, thus reflecting the strain upon central bank reserves that almost immediately resulted from the consternation caused throughout the financial world by the fall of sterling over a week-end."[86] During fiscal 1933, roughly 200 million Gold Swiss francs were withdrawn from sight deposits in the accounts of central banks. Withdrawal of deposits concentrated in April 1933, when the United States prohibited gold exports. The BIS annual report acknowledges this impact as well.[87]

However, when each central bank withdrew its own deposit accounts from the BIS, they converted these to gold and directly deposited such gold with the BIS. While this gold was not included in the BIS balance sheet because it was held under earmark, "its amount and value has been greater during the current, than in any preceding year."[88] What's more, beginning in this fiscal year of 1933, as mentioned above the BIS began accepting deposits of gold bars, and the amount of such deposits – included as credits in the balance sheet, as BIS deposits – were 28 million Gold Swiss francs in that year and 9.6 million Gold Swiss francs in fiscal 1938. Concerning these "stocks of gold," the BIS annual report states, "Experience has shown that the maintenance of a stock averaging at least 25 million Gold Swiss francs is desirable."[89]

Earmarked gold refers to gold bars the management of which was entrusted to the BIS by central banks. It does not appear on BIS financial statements. Also, in most cases the actual gold itself was not sent to the BIS but remained in the gold markets in London, Bern, or elsewhere. While incoming and outgoing gold was recorded on BIS earmark accounts, these were not country-specific accounts. Numbers were merely assigned to groupings of gold. For example, in 1939 the gold earmarked from the Bank of England was split among ten accounts and, what's more, it is impossible to judge from account numbers alone whether this represented gold earmarked from the Bank of England. In fact, if the Bank of

England were to sell some of its earmarked gold to another country the account number would have remained the same, with only the holder of the earmark changing.[90] While in this manner the earmarked gold was not directly related to BIS operations itself, as seen below each country earmarked gold with the BIS for purposes such as preservation of gold reserves during the Depression or preventing confiscation by occupying nations during the war. This means that information on world gold markets was collected at the BIS, and these were very important accounts to the BIS as well – positioned as the point of contact between central-bank cooperation and the banking business.

The BIS annual report's handling of the maturity structure of deposits underwent considerable change at this period. While the annual report for the founding year employed a structure of demand or short-term deposits, as withdrawal of demand deposits and a shift toward longer-term deposits advanced later, calculation of this structure became less meaningful. For this reason, as seen below the BIS annual report began referring to the liquidity ratio of investment of funds – from the standpoint of securing liquidity of investments corresponding to the low level of current liabilities.

With regard to the currency, the makeup of short-term deposits underwent massive changes during this period, and this too was traced in detail in the annual report. As seen in Figure 2.2, the BIS held short-term deposits in the strongest gold-standard currency at the time – the dollar after the pound left the

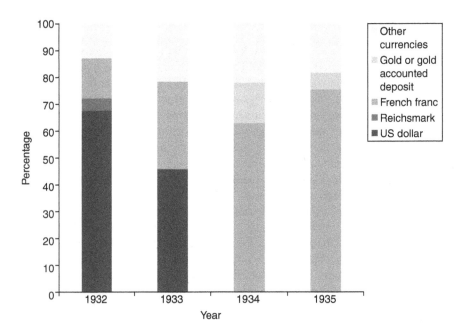

Figure 2.2 Currency composition of short term deposits (1932–1935) (source: *BIS Second–Fifth Annual Reports*).

gold standard, and the French franc after the dollar left the gold standard. As mentioned in the BIS annual report, this was consistent with longstanding BIS policy of "to avoid creating in the various currencies exchange positions."[91] However, after the French franc too was withdrawn from the gold standard, the policy shifted to one of "to maintain, so far as possible, equilibrium between the volume of our assets and of our commitments in a given currency."[92] From the end of March 1936, the annual report discontinued reporting on the data.

In any case, it perhaps can be said that in the middle of the Depression the BIS's way of accumulating deposits by holding short-term deposits in gold-standard currencies primarily and receiving gold in trust (or deposits) from each central bank formed the business background of its policy of continuing to cling to the gold standard.

Trends in the financial statements (2): investment of funds

How did the BIS invest funds (Figure 2.3)? Withdrawal of deposits by each central bank on the credit side had a direct impact on the highly liquid accounts on the debit side of cash, sight funds at interest, and rediscountable bills and acceptances. Commercial bills and bankers' acceptances, which were summed together in the accounts of rediscountable bills and acceptances, in particular showed a rapid decrease in terms of both share and amount in fiscal years 1932 and 1933 when the withdrawal of deposits took place, after accounting for 42 percent of assets in the 1931 fiscal year.

Another account given considerable attention is "gold in bars." In fiscal 1933, when this account first appears, an amount equal to gold in bars on the debit side is booked on the credit side as sight deposits (gold). Later, through fiscal 1936 debits were recorded under gold in bars in amounts slightly higher than those for sight deposits (gold). Beginning in fiscal 1936, gold in bars greatly surpassed sight deposits (gold), indicating that the BIS was buying gold independently on its own. While the amount of gold in bars rose and fell, its share of total assets rose steadily, reaching 6.4 percent in the 1938 fiscal year.

The account time funds at interest was in a decreasing trend, although its total amount rose and fell. Even when funds not exceeding three months maturity, included under this account, are totaled with central bank credits, the result fell to be a very minor account. The drop is impressive only because in the fiscal year in which the BIS was founded this had accounted for 44.7 percent of total assets. This is a sign that the withdrawal from the lending business was conducted at a rapid rate.

In contrast, sundry bills and investments was an investment account whose presence increased. Of the accounts categorized as sundry bills and investments, Treasury bills maintained a certain share despite increases and decreases in amount, and sundry investments also increased beginning in fiscal 1933. From 1933, when the Depression made its effects felt on Europe, for practical purposes the item miscellaneous investments was limited to short-term investments with maturities of no more than three months. In the second half of the 1930s, these sundry bills and investments had become the largest assets account. This

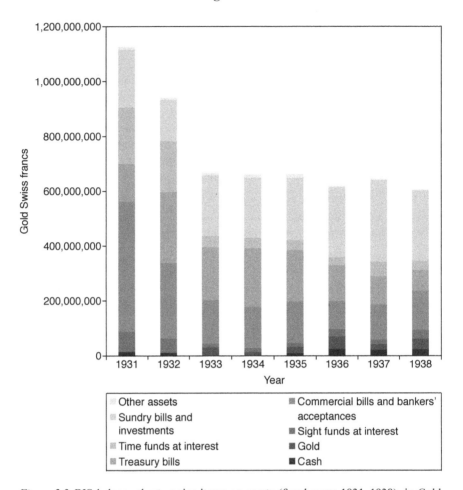

Figure 2.3 BIS balance sheet: major items on assets (fiscal years 1931–1938), in Gold
Swiss francs (source: *BIS Second–Tenth Annual Reports*).

can be seen as a sign of the tendency in the BIS investment business at the time
of shifting "from lending to investment in securities and bonds."

But where were these investments directed? As seen in the preceding chapter,
Article 20 of the BIS Statutes required the BIS to choose investments so that
they were in accordance with the monetary policies of each central bank. A look
at fiscal 1931 shows that 85.9 percent of investments were directed toward
central banks, 10.8 percent to banking institutions selected by the central banks,
and 3.3 percent to other related institutions and other bodies.[93] These shares
largely remained the same in the next year, fiscal 1932.[94] As investment conditions worsened, investment in central banks – effectively, depositing funds with
the central banks – accounted for a high share of investments.

However, these investment categories were no longer released beginning in fiscal 1932. The actual conditions of these investments can be known only from the confidential monthly reports submitted by the Banking Department to the board. The figures in internal documents are clear. According to the report from March 1932, the end of the fiscal year, the total amount of short-term investments at the end of that month was 699 million Gold Swiss francs, of which 610 million francs was in the rediscountable portfolio, with 474 million francs of that amount consisting of bankers' acceptances and the remaining 136 million francs of treasury securities from each country. Investment in bankers' acceptances increased as a result of "the marked growth in our investment in US markets."[95] As such, BIS investments appear to have shifted rapidly from Europe to the United States.

But through what channels were these investments in US markets made? An internal report on investment as of the end of March 1932 provides the following figures: Federal Reserve Bank of New York overdrafts and bills accounted for 90 percent of BIS investments in the United States, followed by Federal Reserve System member bank and trust bank current account overdrafts (accounting for 7 percent), J.P. Morgan deposits at notice and current deposits (1 percent), and other investments (1 percent).[96] These figures show that at this point in time, investments, which were considered official and safe through the FRB system, accounted for the bulk of investments in the United States.

The BIS annual report devoted more attention to asset liquidity than to targets of investment. As seen with liability accounts above, during this period short-term deposits were withdrawn from time to time. During this period, when returns on investment also were low, the BIS made every effort to maintain asset liquidity at or above a certain level. As a result, in each fiscal year readily available assets– although the definition of these varied slightly from year to year – accounted for roughly 60 percent of the total amount of assets. Of course, such liquid investments do not generate many results in the way of profits. The BIS annual report repeatedly referred to this situation as "investment difficulties"[97] or "a dearth of short-term investments."[98]

Profit and loss and distribution of profits: processing of exchange differences

As seen in the preceding chapter, the BIS accumulated its own hidden reserves and kept hidden ledgers in addition to the income statements it released to the public. In this section we will examine BIS income calculation and distribution of profits during the period in which it was impacted by the Depression, looking at these hidden ledgers as well.

First of all, a look at the official figures – the public income statement – shows decreases in both gross profit, as the gross revenue figure, and net balance. The decrease in fee revenues from fiscal 1931 through fiscal 1932 stands out in particular. However, while the total amount on the balance sheet decreased rapidly from fiscal 1931 through fiscal 1933 – with the total amount

Table 2.1 BIS profit and loss account, fiscal years 1931–1938, published and unpublished versions, in Gold Swiss francs

Published account

	Net income	Commissions earned	Transfer fees	Gross profit	Costs of administration	Furniture and office equipment	Constructional alterations to building	Provision for indemnities to and repatriation of staff	Expenditure	Net profit
1931	17,111,750.67	2,287,350.40	1,221.04	19,400,322.11	3,844,660.60	62,798.51	10,044.36	300,000.00	4,217,503.47	15,182,818.64
1932	17,795,368.53	480,901.78	700.80	18,276,971.11	3,656,581.90	5,900.28	0.00	550,000.00	4,212,482.18	14,064,488.93
1933	16,320,646.98	334,868.57	564.88	16,656,080.43	3,549,007.61			100,000.00	3,649,007.61	13,007,072.82
1934	15,842,836.24	300,569.91	633.62	16,144,039.77	2,898,031.11			200,000.00	3,098,031.11	13,046,008.66
1935	11,877,733.88	304,683.41	645.40	12,183,062.69	2,989,391.69				2,989,391.69	9,193,671.00
1936	11,203,938.69	280,814.21	451.99	11,485,204.89	2,413,634.87				2,413,634.87	9,071,570.02
1937	10,977,498.68	229,421.70	436.50	11,207,356.88	2,195,400.35				2,195,400.35	9,011,956.53
1938	10,405,208.62	245,829.78	534.82	10,651,633.22	2,067,768.59				2,067,768.59	8,583,864.63

Unpublished account

	Gross revenue	Interest allowed	Costs of administration	Net balance	Transfers from specific reserves and adjustments	Exchange differences	Total amount available for allocation	Allocations to undisclosed reserves		Revaluation of assets	Administration account	Net balance published
								Exchange differences account	Provision for exchange and other losses			
1931	59,591,000.00	21,610,000.00	3,918,000.00	34,513,000.00	0.00	3,156,000.00	37,669,000.00	3,156,000.00	7,671,000.00	11,359,000.00	300,000.00	15,183,000.00
1932	35,769,000.00	7,492,000.00	3,662,000.00	24,615,000.00	-150,000.00	4,315,000.00	28,780,000.00	4,315,000.00	-150,000.00	10,000,000.00	550,000.00	14,065,000.00
1933	21,866,000.00	2,778,000.00	3,549,000.00	15,539,000.00	968,000.00	25,493,000.00	42,000,000.00	25,493,000.00	4,759,000.00	-1,359,000.00	100,000.00	13,007,000.00
1934	19,472,000.00	2,643,000.00	2,898,000.00	13,931,000.00	0.00	-21,123,000.00	-7,192,000.00	-21,123,000.00	685,000.00		200,000.00	13,046,000.00
1935	19,298,000.00	2,515,000.00	2,989,000.00	13,794,000.00	150,000.00	96,000.00	14,040,000.00	96,000.00	150,000.00	4,600,000.00		9,194,000.00
1936	18,133,000.00	2,248,000.00	2,414,000.00	13,471,000.00	150,000.00	-354,000.00	13,267,000.00	-354,000.00	150,000.00	4,400,000.00		9,071,000.00
1937	16,320,000.00	1,563,000.00	2,195,000.00	12,562,000.00	150,000.00	476,000.00	13,188,000.00	476,000.00	150,000.00	3,100,000.00	450,000.00	9,012,000.00
1938	15,133,000.00	1,131,000.00	2,068,000.00	11,934,000.00	70,000.00	-520,000.00	11,484,000.00	-520,000.00	70,000.00	3,100,000.00	250,000.00	8,584,000.00

Source: BIS Historical Archives, file 7.5, box 1/2, "Disposal of the surplus on the Profit and Loss Account 1949–50", March 28, 1950, *BIS Second–Tenth Annual Reports*.

Stock account of undisclosed reserves (in 1,000 Gold Swiss francs)

	Provision for exchange and other losses	Revaluation of assets	Exchange differences account	Administration account
1930/1931	3,000.00		202.00	400.00
1931/1932	10,671.00	11,359.00	3,358.00	700.00
1932/1933	10,521.00	21,359.00	7,673.00	1,250.00
1933/1934	15,280.00	20,000.00	33,166.00	1,350.00
1934/1935	15,965.00	20,000.00	12,043.00	1,550.00
1935/1936	16,115.00	24,600.00	12,139.00	1,550.00
1936/1937	16,265.0	29,000.00	11,785.00	1,550.00
1937/1938	16,415.00	32,100.00	12,261.00	2,000.00

Source: BIS Historical Archives, file 7.18(6), AUB 3, Situation Generale BRI, IV, "Differentes Reserves".

Note
The figures on "Allocations to undisclosed reserves", which represents the flow account, and the figures on "Stock account of undisclosed reserves" do not coincide properly since the contents of "administrations account" and "provision for exchange and other losses" vary by year.

in fiscal 1933 being roughly 60 percent the fiscal 1931 figure – the decrease in official profit was a gentle one. Both gross profit and net balance in fiscal 1933 maintained levels at roughly 85 percent the fiscal 1931 figures (Table 2.1). A contributing factor appears to be the fact that, while as seen above the decrease in the total amount on the balance sheet resulted in large part from withdrawal of deposits, the BIS also had been assigned businesses such as settlement and transfer of funds, and it secured a certain degree of fee revenues from these services.

However, a look at the unofficial figures on these matters gives a somewhat different impression. A look at gross revenue on the hidden ledgers shows a figure for fiscal 1933 only 36.6 percent of the fiscal 1931 figure, with this rate of decrease being greater than that of the total amount on the balance sheet. However, interest allowed decreased even more – falling to only 12.8 percent over the same period – moderating the decrease in net balance to some degree (Table 2.1).

Now let's look at the characteristics of this period as they concern the relation between the hidden and public ledgers, to identify how hidden reserves were accumulated and official profits derived from gross revenue in the hidden figures.

First we will look at the sources of funding of the hidden reserves. The first source was devised from manipulation of gross revenue and gross profit. In calculation of profit in the founding fiscal year as seen in the preceding chapter, part of the source of funding for reserves was devised through showing a lower figure for gross profit on the public ledger than the amount derived by deducting interest allowed from gross revenue on the hidden ledger. In the founding fiscal year, this amount was allocated unchanged to provisions for exchange and other losses. While this was conducted in fiscal 1931 and later years as well, the source of funding obtained in this way was in a decreasing trend. The amount derived through this handling in fiscal 1931 was 18.58 million Gold Swiss francs – more than the figure of three million Gold Swiss francs in the founding year. However, this amount fell from year to year, dropping to 680,000 Gold Swiss francs in 1934. From fiscal 1935 through fiscal 1938, it decreased gradually from 4.59 million to 3.35 million Gold Swiss francs (derived from Table 2.1). This path largely was in agreement with the trend in deposits.

The second source of funding was foreign-exchange earnings. Exchange differences were not shown on the official income statement. Instead, their entire amount was processed on the hidden ledger. A look at the amount of these gains shows that in fiscal 1931 an amount corresponding to 3.15 million Gold Swiss francs was booked to the hidden ledger, and that this amount reached 25.49 million Gold Swiss francs in fiscal 1933. Fiscal 1933 was a time when, although the dollar had withdrawn from the gold standard, the "gold bloc" currencies such as the French franc maintained the gold standard, and as seen above the BIS shifted deposits from the dollar to the French franc. The massive revaluation gains in this fiscal year appear to have been obtained as a result of the increase in the value of French francs obtained in this manner.

The third source of funding was transfers from specific reserves and adjustments. As touched on in the preceding chapter, this account corresponded to the three items of payment of taxes to the canton of Basel (fiscal 1932–1933), foreign-exchange earnings from transactions in notes with repurchase agreements (fiscal 1933–1934), and interest earnings from loans to the national bank of Hungary (the four fiscal years beginning with fiscal 1935–1936).

How had these hidden reserves been distributed? The point of issue is its handling of foreign-exchange earnings.

In this period, as discussed above a large amount of foreign-exchange earnings was earned temporarily, as the currency in which BIS deposits were held was changed. As seen above, these earnings were accumulated in hidden reserves. However, foreign-exchange losses arose in the three fiscal years 1934, 1936 and 1938. How were these losses handled?

A look at the foreign-exchange losses incurred in fiscal 1934 – the largest prewar amount of loss at 21.12 million Gold Swiss francs – shows that at that time the nonpublic total amount available for allocation fell into deficit. These losses were entirely disposed of by exchange differences in hidden reserves. Almost all of the 25.49 million Gold Swiss francs in foreign-exchange earnings accumulated in the preceding fiscal year were lost through this processing. That is, while in other fiscal years during this period reserves were placed in the asset revaluation account – which in fact was the destination of allocation of the sources of funding of hidden reserves – in fiscal 1934 no reserves were accumulated in that account. In this fiscal year, the funding source of 685,000 Gold Swiss francs obtained through low estimation of public gross profit was allocated to provisions for exchange and other losses, and the provision for indemnities to and repatriation of staff was transferred to the nonpublic administration account.

In comparison with fiscal 1934's results, the foreign-exchange losses in fiscal 1936 and fiscal 1938 were minor.

In each fiscal year, the funding source obtained from underestimating public gross profit was used to appropriate losses, maintaining leeway for transfer of funds to provisions for exchange and other losses (allocation of interest earnings from loans to the national bank of Hungary). In this way, manipulation of hidden reserves on the BIS income statement was fruitful, successfully disposing of the foreign-exchange losses. This successful experience was likely to be referred to repeatedly in later discussions when the continuance of the hidden reserves became an issue.

Appropriation of earnings secured in this way included accumulation of ordinary reserves such as statutory reserves and realization of "6 percent annual dividends on paid-in capital," which could be said to be a responsibility to shareholders (Figure 2.4). Dividends under trust agreements, to which residuals on these reserve accounts were applied, also were maintained through the end of the 1930s, although in very small amounts. While the annual report released to the public bemoaned "a dearth of investment opportunities," on the hidden ledger steady earnings were secured – this hidden face of the BIS comes into view from a look at the BIS's processing of earnings.

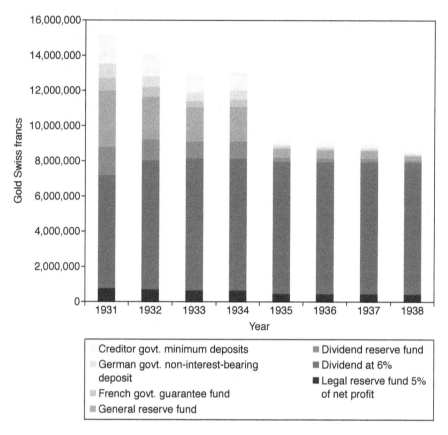

Figure 2.4 BIS profit and loss appropriation account (fiscal years 1931–1938), in Gold
Swiss francs (source: *BIS Second–Tenth Annual Reports*).

6 Conclusion

During the Depression, the BIS's financial utopianism was forced to undergo a
transformation. The concept of securing liquidity in international mid-term credit
was, though giving some results, also unable in the end to counter the Depression. It is inevitable to take the BIS's countermeasures against the Depression as
a record of mistake and failure, particularly in that they failed to avoid the European financial crisis of 1931. The official history by Toniolo also evaluates the
BIS countermeasures against the Depression harshly, pointing out that (1) with
regard to the "timing" of aid, though it never had been possible to intervene
earlier because of the collapse of Credit-Anstalt, its relief measures for the
National Bank of Austria did play an important role; (2) criticism of the amount
of aid was unavoidable; and (3) regarding the conditions of aid the responses
of the BIS and each central bank – in light of the contemporary historical

conditions that required giving priority to prevention of capital flight from Central European markets – were unable to step outside the doctrine of the gold standard.[99]

However, how would these measures be assessed when viewed from the perspective of this book – an attempt to position the history of the BIS within the longer-term history of the twentieth century? Central-bank cooperation on the BIS stage had never ceased even in an age of a beggar-my-neighbor policy. Plans had been developed for international distribution of capital from a line of thought different from the drift toward Keynesianism. Above all, the BIS itself continued operation with gold as one of its foundations. Much later, these historical facts would serve as "another means of countering depression," suggesting the form of central-bank cooperation which restored in the post-Bretton Woods era. The BIS, while responding to the unique demands from France and Japan, survived the Depression era as a "bank for central banks."

On the other hand, how did the BIS respond to the Depression as a "commercial bank"? The Banking Department's motive of securing returns on investment restricted the international countermeasures against the Depression that the Monetary and Economic Department could take. However, the Banking Department itself also aimed for the ideal of contributing to the public good through internal disputes on subjects such as gold settlement. Behind this were the gold earmarking business which showed unexpected vitality during the Depression era, and the steady business policies that managed to avoid foreign-exchange losses through hidden reserves.

Standing behind these unique businesses were the theories and ideas of Jacobsson, the newly appointed head of the Monetary and Economic Department. Jacobsson's theories, blending Wicksellianism and neoliberalism, were likely to see the Depression-era economy in a different way than did Keynesianism at that same time, and to add color to BIS activities.

More than a few persons involved in the BIS died young, for example during the period of the 1930s covered in this chapter, BIS General Manager Quesnay met with an untimely death while still holding that position.[100] Born in 1895 in the French province (*département*) of Eure, after graduating at the top of his class from the University of Paris school of law in 1914 Quesnay served for three years beginning in 1916 as a first lieutenant in the artillery during World War I. He was recognized for distinguished valor twice and was injured once as well. After the war, he took part in reparations and postwar reconstruction policies, starting as an assistant to the French representative to the food controls committee in occupied Austria. In 1925, he served in various posts as a member of the League of Nations secretariat, including serving on the finance committee, and in 1926 he joined the Banque de France's Economic Research Bureau. From his position in the Banque de France, he played an important role in the 1928 legal stabilization of the franc.[101]

His involvement with the BIS began when he joined the French representative team at the Hague Convention and the Baden-Baden Conference in 1929. After distinguishing himself in these meetings, Quesnay was appointed the first

BIS general manger at the urging of the French government and the Banque de France. He was appointed general manager in 1930 at the age of 35, and he was still just 42 years old in 1937 when he died in an accident, leaving behind a wife and five children.

Although a graduate of the elite University of Paris school of law, he was not an inspector of finance (*Inspecteur des finances*), the elite level of finance officials. While it is thought that he might have interacted with Jacobsson and Monnet at the League of Nations, he never acted beyond the framework of his role as a representative of France, and while he earned a reputation as an "*enfant terrible*" for his unprecedented way of working as he supported the BIS administratively during its formative years, as seen in this chapter he deviated from his position as head of an international institution to cooperate proactively in France's intelligence activities. Quesnay's path can be considered to demonstrate the complex, multifaceted nature of the generation that passed through the battlefields of World War I.

3 On the eve of Bretton Woods

The BIS during World War II

Since the start of the Nazi invasions, Geneva, that colorful city on the shores of Lake Léman always bustling with tourists, was enveloped in the extraordinary clamor of refugees seeking to flee to other countries. In July 1940, a tall young American and his pregnant wife came to Geneva in flight from Basel, intending to escape to the United States. The young man, who had been working at the BIS, decided to return to his own country when Paris fell into the hands of the Nazis in June, taking the difficult voyage from Geneva to Lyon, from Lyon to Lisbon, and then to New York, seeing up-close the inspections conducted by the fascists and the sufferings of the Jews. This young man's name was Charles Kindleberger. He was a Keynesian who had confronted Jacobsson in the BIS Monetary and Economic Department. Incidentally, when during his flight Kindleberger attempted to open the window on a shaking bus in consideration for his wife, a man in the seat behind him tried to close the window. That man was Ludwig von Mises, the liberal economist of the Austrian school.[1] The madness of World War II had begun spreading across Europe as well as the Asia-Pacific region, scattering both Keynesians and liberals. This chapter will examine BIS policies and management during the wartime.

When World War II began, the BIS attempted to maintain neutrality, citing the business neutrality prescribed in Chapter III of its statutes. At the same time, the national representatives gathered together at the BIS continued their business activities whether they came from allied or axis nations, which made the BIS a rare case of an international base of communication during World War II. However, this fact would later be a primary cause of significant suspicion regarding the BIS – suspicion that it might have collaborated with Nazi Germany. These suspicions were investigated soon after the end of World War II as the issue of "looted gold," and they smoldered for a long period of time in the postwar years.

The looted gold issue concerns Nazi Germany's seizure of assets including central-bank gold reserves and Jewish assets in the territories it occupied, such as those in Central Europe, and disguising the seized assets as gold in bars to hide the fact of its unlawful seizure. The problem for the BIS was the fact that such gold in bars had been deposited with institutions including the BIS and the Swiss National Bank. While these suspicions came partially to light in an investigation by the US Congress immediately after the war, in recent years there has been a new development, as it has emerged that this gold in bars included the personal gold property of Jews and other victims of Nazi genocide ("gold of the dead"). The full picture of this issue was clarified in the 1990s through the activities of Jewish groups and BIS archival authorities, with resolution reached through the BIS apologizing and compensating the victims.[2]

It goes without saying that this is a grave matter involving human life and human rights. It also was a landmark development in BIS historical research since it served as an impetus for the release of historical materials. However, this chapter will take an approach completely different from that of exposing the issue of looted gold at the BIS during the war: is it not the case that the necessary task today is that of the identification of the BIS business operations during the war and the concepts and thoughts behind them, including such blemishes as its involvement with looted gold, from a historical perspective – within the continuity of BIS history? While of course this chapter will look at the issue of looted gold, it will not restrict itself to that subject matter alone. Instead, from a more broad-ranging perspective this chapter will make a close examination, based on primary materials, of matters such as the structure of international finance as it concerned gold to begin with, relations to the postwar vision of the United States, and positioning of the war years within the history of twentieth-century economic thought.

In this chapter, Section 1 will take a general view of the structure and business of the BIS during the war, touching on its relations to Japan as well. Section 2 will take up the issue of looted gold, focusing on the fact that actually the issue of looted gold resonated in complex ways with the US freezing of BIS assets (and the release of this freeze). Section 3 will examine the concepts and thoughts of the BIS during this period, focusing on Jacobsson, the head of the Monetary and Economic Department. Section 4 will address the BIS banking business and distribution of profits during the war. Each section will attempt to reflect the continuity of history into the postwar period – the eve of Bretton Woods – which is the main subject of this chapter. Section 5 concludes.

1   The structure and business of the BIS during World War II

As fighting on the frontline between Germany and France intensified, in May 1940 the BIS was forced to evacuate from Basel. It evacuated to a hotel in Château d'Oex, in south-central Switzerland. While Basel was originally chosen as the site of the BIS headquarters because it was an important center of transportation, neighboring borders with both Germany and France, these geographical conditions backfired when World War II started. The BIS headquarters in front of Basel Station were located 3 km from the Franco-Swiss border and 3.5 km from the German–Swiss border, and the Swiss authorities even considered a forced evacuation of the entire city depending on how the war developed. During these times, worst-case scenarios such as the possibilities of aerial bombing and occupation by one of the fighting forces were discussed as plausible developments.[3]

In light of these circumstances, General Manager Auboin, through the General Secretariat, immediately began the process of choosing a destination for evacuation. On May 10, 1940 the situation became more serious. "Residents of Basel were awakened early in the morning by the sound of intense gunfire from the German–French border to the north of the city," and "during the morning of Tuesday, May 14, military forces were witnessed moving near the Swiss border." In this situation, the BIS evacuated at once to the Château d'Oex. With only the Banking Department remaining in operation in Basel through May 18, the BIS managed to resume all business operations on May 20 at Château d'Oex. Most of the BIS's decisions during World War II were made at this evacuation site.

The duty of neutrality and future vision

Here, focus will be given to arguments during this era regarding the duty of neutrality by which the BIS was fettered during the war and future plans for the BIS, which were linked closely to this duty of neutrality.

In accordance with the stipulations of its statutes, the BIS declared neutrality during the war. However, the concept of neutrality itself is ambiguous to begin with, and a variety of arguments arose during this period, and even in the postwar era, concerning BIS business operations during the war. In fact, on the matter of the gold issues discussed below the actions of the BIS were seen as having favored Germany.

On the other hand, it can be gathered from private correspondence that General Manager Auboin, a Frenchman, was biased toward the allies. For example, in an unofficial letter sent to Governor Fournier of the Banque de France, Auboin reported on Swiss public opinion and the movements of refugees just like a spy and called for action from the French side.[4] Separately, in August 1939 Auboin wrote a memo titled "Note on the BIS from the Point of View of the French Interest." While as an administrative leader of an international institution General Manager Auboin should have been unconstrained by the interests of his own country, he was discussing in detail "the French interest" just before the outbreak of war. In this memo, Auboin considered "the French interest" breaking it down into the two interests of "shareholders" and "government," providing advice including that "shareholders and the government be united without arising any conflict between their obviously different interests."[5] On September 21, 1939, immediately after the outbreak of war, Auboin also wrote a long memo titled "Measures to Take in the Interest of France Concerning the BIS during the Term of Hostility," declaring that in addition to the interests of the government and shareholders mentioned above "the BIS will preserve its function as an institution for future British–French political cooperation."[6]

The leading BIS member states had a variety of intentions concerning the duty of neutrality. While some argued for utilizing the BIS during the war, with neutrality as a pretext, others were of the view that utilization of the institution should wait until the war ends, understanding "neutrality" to refer to information and human-network functions. Furthermore, as seen in the advice of Auboin above, the understanding of "neutrality" was linked to the future vision of the institution of the BIS itself. Kan Yoshimura, appointed manager of the BIS foreign-exchange section, wrote in 1940 in a letter to President Yanagida of the Yokohama Specie Bank, "Germany and Italy are most aggressive in supporting the continued existence of the BIS... while Britain is very passive on the matter, it has no intent to dismantle the bank," and that while the intents of the French government were unclear, Auboin's opinion was that "France recognizes the need for the BIS to continue" and "the possibility of utilizing it will increase after the war."[7] This observation by Yoshimura on France coincides with the content of the memo by Auboin himself mentioned above.

In any case, it can be said that a consensus had hardened among leading nations – except the United States – about the continuance of the BIS as an organization, while adhering to the duty of neutrality.

But how did the BIS administration itself consider neutrality and the vision of the future? The aforementioned Yoshimura collected valuable comments as he walked around the BIS offices. Here are some of these comments, other than those of Auboin touched on above.[8]

BIS Deputy General Manager Hechler (German) said, "It is the firm intention of Germany that the BIS continue in its current state." However, he believed that "even if Germany were to win the war, every effort would be made to respect the rights and interests of the British in the BIS."

Head of Banking Department van Zeeland (Belgian) held, "the most optimistic view of the future of the BIS, although fully opposed to it politically." Furthermore, he expressed the following to Yoshimura in a "confidential conversation": At the time the BIS was founded, German representative Schacht "focused more on the point of integration into the international financial markets through BIS than on resolution of the reparations issues," while in contrast Britain was not in favor of the rights and interests of the Bank of England being encroached on by Germany and France and adopted "a posture of insisting completely on securing" reparations money. If Germany were "unfortunately" to win the war, these "British and French attitudes would disappear" and "it goes without saying that the BIS would move into a broader scope of activities."

Secretary General Pilotti (Italian) asked, "Why does Japan not use the BIS?" and stated, "You are too optimistic in the face of the worsening situation in the Far East." When Yoshimura joked that the BIS was "a bank with an uncertain future," Pilotti countered, "the recent experience confirmed the necessity of the BIS."

President McKittrick (American), in a statement made when he took office, said that his own hope was "to protect the growing, promising, young man from the threat of gunfire, to bring him up, and in the brighter days to come to send out the completed BIS as a magnificent organization."

The above reflects the collector of the information, Yoshimura, who was experienced as a top member of BIS staff and also was proficient at languages.

From these testimonies one infers the unique atmosphere of the period right after the war began, in which consideration was given to the possibility of a victory by Nazi Germany. The groundwork was laid for Jacobsson's argument accepting *Grossraum* (wide economic zone), discussed below, amid these circumstances. Also, it is notable that despite differences of opinion, representatives of both allied and axis nations argued for the continued existence of the BIS. At the same time, as seen in the next sub-section, Yoshimura launched a scheme under which Japan applied for loans from the BIS during the war on the basis of this information.[9]

The BIS during World War II and Japan

As the hostilities of World War II commenced in Europe and, on the other hand, Japan–US relations grew strained, Japan again began approaching the BIS. Its motive for doing so was to avoid the US government's freeze of Japanese assets and to secure a channel for settlement to the continent of Europe.

To begin with, in 1940 the Bank of Japan made the following two requests to the BIS: one for opening a new account with the BIS in the name of the Yokohama Specie Bank and the other for increasing the balance of deposits in the Bank of Japan's existing accounts with the BIS. In response, the BIS rejected the proposed account in the name of the Yokohama Specie Bank "in light of current circumstances," while it approved the increase in the deposit balances in the Bank of Japan's accounts subject to certain conditions.[10] Then, in 1941 a Bank of Japan representative "Tachi" stopped in Basel on the way back from Berlin to Tokyo and visited the BIS to propose the approval of transactions in Swiss francs between the BIS and the Yokohama Specie Bank and asked if it were "possible to obtain credit from the BIS in any form secured by gold in bars currently somewhere in the Far East."[11] The former proposal was not realized due to the opposition of the Swiss National Bank, and gold-secured loans of the latter proposal also never saw the light of day, as the secured loans requested by the Bank of Japan were not approved.[12] The above process was concluded in May 1941, and the following month, on June 14, 1941, BIS assets in the United States were frozen. From this course of events, one can sense a behind-the-scenes view of Japan–US relations, which culminated in the Pacific War.

On the subject of relations between the BIS and Japan during World War II, there is an important historical fact unrelated to the business of the BIS itself. In July 1945, after the war had ended in Europe and while the war in Asia and the Pacific was moving toward its conclusion, the BIS was the stage for maneuvers aimed at ending the war with Japan. These were conducted through the channels of US Office of Strategic Services European director Allen Dulles on the allied side and Kojiro Kitamura (Japanese representative on the BIS board, formerly with the Yokohama Specie Bank) and the aforementioned Kan Yoshimura on the Japanese side, with Jacobsson, the head of the BIS Monetary and Economic Department, serving as intermediary between both sides. Dulles was in contact with the Truman administration, while Kitamura and Yoshimura had a line to the imperial Court through Lieutenant General Okamoto of the Japanese army, who was stationed in Bern. These maneuvers failed, which led to the atomic bombing of Hiroshima and Nagasaki and eventually Japan's defeat. If those maneuvers had succeeded the war might have ended earlier. The journals and notes of that time edited in later years by Jacobsson's daughter Erin describe the scene of these maneuvers to end the war, conducted in Switzerland under very tense circumstances.[13]

2 The issue of looted gold and the asset freeze

Here we will look at the issue of looted gold, the most important subject in BIS wartime history, in light of its connection with the US asset freeze.

Looted gold: a structural outline of the issue

As World War II hostilities commenced in Europe in September 1939, the central banks of the European nations came to ask the BIS to buy gold. According to the requests received by the BIS, their objectives were to secure on an urgent basis the dollars needed in trade settlement. At the BIS, in November 1939, President Beyen sent a personal letter concerning this matter to Merle Cochran of the US Treasury Department, asking "if American authorities would buy" from the BIS "gold placed on board American ship in neutral European harbor and insured by federal New York with American insurance companies."[14] At this point in time, the United States was still a neutral country, and the BIS and its member countries had taken this opportunity to secure dollars.[15] While in a different context from this gold transaction, Japan asked the BIS to mediate settlement for the shipment of gold to Lisbon via Cape Town, in September 1941 – three months before Pearl Harbor, when it was formally a neutral country as far as the BIS was concerned. BIS authorities held off on the transaction, citing the prospect that "the transport is foreseen for November. Will Japan not be a belligerent then?"[16]

In December 1939, unable to hold a general meeting or a board of directors meeting, the BIS president, Beyen, sent letters to the central banks requesting that they submit approval of the BIS's wartime management principles in letter form. These principles were: (1) the BIS will not conduct transactions involving the accounts of the central banks (or other institutions) of belligerent countries; (2) the BIS will not invest assets or earmarking gold in markets of belligerent countries; and (3) the BIS will demand appropriate statements from transaction counterparties for the purpose of observing the above principles.[17] France and other countries promptly approved these principles. As written, these management principles would appear to be very strict principles befitting the duty of political neutrality in the BIS statutes. The problem was that they were limited to "belligerents." In other words, gold transactions with belligerents would be possible if conducted through neutral countries.[18] While of course the BIS demanded statements in transactions with neutral countries as well, the degree to which these were valid became a problematic point in later years.

The gold-related situation at the BIS grew much tenser immediately the United States entered the war following Japan's attack on Pearl Harbor. Since the United States, which had been treated as a neutral country until then, was now a belligerent in the war, the BIS could no longer conduct gold or dollar transactions with it. At the same time, allied nations ceased trading through the United States, with Switzerland effectively becoming their only remaining liaison with the BIS. It is conceivable that this led to concerns that it would work to the benefit of Germany, which shared a border with Switzerland. Thus, on January 5, 1943 and February 22, 1944 the allies issued statements pressuring the BIS to cease trading in gold from axis nations and their occupied territories. In response to these statements, the BIS finally ceased transactions through neutral countries as well.[19]

The actions of the BIS that became problematic in later years appeared around the time of these allied statements. Here listed are some indications of these problems: (1) After the first statement by the allies, BIS President McKittrick met with Yves Bréart de Boisanger, governor of the Banque de France, to explain the measures taken by the allies. At this time, the Banque de France was under the control of German occupation authorities. In this meeting, McKittrick disclosed, "the Reichsbank is now paying its interest in gold." While the BIS explained that this represented payment of interest on bonds related to the Young Plan and was unrelated to World War II, it deviated from the principles on which the BIS itself had decided. It is hard to understand the logic on which McKittrick was relying when he told the governor of the Banque de France that since the allied statement the BIS "had purchased no gold from the Reichsbank;"[20] (2) According to a summary produced internally by the BIS after the end of the war, in gold transactions during wartime the BIS had checked the origins of gold from transaction counterparties, even when handling gold related to prewar transactions. However, it appears that this check had merely been conducted orally with the Reichsbank and the national bank of Hungary and that later

> we've made efforts to obtain from our correspondents, even on the occasions of simple transfer of interests or reimbursement of capital due to investments made before the war, of declarations ensuring the origin of metals which had been materialized in these transfers.

In other words, they had only "made efforts (*nous nous efforcions*)" and in fact no checking was conducted.[21]

The wartime US freeze of BIS assets

The next issue to be examined is that of the freeze of BIS assets. Specifically, this refers to Freezing Order no. 8389 invoked on April 10, 1940 by the US federal government. At the start of World War II, the BIS sent gold in bars and other assets to the United States, which was a neutral country at the time. These assets were frozen under wartime measures by the US government. These measures not only (1) froze BIS assets in the United States, but also (2) suspended transactions with the BIS itself, which was identified as an enemy organization. From the point of view of the BIS, these measures meant that not only were its assets in the United States frozen, but the assets and liabilities in Germany related to earmarked gold in the United States (i.e., investments in Germany and deposits from Germany) were also frozen.[22]

At this time, while wartime destruction was spreading in Europe, the BIS had evacuated assets to the United States, for example by sending gold to New York. However, these were declared enemy assets, and their withdrawal or transfer required the approval of the US Treasury Department. The BIS, which were informed of the actual situation by an encrypted telegram sent from the Federal Reserve Bank of New York on June 25, 1940, was unable to improve the situation despite the strong counterarguments made to the Treasury Department by President McKittrick, who was an American himself.[23] The BIS considered filing an objection to these measures grounded in Article 10 of the Constituent Charter of the Bank for International Settlements, which prescribed that BIS assets not be seized or commandeered even under wartime. However, since as seen in Chapter 1 of this book the US government had never signed the Hague Convention, which included this charter, the BIS gave up on its plans to object.[24] This matter was resolved after the war on May 13, 1948, when the BIS and the US Treasury Department concluded an agreement on the release of the asset freeze.[25] From start to finish, the United States, and particularly the Treasury Department, had held the initiative on this issue of the asset freeze, and the fact that it had continued to view the BIS as the enemy had lasting effects in various ways in the postwar planning stage.

While relations between the United States and the BIS were worsening, the BIS struck back. In testimony during the United States congressional hearings held (by the House Committee on Banking and Currency) on March 22, 1945 during the last days of the war, Leon Fraser, who had served as BIS chairman of the board and president, severely criticized the Bretton Woods Agreement, which at the time was in the process of ratification hearings.[26] In fact, by this time Fraser had moved to the position of president of the First National Bank of New York. His congressional testimony too was made in his capacity as president of First National, and as such it cannot be said to represent an official view of the BIS. However, since he did discuss his background as BIS president and cited that experience in his testimony, it was not unnatural that the content of his testimony would be taken to represent the position of the BIS. Also, at the time of this testimony the advisory resolution adopted at the Bretton Woods Conference calling for liquidation of the BIS was in effect, and as such Fraser's criticism of the Bretton Woods Agreement and the argument in defense of the BIS probably can be said to be two sides of the same coin.

The main points of this criticism of Bretton Woods by Fraser were as follows: (1) interpretations of the Bretton Woods Agreement differed between Britain and the United States; and actual management of the agreement leaned toward the interests of Britain; (2) in IMF decision-making, the United States, like other countries, had only one representative, leaving it isolated despite holding a controlling share of IMF quota subscriptions; and (3) while it was likely that the World Bank would operate in accordance with the principles of the banking business, the IMF lacked such principles and would be unable to prevent wasting of funds. The following is just one scene from Fraser's testimony.

CONGRESSMAN BROWN: If you had been a delegate, you would not have signed this agreement [at Bretton Woods]?
PRESIDENT FRASER: If I had been a delegate, I would not have signed it; no, sir.
BROWN: However, Lord Keynes signed it because he thought it was in the interest of his country?
FRASER: There is no question about it being in the interests of Great Britain.[27]

Both the wartime issues of looted gold and the freezing of BIS assets in the United States cast a shadow on the postwar years mixed together with the plans for the Bretton Woods structure.

The postwar plans developed on the BIS side will be examined in the next section.

3 Postwar plans made during the war: criticisms of the *"Grossraum"* and of Bretton Woods

The main subject of this section is the postwar BIS plans developed under the extreme conditions of World War II. Once again, Jacobsson appears in a central role. Here is a very simple illustration to help understand Jacobsson's thoughts and ideas during the war.

In general, the following views seem to have been dominant concerning wartime economy, particularly that of World War II:

A   Wartime economies are controlled economies.
B   Wartime economies have had major impacts on postwar economic growth.

However, at this time in Europe there were views that differed considerably in nuance from these views. Namely:

A'   Wartime economies succeeded through the incorporation of market functions within controlled economies.
B'   Wartime economies had no impact on postwar economic growth. In the postwar years, each nation has promptly scraped off the residue of the controlled economy and returned to a market economy.

In the above views, (A) contrasts with (A') and (B) with (B'). However, a close look shows subtle contradictions between (A') and (B') as well. It was the BIS that expressed these views (A') and (B') on the stage of international finance from the wartime through the postwar years and moved on to implement them, and Jacobsson was at the theoretical center of these ideas. But what did this mean in practical terms?

Jacobsson's postwar plans: a focus on the pricing mechanism and small-country theory

The starting point of Jacobsson's theory during the war was the plan to cede the Sudetenland to Nazi Germany in the Munich Agreement right before the start of World War II. This plan, as viewed within the BIS on October 1, 1938, was described in a memo titled "Work for the BIS after the Agreement in Munich."[28] Let's start with a look at this memo.

Written by Jacobsson, this memo was based on a recognition of the situation – greatly mistaken when viewed in the light of subsequent historical facts – that expected that peace would be achieved through the Munich Agreement and that the concern for the future would be that of shifting from preparation for war to a peacetime economy. Based on this assumption, the memo listed the following as roles that the BIS would play under such circumstances: serving as "a possible meeting-place for technical committees," "an intermediary for such committees"; moreover, "when payments are to be made in respect of a loan, both by the Greater Germany and the new Czechoslovakia, the BIS may be made the paying agent for such a loan."[29] It is of considerable interest that Jacobsson expressed the projection that the post-Munich situation would be one of a "general peace" and anticipated economic developments that would result from such situation. That is, a shift to a peacetime footing would direct the flow toward inflationary growth as the economy promptly overheated, and the flow toward government borrowing increase and massive unemployment as the result of shrinkage of defense industry. While in general the forecasting of postwar economic trends is essential to postwar planning, at that time Jacobsson predicted the two opposite developments of inflation and unemployment and proposed achieving balance between them. As seen later, the BIS, and particularly Jacobsson, adopted a theory of economic overheating regarding post-World War II plans, in sharp opposition to the United States and the Keynesians, whose theories predicted an economic slowdown.

As World War II hostilities commenced, while continuing to write for the BIS annual report, Jacobsson energetically gave lectures in response to requests from private-sector organizations such as the Swiss Bankers Association. It is in these lectures that Jacobsson's views developed in a manner relatively free from the restrictions of the BIS organization. Below, the logical structure of Jacobsson's theory will be highlighted, first based on his lectures and related materials, followed by a review of how those opinions were collected in official opinions such as those expressed in the BIS annual reports.

The greatest characteristic of Jacobsson's economic theory during the war was his extolling of the pricing mechanism. His pricing-mechanism theory held that even during wartime prices remained an important signal in the national economy. This argument was developed in a 1942 lecture to the Swiss Bankers Association.[30]

In this lecture, while also mentioning the statement made that year by Japan's minister of finance – pointing out the importance of gold settlement in East Asia – Jacobsson advocated the defense of the gold standard. The logical structure of his argument is outlined below. At the time, criticism of the gold standard was rising in general during the war. The grounds for this argument included not just the theory that the gold standard was ineffectual as the reconstructed gold standard had collapsed, but also the theory that the gold standard was unnecessary, as the Nazi economy had succeeded in re-arming and public-works policies regardless of the fact that it had only a small amount of gold reserves. Jacobsson rejected the latter of these arguments, contending that the success of Nazi Germany relied on high domestic savings rates and keeping wage costs down. Jacobsson pointed out that the Nazi economy, which at a glance appeared to be expansionary, was in fact accompanied by the deflationary factors of high savings and low wages.

In this lecture, the arguments (A') and (B') touched on at the start of this section were expressed clearly along with an assessment of the Nazi economy. That is, the argument that measures of economic control such as the prohibition of the labor movement actually employed the market-economy structure of the pricing mechanism is a claim that leads to argument (A'). At the same time, in this lecture Jacobsson also voiced the position that "a characteristically wartime system would, in many respects, be most difficult to apply under normal conditions."[31] This argument that the market economy, which is realized fictitiously by a wartime system, should be returned promptly to the true pricing mechanism is the argument of (B'). The concept here was that market stability – to use Jacobsson's preferred expression, "balance between cost and prices"– should be realized by force during wartime and through the market after the war.

But how was this argument expressed in the BIS annual report? The introduction to the annual report for fiscal 1939 (April 1, 1939–March 31, 1940) compares World War I and World War II. Based on this comparison, the annual report argues that the following is "the essential features of war economy":

> The fundamental problem arises from the fact that the needs of the state increase twofold or more at a time when the real output of goods and services is reduced by the withdrawal of men through mobilization and by the obstacles placed in the way of foreign trade.[32]

Based on this recognition, the annual report introduces examples of how individual countries were keeping down inflation as a result of excessive military demand. The fiscal 1940 annual report too uses several pages in its introduction to describe the increase in wartime government expenditures in individual countries and the kinds of measures taken to avoid such increases resulting in inflation.[33] In fiscal 1941, the report examined these "inflation-neutral" means in greater detail and compared and contrasted various policies from the "point of view of their effectiveness in counteracting inflation."[34] A similar comparison of policies continued in the fiscal 1942 annual report, which appreciated the forced savings policies seen in both the allied and axis nations.[35]

An assessment of the economic management of Nazi Germany can be seen in the fiscal 1941 annual report as well:

> The success of the German system depends less on the ordinary functions of the cost and price structure than on sound and comprehensive official direction, the efficiency of the control, and the cooperation and discipline shown by the business world and the general public.[36]

Incidentally, the BIS authorities prepared a confidential internal memo after the annual report for this fiscal year had been issued, clearly indicating that the authors of the report had been Jacobsson for chapters 1–3 and Frederick Conolly (a member of the BIS Monetary and Economic Department originally from the Bank of England) for chapters 4–6. The memo stresses that "the authors were under no pressure," listing eight items such as "the fact that the weakness of German wartime fundraising is pointed out" as evidence of the objectivity of its descriptions. This implies that there was debate within the BIS concerning its duty of neutrality simply because of descriptions in this year's annual report that could be seen as favorable to Germany.[37]

The appearance in the BIS annual reports of this position extolling the pricing mechanism became the subject of an important dispute within the BIS Monetary and Economic Department, which had the responsibility for writing the annual reports. In May 1940 – that is, during the process of preparation of the fiscal 1939 annual report – Charles Kindleberger, then on assignment to the BIS from the United States, butted heads with Jacobsson, then head of the Monetary and Economic Department. According to Jacobsson's journal, the young Kindleberger visited Jacobsson "twice and again" regarding the rough draft of the annual report, discussing "inflation-neutral" measures as mentioned above, pressing him to remove from the draft the passages touching on these points. Jacobsson argued with Kindleberger and the matter concluded with the passages not being removed from the draft. Reminiscing on this argument, Jacobsson recalled, "Kindleberger was quick-witted, well-learned, and conversant in both theory and statistics – but he was not a good writer, and he was too influenced by the New Deal to make a good judgment."[38] In contrast, Kindleberger, while expressing a high regard for Jacobsson's ability, recalled his impression of him in his own autobiography, "One might start talking to him in the center of a room, and find oneself after a time backed into a corner with his large frame and thick glasses still in attack" adding, "He was far too much of a monetarist for me." Concerning the wartime annual reports as well, Kindleberger testifies that the analysis for "the 10th Annual Report of the Bank to which I contributed a great deal" – that is, the annual report for fiscal 1939, when the conflict mentioned above took place – "was modestly better than those it followed."[39] Following this conflict, in 1940 Kindleberger left the BIS and returned to the United States. This conflict on the BIS annual report also developed into the dispute with the United States and the Keynesians.

Another important motive behind Jacobsson's wartime theory was "small-country theory." In December 1943, Jacobsson gave a lecture entitled "Small

Countries and World Economic Reconstruction," at the invitation of the Swiss Industrial Association and the Economic Society of St. Gallen. In this lecture, while introducing post-World War II recovery plans he also discussed the roles that small countries in Europe, such as Switzerland, should play.[40] This theory is summarized below.

In his lecture, Jacobsson first reviewed the interwar period, which he assessed as one in which the small countries demonstrated remarkable growth and timely responses to the depression, keeping their unemployment rates below those of the large countries such as Britain and United States. Next, he emphasized that the primary reason of "this superior performance of the smaller countries" was their high level of adaptability to international prices, since they were highly dependent on trade. His argument was that since they were under circumstances in which their choice was "exports or die," the small countries could not simply leave costs and prices in a state of imbalance without adjustment.

Jacobsson then examined the ideal state of the postwar recovery based on an extension of this evaluation of small countries. As will be touched on in the next sub-section, at the time of this lecture the plans for establishing the IMF already had been made clear, and it was thought that some kind of international institution would play a major role in the recovery in the postwar world. While introducing these plans, Jacobsson also pointed out that "it is an almost invariable rule that small countries are not in the least inclined to attempt to increase their competitive power by means of large devaluations," and that "the small countries are, at the same time, aware of the importance of having a sound currency." From these arguments, Jacobsson developed his criticism of the theory behind the establishment of an international institution and deployed his argument in favor of the restoration of the gold standard, advising progress toward the prompt liberalization of trade taking advantage of the strengths of small countries.

Incidentally, this small-country theory had not been worked out at the start of the war. As of October 1940 – that is, when Nazi Germany was expanding its territory across Europe – Jacobsson was projecting that if the Nazis were victorious then the postwar world would be divided into multiple massive currency spheres. Recognizing relations between these massive currency spheres as an "important issue," Jacobsson advised the establishment of an international institution to enforce credit arrangements between these currency and economic spheres. This international institution would carry out the "overall supervision" of capital movements and would provide international credit related to postwar recovery – "relatively small amounts of aid in the form of credit to provide minor aid in meeting budgets." He also argued that "an institution such as the BIS" would be suited to conducting this business.[41]

Whatever the case, during the war Jacobsson's position shifted from acceptance of "*Grossraum*" to a high regard for small countries.[42] Now let's attempt to trace how this change was represented in the texts of the BIS annual reports.

The opening of the conclusion to the fiscal 1941 annual report featured an impressive description that could be read as favorable of "*Grossraum*." "The great war has a double aspect: on the one hand, severance of relations with enemies and, on the other, a close association among countries on the same side of barrier." It then proposed the thesis that "no single country can become wholly self-sufficient, each being of necessity part of a wider economy." However, it argued,

> a difference in conception exists whether this wider economy should be on a world basis or whether collaboration should, in the first place, be worked out in separate, politically defined areas, with arrangements for trade between these areas as larger entities.[43]

This is in accordance with Jacobsson's projection as of 1940 – that after a Nazi victory multiple independent "massive currency spheres" would arise. However, in the fiscal 1943 annual report the keynote of the argument had shifted to the small-country theory. That year's annual report argued that "That there is a close connection between foreign trade and conditions on the home market is, as a rule, more easily appreciated in a small than in a large country," followed by the contention, "But no country – large or small – can afford to disregard the need for restoring balance between costs and prices."[44]

While fluctuating in the assessment of "*Grossraum*," Jacobsson's statements remained unchanged on the point of extolling the pricing mechanism. His focus on small countries too was linked to the issue of working toward cost and price equilibrium in accordance with international conditions. The next sub-section will look at how these arguments of Jacobsson's developed in connection with the international currency system.

A view of Bretton Woods

The Bretton Woods Conference – officially the United Nations Monetary and Financial Conference – opened on July 1, 1944 in the US resort town of Bretton Woods, New Hampshire, ending on July 22 with the conclusion of the Bretton Woods Agreement. Following this agreement, the IMF Articles of Agreement was concluded on December 27, 1945 after ratification by each country. It is common knowledge that the design of the IMF system involved two rival proposals: one from Keynes and one from Harry Dexter White. While the Keynes proposal sought to establish an international settlement institution (an "International Clearing Union") with a credit-creation function, the White proposal envisioned a fund with neither a credit function nor a settlement structure. On the subject of the liberalization of movement of capital too, the Keynes proposal was skeptical while the White proposal was optimistic. These differences between the two proposals expressed the struggle in the background between the interests of Britain and the United States, respectively. In the end, the IMF agreement established a fund fairly close to the White proposal. On the other hand, seemingly to compensate for backing down on the banking function at the IMF, the Bretton Woods Agreement granted to the International Bank for Reconstruction and Development (commonly known as the World Bank) authority for the provision of long-term credit.[45]

While the above developments already belong to the sphere of common knowledge, what is little known is the fact that a BIS representative had crossed the frontlines to visit the United States before the Bretton Woods Conference. This BIS representative was none other than Jacobsson. Jacobsson had ascertained the content of these Keynes and White proposals in secret before they were finalized and became public, and had then criticized both after returning to Switzerland. He also sensed the argument smoldering around the US Congress in favor of liquidating the BIS and deployed lobbying activities in opposition to it. Even more problematic was the fact that after returning to the BIS Jacobsson had communicated his impressions of the allies' postwar plans to Reichsbank vice-president Emil Puhl. How was the BIS planning to respond to the Bretton Woods Agreement and surrounding developments? Jacobsson's words and actions around the time of his visit to the United States offer some clues to answer to this question.[46]

From December 1941 through February 1942, Jacobsson traveled on business to the United States and met vigorously with leading US figures. In doing so, he learned about the postwar plans of the allied nations, centered on the United States. Of these postwar plans, Jacobsson severely criticized Keynes's proposal of an "International Clearing Union," which later would come to fruition as the Keynes proposal. At the same time, urging caution on the difference between the long and short terms, he forecasted shortages of foreign reserves in each country over the short term and revealed a plan for "stabilization loans" to support the stabilization of each country's currency. On the other hand, Jacobsson emphasized trust in the pricing mechanism and also turned his criticism toward the White proposal, which lacked consistency with the gold standard. According to Jacobsson, contributions to a postwar stabilization fund should be made by the United States first, and in gold.

Jacobsson also referred to the issue of a decision on and changes in exchange rates. The drafts that later would come to fruition in the Bretton Woods Agreement adopted systems under which fixed exchange rates would be employed, with little room for fluctuation – what in the future would be called an adjustable peg. Both the Keynes and White proposals adopted this method, and Jacobsson too had high regard for this himself. However, it is of considerable interest that on this matter Jacobsson focused on asymmetries between large and small countries as touched on above. He argued that if a large country such as the United States were to devalue the exchange rate of its currency, it would have an immediate impact on production conditions worldwide. Even if a large country were to devalue its currency for the purpose of adjusting domestic economic conditions, the results would be limited because the world would respond immediately. In contrast, the exchange rates of small countries have no impact on the world as a whole. For this reason, competition through devaluing the currency would work to the benefit of small countries. In connection with the Bretton Woods Conference, Jacobsson demanded that large countries observe fiscal discipline on their own and not be quick to change exchange rates, even under an adjustable peg. This view surpassed the idea of Bretton Woods and seemed to prophesy the 1971 suspension of the dollar's convertibility to gold.

The above concepts were made public in the 1943 lecture on small-country theory referred to above. Since the Keynes proposal was announced in April 1943 and the final version of the White proposal was announced in July 1943, this meant that Jacobsson had already summarized his criticisms of both proposals by the time they were presented. Incidentally, in light of the fact that the Jacobsson lecture was made in the neutral country of Switzerland, it appears that it was communicated quickly to both the American and German sides – with the Americans in particular promptly telegraphing a translation of the content of the lecture to the United States – and made an impression on both the allies and the axis.[47]

Jacobsson's Bretton Woods argument also, while expressed indirectly, was reflected in the BIS annual reports of the time. The fiscal 1942 annual report – published in June 1943 – emphasized throughout "true balance in the cost and price structure," the core of Jacobsson's theory, and particularly discussed in detail the relation between cost adjustments and currency adjustments in a single country. While containing the striking phrase "The distinction between 'adjustment' and 'manipulation' is not easy to establish either in theory or in practice," the annual report also reviewed critically its own claim from the preceding fiscal year – that is, the opinion expressed that "major maladjustments would probably have to be corrected by alternations in exchange rates." Also, this fiscal 1942 annual report recommended a policy of combining "such a step with a direct adjustment of costs and prices" instead of a rapid modification of exchange rates.[48]

Jacobsson's arguments included in the annual reports led to postwar plans that called for not just adjusting exchange rates but also rebuilding the pricing mechanism through cost adjustments made in individual countries, such as decreasing wages, and promoting free trade. In this way, Jacobsson's theory developed the argument calling for market discipline in connection with the adjustable peg of the Bretton Woods Agreement, particularly among the large countries, along the line of the argument for "balance in the cost and price structure" that he had advocated for some years.

However, the plans that Jacobsson had argued for during the war, of the establishment of an international institution and the adoption of the gold standard, would face severe headwinds after World War II.

The dispute with the Keynesians: from wartime to the postwar period

Consistently throughout the war years, Jacobsson continued to declare the above trust in the markets. Naturally, this argument was in conflict with Keynesianism, which was becoming the dominant current of thought at that time. On what points and how did Jacobsson conflict with Keynes and the Keynesians? Examination is needed to elucidate the theoretical and conceptual framework of Jacobsson's theory.

On his wartime visit to the United States described above, Jacobsson met with Alvin Hansen and Paul Samuelson. Concerned about a postwar economic slow-down, these prodigious young American Keynesians were mulling plans to implement extensive Keynesian policies after the war. In response, Jacobsson forecast a postwar boom, emphasizing the need for counter-inflationary policies and discussed his evaluation of the pricing mechanism, Let's attempt to recon-struct this dialogue from Jacobsson's journal, which records the state of affairs in this meeting with Hansen and Samuelson.[49]

At Hansen's invitation, Jacobsson lunched with him on February 28, 1942. In addition to Hansen, Samuelson was invited to this lunch: Samuelson had just been appointed a professor at the Massachusetts Institute of Technology – according to Jacobsson's journal, "one might take him for a bright peasant boy." Jacobsson continued that Samuelson, "does not look more than 28, but is prob-ably 35." The lunch meeting began joyfully but the discussion began when at the table Jacobsson expressed his concern with US price levels.

Jacobsson argued, "American economists seemed to take for granted that most prices in the USA followed those on the world market. But that was not always true," and "After 1931 American prices were much affected by those in the sterling area." In the context of the time, this was an argument warning that the dollar was excessively undervalued and that there was upward pressure on US import prices through the low value of the dollar and the high value of the pound. In response, Hansen asked, "I don't really know what is meant by world prices. Do they exist?" Jacobsson answered that there were some countries that could impact price levels through changing the par value of their own currency and some that could not and pointed out that at that time US price levels were impacted by the sterling economies. Samuelson responded that even if that were the case, the impact would make itself apparent only in the US terms of trade and current-account balance, and that even if these conditions were to worsen the United States could address them using its abundant gold reserves. In response, Jacobsson introduced the examples of small countries such as the Netherlands and Switzerland, arguing that exchange-rate fluctuations were not necessarily reflected in terms of trade and that each country had adjusted costs and prices.

While this dialogue contains many intricate issues, its main points can be summarized as follows. Hansen and Samuelson were skeptical of the existence of "world prices," and saw exchange-rate fluctuations as being adjustable through terms of trade. For this reason, they projected that equilibrium in global markets would be achieved over time even if each country implemented eco-nomic stimulus measures or experienced inflation. In contrast, Jacobsson saw the presence of world prices as important and considered the degree to which indi-vidual countries could influence these world prices through foreign exchange – not just small countries but wartime America as well – as being limited. For this reason, instead of moving quickly to adjust exchange rates each country needed to work to achieve domestic equilibrium – balance in the cost and price structure through the pricing mechanism. This was the framework of Jacobsson's argument as contrasted with the American Keynesians. This is the same point seen in the above perspective of the BIS annual report. This argument can be symbolized by Jacobsson's answer to Samuelson's view. Talking over the adjustment of international price levels, Samuelson stated that the adjustment "would happen if goods moved." In response, Jacobsson answered, "Even without that," and added, "Swiss machines could not be sold without reference to prices of corresponding machines sold abroad." While the Keynesians saw that equilibrium could be restored through exchange-rate fluctuations and movement of goods, Jacobsson emphasized his point that prices had efficacy as signals and that the movement of goods was irrelevant to them when they were functioning as signals.

After returning to Europe following his meeting with Hansen and Samuelson in 1942, Jacobsson set forth an anti-Keynesian argument on business-cycle theory as well. In 1944, he contended with S. Morris Livingston, Nicolas Kaldor and Gunnar Myrdal on the possibility of a "postwar depression." Based on the experience of the economic slump that followed World War I, these European and American Keynesians projected the coming of a "postwar depression" following World War II as well. In response, Jacobsson rejected the possibility of a depression. The grounds for his argument were "wartime interests rates are at their bottom, so that interest rates must rise after the war" and "the difference between World Wars I and II is in the efficacy of price controls."[50] Here we see the appearance of the subtle inconsistency in Jacobsson's wartime economic theory mentioned at the start of this section – the contradiction between theory (A′), which stated that markets functioned during wartime, and theory (B′), which posited that the functioning of markets was assured because of the effects of wartime controls and that these controls should be released after the war.

On the subject of the business cycle alone, Jacobsson's forecasts hit the mark, as there was no "postwar depression" following World War II. To the contrary, focal points in the postwar economy were inflation in each country and there were shortages of dollars in Europe and Asia. His confidence deepened by this process, Jacobsson next took his conflict with the Keynesians further toward criticism of the original Keynes theory itself. The final part of this section will take an overview of this point.

Actually, Keynes and Jacobsson were good friends from before the war. In his papers and lectures, Jacobsson expressed his esteem for Keynes and used a method of argument that separated Keynes himself from the Keynesians.[51] In his paper "Keynes: Costs and Controls" published in 1953, while criticizing the Keynesian views included in UN reports of the time as a "quite astonishing example of almost complete neglect of the question of balance between costs and prices," Jacobsson also expressed his regard for Keynes, noting, "Keynes himself did not rely on 'controls' to achieve the objectives he had in view" and "he remained all his life a believer in the advantage of an economy in which individual initiative and private enterprise would be able to make their valuable contributions."[52]

As an extension of this view of Keynes, Jacobsson focused on Keynes's post-humous 1946 paper "The Balance of Payments of the United States."[53] This Keynes paper looked into the prospect of the US international balance of payments, a prerequisite of a proposed Anglo-American Financial Agreement, based on statistical materials. It probably should be numbered among Keynes's works as a commentary on current affairs, instead of a deeper theoretical or conceptual paper. However, in the conclusion to this paper Keynes expresses the view that "the United States is becoming a high-living, high-cost country beyond any previous experience" and recommends "classical medicine" together with currency adjustments and import controls as balance-of-payments policies for the time being to adjust for these factors.

In this context, Keynes's point of emphasis was the point that "I do not suppose that the classical medicine will work by itself,"[54] and he emphasized the use of IMF and Export–import Bank of America loans as measures to address the international balance of payments. However, with regard to this "classical medicine" which Keynes referred to, Jacobsson interpreted that "in this medicine he would naturally include the ordinary means of monetary policy," and stressed that Keynes had had a final change in thought in this posthumous work.[55] Moreover, Jacobsson introduced this perspective in numerous places. In a luncheon speech held in the United States in 1952, Jacobsson said,

> You may remember that in 1940, in his pamphlet *How to pay for the War*, he was already urging upon his country a quite different attitude, and his last article in the *Economic Journal*, published in 1946, after his death, expounded a policy very unlike the one that he had advocated in the days of depression.

Jacobsson added with a laugh, "I myself feel sure that if Keynes were alive today he would be no Keynesian."[56]

Naturally, the Keynesians reacted strongly to these arguments of Jacobsson. Keynes's leading disciple Roy Harrod authored a review of a Jacobsson book reprinting this lecture, attacking vigorously the closing words of the above lecture: "Mr. Jacobsson seems to regard a Keynesian as an all-weather advocate of cheap money, regardless of the danger that over-investment may cause inflation." However, Harrod claimed that he himself called for direct controls on investment as a counter-inflationary measure after the war and argued for a shift to flexible monetary policies later, once inflationary pressure had receded for a while. "In all this I believe that I was a 'Keynesian'." Harrod dismissed Jacobsson's definition of "Keynesian," saying, "we must leave such nice disputes to the professors of the history of economic doctrines," and went on to express his doubts on Jacobsson's interpretations of Keynes and Wicksell by criticizing, "I do not judge that Mr. Jacobsson has thoroughly understood Keynes's system."[57]

As reviewed in this section, during the wartime and postwar periods Jacobsson continued to criticize Keynes and the Keynesians on business-cycle theory as well, using as his golden rule balance in the cost and price structure. In terms of the schema touched on at the start of this section, while Keynes's theory showed continuity from (A) to (B), Jacobsson's emphasized consistency from (A') to (B'). While there is room for criticism of his aggressive interpretation of Keynes, as touched on in Harrod's review, Jacobsson's argument was included in the BIS annual reports, and probably had a unique impact on the international financial world.

4 The banking business and distribution of profits

This section covers the financial statements for the fiscal years 1939 (ended March 31, 1940) through 1944 (ended March 31, 1945). Counted from the start of BIS operations, these correspond to the tenth through fifteenth fiscal years. The fiscal 1944 annual general meeting, planned for March 1945, was postponed due to the war, and matters that should have been approved in the general meeting, such as distribution of profits, were put on hold.

As touched on earlier in this chapter, during the war the BIS professed neutrality, claiming to conduct its business with no bias to either side in transactions conducted through multiple countries. For this reason, in a case such as the conversion of the currency of Country A to gold at the BIS, sending this gold to Country B, and then converting it to the currency of Country B, it carried out the transaction through the procedures of concluding agreements with both countries and ensuring – at least formally – that no advantage or disadvantage arose in the gold exchange rates used. In the investment business, "considerations of yield have had to take second place in comparison with questions of safety and liquidity." On the other hand, the BIS's business enjoyed various benefits from the "goodwill and sympathy shown by the central banks." The report stated that "certain rules of conduct which the Bank had, as a matter of fact, observed since the month of September [1939] were codified and brought to the knowledge of its clients."[58]

Trends in the financial statements (1): collection of deposits

With repeated increases and decreases, the total amount on the balance sheet during the war remained in the range of 400 million Gold Swiss francs (see Figure 3.1). The BIS annual report published in 1945, which summarized movements during wartime, reported that the BIS's total assets "declined by 10 percent, or a little more than 50 million Gold Swiss francs," from August 1, 1939 through March 31, 1945. This annual report also analyzed this decline as "principally the effect of certain withdrawals of voluntary deposits by central banks." As seen below, this assessment of the annual report hit the mark.[59]

A look at individual accounts shows almost no changes in paid-in capital or long-term deposits (see Figure 3.1).[60]

In contrast, short term and sight deposits fell rapidly. The "Deposits of Central banks for their own account at sight" showed particularly marked decreases, not only remaining in a decreasing trend throughout the wartime

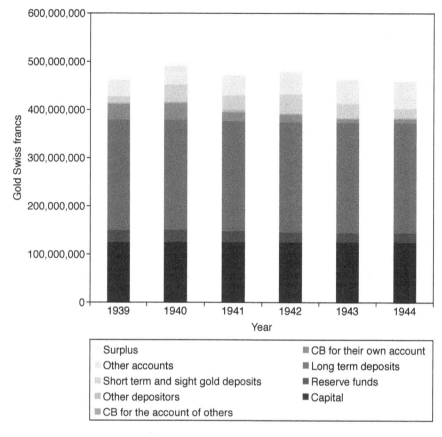

Figure 3.1 BIS balance sheet: major items on liabilities (fiscal years 1939–1944), in Gold Swiss francs (source: *BIS Tenth–Fifteenth Annual Reports*).

period but also changing massively during a single fiscal year. The annual report referred to these accounts using a series of expressions such as "the only variable item" (fiscal 1939)[61] and "some of the most important movements in the composition of the Bank's liabilities" (fiscal 1940),[62] and in fiscal 1941 it reported "abrupt fluctuations and falls."[63] However, the BIS stated that these withdrawals "did not cause any special difficulties" because it held "ample liquid assets" in the currencies and the markets concerned.[64]

As was the case during the Depression, during wartime deposits at the BIS were in a unique relationship to movements in gold. As seen in the preceding chapter, in addition to accepting deposits from central banks and other institutions, the BIS also accepted earmarked gold. During the Depression, while deposits were withdrawn earmarked gold flowed in to the BIS. Since the latter of these, the earmarked gold, did not appear on the BIS balance sheet, the apparent decrease in deposits accompanied an increase in BIS gold holdings. However, during wartime the relationship between deposits and gold showed some more complex aspects, as seen below.

These were: (1) Throughout the period of World War II, BIS gold transactions were in a decreasing trend. While BIS monthly average gold holdings were 21,432 kg in 1938 (73,821,000 Gold Swiss francs), these fell rapidly in 1940, dropping to 535 kg (1,843,000 Gold Swiss francs) in 1945 (see Figure 3.2); (2) While earmarked gold had totaled 73.2 million Gold Swiss francs at the end of fiscal 1939 (March 31, 1940), at the end of fiscal 1940 the figure was 65.1 million Gold Swiss francs, and it would remain around 50 million Gold Swiss francs thereafter through the end of fiscal 1944;[65] (3) A look at a breakdown of earmarked gold by country as of August 1944 shows that allied countries had earmarks of 20.7 million Gold Swiss francs, neutral countries 16.6 million Gold Swiss francs, countries with accounts closed by the BIS (Denmark, the Baltic states and the Free City of Danzig) 14.4 million Gold Swiss francs, axis countries 3.1 million Gold Swiss francs, and countries that had signed peace treaties (such as Italy) 100,000 Gold Swiss francs. The markets in which earmarked gold was placed were Amsterdam and Bern for allied countries; Bern for neutral countries, axis countries and countries that had signed peace treaties; and New York and London for countries with accounts closed by the BIS;[66] (4) In contrast, as seen above central bank deposits and other accounts were withdrawn. The indicator commitments, which expresses these deposits in weight in gold, decreased throughout the wartime period; and (5) The bank's own stock of gold, which represents the total of gold in bars and earmarked gold held by the BIS minus commitments expressed in a weight of gold, swelled rapidly beginning in fiscal 1941, as seen for asset accounts below.

Through comparison of these trends with the period of the Depression, we can identify the following characteristics. During the Depression, withdrawal of deposits corresponded to inflows of earmarked gold. Each country's central bank withdrew deposits in each country's currency, for which future prospects were uncertain, bought gold on gold markets, and deposited this gold with the BIS. In contrast, during the wartime period earmarked gold remained largely unchanged, with only withdrawal of deposits standing out. A further issue with the wartime period is the fact that regardless of the above BIS's own stock of gold increased, rising from roughly 20 percent of the balance sheet in fiscal 1943 to 21 percent the following year in fiscal 1944, reaching an "all-time maximum" of 95.2 million Gold Swiss francs.[67] Since these gold assets had been no more than ten million Gold Swiss francs at the start of World War II, the increase in this account truly corresponded to the consequences of wartime.

But what was the specific form of non-earmarked gold? The main component of commitments expressed in a weight of gold was the gold deposit account. About 26 central banks and international institutions had opened gold sight deposit accounts with the BIS (as of fiscal 1942).[68] Regarding these gold deposits, the BIS has evaluated them highly for their role in wartime settlements. In fact, most of these deposits were sight deposits, apparently used for trade settlement instead of savings.[69] While delivery of this gold originally took place in

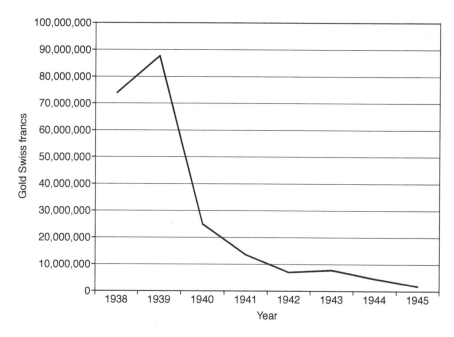

Figure 3.2 BIS gold holdings during the wartime, monthly average, in Gold Swiss francs (source: BIS Historical Archives, 7.18(6), AUB 1, "Movement of Gold held for our Account during December 1946").

London, as the war progressed it came to be concentrated in New York. However, even these gold deposit accounts fell rapidly from 39.7 million Gold Swiss francs at the start of fiscal 1943 to 29.6 million Gold Swiss francs at the end of the fiscal year.[70]

Earmarked gold remained unchanged for the most part, while central-bank deposit accounts and other commitments expressed in a weight of gold decreased. At the same time, gold deposits, while increasing for a time, decreased rapidly in fiscal 1943. These were the trends in deposits and gold at the BIS during wartime. Thus, while the wartime BIS performed something of the role of a venue for settlement via gold accounts while the warfront was at a standstill, as the war situation intensified this business was affected as well.

Trends in the financial statements (2): investment of funds

But how did the impacts of wartime make themselves felt in the investment of funds? A look at highly liquid accounts shows that while in some years cash, sight funds at interest, and rediscountable bills and acceptances did indeed decrease substantially, for the most part they remained largely unchanged. In contrast, Treasury bills showed marked decreases (see Figure 3.3). Treasury bills fell severely in fiscal 1940, the same year in which own accounts of central

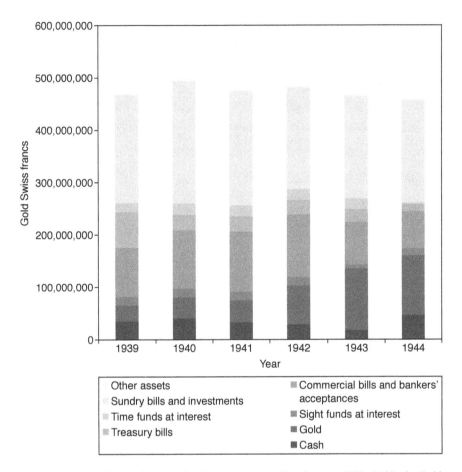

Figure 3.3 BIS balance sheet: major items on assets (fiscal years 1939–1944), in Gold
Swiss francs (source: *BIS Tenth–Fifteenth Annual Reports*).

banks on the credit side dropped by one-half, and later Treasury bills demonstrated movements correlating to those of deposits. It would appear that the withdrawal of deposits was handled through the sale of Treasury bills.

On the other hand, gold in bars increased steadily during wartime. As seen
in Figure 3.3, after rising gradually through fiscal 1941 gold in bars increased
rapidly in fiscal 1942. Incidentally, gold in bars as shown here refers to what
one might call gross gold assets, and as seen above net gold holdings represents this amount (after totaling it with off-the-books earmarked gold) minus
commitments expressed in a weight of gold. On this point, the gold-assets situation was a severe one in the fiscal years 1939 and 1940, at the start of the war.
With regard to the balance of gold holdings in fiscal 1939, "The average of the
five last months of the financial year, however, has barely exceeded 15 million
Gold Swiss francs," and this was said to "equivalent to less than 5,000 kg of

fine gold."[71] Net gold holdings at the end of the 1940 fiscal year (March 1941) were reported to have fallen "from 17.6 million Gold Swiss francs on March 31, 1940 to 4.5 million a year later."[72] At that point in time, more than 75 percent of BIS gold holdings were invested in New York and 14 percent in London, indicating that the sending of gold away from continental Europe largely had been completed (see Table 3.1). However, this movement reversed in fiscal 1941. At the end of July 1941, Bern, which until then had been the BIS's third-ranked destination for investing gold, suddenly overtook London to rise to second place. As touched on above when discussing deposits, this increase in gold assets resulted from an increase in BIS own accounts – as loans to the national bank of Hungary were repaid in gold. Later, gold invested in Bern would increase rapidly, reaching 2.717 million Gold Swiss francs at the end of November 1941 (see Table 3.1). This amount is more than ten times the amount of gold the BIS had invested in Britain at that time, and it corresponds to 42 percent of total BIS gold investments. Gold in bars on the debit side too coincided with the increasing trend in BIS own accounts starting in this fiscal year.

While gold in bars increased massively in December 1943 – from 81.5 to 137.1 million Gold Swiss francs – this resulted from the BIS rediscounting investments in Italian markets, converting the resulting sales to gold, and then delivering them to Switzerland under Article 10 of the Hague Convention. The BIS notes, concerning this business, "the Bank's holdings, in Switzerland, of assets belonging to it in Swiss francs and gold represented more than 20 per cent of the paid-up capital."[73] Thus, effectively BIS gold-related investments during World War II were conducted based in Switzerland, and this point is the background behind the gold issue mentioned above.

The issue regarding the investment of BIS funds was whether these gold holdings were intended as long-term investments with high returns or as liquid reserves for payment. As seen above, the BIS increased gold in its own account. Put another way, this means that assets that could be invested without receiving demands for the withdrawal of deposits increased. However, the description of these gold investments in the annual reports changed subtly. In fiscal 1941, the

Table 3.1 BIS gold investments, in 1,000 Gold Swiss francs

	March 1941		June 1941		July 1941		November 1941	
	No.	%	No.	%	No.	%	No.	%
New York	3,415	75.6	3,415	77.4	3,415	64.4	3,415	53.8
London	631	14.0	631	14.3	631	11.9	207	3.3
Bern	408	9.0	303	6.9	1,195	22.5	2717	42.8
Paris	61	1.4	61	1.4	61	1.2	8	0.1
Total	4,515	100.0	4,410	100.0	5,302	100.0	6,347	100.0

Source: Rapport sur les opérations de la Banque du 1er au 31 mars 1941, p. 3; du 1er au 31 juillet 1941, p. 3; du 1er au 30 novembre 1941; p. 3.

report indicated an inclination toward high-return investments, using the phrasing,

> The lengthening of the average period of investment is connected with an increase in the proportion of the Bank's own funds in relation to its total liabilities and reflects a tendency on its part to improve, in some measure, the earnings on the amounts invested in the different markets.[74]

However, the next year in fiscal 1942 the report evaluated critically the main causes of developments such as a shortening of average terms of investments, including "increase in the aggregate amount of gold and cash holdings," stating that these "have necessarily had an effect upon the profits for the fiscal year."[75] In the end, in fiscal 1944 it settled on the assessment "one of the main considerations in framing the policy of the Bank ... has been to maintain the greatest possible liquidity backed by a strong position in actual gold."[76] It would probably be appropriate to say that while the wartime BIS attempted holding its own gold for a time, due to interruptions in the sending of gold and decreases in trade itself it was forced into an investment policy of stocking up on liquid assets, whether it wanted to or not.

Finally, a section in the annual report reviewing the investment of funds during wartime summarized it this way:

> Between 31st August 1939 and 31st March 1945 the liquid assets of the Bank on the American, British and Swiss markets, held in gold, dollars or Swiss francs, rose in the aggregate by more than 117 million Gold Swiss francs.[77]

At the base point of the start of the war used here (the end of August 1939), a look at deposit positions by currency shows that of the total of 54 million Gold Swiss francs 29 million was in dollars, 11 million in gold, six million in British pounds, three million in Swiss francs, one million each in French francs and Dutch florins, and one million in other currencies. Over the three-month period to this point in time on the threshold of war, the amount in French francs had decreased by 41 million and that in dollars had decreased by 32 million.[78] The trend toward a decrease in dollars and relative increase in Swiss francs was a characteristic that remained throughout the wartime period.

In contrast, after the war this trend reversed. A look at deposit positions by currency shows that as of the end of December 1946 of the total amount of 335 million Gold Swiss francs 223 million was in dollars, 45 million in gold, 48 million in British pounds and 19 million in Swiss francs. Over the three-month period to this point in time at the end of 1946, the shares of the pound and the dollar increased by 31 million and 21 million, respectively, while the amount in Swiss francs fell by four million. An internal business report points out, "New deposits are being received in pounds sterling and dollars, while deposits in Swiss francs are in a decreasing trend."[79] One notes that on BIS accounts, together with the postwar fall of the Swiss franc as an emergency currency, gold continued to increase at this point in time.

Profit and loss and distribution of profits: processing of exchange differences

Regarding indicators of profit in the postwar period, first of all a comparison with trends in total amounts on the BIS balance sheet should be examined. As seen above, the total amount on the balance sheet shows a decrease of 10 percent from August 1, 1939 through March 31, 1945. Comparison over the period of fiscal years for which reports were published – March 31, 1939 through March 31, 1945 – to contrast this figure with profit indicators shows that the total amount on the balance sheet in March 1945 retained 97.6 percent of the figure for March 1939. In contrast, over the same period announced total revenue (gross revenue) retained 63.3 percent and announced net balance retained 55.6 percent of the figures for March 1939, showing a marked decrease in income. Unpublished indicators too largely decreased in the same manner, with gross revenue falling to 62.8 percent and net balance to 59.5 percent of the March 1939 figures.

As seen in Table 3.2, the main causes of the decrease in profits in comparison to the balance sheet total can be derived from the rapid decrease in commission revenues and the continuing high costs of administration. During the period of the Depression, strong commission revenues had been received because the remittance business and other operations continued despite the decrease in business overall. However, during wartime this source of revenues dried up. The announced indicators show a rapid drop in commission revenues beginning in fiscal 1942, and this trend matches the trends in deposits and gold seen above.

On the other hand, net income in Table 3.2 remains largely unchanged during wartime. The bulk of net income consists of gains on investments in Germany, and it is said that in 1943 these accounted for 80 percent of net income. While as seen in this chapter the BIS was criticized after the war by those who argued that it should have suspended gold transactions with Germany through strict application of its duty of neutrality, since the BIS was based on this revenue structure "it would have been impossible to stop the gold flow from Berlin without virtually closing the Bank."[80]

The next issue concerns the processing of gains and losses on foreign exchange. While gains and losses on foreign exchange had arisen since the Depression, the BIS had processed all of these gains and losses on its unofficial books, without covering them in its official income statement. While it continued this policy through the war years, attention is drawn to transfers from specific reserves and adjustments. In this account, while 968,000 Gold Swiss francs were transferred to gain/loss accounts in fiscal 1933, at the peak of the impact of the Depression, a level of 150,000 Gold Swiss francs was maintained for the following several years, falling to 70,000 Gold Swiss francs in the 1938 fiscal year (see Table 2.1 in the preceding chapter). However, during the war years the amount

Table 3.2 BIS profit and loss account, fiscal years 1939–1944, published and unpublished versions, in Gold Swiss francs

Published account

	Net income	Commissions earned	Transfer fees	Gross profit	Costs of administration = total expenditure	Net profit
1939	9,793,039.34	156,644.89	298.55	9,949,982.78	1,987,802.13	7,962,180.65
1940	7,022,432.10	124,819.22	53.00	7,147,304.32	1,853,395.20	5,293,909.12
1941	6,976,870.40	110,305.12	18.28	7,087,193.80	1,901,507.90	5,185,685.90
1942	6,389,808.56	66,000.42	13.67	6,455,822.65	1,946,868.76	4,508,953.89
1943	7,119,389.97	71,406.27	21.33	7,190,817.57	1,936,914.45	5,253,903.12
1944	6,238,892.80	60,851.05	31.00	6,299,774.85	1,870,212.44	4,429,562.41

Unpublished account

	Gross revenue	Interest allowed	Costs of administration	Net balance	Transfers from specific reserves and adjustments	Exchange differences	Total amount available for allocation	Allocations to undisclosed reserves				Net balance published
								Exchange differences account	Provision for exchange and other losses	Revaluation of assets	Administration account	
1939	13,291,000.00	441,000.00	1,988,000.00	10,862,000.00	−77,000.00	−82,000.00	10,703,000.00	−82,000.00	2,673,000.00		150,000.00	7,962,000.00
1940	10,483,000.00	63,000.00	2,026,000.00	8,394,000.00	0.00	−73,000.00	8,321,000.00	−73,000.00	3,100,000.00			5,294,000.00
1941	10,022,000.00	35,000.00	1,901,000.00	8,086,000.00	720,000.00	43,000.00	8,849,000.00	43,000.00	3,120,000.00		500,000.00	5,186,000.00
1942	9,086,000.00	30,000.00	1,947,000.00	7,109,000.00	285,000.00	65,000.00	7,459,000.00	65,000.00	2,885,000.00			4,509,000.00
1943	9,201,000.00	25,000.00	1,937,000.00	7,239,000.00	1,161,000.00	54,000.00	8,454,000.00	54,000.00	2,396,000.00		750,000.00	5,254,000.00
1944	8,352,000.00	18,000.00	1,870,000.00	6,464,000.00	308.00	227,000.00	6,999,000.00	227,000.00	2,043,000.00		300,000.00	4,429,000.00

Stock account of undisclosed reserves

	Provision for exchange and other losses	Revaluation of assets	Exchange differences account	Administration account
1939	16,485.00	35,200.00	11,741.00	2,250.00
1940	19,158.00	35,200.00	11,659.00	2,400.00
1941	22,258.00	35,200.00	11,586.00	2,400.00
1942	25,378.00	35,200.00	11,629.00	2,900.00
1943	28,263.00	35,200.00	11,694.00	2,900.00
1944	30,659.00	35,200.00	11,748.00	3,650.00

Source: BIS Historical Archives, file 7.5, box 1/2, "Disposal of the surplus on the Profit and Loss Account 1949–50", March 28, 1950; BIS *Tenth–Fifteenth Annual Reports*.

of 77,000 Gold Swiss francs was returned to this account in fiscal 1939 – this appears to be a repayment from the previous fiscal year – and from fiscal 1941 through fiscal 1943 funds were transferred to this account in large amounts. Particularly, in fiscal 1943 a transfer took place in the amount of more than one million Gold Swiss francs, implying that there was a decrease in revenues that could not have been covered using unofficial income for the previous fiscal year alone (see Table 3.2).

What is problematic here is the accumulation of hidden reserves. During the war, while transferring funds from specific reserves and somehow padding the unofficial total amount available for allocation, in the hidden reserves account the BIS booked provision for exchange and other losses as in an ordinary year. As soon will be seen, in the fiscal years 1942 and 1943 in distribution of profits the dividends of 6 percent per year on paid-in capital would decrease in amount, but in these years too for the most part increases in provision for losses were accumulated steadily and funds were accumulated under the title of the administration account as well. Put another way, if these reserves and accumulated funds had been allocated to dividends it would for the most part have been possible to pay regular dividends in the ending period of the war as well. This situation tells the story of how the management of hidden reserves during this period deviated from the dividend policy obligated under Article 53 of the BIS statutes.

On the official financial statements, a note was added beginning in fiscal 1943, which corresponds to the second year after dividends began to decrease in amount. This proviso stated,

> Dividends declared prior to the date of the balance sheet, compared to the 6 percent cumulative dividends set forth under item (b) of Article 53 of the BIS statutes, are in short by Gold Swiss francs ___ per share or in total Gold Swiss francs ___.

In this way, the BIS annual reports announced in numerical terms in the official books that the BIS had been unable to pay dividends in accordance with the statutes. This point developed into a major problem after the war.[81]

On the other hand, appropriation of profits was conducted in accordance with officially announced profits (see Figure 3.4). In the officially announced total amount available for allocation in the period, all the BIS managed was to secure legal reserves, and after fiscal 1940 it had quickly ceased accumulation of both reserves for dividends and general reserves. As seen above, the dividends of 6 percent per year on paid-in capital also decreased in amount. Reserves for dividends were short in the 1943 fiscal year.

In fiscal 1944 distribution of profits, appropriation was put on hold because the BIS could not hold a general meeting due to the war. In this fiscal year as well, while the hidden ledgers showed a total amount available for allocation of roughly seven million Gold Swiss francs, two million francs of this figure was subtracted to hidden reserves and official net income was just 4.42 million francs (see Table 3.2). In light of the "exceptional circumstances" of wartime, the board

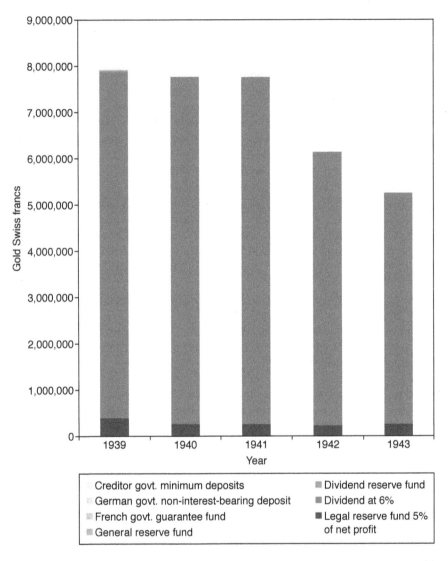

Figure 3.4 BIS profit and loss appropriation account (fiscal years 1939–1943), in Gold Swiss francs (source: *BIS Tenth–Fifteenth Annual Reports*).

Note
For the fiscal year 1944, appropriation of profit was suspended due to cancellation of the annual meeting.

of directors decided to transfer this profit to a special account instead of considering it to be net profit.[82] While the BIS general meeting, which should have deliberated on this special account, as mentioned above failed to meet due to the war, this account came to represent the nucleus of BIS management over a period of time from wartime into the postwar years. The outcome of this matter will be seen in the following chapter.

5 Conclusion

Despite declaring its neutrality, the wartime BIS suffered a freeze of its assets and had its hands tainted by looted gold. The conclusions of this book are in complete agreement with the harsh criticisms of the wartime BIS found in Toniolo's official history: "Mistakes were made even before the war began, and numerous misunderstandings were created," and "Overlooking warnings about looted gold was also a serious error."[83]

However, it might be appropriate to look at the BIS's business and plans during wartime from the point of view of the eve of Bretton Woods. As a forum for central-bank cooperation, the BIS had functioned even during wartime as a venue for exchange of information between representatives of allied and axis nations. In the area of the banking business as well, during wartime transactions in gold in bars – while including looted gold – demonstrated unexpected vitality. The set consisting of "the perspectives of central bank" and "gold transactions" is poles apart from the set consisting of "the Keynesian perspective" and "the IMF system" in Bretton Woods. From this unique position, the wartime BIS served as a cradle for postwar plans.

In BIS theoretical activities, these plans were embodied in Jacobsson's theory. Jacobsson, whose supreme thesis was that of balance in the cost and price structure, placed gold at the foundation of his postwar plans. Jacobsson's theory was reflected in the opinions of the BIS annual reports and was the subject of dispute with American Keynesians. While Jacobsson's arguments showed some variation with the times, his fundamental opinion emphasizing markets and the gold standard remained unchanged and demonstrated a firm continuity through to the postwar years. On the eve of Bretton Woods, it was the wartime BIS that shaped an alternative that attempted a fundamental criticism of Bretton Woods.

John Maynard Keynes died in 1946 at the age of 62, soon after he contributed to the design of the postwar world economy at the Bretton Woods Conference. In Jacobsson's journal entry for that day he pasted a number of newspaper clippings reporting Keynes's death and wrote the following in a shaky hand:

> Keynes is dead! A brilliant man. He combined literary and scientific gifts – he was a mathematician and an artist. Was he a very great economist? I wonder. He has enriched economic thinking – he was full of ideas – he could develop ideas – he could feel in what direction the current of ideas went. But he had not the gift of making a system – his General Theory is no general theory! ...

> Keynes has not seen as clearly as Wicksell what is the effect of gold movements arising from newly produced gold – but he has been on the threshold of the right solution, he just missed it.[84]

As seen in this chapter, Jacobsson had long respected Keynes, and the two had even dined together with their wives.[85] However, Keynes died first, with their theoretical positions still greatly differing. Keynesianism soon entered its golden age in the postwar years, while Jacobsson turned his back to that age and continued extolling the importance of gold and free markets. The meeting and separation of Keynes and Jacobsson – two intelligences deeply related to the BIS – seems to symbolize the fate of the postwar capitalist world.

4   The road to a gold–dollar standard

The BIS in the postwar reconstruction period

The scene returns to Paris, in March 1957. Every morning, a black Citroën carried a bespectacled foreign gentleman from a luxurious hotel on the Rue de Rivoli to the Ministry of Finance or the Banque de France. This gentleman, who had been staying in the Paris hotel for nearly one month, was overwhelming the officials in the French finance ministry with his bold gestures, despite working late into the night day after day. In France at this time, with restoration of convertibility of the franc imminent, the gentleman made the rounds arguing for discontinuation of provision of medium-term credit by the Banque de France and controlling inflation, having great influence over the political and official worlds of Paris as an advisor. This gentleman, already familiar to us, was the third IMF managing director, Jacobsson. Now seeing as problematic the fact that the liquidity policies of medium-term credit that he himself had participated in advocating before the war had been applied without restriction to the French housing sector, Jacobsson remained in Paris burning with the conviction that this system needed to be discontinued in order to have France reintegrated to free markets.[1] Just what kind of a system was this Bretton Woods system, under which the IMF managing director himself marched in to provide guidance on a course of action of liberalization? Through what route was a former head of the Monetary and Economic Department at the BIS appointed to the top position at the IMF? And what was the BIS's position in this system? These are the topics addressed in this chapter.

Below, this chapter will proceed with a study of these topics in the following order: Section 1 will discuss the issue of liquidation of the BIS, Section 2 will look at the process of establishment of the European Payments Union (EPU) and Section 3 will look at the rise of the key-currency approach and the BIS. This chapter argues that the ideas of Jacobsson and others on the BIS side, who opposed Keynesianism, and the facts related to BIS management concerning the issue of looted gold and the freeze of assets had an important impact on the process of establishment and transformation of the Bretton Woods system.

1 Establishment of the IMF and the issue of BIS liquidation: conflict with the new dealers

When the decision was made in the Bretton Woods Agreement to liquidate the BIS, the BIS began lively maneuvering toward rehabilitation, led by the governors of the central banks of participating states. This process exposed the conflict between the BIS and the New Dealers on postwar plans.

The Bretton Woods decision: the shock of BIS liquidation

Voices arguing against leaving the BIS unscathed for its wartime state, in which, due in part to its geographical location surrounded by axis powers and their occupied territories, representatives of Nazi Germany were active on a daily basis, appeared at an early stage in the US Congress and elsewhere. Outside the venue of the Bretton Woods Conference, Harry White denounced the BIS, stating, "There is an American president [of the BIS] doing business with the Germans, while our boys are fighting Germans."[2] This issue continued to smolder after the war, forcing considerable difficulty in the BIS's return to the world of international finance.[3]

Incidentally, at a deep level in these arguments over the liquidation of the BIS an even greater structural conflict was spreading. This was what would be called the "New Deal Antagonism." An American business newspaper of the time, which presented this viewpoint, analyzed it as follows. Behind the argument to protect the BIS was the banking world, centered on the Federal Bank of New York. On the other hand, it was the US Treasury Department, controlled by New Dealers, that supported the argument for the liquidation of the BIS. The bankers supported the BIS because it had served as a base for central-bank cooperation that made it possible to invest in Europe before the war. The Treasury Department, in opposition to the BIS, which was made up of representatives of central banks, was trying to make the new IMF an organization managed by the governments and fiscal authorities of member nations. The decision in the Savannah Conference in the spring of 1946, two years after the Bretton Woods Agreement, to relocate the headquarters of the IMF from New York to the federal government's capital of Washington, DC, was an extension of this conflict.[4] In the BIS at that time, a typed special copy of this story was provided to core management, including General Manager Auboin, for their perusal.[5] The diagrams "Treasury vs. the Banks" and "New Deal vs. Central Banks" can be seen as having had a certain impact on the awareness of parties involved in the BIS, faced as they were with the postwar crises. The governor of the Nederlandsche Bank, Marius Holtrop, who worked busily to avoid the liquidation of the BIS, testified that the decision to liquidate the BIS was based on an "anti-central-bank attitude" which had existed since before the war and that this was "partly due to the influence of Lord Keynes."[6] It is likely that this recognition had an effect on the machinations to rehabilitate the BIS.

There was one other motive behind the argument over the liquidation of the BIS. This involved the relations between the newly established IMF and the BIS, which had been in existence since before World War II. A US congressional report reviewing the decision to liquidate the BIS in later years noted that the motive behind this decision was concern that the BIS might compete with the operations of the IMF.[7] Oddly, this analysis by the US Congress is in agreement with the argument about Bretton Woods circulating in Japan during the war. The decision to liquidate the BIS was communicated to Japan through the Yokohama Specie Bank. A Yokohama Specie Bank memo analyzing this information stated the following: The decision to dissolve the BIS was

> an understanding which only represents that the BIS and other institutions should be dissolved because it could be an obstacle to the proposed new international bank established by the anti-Axis powers, or rather, because it had been used by the Axis powers.

It also described, "The BIS itself is not so prevailing as to maneuver for its liquidation, which the United States and Britain worked on feverishly." The memo was sardonic concerning the prospects for the decision:

> In consideration of matters such as the current state of the BIS and the fact that the decision on dissolution itself has the nature of a prize for the currency conference, perhaps the best that could be hoped for is that some of the board members from anti-Axis powers would withdraw out of spite.[8]

While the author of the memo is unknown, the recognition described therein for the most part had hit the mark.

The Bretton Woods resolution adopted in July 1944 called for "The liquidation of the Bank for International Settlement at the earliest possible moment." However, after the adoption of this resolution movement began toward a compromise. At first, the draft resolution submitted by the Norwegian representatives included together with the liquidation of the BIS a proposal that the governments of the allied nations at war with Germany establish a research committee to study the management and transactions of the BIS during the current war. However, in the subcommittee that considered this draft the latter text concerning the research committee was removed with the acceptance of a draft revision by the Netherlands.[9] In this way, the hurdle to rehabilitation of the BIS already had been lowered starting at the time of the Bretton Woods resolution.

After the end of World War II, parties connected to the BIS and the governors of the central banks began machinations to roll back the proposal and put a stop to liquidation. While ordinarily a BIS regular general meeting would have been held in May 1946, it was postponed due to the disorder following the war, and instead a round-robin meeting was held in writing. However, despite the fact that no general meeting was held, Niemeyer (Bank of England), Ruth (Swedish National Bank), Frère (National Bank of Belgium and BIS vice-president), and Weber (Swiss National Bank) converged on Basel on their own and began an unofficial exchange of opinions. It appears that even General Manager Auboin had not expected this development, and he quickly telephoned the Banque de France in his home country and urged that France respond so that it did not get left behind. In addition, in this unofficial conference unofficial decisions were made to ask President McKittrick to retire and to promote Frère; how to respond to the pressing issue of looted gold was discussed as well. Also in this meeting, the decision was made with great care to lay the groundwork by "reaching an unofficial agreement with the Banque de France prior to communicating this matter officially to the central banks of Britain, the United States and France."[10] The fact that soon after the end of the war, and through coordination between the central-bank governors, such a meeting was held suddenly and the groundwork begun perhaps can be seen as an exhaustive demonstration of the function that the BIS had built up as a "club" for central-bank cooperation.

It was the governors of the central banks who played the central role in these rehabilitation machinations. According to the recollections of such governor, Banque de France Governor Emmanuel Monick, it was at the 1946 Savannah Conference that these machinations reached a turning point. Monick, who attended that conference, met with Fred Vinson, then the US secretary of the Treasury, and Harry White, one of the central figures in the IMF, and was given the impression that the BIS would be allowed to remain in existence. As mentioned above, the Treasury Department was seen as a stronghold of the New Dealers, and Monick's moves were targeted at senior Treasury officials. According to Monick, "A danger was avoided by September 1946." He says that the decision to keep the BIS in existence was the fruit of the fact that the BIS had quickly begun operations in 1945, prior to the implementation of the Bretton Woods Agreement, and had established as a fait accompli a firm position as an international bank.[11] In fact, as of 1946 the BIS was continuing operations with a team consisting of top management and the three department heads – General Manager Auboin; Secretary General Pilotti (Italy); the head of the Banking Department, van Zeeland (Belgium); and Jacobsson, the economic adviser/head of Monetary and Economic Department,– with its experienced staff who had been working since before the war, including the manager of the foreign-exchange section, Kan Yoshimura.[12]

However, when viewed in light of the historical facts of the time, these recollections of Monick – although proper in that in the end the BIS did avoid liquidation – were a little too optimistic. In reality, the United States did not give up arguing for the liquidation of the BIS until around 1948. Behind this fact were the issues of looted gold and the asset freeze, as seen in the preceding chapter.

Development of the looted-gold issue

The course by which the matter of looted gold became open in the postwar period can be outlined as follows. In August 1945, Auboin travelled on business to Paris to gather information on subjects such as negotiations toward ratification of the Bretton Woods Agreement. In the process of doing so, Auboin obtained "grave information about the matter of Belgian gold." This was the information that Reichsbank Vice-President Puhl – the person to whom it is said that Jacobs-son communicated an outline of the Bretton Woods Conference during the war – had been taken into custody by US occupation authorities in Germany and was being investigated on suspicion of embellishment of Reichsbank account books. In a letter to BIS President McKittrick, Auboin described his expectation that this investigation would involve Puhl and "all related parties" and stated that this requires "the utmost care on our part."[13] Head of the Banking Department van Zeeland prepared an internal memo in which he stated, "It would be a mistake at this point in time to try to prove that we made no mistakes at all" and advising an investigation into the facts of the matter, including "the atmosphere at the time," of the gold transactions conducted through "wartime blackmail" (*bribes et morceaux*).[14]

Auboin then collected information based at the Banque de France and the French finance ministry, and a full view of the issue of looted gold gradually became clear to the BIS. An outline of what was clear about the looted-gold issue at that point in time was as follows: During the war Nazi Germany unlaw-fully transferred 198 tons of gold from the National Bank of Belgium in occu-pied Belgium, "of which 145 tons was exported to Germany, and 112 tons [of that 145 tons] to Switzerland. Exports continued from January 1, 1943 until the end of February 1944." The BIS reported having "accepted 12,000 kg of gold from the Swiss National Bank" during this period, and just how much looted gold was contained in this amount became the focal point of the issue.[15]

Results of a survey conducted through related central banks showed that Reichsbank gold deposits included the following three types of improperly seized gold: (1) approximately 1,607 kg of gold deposited January 5, 1943, cast into 129 gold bars by the Prussian mint; (2) approximately 1,261 kg of gold in 127 gold bars, deposited on the same day in 1943 and including Dutch gold coins recast by the Prussian mint; and, (3) gold deposited prior to 1943, consist-ing of approximately 827 kg in 71 gold bars cast in the United States and approx-imately 12 kg in one gold bar cast in France.[16] In the end, the US State Department estimated the total amount of looted gold that the BIS needed to return to Belgium, the Netherlands, Italy and other countries at 3,738.5 kg.[17]

At the same time, in light of the investigation the US departments of Treasury and State instructed the special US envoy in Berlin to clarify the matter in its entirety. The order, sent in December 1945 by official telegram signed by James Byrnes, identified the issue as follows, bringing the BIS into the picture: "During the war, a massive amount of gold was deposited from the Reichsbank in the Swiss National Bank"; "Of the gold in the possession of the National Bank of Belgium, an amount as high as $123 million was melted down and sent to the Swiss National Bank."; and "Some of this was sent to the BIS." The detailed tel-egram instructed that specialists be sent to the Swiss National Bank and the BIS to conduct a thorough investigation, and even envisioned conceivable questions and answers, instructing that "if the Swiss government were to object that BIS assets were protected under Article 10 [of the BIS statutes], answer that the Statutes do not apply to looted property."[18]

This was a time at which the Bretton Woods Agreement established the IMF and the International Bank for Reconstruction and Development (IBRD, commonly known as the World Bank) and the BIS found itself facing the possibility of a decision for liquidation as it was seen no longer to fit the international currency system. As seen in the preceding chapter, Jacobsson took on Keynes and the Keynesians in the press, criticizing the Bretton Woods Agreement, and former BIS President Fraser too supported the BIS from his position as a private citizen. It was right at this point that the wartime scandal was revealed. No matter how much one advocated on a theoretical basis for the superiority of the gold standard and the balance in the cost and price structure, it would be a very serious matter if the BIS's performance in the areas of gold settlement and gold holdings were originally based on looted gold. The fact that shortly after the Byrnes official telegram BIS President McKittrick revealed confidentially his intention to resign for "family matters" testifies to the degree to which the organization was shaken at this time.[19]

In the end, an agreement was concluded in Washington on May 13, 1948, and at that time 3,740 kg in currency gold identified as gold looted by the Nazis was deposited by the BIS with the Bank of England, for the purpose of returning it to its owners. Ultimately, the amount returned at this point in time would be 3,366 kg, as the amount refunded to the BIS in advance by "a central bank" was deducted from the total.[20]

However, this handling of the issue of looted gold developed in an unexpected direction in connection with the BIS. Here it was the issue of the freeze of assets that became involved in the situation.

Removal of the asset freeze

When the allies, particularly the United States, demanded through strict handling of the looted-gold issue that the BIS return the gold to victim nations, the BIS responded that "since most of the gold has been sent to the United States, in order to return it the freeze of enemy assets targeting the BIS would need to be released."[21] Release of the asset freeze would lead to acceptance of subsequent BIS activities, which would have no small impact on plans for the postwar international currency system.

At the time of the Bretton Woods Conference, when the continued existence of the BIS itself was in danger, the release of the freeze of assets had not been considered problematic. However, in 1947 when it was confirmed that the US government wanted the BIS to remain in existence, BIS officials began machinations toward the release of the asset freeze. Already, in April 1947 BIS President Frère and General Manager Auboin had visited Treasury Secretary John Snyder.[22] Furthermore, in October 1947 US government representative Overby visited Switzerland. While the purpose of his visit was to make arrangements for the release of Swiss bank assets frozen in the United States during the war, Auboin took this opportunity to argue within the BIS that "if we were considered an ordinary Swiss bank, then the freeze on our assets would be released as well."[23] In response to this view, BIS officials instructed legal staff to begin studying conditions for release of the asset freeze.[24]

Through these studies, it became clear that the situation was involved in a complicated manner with wartime gold issues. In particular, in exchanges between the Office Suisse de compensation and the BIS Legal Advisor Henri Guisan, the focal point became the share of stock issued by the BIS that was owned by the enemy states – Germany and Japan. At the time the war ended, the Japanese and German shares were 22.8 percent, lower than the 25 percent level of capital participation by enemy states specified by the Swiss authorities. However, Japan and Germany accounted for 33.8 percent of minimum accepted deposits, and if these were included in capital then these two nations' shares of capital thus broadly defined would be 29.2 percent. Also, BIS German assets related to the Young Plan had reached 291.16 million Gold Swiss francs. This had risen to 64.5 percent of total assets in fiscal 1945.[25] While the BIS had shown these figures to the Office Suisse de compensation and sought its opinion, the Swiss authorities put off making a formal reply, in light of the "extremely unique nature of the BIS."[26]

It was February 1948 when the moves of the United States on this point became clear. Treasury Secretary John Snyder, chairman of the National Advisory Council on International Monetary and Financial Problems, sent a letter to Arthur Vandenberg, chairman of the US Senate Foreign Relations Committee, arguing for release of the freeze of BIS assets. It should be noted that this letter argued for release of the freeze in connection with the European Recovery Program, which was being debated at the time. In this letter, Snyder presented the argument that European private-sector capital also should be appropriated toward recovery and that for this reason there was a need to release frozen assets in the United States, including Swiss assets.[27]

Next, in May 1948, a conference was held between the governments of the United States, Britain and France and BIS representatives on the issue of wartime looted gold at the BIS. In response to the end of this conference, which finalized the amount of gold seized by the Nazis that the BIS had accepted, new BIS President Frère sent a letter to US Treasury Secretary Snyder expressing full agreement with the reporting obligation concerning matters such as the locations of related assets imposed on the BIS by the conference and pressing the following points: (1) most of these assets were frozen in the United States; (2) assets corresponding to seized gold should be excluded from frozen assets and transferred to a special account from which they could not be withdrawn without the permission of the US Treasury Secretary; and (3) at the same time, the BIS ask that the US Department of the Treasury release from the freeze the remaining assets in the United States.[28] The strategy was an attempt to barter the BIS asset freeze against the issue of looted gold. In the end, through this conference the freeze on BIS assets in the United States was released.[29]

As above, the resolution of the issue of looted gold and the release of the freeze on BIS assets in the United States were two sides of the same coin.[30]

While ultimately released, the asset freeze had a significant impact on BIS officials. In 1949, the BIS general secretariat was studying how to preserve its assets in the event of another asset freeze. According to a memo on these studies that would appear to have been initialed by Legal Advisor Guisan, the conclusion reached was that the best plan for preserving assets would be for the BIS to open a branch in the United States.[31] While these discussions later disappeared, they demonstrate the fear that resulted from the asset freeze.

The Marshall Plan and intra-European settlement: toward rehabilitation of the BIS

The Marshall Plan was announced on June 5, 1947, making it clear that provision of funds under the plan would begin the following year. The outcome of the BIS liquidation issue was decided over the truly short period of time between the announcement of the Marshall Plan and the shift to its implementation.[32] The course of these events was as outlined below.

In June 1947, US Secretary of State George Marshall announced in a speech at Harvard University the massive aid plan that later would be known as the Marshall Plan. At that point in time, it appeared that sooner or later the convertibility of the pound sterling would be restored, and it was expected that after enactment of the Marshall Plan the pound sterling, with its convertibility restored, would function as the settlement currency within the region. However, the circumstances changed as, although the pound sterling was restored to convertibility in July of that year, the restoration failed after just five weeks. The impossibility of the multilateral approach was decisive, and there was no choice but to reconsider how to handle settlement within the European region after enactment of the plan.[33] Under these circumstances, pessimistic and resentful voices arose in Britain, leading to comments such as "The return to the gold standard in 1925 was an act of purely British pride; the return to convertibility on July 15th last was an enforced condition of the American loan."[34] Thus, during the period from the development of the Marshall Plan until its implementation, the failure of the restoration of convertibility of the pound – and by extension the impossibility of the immediate stabilization that was an ideal of Bretton Woods – was exposed.

It was in this phase that the BIS asserted itself. First, in November 1947 an Agreement for Multilateral Monetary Compensation was concluded. Signed only by France, Italy and the three Benelux countries, the basic principles of this agreement were no more than a collection of arrangements for reciprocal settlement. However, under this system the signatory states reported their balances of trade with each other state to the BIS monthly, and this was the starting point for building the subsequent relations between the EPU and the BIS.

In response to this course of events, the issue arose of how to distribute funds provided to Europe in connection with the Marshall Plan. The debate began with a French proposal that the BIS handle the settlement function within the region on behalf of the IMF. This was right before the start of the debate toward ratification of the Marshall Plan in the US Congress – a debate that anticipated turmoil. Sensing France's moves, the US Treasury Secretary, in a December

1947 internal memo, advised that the Treasury Department decide on its position on the liquidation of the BIS prior to the start of congressional debate. This memo, given to the assistant secretary of the Treasury, Frank Southard, argued that if Treasury were to support liquidation of the BIS then enforcement of the Bretton Woods Agreement should be moved ahead urgently, while if the argument for liquidation were to be abandoned then there was a need to prepare for disputes that would arise in connection with the Marshall Plan.[35] It is worth noting there that at the end of 1947 abandoning the argument for liquidation was already considered an option.

Next, in October 1948 the Intra-European Payments and Compensations Scheme was concluded. All member states of the Organization for European Economic Cooperation (OEEC), which had been established in response to the Marshall Plan, were parties to this scheme. Again it was the BIS that undertook the operations related to this scheme.[36]

The 1948 Intra-European Payments and Compensations Scheme created a system of drawing rights. These drawing rights were a system under which part of the Marshall Plan aid corresponding to the estimated surplus in receipts on the part of a country in the European region with a trade surplus was delivered to the surplus country and that recipient country established drawing rights denominated in its own currency vis-à-vis a counterparty country in the region running a deficit. However, drawing rights under this system strongly had the character of gifts to deficit countries, and they lacked motivation for structural deficit reduction.[37] BIS General Manager Auboin noted that the BIS's role under this Intra-European Payments and Compensations Scheme was "purely technical" and described the BIS as having become an agent for the governments of OEEC member states.[38]

Around the time the agreement was concluded on this scheme, in January 1948 Andrew Kamarck of the US Treasury Department exchanged opinions with IMF officials on how intra-European settlement should be conducted. During this meeting, Kamarck expressed the views that "the functions of the BIS in the Clearing Organisation were slightly more than mere bookkeeping," and that "if the BIS has capable personnel and they become skilled, they may become the center to which countries will turn for advice in handling clearing and payments agreements."[39]

In this way, in the process of rehabilitation of the BIS a decisive motive was the plan to have the BIS handle the intra-European settlement function.

Three months after this meeting with Kamarck, in April 1948 the continued existence of the BIS was finalized formally through a declaration announced by the US representative in an IMF and IBRD board meeting.[40] After this statement, the BIS held an important position in intra-European settlement.

Relations between the United States and the BIS developed in complex ways from the wartime through the postwar periods: a sense of distance from the United States at the time the BIS was founded, the dispute over the wartime asset freeze, the BIS opposition to the Bretton Woods Agreement and the decision in the Bretton Woods Conference to liquidate the BIS, criticism of the BIS over the issue of looted gold, return of the looted gold and release from the asset freeze, and the machinations and arrangements toward abandonment of the liquidation plans and rehabilitation. While the circumstances were complicated, from the point of view of this chapter these developments can be read in accordance with a single line of thought: that the BIS's rehabilitation correlated with change in the Bretton Woods system. The Bretton Woods concept of immediate stabilization, which had broken down over several years after the war, had been replaced by the key-currency approach and intra-European settlement. Together with this change in the nature of the Bretton Woods system, it was the BIS that took the responsibility for the restoration of market economies in Europe.

But what kinds of arguments were deployed in the above avoidance of liquidation of the BIS? A look at the testimonies of contemporaries involved in these developments shows no logical argument over the years 1945 and 1946 that the continued existence of the BIS could contribute proactively to the IMF system. Instead, what was emphasized was the assessment of the BIS's past legacy, such as the function it had performed since before the war as a venue for cooperation between central banks or the accumulated analysis of currency conditions that had borne fruit in the BIS's annual reports.[41] While in the end it approved the continued existence of the BIS, the US Treasury Department maintained through the spring of 1947 the course of multilateral currency adjustments centered on the IMF. As such, it had not seen the BIS as being responsible for a new international currency scheme.[42]

However, within the newly enacted Bretton Woods system the BIS would gradually build its own position. First, in the fall of 1946 an exchange of opinions between the BIS and the IBRD began, with a written agreement exchanged in April 1947 between the two parties. According to this agreement, the BIS confirmed that it would provide to the IBRD information collected by the Monetary and Economic Department.[43] Furthermore, the following month in May 1947 it was announced in a BIS board meeting that the BIS had contacted the IMF.[44] In October 1947, van Zeeland, the head of the Banking Department, met with the leadership of the US Export–import Bank, discussing matters such as the impact on the BIS of the asset freeze.[45]

Jacobsson played an important role in the above rapprochement between the BIS and the IBRD. Jacobsson, who remained at the BIS even after the Bretton Woods Conference, was named in October 1946 as an economic advisor for the newly established IBRD. In December of the same year, he was promoted in the BIS from department head to board member.[46] With important appointments in both the IBRD, which played a key role in the Bretton Woods system, and his old haunts of the BIS, he contributed to moving the two institutions closer to each other. In fact, the BIS reported to the IBRD on its moves seeking release of the asset freeze. In April 1948, General Manager Auboin sent a letter to Eugene Black, a US representative on the IBRD board, divulging the efforts targeting the Treasury Department and informing him that he would visit the IBRD during a trip to the United States at the end of that month.[47]

Having avoided the worst-case scenario of liquidation, the BIS emerged with a new role in the international currency system beginning in 1947. As the IMF ideal of multilateral currency adjustment reached a dead end while an intra-European settlement network came together, the BIS's role became more practical and grew in importance.

2 Abandonment of the multilateral approach, and intra-European settlement: the BIS and the process of establishment of the EPU

As seen in the preceding section, the multilateral currency adjustment approach that was the ideal of the Bretton Woods Agreement had reached a deadlock in the first half of 1947. The principles of "immediate stabilization" and "multilateralism and nondiscrimination" – the multilateral approach – that had dominated US plans for the international currency system were abandoned, and in this period the idea of restoring the convertibility of individual currencies while permitting exceptional measures on an interim basis gained force. This new idea arose among US government leaders beginning around the start of 1947 and led to the announcement of the Truman Doctrine in March of that year and the speech in June at Harvard University by Secretary of State Marshall that announced the Marshall Plan.[48] Subsequently, the actual state of the international currency system moved away from the ideas in the Bretton Woods Agreement and, through enactment of the Marshall Plan, shifted toward development of intra-European settlement. In this section, we will examine developments at the BIS within this intricate process.

The BIS in the EPU: an agent or a trustee?

Spared liquidation, the BIS began to discover its role in intra-European settlement around the time the Marshall Plan was enacted. This course peaked along with the establishment of the EPU. Now let's take a look at the course of these developments.

What courses of action did the BIS seek out prior to the establishment of the EPU? General Manager Auboin left behind a very interesting memo on this point, dated December 9, 1949. First, Auboin argued that the various competing plans proposed by each country in advance of the establishment of the EPU were likely to result in the establishment of a "fund" that differed from the various preceding intra-European settlement systems. This fund was likely to be managed "in accordance with the methods of the banking business." If so, the BIS should undertake such operations, since it had "shown that it was possible to maintain full liquidity making it possible to meet the demands of each country's central bank through the provision of truly short-term credit with a relatively small amount of revolving funds." In accordance with this policy, the role of the BIS would be that of a "trustee," and not an "agent."[49] As seen in Chapter 1 of this book, both "agent" and "trustee" were forms of operation established in the BIS statutes. If things went as Auboin anticipated and the BIS were upgraded from its existing role as an agent handling settlement to that of a trustee managing a fund, then it was likely that it would perform an important role in intra-European settlement.

But what kind of role did the BIS play in the EPU, established in 1950? Let's review the negotiations on establishment of the EPU. A study by Kaplan and Schleiminger has shown that the process of these negotiations was characterized by various competing proposals.[50] While there were diverse points of difference between these proposals, among these debate was focused chiefly on how gold–dollar settlement between EPU member states should be handled and on how to rectify trade imbalances between member states. Overall, the US plan – led by the United States Economic Cooperation Administration (ECA) – focused on trade liberalization and a settlement union combined together as a set, which tolerated the provision of credit to countries running deficits, while the British plan, while taking into consideration the use of sterling by continental states, was opposed to the establishment of a new system. In contrast, the basic framework argued for by the European states was the proposal from the expert committee led by Hubert Ansiaux, chairman of the OEEC Intra-European Payments Committee. This proposal, adopting the name "European Payments Union," also included asking the BIS to serve as the secretariat. While proclaiming the goal of rectifying trade imbalances between EPU member states, the Ansiaux proposal also called for even stricter conditions on provision of medium- to long-term credit using dollar funds than did the British and American proposals. On the other hand, it left room for credit provision between member states using gold. After passing the OEEC board and then earning the approval of an OEEC cabinet-level meeting in February 1950, the Ansiaux committee's proposal was presented as the OEEC proposal. After its announcement, the Ansiaux proposal, which originally had been a compromise, was criticized severely by the United States, Britain, the IMF and others.[51]

Here, it was Jacobsson of the BIS who intervened. While Jacobsson was critical of the Ansiaux proposal, the points of his criticism differed somewhat from those of Britain, the United States and others. Jacobsson argued that the medium- and long-term credit-provision function should be removed from this Ansiaux proposal. Jacobsson's argument was that the EPU should be refined into a provisional settlement system, and the central-bank governors in each country were influenced strongly by this argument. General Manager Auboin too – despite having in the past sought to make the BIS a trustee handling the fund for intra-European settlement – was acting in accordance with this Jacobsson roadmap.[52] In the end, Ansiaux revised his initial proposal, removing the credit-provision function from plans for the EPU, and means of adjusting for imbalances between member states were more restricted than initially planned in the EPU that actually was established. The role of the BIS too was positioned as that of an agent handling EPU operations.[53]

But in contrast to the policy advocated until then by Auboin that aimed to make the BIS function as a trustee, why did Jacobsson argue for limiting its role to that of an agent? Let's trace Jacobsson's footsteps around the time the EPU was established.

Beginning immediately after the announcement of the Marshall Plan, Jacobsson had argued vigorously on the subject of a shortage of dollars. A dollar shortage would need to be resolved through tight fiscal policy implemented by Europe on its own. European nations would need to restore balance between savings and investment and between income and expenditures through means such as raising interest rates. Marshall Plan aid should not be used to finance domestic investment.[54] Jacobsson was also critical of the bilateral nature of the Intra-European Payments and Compensations Scheme mentioned above, pointing out that the drawing rights would in effect be a structure that would preserve trade deficits.[55] From the point of view of Jacobsson's argument, the Ansiaux proposal envisioning the provision of medium- and long-term credit appeared to be one that would either be ineffective at reducing deficits in each country or encourage lax fiscal policy. Just before the unofficial meeting of central-bank governors in which Jacobsson intervened in March 1950, at the start of that year Jacobsson wrote the following in a manuscript: "The continental monetary system [is] precarious and vulnerable without sterling," and "one is brought back to the problem of Great Britain and the position of sterling."[56] This longing for the swift rehabilitation of a market mechanism centered on sterling is a very important point of view.

But to what kinds of policies did Jacobsson's argument pressing for restoration of convertibility of European currencies lead in connection with the United States? Let's examine this point by focusing on a venue in which Jacobsson's opinion was expressed clearly – a secret meeting held in July 1949, just before the start of the EPU, between top BIS leaders and US Treasury Department representatives.

The secret July 14, 1949 meeting: rapprochement between the United States and the BIS

This meeting was held on July 14, 1949 in a room in a Geneva hotel.[57] Attendees at the meeting, which began at 4.30 p.m. on that day, were Auboin, the BIS general manager; Jacobsson the head of the Monetary and Economic Department; Snyder, the secretary of the Treasury, William McChesney Martin Jr., the head of the Export–import Bank in Washington, and Walter Ostrow, Treasury representative in Bern. Negotiations between the BIS and the United States took place through the mediation of the central-bank governors of nations participating in the BIS, through the process of the machinations toward rehabilitation of the BIS conducted up to that point. The fact that this meeting, while unofficial, was the first direct meeting between BIS leaders and US representatives, including the Treasury secretary, was highly significant, particularly to the BIS. Sensing the infeasibility of the principles of immediate stabilization and of multilateralism and nondiscrimination, the United States, which had argued for the liquidation of the BIS since the Bretton Woods Conference, approached the BIS. In response, the BIS, which had steadily realized rehabilitation in the face of the establishment of the EPU, brought a new demand to the table. Jacobsson's views of currency and the markets identified in this meeting included an important point that would predict the shape of the subsequent IMF system. Below will trace the course of the meeting on that day, relying on the minutes of the meeting.

First of all, Auboin led off the meeting with the following explanation of postwar BIS business operations: While prewar European central banks had held adequate gold reserves, in the postwar period a "general scarcity of gold and dollars" had appeared, so that "even central banks in the larger countries were glad to turn to the BIS for short-term credits." Auboin emphasized that an important role demanded of the BIS was that of such provision of short-term credit to central banks, and that the BIS did not compete with the IBRD, a provider of long-term credit.

Next, after discussing the roles of the BIS in the Intra-European Payments and Compensations Scheme mentioned above, Auboin touched on the relations between the BIS and the IMF, stating that "the BIS was anxious to keep in contact" with the IMF and the IBRD. In response to Auboin's wishes, Treasury Secretary Snyder revealed that negotiations were underway with IMF Managing Director Camille Gutt on cooperation with the BIS. While, as seen in the preceding section, contact between the BIS and the IMF had already begun as part of the process of rehabilitation of the BIS, it turns out that the United States and the BIS had simultaneously prepared parallel policies of strengthening and restructuring relations between the two institutions in connection with the retreat of the multilateral approach.

Later, after some discussions Treasury Secretary Snyder left the meeting and just Auboin, Jacobsson, and McChesney Martin of the Export–import Bank in Washington moved to a separate room where they took part in "some thirty to forty minutes" of sharp discussion of currency issues in general.

In these discussions, BIS economic adviser Jacobsson stepped to the forefront of the meeting. Regarding the currency situation in Europe, Jacobsson brought up the fact that at present there were "two different approaches": Italy, France and Belgium, which had set up "free markets" and were lessening the difference between actual exchange rates in these markets and official rates through ratification of market rates, and other countries whose official rates were fixed.

The free markets he spoke of here had been established through the following process, using France as an example. Immediately prior to implementation of the Marshall Plan, in January 1948, the franc was devalued. While this was a standard par-value adjustment devaluing the franc by 44.444 percent to the dollar, the additional policy was decided on of creating a free market in Paris, subject to certain conditions. This free market would be established for gold, dollars and Portuguese escudos only, and the market would be managed through the following steps. If they sold one-half of their gold, dollars, or escudos on hand to the currency authorities at the official rate, French exporters could sell the other half on the free market. importers could purchase gold and foreign currencies on the free market, only if they were importers of nonessential products. This was a decision to acknowledge, albeit only partially, free-market rates in addition to official rates, a clear violation of the spirit of Bretton Woods. In fact, while the IMF and Britain strongly opposed this decision, France rammed through this devaluation and establishment of free markets, taking an approach that refused to rule out withdrawal from the IMF.[58] At the time, the United States, in a special report by the National Advisory Council on international monetary and financial problems, criticized France's creation of a free market and made clear its position in support of the IMF.[59]

However, in the secret meeting in 1949 Jacobsson praised France's free market and expressed approval of advancing par-value adjustments in reference to free-market exchange rates. In response, McChesney Martin of the Export–import Bank answered that the United States too understood "greater flexibility" in the field of foreign exchange and stated that American IMF representative Frank Southard Jr. had been given instructions on such a course of action. On this point too, apparently the US change in strategy and Jacobsson's policy had shifted independently but in the same direction.

Next, Jacobsson, together with Auboin, argued for the need for tight fiscal policy as a means of achieving currency stability. While these arguments – that devaluation alone was insufficient, that budget cuts and credit restrictions were needed, and that balance between costs and prices should be strived for through wage restrictions – were ones that later would come to characterize the IMF, they were an extension of views Jacobsson had cherished for years. It was the BIS that made these arguments to the United States.

Later, in this separate room the discussion turned to an assessment of the pound sterling. The BIS representatives and McChesney Martin were in agreement in their recognition that confidence in sterling had narrowly been protected by Marshall Plan aid. McChesney Martin described his concern that if sterling were to continue as it was then a dollar shortage could arise, and he also introduced "quite a dangerous feeling" in the United States – the criticism that Britain was "using Marshall aid to their own advantage and the American disadvantage." This secret meeting was interrupted by a telephone call at the McChesney Martin's room.

The essentials of this meeting can be summarized as follows. Jacobsson's views on currency and markets discussed in the July 14, 1949 meeting were an effort to reflect his assessment of free markets in European currency adjustments. This point of view was based on the trust in the market mechanism even before the currency convertibility was restored completely, which means to criticize the spirit of the Bretton Woods Agreement from the marketist perspective. Here it should be noted that at the time the United States was in the process of shifting to a policy of reviewing the Bretton Woods system and that the BIS also had prepared such a course of action in a similar way. In particular, the BIS developed a criticism of the Bretton Woods system based on actual performance in settlement operations from before the war. Thus, at a turning point in the international currency system not constricted by a Bretton Woods-centric view of history, the BIS's policy choice, which also positioned the US strategy relatively, appeared in this form. In the background were Jacobsson's views on currency and markets.

But how would these views on currency and markets assess the actual conditions of the EPU after its establishment and the IMF, which was facing a crisis? In the next section, a review will be conducted of the regionalism that appeared in the 1950s and Jacobsson's response to it.

3 Crisis at the IMF and the development of the EPU: toward restoration of convertibility

As a preliminary to tracing Jacobsson's footsteps and looking at the BIS's choices from here on, let's turn our gaze to the IMF.

Crisis at the IMF

Viewed from the philosophy of the Bretton Woods Agreement, the IMF should have conducted multilateral currency adjustments. However, since beginning its activities in March 1947 the bulk of the IMF's lending performance had consisted of loans in US dollars, and these dollar loans had been decreasing since the enactment of the Marshall Plan.[60] At the start of the 1950s, when the EPU began functioning, the crisis at the IMF deepened further. Here, let's take a look at a speech made by the IMF's first managing director, Gutt, at the IMF board meeting held on March 19, 1951, the day he left the IMF.[61] In a conversational manner, Gutt said the following: "the current topic is, just take the OEEC and enlarge it. It will advantageously replace IMF," and "Well, many people in the United States are now in love with BIS." On the whole, this speech can be seen to describe a structural outline of the crisis the IMF faced at the start of the 1950s – the IMF having been forced into a supporting role, the BIS having been rehabilitated around the time of the establishment of the EPU, and a recovery in relations between the United States and the BIS.

When viewed in terms of the ratio of the annual amounts drawn to the quota subscriptions, IMF activities were slow. The amount drawn from the IMF fund had risen to $467.7 million in 1947, which was 9 percent of the year-end balance of member nations' quota subscriptions (not including that of the United States). This ratio of annual amounts drawn to the quota subscriptions was not exceeded through 1955. In 1948, when the Marshall Plan began, the amount drawn fell by half to $208 million, and its ratio to the quota subscriptions fell to 3.9 percent as well. Subsequently these remained sluggish into the first half of the 1950s, and despite a slight increase seen in the amount drawn in 1953, in 1955 both the amount drawn and the ratio set new record lows.[62] Slumping in this manner, the IMF had a poor reputation: "There was a time when Bretton Woods was almost a dirty word in the American banking circle."[63] The slump at the IMF meant that

> there must be something profoundly wrong with the constitution or management – or both – of an institution which has in ten years of life failed so

obviously to adjust itself to the world and the conditions in which it has been called upon to function.[64]

But how did Jacobsson assess this slump at the IMF and the development of the EPU? Let's return now to the responses of Jacobsson and the BIS.

Toward the key-currency approach

Jacobsson was sensitive to signs of trouble in the trend in public opinion at the time – toward attacking the IMF while praising the EPU. According to Jacobsson, the EPU was a temporary detour toward the more ambitious goal of multi-lateral settlement, and it needed to be no more than a "means" to an end.[65] However, within opinion in favor of the EPU had appeared an orientation toward a "closed Europe" through enhancement of intra-regional settlement. An example is a piece in *The Economist* issue of July 15, 1950. According to Jacobsson, this article saw the EPU not as a "means" but as an "end." Alarmed at this tone of argument, immediately following the establishment of the EPU Jacobsson began advocating speeding up the restoration of convertibility.[66]

At this time, Jacobsson went to West Germany, which was facing the largest foreign-exchange crisis in the EPU, to execute special EPU loans and ensure the continuation of liberalization. Thus, not only through words but through deeds as well Jacobsson backed up his cherished views on the continuation of liberalization and on the EPU as a means to an end.[67]

Then, a perfect opportunity for Jacobsson's argument appeared in 1953. This was the EPU's easing of restrictions on movement of funds, on May 18 of that year. This easing made it possible for authorized banks within the region to carry out interbank spot trades freely in any of the currencies of EPU member states. As a result, the bilateral exchange-rate spreads between EPU members, which until then had expanded to as high as 1.5 percent, began to converge. As of June of that year, less than one month after the easing of restrictions had taken effect, the spread between the strongest currency (the Dutch florin) and the weakest (the French franc) had contracted to 0.75 percent, and the French franc, the Belgian franc and the Swedish krona, which earlier had fallen greatly against the pound, had reached parity with the pound.[68] Here it should be noted that Jacobsson was observing these movements in foreign-exchange markets in close cooperation with the responsible BIS personnel. The argument for restoration of convertibility at this time was not simply Jacobsson's own personal argument but had developed within his organizational relationship with the BIS.[69]

Seeing these circumstances as a good opportunity for the restoration of convertibility, Jacobsson again declared the need for such restoration. At this time, Jacobsson spoke about not just the efficacy of free markets but also the subsequent prospects of dissolution of the EPU and easing of restrictions. These prospects were those of managing the volume of credit through the introduction of "credit policy." He also argued that it would be the central banks that would be responsible for such credit policy.

by now most governments and the majority of the public seem to have accepted once more the idea that the central banks should be allowed to exert their influence on the volume of credit by employing the usual means at their disposals.[70]

At the same time, Jacobsson deployed an argument which was harshly critical of Keynesian policies, sounding the alarm about inflation.[71]

However, during this period too the EPU board was split into two camps. One consisted of nations running surpluses, who attempted to realize a "broader multilateral system" through expanding the scope of gold settlement in the EPU and to link this to restoration of convertibility, while the other was made up of deficit nations who were cautious about restoration of convertibility.[72] In response to this conflict, BIS General Manager Auboin released a journal article in which he noted, "At the very least, the issue of restoration, sooner or later, of convertibility of the leading European currencies has again begun a contemporary topic of discussion" and argued that the goal of establishing the EPU had been "to promote overall restoration of convertibility of each currency."[73]

On this point, Jacobsson once again contacted the United States. This time, his counterpart was the Commission on Foreign Economic Policy (generally known as the Randall Commission), organized by the Department of State and made up chiefly of congressional representatives.[74] The Randall Commission announced its report in January 1954, summarizing the American conditions for restoration of convertibility of European currencies. Jacobsson met with the commission at the US embassy in Paris in November 1953, to give a report and take part in a discussion. Jacobsson's assessment of the IMF was also mentioned in this meeting. Now let's examine the contours of this meeting.[75]

When this meeting shifted to a discussion, Jacobsson stressed the point of "why restoration of convertibility is necessary and beneficial to the US," and the Americans questioned him about specific policies. Jacobsson's explanation was as follows: First, once US aid to Europe ended American and European exporters were likely to be on even terms with each other. By then, currencies would need to be liberalized in Europe. Second, under current conditions there were signs of an economic downturn in the United States. There was a need to secure free export markets as an economic policy as well. Perhaps out of an awareness that his counterparts were congressional representatives, Jacobsson deployed the argument that restoration of convertibility would be beneficial based on trade and industry interests – a somewhat different argument from the one he made to Europe. Then, in response to questioning from the US side, Jacobsson advocated the following measures: First, US authorities should declare clearly the goal of restoration of convertibility. Then, American import procedures should be simplified and tariffs cut. In this venue, Jacobsson did not touch on abandonment of Keynesian policies, for which he had argued widely in Europe.

The record of the above meeting shows vividly that, even right before preparing its report, the Randall Commission had not yet established its own views and how Jacobsson, in response, deployed his long-held argument showing the route toward restoration of convertibility. Here too, Jacobsson of the BIS had got a jump on the US strategy.

At the very end of the meeting, Jacobsson had the following highly memorable exchange with attendees Senator Prescott Bush and Harvard University professor, John Williams.[76] This exchange shows Jacobsson's frank assessment of the IMF. We will close this section by citing it in full.

SENATOR BUSH: Do you think it would be a good trade to dissolve the IMF, take over money out and put it in the stabilization fund?
JACOBSSON: I don't think so, because I think the Fund can do the work for all the other 54 nations [...]. I think it can be better done internationally.
PROF. WILLIAMS: Would this be the key-currency fund we used to talk about?
JACOBSSON: Yes, I think this is the key-currency approach. I think the key-currency approach has been quite right.

This discussion would lead directly to the Randall Commission's report, the appointment of Jacobsson as an IMF managing director, and currency adjustments through the key-currency approach.

Jacobsson was appointed IMF managing director in 1956.[77] At the IMF, Jacobsson seized the opportunity to revive the organization, successfully implementing a series of standby arrangements. A newspaper story at the end of the 1950s reported,

> Up to the time that Dr. Per Jacobsson took over its top job towards the close of 1957, the IMF made only the feeblest of efforts to influence the economic behaviour of its members. ... But the Doctor, coming straight from the Bank for International Settlements with a banker's ideas of the way to run a country, soon altered all that.[78]

This is the start of the period in which the gold–dollar standard was established.

Raising foreign currency prior to restoration of convertibility: BIS plans and operations

The roles played by the BIS in designing the gold–dollar standard have been reviewed above with a focus on Jacobsson of the Monetary and Economic Department. Now let's look at another role played by the BIS during this period – namely, that of international allocation of credit centered on raising foreign currency. Prior to the restoration by each country of the convertibility of its currency, securing foreign currency – effectively, dollars – was a most difficult task. Under these conditions, the BIS enhanced the foundation of its business operations on its own by distributing foreign currency to each country through various routes, utilizing its business experience from before the war. Now let's take a look at these operations, which were positioned in between those of central-bank cooperation and the BIS's operating as a bank.

The Banking Department had discussed the plans for these operations beginning in 1947. Head of the Banking Department van Zeeland proposed the following plans based on the context that in order to reconstruct the BIS, which was shaken by the asset freeze and the gold issue, it was necessary for the BIS to be able to supply the strong currency – i.e., the dollar – that each country wanted: (1) The BIS would discount the bills of each country in foreign currency (such as the dollar), with the central bank handling that currency accepting these for rediscounting; (2) Similar bills would be presented for rediscounting to "a newly established international currency agency, such as the IBRD or the US Export–import Bank," signed jointly by the BIS and the central banks of exporting countries; and, (3) Private-sector banks would be asked to discount similar bills. Regarding the third of these plans in particular, as of 1947 it already had been reported that Swiss bank Credit Suisse was "prepared to discount in dollars, in the same way as Swiss francs" Belgian Treasury bills held by the BIS.[79]

Part of this plan moved to the implementation stage. The actual conditions of these operations, not apparent from the financial statements, appears to have been as outlined below:

1   The operations take place between the BIS and the central banks of countries with seats on the BIS board;
2   The BIS acquires the currency of the counterparty country by swapping gold for it, and furthermore invests this currency in Treasury bills of the relevant country;
3   The BIS invests some or all of this investment in Treasury bills in instruments such as export bills of the relevant country. The BIS will "have [porté] these, for example by holding bills with maturities of 18 months for up to 12 months, or present them to Swiss banks for discounting";
4   The relevant country's central bank accepts the bills for rediscounting;
5   The BIS receives the amount corresponding to the discount in the currency of the country to which the goods were exported, rather than in the local currency. "The gold lent at the start of the transaction will change into foreign currency from the export proceeds for which credit was provided at the start of the transaction."[80]

The following circumstances were in the background behind these operations: While each country needed to stimulate exports in order to secure foreign currency, no trade finance system for exports had yet been developed. Also, intervention by central banks was limited by factors such as the maturities of bills. These operations were characterized by the fact that the BIS intervened here based on gold swaps, providing credit to export industries. It should be noted that these operations made use of the unique management resources of the BIS, such as the gold it had accumulated through the war and the securing of liquidity of mid-term credit it had conducted since before the war, and that the BIS's relations of trust with each central bank were utilized in performing these operations. Incidentally, it is said that the profit the BIS received on these operations was 2.25 percent per year.[81]

Next, let's examine the BIS during the postwar reconstruction period from the perspectives of France and Japan.

4 The BIS and France: currency diplomacy on "two different fronts"

During this period, French currency diplomacy – and in a sense, uniformly through today – employed a "two-front" approach vis-à-vis the United States and vis-à-vis Europe. On the one hand, there was the rivalry between acceptance of US aid from the France–US currency agreement through the Marshall Plan and de Gaulle's course of an independent recovery. On the other hand, while employing this two-sided approach on the front of its posture vis-à-vis the United States, a course was apparent of claiming supremacy within the region, looking toward European unification. Relations between the BIS and France too moved together with the progress of these two fronts.

France's moves to ensure the continued existence of the BIS and maneuverings regarding the IMF

After the decision was made at the Bretton Woods Conference to liquidate the BIS, France, which was one of the cornerstones of the BIS, began moves toward ensuring the BIS's continued existence. As touched on in the preceding chapter, since the BIS's founding France had secured successive general manager posts, including the able officials Quesnay and Auboin. As we already have seen, during the period addressed in this chapter Auboin was acting as the center of France's machinations regarding the BIS.

France's machinations on behalf of the continuation of the BIS continued thoroughly even after the United States had effectively shifted to an approach of acceptance of the BIS. For example, from June through July 1949 France's finance ministry and the Banque de France exchanged letters considering a rumored development at the United Nations at the time – a proposal to reorganize the BIS as an institution under the umbrella of the UN's Economic and Social Council – and confirming their opposition to this UN proposal.[82] While the UN plan never was realized, the correspondence demonstrates the atmosphere around the argument to liquidate the BIS, which still was smoldering at that time in 1949, and France's resolve to resist it.

Incidentally, behind France's determination that the BIS remain in existence was a state of affairs related to the European component of the two fronts seen above. French authorities saw Japan's withdrawal from the BIS as having strengthened the BIS's nature as a European institution, and they had devised a strategy for deploying France's currency diplomacy vis-à-vis Europe based on the BIS.[83] This argument shows the background that made it possible for the BIS to remain in existence by gathering the support of not just France but the other continental European states as well.

If the base for the European front was at the BIS, the base for the American front was at the IMF and the French embassy in the United States. Even in the process of negotiations on the EPU as seen above, France's maneuvering vis-à-vis the United States was advanced thoroughly. French representative director Jean de Largentaye[84] was on the scene at the IMF and Pierre-Paul Schweizter was posted as financial attaché at the French embassy, each reporting in detail to the French finance ministry on progress in the situation. Both Largentaye and Schweizter were heavyweight bureaucrats and theorists who led the fiscal policy and financial worlds in postwar France.

The manager at the finance ministry referred to in the letters from these two men as "Dear Guillaume" was Guillaume Guindey, director of the International Finances Bureau. Guindey managed in France the nation's "two-fronted" currency diplomacy and furthermore, in 1958, succeeded Auboin as the third BIS general manager.[85] The fact that France sent to the BIS an individual with thorough knowledge of both sides of its currency diplomacy vis-à-vis both Europe and the United States shows the enthusiasm with which it focused on the BIS.

But specifically what kinds of arguments did France deploy as it took on postwar currency diplomacy with this splendid lineup? Let's take a look at this point by focusing on the negotiations on establishment of the EPU.

The EPU, the BIS, and France's response

In the negotiations on the establishment of the EPU, which we touched on above in connection with the BIS, France took a complex position. While the negotiations took a complicated course, France's handling can be summarized into the following three aspects: (1) opposition to British and American proposals, representing the intention of continental Europe, (2) while also seeking a compromise with the British and Americans under the surface, to avoid a breakdown of negotiations, and (3) on the other hand supporting the wishes of the central-bank side on the BIS stage, from its position in support of the BIS general manager. France handled each of these three aspects, which included some mutual contradictions, as outlined below.

First, let's look at the first aspect of opposition to Britain and the United States. In 1950, France – thanks to protective regulations – was running a trade surplus within the European region. With these circumstances in the background, France is said to have demonstrated an understanding of German membership in the EPU and repeatedly came to play a coordinating role among European states. When the Ansiaux proposal mentioned above met with a flood of criticism, Guindey established a task force and set up unofficial meetings in the offices of the Ministry of Finance, housed inside the Louvre in Paris. In these, the tone of France's strategy was one that should be called anti-IMF rather than anti-American. In fact, the French finance ministry, particularly de Largentaye at the French embassy in the United States, clearly was opposed to the Ansiaux proposal, albeit on the grounds that the authority of the IMF would expand in the distribution of credit to each country that was implied in that proposal. Even when European states were swayed by the Ansiaux proposal, de Largentaye submitted a report to Guindey that stated, "It would appear highly dangerous to abandon our general principles on drawing rights in exchange for the flimsy advantages that might come from the IMF intervening in the EPU mechanism."[86]

On the second aspect – although this is the other side of the coin in relation to the first aspect above – France, and particularly the Ministry of Finance, had from an early stage seen the US ECA proposal as proper and settled on a policy of building a compromise based on this line of reasoning. "On the subject of the overall ratios of use of gold payments and credit, the method proposed by the ECA can be considered satisfactory, together with categorization of gold payments by levels."[87] Auboin at the BIS appeared to have a similar view.

> Above all, the best method of making the most of the opportunity to get all interested countries to participate in EPU planning can be considered to be one based on the essential principles summarized in the memorandum submitted by the ECA to the (US) House of Representatives Foreign Affairs Committee.[88]

In light of the current of disaffection between the United States and the IMF touched on above regarding Jacobsson as well, this strategy appears to have been a highly coherent one.

However, it was the third aspect that was problematic. The BIS board, and furthermore both official and unofficial meetings of central-bank governors, had chosen a policy course that differed from that of France as seen above and from both those of the US–ECA proposal and the OEEC Ansiaux proposal. Led by Jacobsson, this path of liberalization – as expounded on by Kaplan and Schleiminger – would delineate clearly the BIS's position as a club of central banks, based on the assumption of structural antagonism between government and the central bank in each country.[89] From the point of view of France, where a system was in place under which the Ministry of Finance took the lead in currency diplomacy, this must have appeared to be a radical response. But at the same time, it was difficult for France to take action in light of its position as having sent to the BIS its general manager, Auboin, who supported the BIS's path administratively. As seen above, Auboin himself had taken the lead in extolling Jacobsson's proposal. In light of this background, even on the French side it was expected that a state of affairs would develop under which compromise was reached at a high level.

5 The BIS and Japan: from the prewar to the postwar era

In comparison with France's flourishing activity in international currency diplomacy during this period, Japan's situation was a severe one.

The San Francisco Peace Treaty and Japan's withdrawal from the BIS

As seen in the preceding chapter, while the United States had frozen all BIS assets as enemy assets, on May 13, 1948 an agreement was concluded between the BIS and the US Treasury Department, releasing the asset freeze. However, Japan's BIS accounts were not released from the freeze, along with "accounts of governments and nationalities specified by the US Department of the Treasury."[90] At this point in time, Japan's assets at the BIS consisted of approximately 474 pounds in Bank of Japan accounts ("N Accounts") and approximately 11,901 pounds in Japanese government accounts (held in the BIS Bank of Japan account). The entire amount of these assets was moved from Federal Bank of New York accounts to a frozen account and then to a special account of the US Attorney General.[91]

The BIS had considered lodging a complaint about these measures, grounded in Article 10 of the BIS statutes, which specified that BIS assets would not be seized or commandeered even during the war years. However, it gave up the idea of the protest in light of the fact that the US government had not originally signed the Hague Agreement – it had been a private-sector banking syndicate consisting of Morgan and others that had participated in the BIS.[92] In January 1951 the Bank of Japan made an inquiry to the BIS through the lawyer George Yamaoka, this did not lead to any breakthrough in the situation. In the end, the exchange between the BIS and the Bank of Japan through Yamaoka was the final negotiation prior to Japan's withdrawal from the BIS.[93] In September 1951, the San Francisco Peace Treaty was signed, with the Japanese government relinquishing claims on all assets it had secured overseas through 1945.

In parallel with the issue of the freeze of Japanese assets seen above, the issue of Japanese representation in the postwar BIS was debated as well.

This started with a proposal made in January 1946 by the BIS president – chairman of the board McKittrick – to Kojiro Kitamura. In a meeting with Kitamura held at the Swiss National Bank, based on the example of Belgium during the war – which had been granted a position in which both competing representatives, the Nazi puppet regime and the government in exile in London, were represented on the board but with no voting rights – McKittrick proposed for postwar Japan the position of a nonvoting shareholder. In response, Kitamura replied that since unlike in Germany's case the government of Japan had remained in power continuously from the prewar through the postwar years its voting rights should be maintained, and the meeting ended without an agreement being reached.[94] When taking into consideration the facts that among the other axis powers Germany's representation had been transferred to West Germany and Italy's had remained unchanged, it cannot be denied that McKittrick's proposal seems to stand out.

While the circumstances remained unchanged for a while afterward, it was Britain that introduced the next phase. In July 1948 the British foreign ministry held an internal meeting in which Japanese representation in the BIS was discussed.[95] Based on these discussions, the Bank of England made a series of proposals in October and November 1950, advising the BIS to seize BIS shares held by Japan and force Japan's withdrawal from the BIS.[96] At this point in time, the idea already had been floated of making the BIS a European bank.

On the other hand, at the level of intergovernmental negotiations the BIS issue had been set aside somewhat. In fact, a Dulles memorandum (February 1951) discussing the draft text of the San Francisco Peace Treaty did not mention Japan's withdrawal from the BIS. However, in the following month the British government insisted that Japanese withdrawal from the BIS be incorporated into the treaty, to fit in with BIS plans.[97] Here too, the British initiative stands out.

In the end, it was decided that the San Francisco Peace Treaty would, as argued by the British government, explicitly call for Japan's withdrawal from the BIS. Just before the treaty was signed, in July 1951, after returning to Japan Kan Yoshimura sent a letter to BIS General Manager Auboin asking for his interpretation of the San Francisco Peace Treaty.[98] The response to this letter came not from Auboin but from BIS legal advisor H. Guisan. This reply from Guisan adroitly described Japan's prewar and postwar positions in the BIS and the course by which the BIS aimed to grow in the postwar era. Let's look at some passages from the letter:

> As you know, the Bank for International Settlements, in conformity with the obligation imposed on it by its statute always completely dissociated itself from political questions. The problems raised by Articles 8(c) and 16 of the draft treaty with Japan only concern the Governments involved.

> Although those Governments have not advised us of their intentions with regard to those Articles, I think I am right in saying that the demand made to Japan by those Governments to renounce her participation in the Bank for International Settlements is in accordance with the conception that the bank should remain an essentially European institution.[99]

This concept of the BIS as a European institution was at the heart of the BIS's postwar plans. While the above letter from Guisan stated that this concept of the BIS had been in existence for a long time, this is not an accurate assertion. The concept of the BIS as a European institution was a desperate response devised in response to the argument for liquidation of the BIS that had welled up out of the United States after World War II.

Whatever the case, in this situation Japan had no choice but to withdraw from the BIS. As a legal formality, Japan's withdrawal was completed through abandonment of "all rights, title and interests" it had acquired under the January 1930 Hague Convention and other agreements. The renunciation was communicated from Japan to the Swiss government on October 31, 1952, via the French foreign ministry. Also, Japan's shares in the BIS were transferred to European central banks at face value. These procedures were approved at an extraordinary BIS general meeting held on June 9, 1952, completing Japan's withdrawal.[100]

The Bank of Japan's maneuvering for reentry

Later, after the San Francisco Treaty took effect in April 1952, Japan began returning to and joining international institutions. In August 1952 it joined the IMF and the World Bank, and in April 1964 it became one of the IMF's Article VIII members. It achieved provisional GATT membership in 1953 and official membership in September 1955, and in February 1963 it acceded to GATT Article XI membership.

Japan's rejoining BIS membership – examined in Chapter 4 of this book – is related to the process of the formation of the meeting of the ministers of finance and central-bank governors of the Group of Ten (G10). Japan was permitted to take part in the G10 from its start in 1961. With this G10 as the point of contact, Japan negotiated on matters such as rejoining the BIS and accession to board membership. This started with a visit to the BIS – unannounced to the BIS – by Bank of Japan London branch director Kazuo Fukano in February 1961 to demand trading in gold and opening of an account with the BIS.[101] Next, in October 1961 the BIS invited a visit by Tetsusaburo Tanaka, who had served as a director before the war. On his return from Basel, Tanaka visited Jacobsson, who at the time was serving as managing director at IMF headquarters in Washington, where he was told, "it was a mistake for Japan to withdraw from the BIS" and promised "support for Japan's OECD membership."[102] Later, beginning in 1963 Haruo Maekawa (a Bank of Japan director at the time) visited the BIS monthly, and through 1964 Japan was allowed to attend BIS Eurocurrency meetings and other meetings as a member. In 1967, Maekawa was permitted to attend the monthly meeting of central-bank governors as representative of the governor.[103] Japan once again secured shares of BIS stock in 1970, and in 1994 it returned to the board member nation status (see Chapter 1).

6 The banking business and distribution of profits

This section covers the financial statements for the fiscal years 1945 (settlement of accounts conducted March 31, 1946) through 1957 (settlement of accounts conducted March 31, 1958). Counted from the start of BIS operations, these correspond to the sixteenth through the twenty-eighth fiscal years. Some notes are required concerning the balance sheet during this period.

The first concerns the currency in which figures are denominated. While the basic currency unit of BIS financial statements is the Gold Swiss franc, the gold price on which it was based was set to be "based on the US Treasury's official selling price for gold and on the exchange rates quoted for the various currencies against dollars on the date of the closing of the Bank's accounts." In other words, while fluctuations in each country's currency were reflected, during this period they "are of no practical importance so far as the Bank's accounts are concerned."[104]

The second concerns handling of matters related to the prewar Young Plan. The method of indicating on the financial statements accounts related to payment of German reparations annuities based on the Young Plan changed beginning in the 1949 fiscal year. As seen in Chapter 2, the payment of German reparations which had been handled by the BIS was frozen by the 1931 Hoover Moratorium, but its legal standing, such as the right to demand payment of annual install-ments of reparations, was maintained. When in fiscal 1949 the BIS organized the legal interpretations on payment of these annual installments and sounded out the states holding rights to demand payment, it attained the agreement of four states: France, Britain, Italy and Belgium. According to this development, the account items on payment of annual installments on reparations in connection with the Young Plan (Hague Convention), which until then had been shown on the financial statements, were moved off the books.[105]

The third note concerns the impact of the asset freeze. As seen above, when the freeze on assets in the United States was released under the agreement con-cluded between the US government and the BIS on May 13, 1948, "the greater part of the Bank's working funds once more consist of dollar holdings, as was the rule before the war."[106] While the amount of gold in bars to be restituted from the United States to the BIS under this agreement had been shown on the balance sheet since before enactment of the agreement, separately six million Gold Swiss francs were added to both the debit and credit sides in connection with this return of assets.[107]

Trends in the financial statements (1): collection of deposits

First, let's check the movement of the total amounts on the balance sheet (Figure 4.1). During this period, the total amount on the BIS balance sheet increased steadily. In fiscal 1948, three years after the end of the war, the balance sheet total already exceeded the immediate pre-war level (as at August 31, 1939) and, furthermore, set a new record high among monthly reports since April 30, 1933, "just after the devaluation of the dollar."[108] Both the fiscal years 1954 and 1955 showed particularly rapid growth. The BIS annual report for fiscal 1954 reports, "The total volume of business handled by the Bank during the financial year under review was about 50 per cent greater than in the previous year, this being the largest turnover so far recorded" and describes this growth as "the largest turnover so far recorded."[109] A rough estimate with fiscal 1945 as the base year shows that the total amount on the BIS balance sheet in the postwar period more than doubled over five years and grew fourfold over 11 years. This is in stark contrast to prewar and wartime developments – in which the total amount on the balance sheet fell over the ten years from the start of operations in 1931 to less than one-half its initial level.

Next, let's look at the key factors in liabilities (on the debit side) that led to this growth in the balance sheet (Figure 4.1).

First, paid-in capital showed no changes. Also, long-term deposits were moved off the balance sheet beginning in fiscal 1949 in accordance with the pro-cessing related to the Young Plan as seen above, so that this account effectively was removed from the debit side. On the other hand, short-term and sight

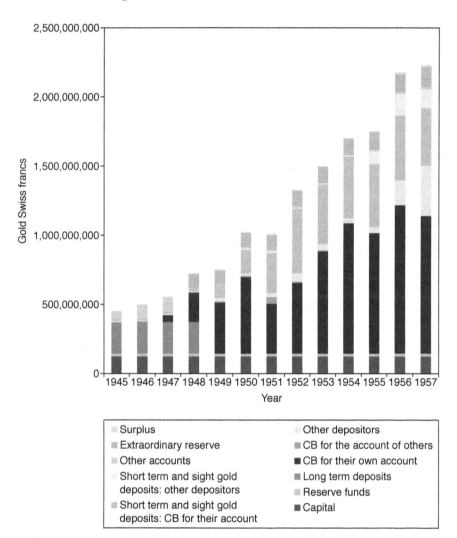

Figure 4.1 BIS balance sheet: major items on liabilities (fiscal years 1945–1957), in Gold
    Swiss francs (source: *BIS Sixteenth–Twenty-eighth Annual Reports*).

Note
"Annuity trust account" and "German government deposit" which constituted the "Long term
deposits" have been released out from the BIS balance sheet from fiscal year 1949 on.

deposits increased steadily. The main type of deposit that increased here was not
sight deposits but time deposits. In particular, central banks' own accounts (with
terms not exceeding three months) leapt into the position of the largest item in
liabilities accounts as long-term deposits were removed from the balance sheet.
The ratio of short-term time deposits to total BIS deposits (total deposits denominated in gold and currencies) grew from 1.38 percent at the end of fiscal 1945 to

32.8 percent at the end of fiscal 1948 and, furthermore, to 61.5 percent at the end of fiscal 1948.[110] While long-term deposits related to the Young Plan accounted for a large proportion of the total amount of deposits when deposit operations were suspended during the war, as business returned to normal after the war the ratio of short-term deposits showed an increase. In fiscal 1946, of cash and current deposits "the cash holding in Swiss francs then accounting for about 80 percent of that total."[111] Incidentally, this ratio changed considerably over the following several years. First, in October 1947 the proportion in pounds surpassed that in Swiss francs,[112] and then in January 1948 the dollar overtook the Swiss franc to take the second-place (third place when including gold) currency.[113] In March 1948, the dollar leapt ahead of both gold and the pound, so that at the end of that fiscal year the dollar accounted for roughly 80 percent of BIS sight and short-term deposits.[114]

But why did this increase in deposits take place through time deposits instead of sight deposits? This involves the relation between BIS deposits and gold, also touched on in the preceding chapter. Put plainly, use of earmarked gold spread, so that the settlement function that until then had been performed by sight deposits came to be performed instead by gold, in particular earmarked gold not reflected on the BIS financial statements at that. The earmarked gold had totaled 51.4 million Gold Swiss francs on March 31, 1945, but then rose to 169.5 million in March 1949, with the markets in which it was invested growing from the previous number of four to six. In March 1954 earmarked gold grew to 302.2 million Gold Swiss francs, and the BIS annual report noted, "At the latter date, this gold was distributed between seven different centres."[115] According to the analysis of the BIS annual report, the increase in earmarked gold was partly due to fresh deposits in gold and partly to the conversion of currency deposits into gold held under earmark.[116]

How did the BIS react to this growth in deposits, and time deposits for which interest was demanded at that? On one hand, the BIS was in a situation in which it proved unable to increase investment in response to this growth in deposits. Once the EPU had begun in 1950, deposits denominated in each currency came to fluctuate massively throughout the year. According to the BIS annual report, this was because "the central banks utilize their deposits to make current payments, including the monthly settlements in connection with the European Payments Union."[117] To the BIS, this state of affairs was a factor limiting investment, in that the BIS needed to maintain cash balances in large amounts. On the other hand, in fiscal 1957, when market functions were restored internationally, the BIS still would maintain a "policy of ... allowing interest ... at market rates" to these deposits. While this policy involved risk when interest rates were falling, the BIS "thought it desirable, in view of its strong financial position, to take the risk of paying interest on relatively large deposits."[118]

What about deposits denominated in gold? At the end of fiscal 1946, the number of gold deposit accounts, representing gold other than earmarked gold, was 25 (reflecting a decrease of one account from the previous fiscal year).[119] Gold holdings of the BIS itself fell from 103.2 million Gold Swiss francs on

March 31, 1946, to 88.6 million on March 31, 1947.[120] This was due to the gold sale measures seen above. However, later gold deposits began to increase again, and in fiscal 1952 the sight deposits component of central banks' own accounts (gold) overcame the central banks' own accounts (with terms not exceeding three months) seen above to become – while only for that one fiscal year – the largest item in liabilities accounts. It appears that as the EPU began functioning prior to restoration of convertibility of European currencies each country increased, albeit temporarily, the amount of its gold deposits with the BIS. From the BIS's point of view, this was a welcome state of affairs since the larger the amount each central bank deposits with the BIS the more it benefits from the opportunity to offset or exchange gold position with other regions at the minimum cost through the functions of the BIS.[121]

During the postwar reconstruction period, BIS deposits broke free from their wartime stagnation and showed an increase in restricted deposits and in off-books earmarked gold. On the other hand, the start of the EPU introduced a new issue concerning how to hold liquid deposits. In this way, BIS liabilities accounts would make their way toward the 1960s while being impacted by the progress of trade settlement in the postwar world and in Europe.

Trends in the financial statements (2): investment of funds

The BIS annual report issued right after World War II contained the note, "The Bank's new operations are rather different from those which it handled before the war." According to the annual report, while its prewar investment had been conducted through investing "comparatively large amounts on a small number of markets," in the postwar period it would try to invest: "In making its investments, it aims at securing a type of paper which is, in many cases, remobilisable before maturity, and in such a way that the creditor markets become connected with the operations of the Bank."[122] This was a shift from concentration on a small number of markets to distribution across a large number of markets. A change in policy was declared concerning how to maintain liquidity as well. While during the war the BIS had given top priority to securing liquidity, in fiscal 1946 it began measures "for a progressive re-establishment of equilibrium between current income and expenditure."[123] How would these changes in policy make themselves felt in the BIS's assets (on the debit side of the books)? Let's look at these in order of liquidity, from high levels to lower. Also, while as shown in Figure 4.2 the categories of asset items were changed beginning in fiscal 1955, this does not introduce any difficulties in looking at overall trends.

The first items we will look at are cash and gold in bars. At the end of fiscal 1950, total gold and cash holdings accounted for 42.4 percent of the total amount on the balance sheet.[124] This ratio would rise to 52.4 percent at the end of fiscal 1951[125] and 57.4 percent at the end of fiscal 1952.[126] However, it then would fall to 44.2 percent at the end of fiscal 1953[127] and 37.5 percent at the end of fiscal 1955,[128] and it was 26.1 percent at the end of fiscal 1956 and 28.4 percent at the

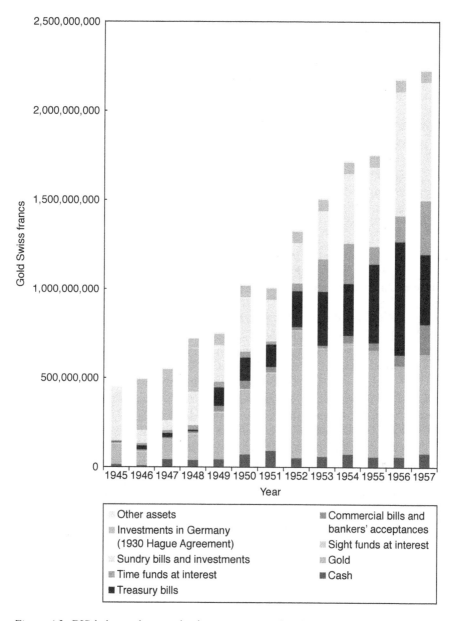

Figure 4.2 BIS balance sheet: major items on assets (fiscal years 1945–1957), in Gold Swiss francs (source: *BIS Sixteenth–Twenty-eighth Annual Reports*).

end of fiscal 1957.[129] The main reason these items showed a decreasing trend in the 1950s was due to movements in central banks' own accounts (gold). That is, in this account sight deposits (gold) decreased while those with terms not exceeding three months increased instead (Figure 4.2).

In fiscal 1946, the amount of gold in bars (gold bars and specie) decreased as part of the amount of gold sold was used in investment activities to increase returns on BIS assets. The BIS annual report insists that the sum "entailed a forward repurchase."[130] While the BIS had been accepting gold as deposits and investing it, in this fiscal year it conducted gold sales with central banks for the first time. The BIS annual report described this as an "interesting experiment."[131] Furthermore, in fiscal 1947 European central banks became able to acquire dollars for gold within the European region through the BIS, and as a result there was no longer a need to send gold to the United States:

> Thanks to the size of the Bank's gold holdings, their geographical distribution can be arranged in such a way as to make it possible to meet the requirements of the central banks without recourse to more than a minimum of physical shipments.[132]

In connection with this point, categorization of the gold held by the BIS in its own accounts by the location in which it was invested shows the following tendencies: Immediately following World War II, Berne, Switzerland held the top position, reflecting the locations of gold during the war. In the investment structure as of the end of fiscal 1948 (March 1949), New York and London accounted for largely the same amount of investment, followed by markets in former neutral European countries, such as Lisbon and Berne. In the 1950s New York's position rose rapidly, so that at the end of March 1957 New York alone accounted for 66 percent of gold holdings. Over this period, the proportion invested in London showed no major change (other than a temporary rapid decrease).[133] In other words, gold investment can be seen to have been withdrawn from continental Europe and concentrated in the United States (Figure 4.3).

Next, a look at sight funds at interest shows that while the amount in this account grew, its weight in asset accounts fell to less than 1 percent.

In contrast, various types of term loans increased greatly. In fiscal 1945, "even more than in preceding years," "every care was taken to keep the Bank's investments as liquid as possible."[134] However, this trend reversed in fiscal 1948, when loans and miscellaneous securities with maturities of nine months or less increased, as did those with maturities of nine months or more. This rate of growth even surpassed that of the balance sheet as a whole.[135]

Rediscountable bills and acceptances would appear to be an account related to the BIS export finance, touched on in the preceding section. While at the start of the postwar period this item as a percentage of the total amount on the balance sheet was very small, in fiscal 1950 it grew to 4.5 percent, reaching a peak. While subsequently it would experience repeated ups and downs, in fiscal 1957 it would reach a level of more than 7 percent of the total balance-sheet amount. As implied by the Banking Department memo seen above, this business was related to the holding of Treasury bills that we will look at next.

Treasury bills made up the second most important credit account after gold in bars. The increase in Treasury bills in fiscal 1946 resulted from sale of gold.[136]

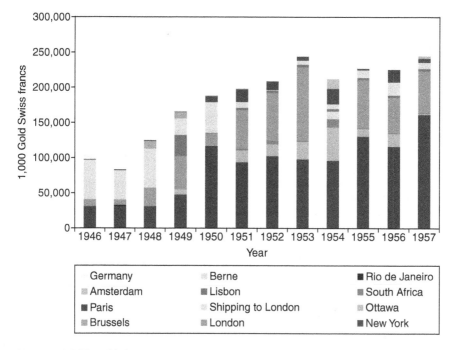

Figure 4.3 BIS gold investments, 1946–1957, in 1,000 Gold Swiss francs (source: Rapport sur les opérations de la Banque du 1er au 31 mars 1946, p. 3; du 1er au 31 mars 1947, annexe 97/D(2), p. 3; le mois de mars 1948, annexe 104/D, p. 2; le mois de mars 1949, annexe 114/D, p. 4; le mois de mars 1950, annexe 125/C(1), p. 5; le mois de mars 1951, annexe 134/D, p. 5; le mois de mars 1952, annexe 146/C, p. 5; le mois de mars 1953, annexe 154/D, p. 5; le mois de mars 1954, annexe 164/D, p. 4; le mois de mars 1955, annexe 175/C(1), p. 5; le mois de mars 1956, annexe 184/D, p. 4; le mois de mars 1957, annexe 194/D, p. 6).

Note
Stock data as of the end of March of each fiscal year.

After the cutoff date for accounts in fiscal 1947, the BIS concluded with the IBRD an arrangement to purchase public bonds bearing interest of 2.5 percent, denominated in Swiss francs. The BIS would profit indirectly on this arrangement by providing Swiss francs to the IBRD, which the IBRD would use in loans to the Netherlands.[137] While growth in Treasury bills was at a standstill in fiscal 1948, they later would undergo continued steady growth, accounting for the second largest proportion of credit accounts in fiscal 1949 and the largest, albeit temporarily, in fiscal 1956. It also was reported that a considerable portion of these Treasury bills was in US treasuries.[138] In fact, using indicators from the end of fiscal 1948 as was conducted above, Treasury bills accounted for the largest share of investments in the United States, at $42 million (70.1 percent) of the total amount of $59.911 million. Next came investments such as the FRB cash account at $11.823 million (19.7 percent) and bank acceptances at $3.516 million (5.9 percent).[139] This investment structure would later show a rapid decrease in the cash account, replaced by increasing investments in bonds such as treasuries. While figures fluctuated greatly by fiscal year, in the second half of the 1950s Treasury bills and public bonds related to the Treasury Department together would in general account for a share of 70–80 percent of investments in the United States (Figure 4.4).

Incidentally, the BIS also carried out transactions not shown on the balance sheet. This refers to the acceptance of earmarked gold in liabilities accounts and corresponding gold transactions in assets accounts. Below, we will look at these off-the-books transactions with a focus on gold-related business.

Of the transactions not shown on the balance sheet, it was futures trading in gold that showed the most important developments during this period. Beginning with the fiscal 1949 annual report, a small number of statistics were provided concerning the futures position. According to these, while on March 31, 1949 gold holdings in a total of 129.1 million Gold Swiss francs – consisting of 150.8 million in gold in bars and 21.7 million in gold-denominated deposits – were shown on the balance sheet, the amount of solid gold held for futures adjustments was 166.2 million Gold Swiss francs. Calculation of the ratio of the

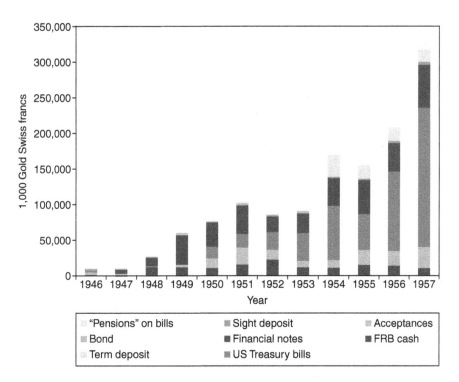

Figure 4.4 BIS investments in the United States, 1946–1957, in 1,000 Gold Swiss francs (source: as for Figure 4.3).

amount of futures holdings to that of gold holdings on the balance sheet shows that at the time under consideration here of the end of March 1949 the amount of futures holdings was about 1.3 times (128 percent) that of holdings on the books. During this fiscal year, this ratio moved within the 108–140 percent range.[140] The range of fluctuation in this ratio would broaden in fiscal 1951 to 44–165 percent.[141] Beginning in fiscal 1950, the BIS annual report even mentions swap transactions between spot gold and gold futures.

The BIS's net gold holdings are derived by adding the amount of gold currently being managed in trades such as spot sales and futures purchases and subtracting gold involved in futures sales and that for which weighing requests were being made, i.e., short-term and sight deposits (gold) in liabilities accounts. This net holdings amount was 83 million Gold Swiss francs at the end of March 1947, 124.9 million at the end of March 1948, and 166.2 million at the end of March 1949.[142]

After World War II, in investment of funds the BIS pursued a policy of a more long-term investment orientation. However, actual change was limited roughly to investments related to very short-term loans in the form of call loans with terms of three months or less. Still, as investment in treasury bonds and miscellaneous securities increased, perhaps one should say that the germ of new investment management had been cultivated. In off-the-books gold trades, the BIS carried out transactions such as trading gold with central banks and futures and spot swap trades on gold markets and attempted to handle investment in a manner in line with the new developments in the global economy, which was moving toward a postwar growth period.

Profit and loss, and distribution of earnings: the end of the use of hidden reserves

An important change was made concerning the income statement during this period. As seen in the preceding chapter, net profit in fiscal 1944 was transferred to a special account without submitting this move for discussion in the general meeting. This special account later functioned through fiscal 1948 as a BIS hidden ledger. That is, from fiscal 1945 through fiscal 1948, even if actual net profit showed an increase they were all transferred to the special account established during wartime instead of affecting the total amount available for allocation in the period.[143] As seen in Table 4.1, beginning in fiscal 1946 exchange differences were included in calculation of official net profit. For this reason, profit and loss on the hidden ledger and the official ledger came into agreement.

The BIS paid no dividends during this period. In the fiscal years 1945 and 1946 the provision to the balance sheet seen in the preceding chapter continued to be included, and the amount corresponding to dividends in fiscal 1945 was lower than the standard specified in the BIS statutes by 95.50 Gold Swiss francs per share,[144] while in fiscal 1946 too dividends were lower than the standard by 133 Gold Swiss francs per share.[145]

Beginning in fiscal 1947, the qualifier "after deducting provisions for contingencies" that until then had modified the term net profit during peacetime was

removed, replaced with a note to the income statement stating that certain processing of income would be conducted subject to resolution by the board of
directors. In fiscal 1948, the amount subject to this processing was the same as
the amount corresponding to net profit in an average year – in other words, all
profit for that fiscal year was allocated to the special account so that no net profit
resulted.[146] While in fiscal 1949 a final amount available for allocation in the
period did arise, it too was allocated to special expenses and special reserves.
Beginning in the 1950s, the BIS finally would begin recording dividends to
shareholders (Table 4.1).

To summarize the course of developments to this point, it can be seen that use
of hidden reserves gradually was abandoned through the following process: (1)
the separation between official and unofficial books from the prewar period
functioned only through fiscal 1945, (2) beginning in fiscal 1946 exchange differences were counted on the official books, reducing to a mere shell the function of the unofficial books, (3) but still, through fiscal 1948 all these profits

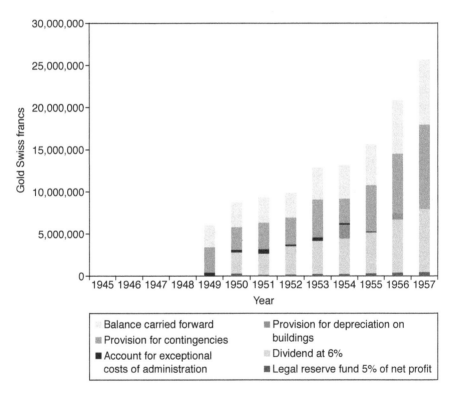

Figure 4.5 BIS profit and loss appropriation account (fiscal years 1945–1957), in Gold
Swiss francs (source: *BIS Sixteenth–Twenty-eighth Annual Reports*).

Note
The undistributed balance from the fiscal year ended March 1944 has been included into the balance
carried forward of the fiscal year 1950.

Table 4.1 BIS profit and loss account, fiscal years 1945–1957, published and unpublished versions, in Gold Swiss francs

Published account

	Net income	Commissions earned	Transfer fees	Gross profit	Costs of administration = total expenditure	Less: amounts recoverable for expenses as Agent of the OEEC, etc.	Net profit
1945	1,242,567.54		86.73	1,242,744.27	1,859,325.72		−616,581.45
1946	2,591,283.34	248.37	68.30	2,591,600.01	1,898,813.00		692,787.00
1947	11,788,994.12		95.00	11,789,089.12	2,247,655.32		9,541,433.80
1948	7,614,851.44		884.75	7,615,735.19	2,625,508.51	111,629.23	5,101,855.91
1949	8,874,596.29		455.23	8,875,051.52	2,847,778.57	284,417.85	6,027,272.95
1950	8,957,262.29		564.35	8,957,826.64	3,381,250.43	512,117.10	6,088,693.31
1951	9,730,051.93		680.61	9,730,732.54	3,894,689.46	563,558.14	6,399,601.22
1952	10,157,762.92		462.83	10,158,225.75	3,843,092.00	573,463.12	6,888,596.87
1953	13,244,598.56	246,212.58	418.18	13,491,229.32	4,109,531.86	569,090.35	9,950,787.81
1954	12,474,244.37	547,912.56		13,022,156.93	4,235,254.50	569,615.10	9,356,517.53
1955	15,044,018.00	619,759.00		15,663,777.00	4,594,027.00	572,933.00	11,642,683.00
1956	19,536,479.00	679,568.00		20,216,047.00	4,767,939.00	566,354.00	16,014,462.00
1957	23,185,449.00	592,527.00		23,777,976.00	5,028,910.00	568,672.00	19,317,738.00

Unpublished account

	Gross revenue	Interest allowed	Costs of administration	Net balance	Transfers from specific reserves and adjustments	Exchange differences	Total amount available for allocation	Allocations to undisclosed reserves				Net balance published
								exchange differences account	provision for exchange and other losses	revaluation of assets	administration account	
1945	1,260,000.00	17,000.00	1,859,000.00	−616,000.00	−58,000.00	218,000.00	−456,000.00	218,000.00			−58,000.00	−616,000.00
1946	1,323,000.00	20,000.00	1,898,000.00	−595,000.00		1,288,000.00	693,000.00					693,000.00
1947	6,516,000.00	77,000.00	2,248,000.00	4,191,000.00		5,350,000.00	9,541,000.00					9,541,000.00
1948	5,587,000.00	1,129,000.00	2,625,000.00	1,833,000.00		3,269,000.00	5,102,000.00					5,102,000.00
1949	8,950,000.00	2,200,000.00	2,850,000.00	3,900,000.00		2,100,000.00	6,000,000.00		35,200,000.00	−35,200,000.00		6,000,000.00
1950												
1951												
1952												
1953												
1954												
1955												
1956												
1957												

Source : BIS Historical Archives, file 7.5, box 1/2, "Disposal of the surplus on the Profit and Loss Account 1949–50", March 28, 1950, *BIS Sixteenth* –*twenty–eighth Annual Reports.*

Note

"Commissions earned" after fiscal year 1953 represent the commissions earned as trustee (or fiscal agent of the trustees) for international loans.

were diverted to a special account instead of resulting in a net profit figurc, and (4) allocation of funds to this special account was conducted on a partial basis in fiscal 1949, and then in fiscal 1950 dividends were restored.

The point is that in connection with these changes the argument arose within the BIS that use of hidden reserves itself should cease. A memorandum prepared in March 1950 made the following arguments, while also tracing the history of hidden reserves and reviewing processing of profit, particularly during the period when no dividends were paid: (1) While it was a fact that BIS revenues had come to be affected by factors of uncertainty to an even greater extent than in the past, the fact of a certain irregularity in income from year to year, despite realizing sufficient profits for distributing dividends, is alone insufficient reason for failing to pay dividends. (2) The practice of making deductions from net income for various reasons was likely to invite errors regarding valuation of the BIS's assets in general. (3) In the past, payment of dividends was an important means of earning profits for the central banks that owned stock in the BIS, particularly central banks of countries without seats on the board of directors. Nevertheless, for a long period of time no dividends had been paid. This issue called for special concern if only because at that time some countries were withdrawing from new international institutions and amendment of the statutes had made it easier for new members to join the BIS.[147] Thus, in the peculiar context of the postwar reconstruction period the use of hidden reserves ceased in 1950.

Now, in light of the above background let's confirm the trends in BIS profit as a ratio of the total amount on the balance sheet. As seen in Table 4.1, a look at official net profit shows that after recording a loss of more than 600,000 Gold Swiss francs in fiscal 1945, profitability was restored beginning in fiscal 1946, with profit showing record growth to nine million Gold Swiss francs in fiscal 1947 – even higher than the official net profit of fiscal 1935. However, the subsequent stagnation should be noted. From fiscal 1948 through fiscal 1952, official net profit remained unchanged in the vicinity of six million Gold Swiss francs. During the same period, the total amount on the balance sheet doubled from 722.48 million (in fiscal 1948) to 1.32981 billion (in fiscal 1952). For this reason alone, this stagnation in profit stands out even more. Later, net profit shows rapid growth. While the total amount on the balance sheet rose by 67.9 percent over the fiscal years 1952 through 1957, from 1.32981 billion Gold Swiss francs to 2.23234 billion, official net profit grew rapidly by 180.6 percent over the same period, from 6.88 million Gold Swiss francs to 19.31 million (Table 4.1).

Here, the topic of interest is a look at the changes in the revenue structure behind this transition from the recovery of profitability immediately after the war through stagnation at the start of the 1950s to the subsequent rapid recovery.

Behind these circumstances was a change in the revenue conditions related to the Young Plan (Hague Convention). This was first identified as early as the BIS annual report for fiscal 1945. In that fiscal year, no payment of interest or principle was received on investments in Germany based on the Hague Convention, and the report states, "This has meant a very important reduction in the income of the Bank."[148] In that same fiscal year, the BIS recorded on its income statement expenditures in excess of receipts, and in the years 1944–1945 it transferred 616,581.45 Gold Swiss francs from the special account to cover this deficit. In fiscal 1946, official net income was back in the black. According to the assessment of the situation in the BIS annual report, a large amount of net gains on exchange differences contributed to this surplus.[149] Trading in gold and gains on exchange not only covered the deficit at the start of the fiscal year but also generated enough surplus to offset the deficit in the previous fiscal year. While in fiscal 1947, as seen above, official net income had recovered to a level rivaling the results achieved several years before the war, according to the BIS's analysis the regular income from investments in Germany seen in the prewar years largely had disappeared, replaced by a dependency on income from timely management of investments.[150]

In short, income from investments and fees related to German reparations had stopped coming in, and instead the BIS found itself in a situation in which it needed to rely on revenues from the timely management of investments in the form of gains on exchange differences. Gains on exchange differences as a percentage of official net income was 56 percent in fiscal 1947, 64 percent in fiscal 1948, and 35 percent in fiscal 1949.[151]

Income was processed in accordance with official profit. While no amount available for allocation was recorded in the fiscal years 1945 through 1948, dividends were paid to shareholders during these years.

Beginning in fiscal 1949, the BIS allocated funds to various reserves, including dividend reserves. Beginning in fiscal 1954, together with stabilization of the business environment transfers to the special expenses account decreased, and two years later this account was eliminated. In its stead, accumulation of funds to building depreciation reserves began, and starting in fiscal 1956 dividends to shareholders also increased substantially in response to a rapid increase in net income (Table 4.1). Thus in terms of profits as well, during the postwar reconstruction period the BIS can be said above all to have got off to a good start.

7 Conclusion

To each country's central bank, and to the BIS as a "club" of central banks, the postwar reconstruction period began amid severe circumstances. The Bretton Woods Agreement had pronounced a sentence of liquidation for the BIS, and the prewar cooperation between central banks appeared to have been overcome by the IMF, in which each country's fiscal authorities were deeply involved. However, as the infeasibility of immediate stabilization was exposed the key-currency approach rose, and the postwar world quickly rewrote its scenarios. The BIS too addressed this situation by moving to implement strategies to resolve simultaneously the issues concerning looted gold and the asset freeze, successfully ensuring the continued existence of the organization.

At the same time, the continued existence of the BIS meant its rebirth as a European institution. The postwar BIS can be seen as having started on a path that differed from that of Bretton Woods, while also confining itself to Europe as the natural outcome of participation in the European settlement framework leading to the EPU or of French and Japanese currency diplomacy.

In the area of BIS business operations, together with the rapid recovery of dollar deposits and stability in its lines of business in the postwar reconstruction period businesses appeared that led into the next era, such as gold trades with central banks and futures and spot swap trades in gold markets.

The theoretical and ideological backbone for this continued existence of the BIS was neoliberalism, broadly defined, which saw gold as the foundation of economic growth. Exemplified by Jacobsson, as described by Toniolo this neo-liberalism at the time was "conspicuously isolated and looked somehow old-fashioned." However, "Today, as the philosophy underlying economic thinking and policy making has gone almost full circle to where it stood before the Depression, one cannot fail to note the 'modernity' of the BIS's postwar economic thinking."[152] The continuity of neoliberalism, Europe and gold embodied in the BIS was a historical continuity linking the traditions of the BIS as well as an organizational and management consistency penetrating the Monetary and Economic Department and the Banking Department.

In April 1945, Fraser who had served as governor and president of the BIS from the time of its founding killed himself using a pistol.[153]

Seemingly more strongly constituted as a practitioner than as a theorist, Fraser left behind no high-flown arguments. His policy advisory memos too were much fewer in number than those of, for example, Jacobsson. Hisaakira Kano of the Yokohama Specie Bank has described the natural voice of Fraser laying out his true feelings. Kano, who was stationed at the BIS for a long time as a Japanese representative director, gave his strong impressions to Fraser and other core members of BIS management and central-bank governors. In 1935, Fraser called Kano into his own office to discuss his own future.[154]

Fraser told Kano, "Regarding my own resignation, while later there will be much talk about choosing a successor, since I already have made my decision I will leave without getting involved in the issue." Fraser had in mind as his successor J. Trip, governor of the central bank of the Netherlands. The gist of the discussion between Fraser and Kano was that while this choice involved some issues, such as whether Trip could serve simultaneously as a central-bank governor and in the appointment of a representative, arrangements should be made on these matters in a meeting of central-bank governors. This appointment plan was realized as Fraser had wanted.

What is highly interesting on this point is the atmosphere of the BIS that emerges from Fraser's words. "BIS core management is formed through selection of the most outstanding experts from each country. However, it is made up of a large number of theorists and few practitioners." As Fraser saw it, the role of the BIS president was to "gather together and weed out the arguments of these so-called theorists and move them into the realm of practical theory." If the president did not "show up for work every day even if there were nothing to do, then the BIS could get overcome by theory and become unable to move." Fraser said that he himself had experienced "considerable pains" on this point. While Kano asked if there were not "any good candidates who could come from the US" as Fraser's successor, Fraser replied that – as seen in this chapter – the United States had adopted a policy of nonintervention in not just the BIS but the entire European reparations issue, and the FRB was legally restricted from holding shares of BIS stock.

Fraser's path embodies something of a negative image of the relationship between the United States and the BIS – or more generally speaking, relations between the United States and Europe. When Europe was entangled in the issue of reparations from World War I, it was the American outsider Fraser who was sent to the leadership of the new BIS. As seen in the preceding chapter, after returning from Europe to the United States, Fraser spoke up as a firm critic of the Bretton Woods system. At a time when the United States and Europe were at a distance from each other, he went to work at a new bank in Europe, but when the IMF was established under US sponsorship and was ready to welcome in the nations of Europe, he was an outspoken critic of this system. From the footsteps of Fraser, who took his life right before the end of World War II, emerges an alternative vision for the twentieth century.

5   Neoliberalism as an alternative

International currency issues and the
Bank for International Settlements in
the 1950s and 1960s

Washington, DC, 1971. Just before the Nixon Shock, in June 1971 a man testified before a hearing of the US Congress. He was Milton Gilbert, Jacobsson's
successor as head of the BIS Monetary and Economic Department. He testified,

> I would like to say, finally, that a very important factor in keeping the
> expansion of the Euro-currency market in check would be a fundamental
> readjustment of the United States' balance-of-payments deficit. While it is
> possible to imagine there being a Euro-currency market without this persist-
> ent deficit, I believe the deficit has been a major force which explains the
> dynamic expansion of the market.[1]

The postwar international currency system had, with restoration of convertibility
of European currencies at the end of the 1950s, appeared to be as firm as a rock.
However, this system – the controversial Bretton Woods system – had reached a
turning point soon after the start of the 1960s. In the face of the development of
circumstances unexpected under the Bretton Woods structure – loss of confidence in the pound and the dollar and, furthermore, the growth in the Eurocurrency markets discussed above by Gilbert – Gilbert argued that the US
international balance of payments deficits were the root of the problem, which
was obviously different from the arguments for easing international regulation
and welcoming Eurocurrency markets.

   But why did the head of the BIS Monetary and Economic Department present
before Congress a point of view that differed from the argument welcoming the
Eurocurrency markets? And what was the meaning of the readjustment of the US
balance of payments deficits? The subject of this chapter is an examination of developments at the BIS in the 1950s and 1960s from the perspectives of trends in the
international currency system during this period – at a "market" level – and the
development of neoliberalism – at the level of "ideas" – starting from these questions. While the subject of neoliberalism was touched on in the Foreword, here we
consider neoliberalism to represent the general system of thought oriented in Europe,
that tolerated national intervention while based on trust in markets – and as such it
was not simply an argument for deregulation – and valued currency stability above
all – and as such it aimed to restrict unregulated growth in financial instruments.

Below, Section 1 will examine the point of view of the BIS on gold and the dollar crisis, and Section 2 will look at the responses of the BIS in the early years of the Eurocurrency markets. Section 3 will look at the arguments over international capital movements during the 1960s, and Section 4 will take up the turning point in the BIS's response in the face of the sterling crisis. Section 5 will examine the BIS banking business and distribution of its earnings. Section 6 concludes.

1 Gold and the dollar crisis: another prescription

Around 1958, the leading nations had restored convertibility of their currencies, and at this point it appeared that the gold–dollar standard had entered a period of stability. However, as the weaknesses in this system gradually were exposed over the 1960s, uneasiness about the dollar, the core currency in this system, developed. The economist Robert Triffin described his views on these circumstances in "Gold and the Dollar Crisis,"[2] turning the focus once again to problems with the design concepts of the international currency system regarding gold.

In this situation, the BIS played its unique role based on its experience since the prewar era in gold-related businesses. The subject of this section is to examine this course of developments from the BIS's point of view. The examination will begin from the developments in the 1950s, a little earlier than the period covered by this chapter.

BIS gold operations: business and concepts in the 1950s

While the gold operations by the BIS went through a downturn since the end of World War II, trading between the BIS and central banks of member countries became active in the 1950s. In this business, in light of "recent practices," the BIS Banking Department permitted the BIS gold position to "fluctuate between 1 ton above and 10 tons below the limit we fixed."[3] This base amount is that corresponding to BIS equity (as of 1951, 196 million Gold Swiss francs).

To the BIS at that time, the focal point was this breadth of fluctuation. This band of 11 tons from maximum to minimum was "small if circumstances normalized quickly and if event buying and selling trades were to become more active," but also "too large in the lack of buyers at reasonable prices." This meant that, if central banks instructed conversion of their gold deposits with the BIS into dollars, then the BIS would suffer losses if it could not arrange the required amount in dollars. There were concerns about the cases where the BIS were to "hold 'abundant' gold – that is, 10 tons more than the base amount."

What were conceivable measures to be taken by the BIS at that time? The BIS Banking Department considered the trading of gold certificates (*certificats d'or*) or the intervention in gold markets through brokers. The latter market intervention in particular – which the Banque de France had already implemented but appeared to have abandoned completely – was a measure that might impede free trade in gold and dollars. The Banking Department saw such intervention in gold markets as involving "the risk of blame" of the BIS by the new international institution the IMF. However, it also argued that the "moral position" of the IMF would be limited because "this institution [the IMF] is not unified, with part of members supporting the BIS's view." In its conclusion, this Banking Department memo expressed the view that if through the above intervention measures European central banks came to recognize that the "BIS is always in the precious metals markets," then such central banks would be likely to "place dollar deposits with the BIS particularly for the purpose of forming pools."[4] The BIS paid attention to the imbalance between gold and the dollar as early as in 1951 and made plans for market intervention which might violate the terms of the IMF agreement. The BIS expected that pools of dollars would be created within the BIS through such intervention, pressing for the cooperation of European central banks – one can see here the unique position of the BIS drawing a line between it and the IMF.

In fiscal 1954, the London gold markets reopened. The BIS annual report stated that in the London markets "under normal conditions as it did before the war ... the Bank was able to maintain a certain volume of operations and thus to continue to be of service to the central banks." However, it noted that the BIS obtained no appreciable profit.[5] Following is an example of the Banking Department's gold operations against this background – gold operations in connection with the support for the Bank of England in 1955.[6]

1   In October 1955, the BIS sold 3,200 kg in gold at a price of $34.96⅞ cent per ounce, receiving the proceeds in dollars. It lent these dollars at an interest rate of 2 percent per year.

2   The BIS had to purchase gold at a market price of $34.99⅛ cent per ounce or less to cover the amount equivalent to the annual interest rate and to ensure the bank could repurchase the same weight in gold without suffering losses. However, it could not find any offers to sell gold at this price.

3   For this reason, first of all three tons of gold would be purchased from the Bank of England at 34.985 dollars per ounce, "to square our gold position and to assist the Bank of England."

4   The Bank of England would receive, in its own account with the BIS, approximately $7 million in gold proceeds. The BIS would immediately exchange $5 million of this amount for US Treasury bills (maturing at the end of the year, discounted at 2.10 percent).

5   The BIS would use the $5 million received from the Bank of England to purchase sterling and immediately buy British treasuries.

In summary, this was an operation in which gold that could not be bought on the market was sold by the Bank of England at a beneficial price, with the pound bought to support and British treasuries purchased it in return. The BIS made the following calculations for this transaction:

Assuming a yield of $3^{15}/_{16}$ percent p.a. on the UK Treasury Bills our return on this transaction will be at the rate of $2^{5}/_{8}$ percent p.a., i.e., a net gain of $^{5}/_{8}$ percent p.a. or approximately SF 24,000.

If the position could not be restored in the gold markets, then as part of central-bank cooperation central banks would be asked to provide beneficial prices. However, even in such a case the BIS would secure profit as a bank. These were the operations that the Banking Department advanced during this period. While the BIS annual report described such gold operations left the BIS "a very narrow margin"[7] of remuneration because the purchases, sales and exchanges of gold were "effected on the basis of the official prices applied by the central banks." This probably should be seen as the indication that the BIS pursued profits enough to ensure that no losses were suffered in normalization of the gold position at the very least.

The course of developments to that point can be summarized as follows. Until the reopening of the London market, the BIS accepted large amounts of gold deposits in place of this market and achieved a good performance in gold operations. This appeared in the form of actions to provide gold options in accordance with the interests of European central banks in particular and to earn income on its own as well. Even after the London markets reopened, this stance continued. However, at the same time these operations triggered a dollar crisis as they involved purchase of gold from the FRB (i.e., sale of dollars by the BIS).

But how did the BIS in the second half of the 1950s recognize the relationship between gold and the dollar as these gold operations by the BIS advanced? A theoretical consideration indicating this recognition was completed in November 1956 by the deputy head of the Banking Department, Donald MacDonald, and provided for core management to read.[8] Let's take a look at this document.

After overviewing the relationship between gold and the dollar at the time, in his memo MacDonald then asked himself whether it was a good policy to hold gold in preparation for circumstances such as those of a world war. He stated that even when holding gold, doing so would be ineffective if the gold could not be converted to currency – in fact, the only buyer of gold for dollars was the United States. He also summarized US plans concerning then current gold prices as follows: (1) The US Treasury Department was the residuary buyer of the world's residual gold production. Without the support of Treasury, the price of gold would drop; (2) It chiefly was the Soviet Union that would gain from rising gold prices. In summary, he analyzed that on these two points the price of gold, whether increasing or decreasing, was not a primary factor to the United States. In light of these views – that buying gold was meaningless and the price of gold would remain unchanged – MacDonald concluded that "no political tension in Europe or Asia can immediately change the par value of the dollar."

At the same time, MacDonald, touching on a memo submitted in the same period by the head of the Banking Department, van Zeeland, analyzed traditional BIS gold policies and commented that the BIS had put such great value on gold as to "keep its own funds in gold" and that it had given the highest priority to "the value which our [the BIS] operations have for the community of central banks." He described these policies as being oriented toward stability, stating that their objective had been "to smooth out fluctuations in the relationship between the US dollar and gold." Disagreeing with this existing policy, Mac-Donald recommended a standard of holding roughly five tons in gold over the short term instead of holding excess gold. He also clearly called for a policy of securing operating income. "We aim primarily to give service to our customers but we like to run our banking operations on a commercial basis." At the end of this memo, he concluded with the recognition that the BIS is "beginning to occupy a very special position in the field of gold." Reviewing the traditional BIS recognition of the gold markets as having been "proved wrong many times," he stated that the BIS seemed "to exaggerate the short-term potential value of holding a surplus in gold and the risk of being short on the spot of a few tons of gold."

Later, BIS gold trading grew in leaps and bounds, becoming more technically precise as well. In April 1959, the Banking Department considered the possibility of options trading in gold and US Treasuries.[9] In June of the same year, gold and dollar options trading was considered between a European central bank and the BIS.[10] The following day, June 19, 1959, MacDonald again completed an internal memo titled "Gold."[11] This memo systematically outlined the BIS's gold operations through that point in time and indicated a course of action for the future. Now let's take a look at this memo.

First, the memo described three objectives of BIS gold option trades: (1) having European central banks buy gold at low prices on spot markets, without relying on the FRB, (2) decreasing gold demand from the US Treasury Department, and (3) earning income by the BIS. This memo was somewhat self-congratulatory in that it stated that the BIS gold operations satisfied the demands from Canada, the Soviet Union and other countries for sale of gold while also providing appropriate prices to the central banks, the buyers, and "tended to stabilize the price and to give a certain solidity to what could otherwise be a very thin London market." Furthermore, over about a half-year period from January 1 through June 16, 1959 the BIS purchased 286 tons of gold (averaging 52 tons per month) "to cover options not exercised during that time." During the same period, the BIS purchased only 28 tons of gold – no more than 10 percent of the gold purchased during the period – from the Federal Bank of New York. The BIS memo stated that the Federal Bank of New York "has every reason to be pleased with this result." However, since the purchase of gold from New York evidenced that gold options had swollen so excessively that the BIS was unable to purchase enough gold to cover them on the London market, the Banking Department expressed its view that, "25 tons per month would be manageable and would create a valuable stabilizing force for the London market." In light of the above considerations, the Banking Department forecasted that the BIS could maintain sufficient ability to buy gold in response to seasonal sales from the Soviet Union and Canada in the second half of 1959 by setting a target of 25 tons per month for options trades.

In October 1959, the possibility of gold–dollar swaps was studied. A memo studying these swap operations – also authored by MacDonald – described swaps as grounded in a "different philosophy" from that of ordinary lending operations. That is, in swaps "no-one is a borrower, no-one a lender." The memo expressed its view that, for example, by entering into gold–dollar swap contracts with central banks the BIS would support the gold and foreign reserves of those countries and, at the same time, these swaps would assist the BIS "to get gold deposits/currency deposits a little cheaper by appealing to someone wanting to place gold with us."[12]

These business concepts and performance by the Banking Department each can be said to indicate that the BIS was on the path of attempting to secure business profit while keeping in mind its role of holding "a very special position in the field of gold." It was MacDonald, the deputy head of the Banking Department, who had leadership in this area.

At the same time, it is quite interesting that these concepts of the Banking Department often took the form of criticism of van Zeeland's plans. At the time the above memo was submitted, van Zeeland was head of the Banking Department (he resigned in 1962) – the direct superior to Deputy Head MacDonald. Here one can sense some discord between the younger generation in the Banking Department, including MacDonald and van Zeeland, who stood on his experience since the prewar years.

Through the end of the 1950s, BIS gold operations attempted to secure revenues for the BIS itself while also serving the interests of the "community of central banks" of stabilizing the London gold markets and restraining outflows of gold from the FRB. Overall, there was an optimistic tone to views of this crisis in the Bretton Woods system itself.

But how did this business and these concepts develop in the face of the gold and dollar crisis? The policy arguments of neoliberalism reemerged to the forefront.

The gold and dollar crisis as seen from the BIS

Already there has been an abundance of research on the crisis in the Bretton Woods system which became apparent in dollar instability and on the various plans to overcome that crisis. The process of intensification of the crisis, which led to the suspension of gold–dollar convertibility, also has been studied from various theoretical positions, and this book will not offer any comprehensive new theory on these subjects. Here we will attempt to provide an answer to the question of how the BIS viewed the Bretton Woods system at that time. While the BIS responded to this crisis as a venue for cooperation between central banks and a backstage player, at the same time, as touched on above it also presented its own unique plan as one actor. This plan – to go straight to its conclusion – took a perspective slightly different from the arguments of the time concerning "the gold and dollar crisis" and "gold or the dollar," while resonating with the theoretical positions of Jacobsson, who at the time had already left the BIS for the position of IMF managing director. While this point of view would appear somewhat dimmed amid later arguments seething around the Nixon Shock, it can be considered to be an extension of the neoliberalism focused on in this chapter and has had a significant impact on international currency-system theory until now.

But just what was the gold and dollar crisis to begin with? As is well known, the relevant theory is of crisis based on a liquidity dilemma theory as argued by Triffin. The liquidity dilemma theory argues that even as US current account deficits continued to provide international liquidity, they simultaneously led to decreased confidence in the dollar as reserve currency. Triffin warned that the Bretton Woods system eventually would reach a dead end due to this liquidity dilemma. His proposed response of "internationalization of foreign-currency reserves" was tinted by Keynesian utopianism. Triffin also criticized the "revisions to gold prices" and "floating exchange-rate systems," which became hot topics at the time as proposed solutions to the situation.[13]

How did the BIS response to these circumstances? First of all, let's look at the BIS's actual response to the gold and dollar crisis. In 1961 central banks entered into a succession of international currency adjustment arrangements – the Basel Agreement (March 1961) and the Gold Pool Agreement (October 1961) – aiming to stabilize the relationship between gold and the dollar.[14] The BIS supported these countermeasures against the gold and dollar crisis behind the scenes. These measures were oriented toward the stabilization of gold prices more than anything else, as extensions of the course seen above advocated by the Banking Department – securing the revenues of the BIS itself while providing preferential treatment to central banks in forms such as gold, dollar and options trading – clearly distinct from the plans offered by Triffin.

Incidentally, from a theoretical perspective the BIS, in its annual report released in 1963, offered a direct counterargument against Triffin, without identifying him by name:

> As international financial co-operation has been active in extending the scope and flexibility of resources available for liquidity needs, it is surprising to find in much of this criticism the implication that obstinate financial conservatism is the essential barrier to the solution of what are in fact profound difficulties.[15]

The BIS countered this as follows: (1) "There is no simple functional relation between the need for some aggregate of official liquid resources and the volume of world trade"; (2) "the liquidity available to a particular country" to meet payment imbalances is not limited to its reserves but includes "the international credit to which it can have access"; (3) "while reserves of foreign exchange are liquidity to the country which holds them, they mean reduced liquidity to the country whose currency is being held abroad"; and (4) "Hence, the adequacy of liquidity cannot be evaluated in global terms."[16] In the conclusion to the Annual report, Gabriel Ferras, the BIS general manager, touched on the results of reforms such as those to special IMF arrangements and then, in the final paragraph, provided the statement quoted below. Incidentally, as Guillaume Guindey's successor Ferras was the fourth BIS general manager from France.[17]

> None the less, there has been a steady stream of suggestions for more fundamental redesigning of the international financial system to increase the volume of liquid resources and to make them available more easily. What must be recognized, however, is that behind liquid resources there must be real resources, and that none of the main industrial countries considers it reasonable to supply a continuous stream of real resources to any other member of the group. The functioning of the international payments system depends less in the end on the technicalities of the mechanism itself than on the policies pursued in the different countries.[18]

The outline of the criticisms of Triffin that one can sense from the implicit descriptions of this BIS annual report perhaps can be summarized as follows: The proposals for "fundamental reforms" to the international financial system – Triffin's argument – lacked the backing of such real resources. A proposal like Triffin's, calling for reorganization of the IMF and regional currency union concerned no more than "the technicalities of the mechanism itself." Instead of that, what was needed at the time was "the policies pursued in the different countries" – needless to say the US international balance of payments policies.

Jacobsson too shared the above BIS criticisms of Triffin. Jacobsson, who met with Triffin in 1962, was sharply critical in his journal: "There is something pathetic about Triffin – he is not an intelligent man and has a fair amount of knowledge – but he has no deep insight, and he thinks in terms of 'gadgets'."[19]

Of course, at the time the BIS's criticisms of Triffin were written Jacobsson had moved on to the position of IMF managing director, and at the time the report was published he already had passed away. For this reason, one cannot see Jacobsson as having contributed formally to the argument in the BIS annual report. For this reason, perhaps Jacobsson's criticisms of Triffin will provide a clue to the existence of a larger current of thought including both BIS authorities and Jacobsson.

But just what was this current of thought? For now, let's look at just two illustrations. One is a book of journalism cited by Triffin himself in the first edition of his *Gold and the Dollar Crisis*. Here Triffin cited the following criticism of the mass media as a description of old-fashioned theory in opposition to his own: The villains pulling the strings behind inflation were identified as Harvard's Gottfried Haberler in the area of money supply, Jacques Rueff of Paris in the area of fiscal policy with no government restrictions, Harvard's Edward Chamberlain in the area of labor unions, and Erik Lindhal of Uppsala in Sweden in all of these areas plus antitrust.[20]

Haberler, Rueff, Lindahl and the others cited here by Triffin – with some scorn – all are neoliberals who either knew Jacobsson or were admired by him.

These neoliberals focused – to use Jacobsson's own expression – on the "balance between costs and prices."

Another illustration is in a letter by Jacobsson himself. Dated January 23, 1963, this was a long letter sent by Jacobsson to the Japanese researcher Zentaro Matsumura. Here he discusses dollar countermeasures deducing the policy theory of the above neoliberals. At the time, as IMF managing director, Jacobsson had announced dollar countermeasures based on IMF loans – known as the Jacobsson Plan – and this announcement had created a stir as it was misunderstood in some quarters as a call for restoration of the gold standard. This letter is a response to Matsumura, who had asked Jacobsson's true views at that time. It included the statements, "US balance of payments deficits have played an important role in economic recovery in the nations of Western Europe and helped those nations accumulate foreign reserves to satisfactory levels"; "The job that remains is that of achieving an appropriate restoration of equilibrium on both sides of the Atlantic"; and,

> If wage controls continue in the US in the future and interest rates are not reduced, then my hope is that eventually a state will be reached in which US gold reserves do not fall massively and dollar balances held by foreign countries do not increase massively.[21]

Viewed from today's point of view, it might be easy to be struck by the optimistic tone of Jacobsson's forecasts or to point out the lukewarm nature of the Jacobsson Plan among the various proposals for IMF reform. However, what is highly interesting from the perspective of this chapter is the fact that the BIS and Jacobsson shared the perspective that the gold and dollar crisis could be avoided through achieving balance between costs and prices and that originally the gold and dollar crisis did not exist in the form argued by Triffin, and furthermore that this point of view represented a firm level of continuity along the line of neoliberal economic thinking that spread across Europe in the twentieth century.

Next, we will focus on the Eurocurrency markets as another factor shaking the Bretton Woods system together with – or resonating with – uncertainty about the dollar.

2 Eurocurrency markets and the BIS

What are the Eurocurrency markets? According to the definition used by BIS authorities at the time, the most important currency in the Eurocurrency markets, the Eurodollar, referred to "ordinary dollars at short term or sight by the owner (who is usually resident outside the United States) with a bank or financial institution outside the USA."[22] While such deposit currencies also were in existence prior to World War II, what was new about the Eurocurrency markets was "the scale on which it is now taking place, the extent to which operations are conducted across national frontiers and, perhaps, the degree of competition among banks for foreign currency deposits."[23]

It is said that the Eurocurrency markets has its roots in the operations of private-sector British banks at the end of the 1950s. That is, in response to the restrictions on capital movements enacted in Britain at that time Midland Bank and other corporate banks began investing deposits accepted in foreign currency (in this case, dollars) as foreign currency, instead of converting it to domestic currency (pounds sterling).[24]

But what was the BIS's recognition of this formation of Eurocurrency markets? Actually, this question embodies two separate questions stemming from the dual nature of the BIS itself. The first is the question of when the BIS, as a "regulator" of international markets, recognized the existence of these Euro-currency markets, and the second is that of how the BIS, which itself was a "commercial bank" too, acted in response to these markets.

Delays in market recognition and proximity to international institutions

Let's start by looking at the first point. The first meeting held by the BIS regarding the Eurocurrency markets was a meeting of personnel responsible for foreign exchange, convened May 6, 1961 by the Monetary and Economic Department. This meeting in Basel, which gathered together officials involved in actual operations at each central bank, merely exchanged information on markets.[25]

It was in 1962 that the BIS formally began setting up an organization to specialize in handling such markets – the Meeting of Experts on the Eurocurrency Market. This meeting of experts was periodically timed to coincide with the monthly meetings of central-bank governors at the BIS, providing opportunities for exchange of information and policy proposals concerning Eurocurrency markets.[26] The BIS Monetary and Economic Department provided information to and coordinated discussions in this meeting of experts.

At first, this meeting of experts merely discussed defining of the nature of Eurodollars, without conducting specific collection of statistics or analysis of information,[27] demonstrating that the BIS's response to the formation of the Eurocurrency markets got off to a fairly late start.

At the same time, the BIS acted quickly on the stage of international currency negotiations. In this aspect, its participation in Working Party 3 (WP3) of the Organization for Economic Co-operation and Development (OECD) was quite important to the BIS: the BIS claimed both to itself and to others to serve as "a club of central banks," it had not participated in the OECD, in which governments and fiscal authorities held considerable authority. However, in 1963 the BIS began participating in the WP3 as an observer, to provide information on international financial markets.[28] The fact that the BIS had stepped away from its previous identity as a club of central banks to take part in an international network was highly significant. First, while as seen in the preceding chapter in the 1950s the BIS was in charge of practical operations for intra-European settlement in the 1950s as an agent for the EPU. However, it had lost some of its business in Europe with the dissolution of the EPU (in 1958).[29] The BIS was required to participate in international institutions to secure new domains for its business activities. Second, the proximity between the BIS and the OECD in response to the formation of the Eurocurrency markets served as the basis for the later formation of the meetings between finance ministers and central-bank governors of the leading ten industrialized nations, or the G10.[30] The G10 was a venue in which the fiscal authorities and central banks of industrialized nations came together in one place to discuss international currency issues and other matters. As seen in the preceding chapter, the relations between fiscal authorities and central banks in each country showed discord around the time of World War II and relations between the US Treasury Department and the BIS in particular were strained in connection with the issue of Nazi gold. This participation by the BIS in the WP3 served as an opportunity for close cooperation between the fiscal authorities and central banks of each country and the BIS, overcoming such background.

The BIS swap business

Now, how did the BIS conduct itself in the markets? As seen above, unlike funds and institutions such as the IMF the BIS also had aspects of a commercial bank, taking deposits and creating credit. Facing the formation of Eurocurrency markets, the BIS acted as a market participant in its own right while also carrying out surveys and research and exchanging information with international institutions. The Banking Department was in charge of these activities, which were conducted through the method of the "swap" business.[31]

A swap is an arrangement by which multiple participants – central banks, private-sector banks, and international institutions such as the BIS – swap currency on hand under certain conditions. While the actual exercise of these arrangements was subject to each agreement by the participants, swap arrangements functioned to send the market messages that speculation would be restrained even if not exercised. Also, since swaps were conducted off the balance sheet they also had the benefit of being able to be concluded and exercised dynamically without relying on the intents of regulators, shareholders, or others.

To the best of my knowledge, the BIS swap business appears to have begun at the end of the 1940s. To use the example of France, in August 1949 the term "swap" was used between the Banque de France and the BIS, and an actual arrangement was concluded between them.[32] Beginning at the start of the 1950s, the BIS concluded swap arrangements mainly with the Bank of England, which called for the BIS to provide dollars and the Bank of England to receive pounds.[33]

Viewing from the standpoint of the BIS Banking Department, this swap business involved two aspects. In the first, it served as a means of emergency aid to enable BIS member states to avoid currency crises, and in the second it served as a means by which the BIS itself could earn revenues. The BIS swap business developed in a manner that intertwined these two aspects. Let's look at an example from Great Britain. The swap arrangements concluded with the Bank of

England in the 1950s served as an arrangement by which the BIS could receive pounds and invest them in British Treasury bills. However, some within the BIS criticized this investment in Treasury bills as not providing sufficient returns.[34] For this reason, the BIS opened special accounts with city banks in London as substitute targets for investment. The BIS could place deposits in these banks up to a maximum equivalent to $50 million.[35] As seen here, BIS swap arrangements in response to the sterling crisis were, at the same time, grounded in the Banking Department's own motivation to secure revenues. Incidentally, the BIS, which at this point in time had not yet recognized the existence of the Eurocurrency markets, later would list the amount of its own swap operations in statistics as a structural element of Eurocurrency.[36]

Together with the development of the Eurocurrency markets, BIS swaps came to be used as a means of regulating and adjusting markets – that is, as the aid measured mentioned above. Under the Basel Agreement touched on in the preceding section, swap operations were used as a means of intervention. A member of the staff of the US State Department who analyzed the BIS swap business independently in the late 1960s assessed this swap business based on the Basel Agreement as "the primary activity of the BIS in recent years," noting that

> this activity in the swap network has given the BIS a new lease on life as its assets have increased by one billion dollars in the three years after 1963, as much as the increase that took place in the previous seven years.[37]

Furthermore, in December 1963 Hans Mandel, the head of the BIS Banking Department, proposed the formation of a network of central banks for multilateral swaps known as gold exchange swaps. According to Mandel, restoration of convertibility of European currencies at the end of the 1950s had been incomplete because it was dependent on the dollar. He envisioned European states countering a likely dollar crisis through building a network, based in the BIS, for swaps between gold and each country's currency.[38] While this plan was not realized, it shows that the BIS itself overlooked a crisis of the dollar as the Eurocurrency markets and swap networks were developing.

3 Dispute on international capital movements: regulation or laissez-faire?

As seen in the preceding section, in the first half of the 1960s the BIS came to recognize the existence of the Eurocurrency markets and even actually took part in such markets through swaps. On this aspect a dispute arose concerning whether Eurocurrency markets should be regulated or left to grow on their own.

December 1963: the start of the dispute

The dispute began at the BIS in December 1963. Milton Gilbert, the head of the Monetary and Economic Department at that time sent questionnaires to the governors of the central banks of leading BIS member states asking how the Eurocurrency markets should be addressed. Those questionnaires were also intended to gather opinions for arrangement of the agenda for the monthly meeting of central-bank governors to be held in January of the following year.

As responses were sent back to the BIS, a backstage dispute began even before the formal debate started. The first impetus was the response from France. The response, sent in the name of the director-general of foreign services of the Banque de France, sounded the following warning about the Eurocurrency markets: "One must not underestimate the risk of using short-term deposits for longer-term lending." Citing the example of the bankruptcy of a borrower of funds in the Eurocurrency markets, Banque de France authorities made demands concerning the BIS's handling, calling on the BIS Monetary and Economic Department to describe these risks of the Eurocurrency markets "in a more detailed form" in its reports.[39]

Upon receiving the response from France, Gilbert, immediately responded to France. Gilbert wrote a letter to André de Lattre, the director of Foreign Finance in the French finance ministry, who had attended the G10 meeting mentioned above. There he stated that "care must be taken not to give up the advantages of the present system." And France's criticisms of Eurocurrency markets were "a bit like locking the stable after the horse has gone." Also, regarding the bankruptcy example, he wrote that "a new situation of danger does not arise again in the future," because each central bank had stored up sufficient foreign reserves "because of an excessive outflow of dollars from the United States."[40] As can be seen from this text, Gilbert was of the optimistic view that saw excessive dollars as a source of funding to avoid risks in the Eurocurrency markets. Its logical framework differed completely from the above foreign-exchange swap plans of the head of the Banking Department, Mandel – which proposed swaps of gold and each country's currency based on the premise of lack of confidence in the dollar.

Following the above preparatory stage, on January 23, 1964 the meeting of central-bank governors was held in Basel. The meeting, which BIS President Holtrop presided at, became the site of intense argument over the Eurocurrency markets between the two extremes of laissez-faire approach and regulation approach.

In the meeting, the representatives of the British, American and West German central banks each expressed optimistic views of the Eurocurrency markets. Alfred Hayes, president of the Federal Bank of New York, emphasized the strong points of these markets as follows: the Eurocurrency markets brought "greater efficiency in the channeling of short-term capital" and "facilitated a leveling of interest rates." George Baring, third Earl of Cromer governor of the Bank of England, stated, that he was "not worried about the Euro-dollar market in London; no limit had been put on foreign deposits in united Kingdom banks, although some ceilings had been imposed on foreign exchange spot and forward positions." Even in the event of losses in New York markets, "no serious difficulty had arisen so far and that the banks were acting soundly," said Cromer.

Also, Bundesbank president, Karl Blessing, after noting that some observers "have been trying to make comparisons between the present situation of the euro-dollar market and what had happened in the early 1930s," denounced that there are "no grounds for such comparison."[41]

In contrast, Banque de France Governor Jacques Brunet argued for caution. While Brunet did not discuss "whether the market was good or bad," but insisted that "the central banks were justified in regarding it with a certain amount of suspicion." He made an important remark that "the French authorities would not allow the conversion of Euro-dollars into French francs."[42]

While conflict between central banks became clear, at the same time a consensus also was formed. President Hayes of the Federal Reserve Bank of New York "saw some danger of over-extension of credit to one or a few borrowers and of inadequate checking between countries of the credit-worthiness of borrowers"; Cromer too pointed "that when the [commercial] banks conduct Euro-dollar business they should be clear as to whether they are granting credits or carrying out foreign transactions"; Brunet, for his part, said that "there was no necessity for rigid controls" and "as regards capital movements, some flexibility had to be maintained." Holtrop, as the president of the meeting, summed up these discussions, as follows: "there might be problems in connection with the Euro-dollar market but they were not essentially different from the problems that existed in relation to international short-term capital movements in general."[43]

Specifically, the problem in the Eurocurrency markets brought up in this meeting of central-bank governors was the fact that Eurocurrency funds, separated from the regulations of the authorities, were used in loans where actual conditions were unclear, posing a threat to credit in the market as a whole. At the time, a number of examples already had been reported. For example, in May 1963 – about half a year prior to the above governors' meeting – the Bank of England circulated an internal memo on the state of improper use of Eurodollars. The memo stated, "One banker [American] told me today that Euro-dollars were being used in one instance by a mortgage and loan association in Munich to lend on long-term mortgage although the funds were borrowed at short term." The writer of this note closed his correspondence: "A case for flying some danger signals?"[44] This unease proved on the mark in November 1963 – one month before the above governors' meeting. A credit crisis that erupted in a chain of events arising from a scandal concerning product handling by a New York cooking oil firm involved other parties including London banks as well, in the end leading to the bankruptcy of well-known New York Brokerage Ira Haupt and Co.[45]

When compared to these scandals that had arisen immediately before the meeting of central-bank governors, the tone of the January 1964 meeting seems quite optimistic. At that time, the BIS Monetary and Economic Department too took a passive approach to adding restrictions to Eurocurrency markets. These circumstances changed completely over the second half of the 1960s. The impetus for this change was a sterling crisis.

The Bank of England and the BIS: responding to the sterling crisis

In 1964, Eurocurrency markets underwent further growth. While following the bankruptcy drama on the stage of the Eurocurrency markets mentioned above the market growth had lulled temporarily from the end of 1963 through the start of 1964, later the scale of the markets showed growth again. By the end of 1964, the number of banks participating in the markets grew to 400, and the number of nationalities of participating banks rose from 25 to 35. According to a BIS report, the dollar positions of the reporting countries, between March and September 1964, "showed an increase in total liabilities by 13 percent, from $11,340 to 12,780 million." "The main factor behind the growth of the market," analyses the report, "was the increase in the UK banking system's foreign indebtedness."[46]

During the same period, the international currency and financial systems too experienced important changes. An increase in the US international balance of payments deficit accelerated the decrease in the value of the dollar. In response to these circumstances, the US Treasury Department and other authorities began restrictions on external investment. Starting with the 1963 tax reforms, the US government came to restrict investment in dollars from the United States to other countries, followed by the voluntary restraints on foreign-investment and com-pulsory investment restrictions.[47]

These defensive measures to protect the dollar exerted a major impact on the Eurocurrency markets. The US restrictions made it more difficult for European banks to receive dollar deposits. As a result, Eurodollar interest rates in Europe rose rapidly. This was "the tightening of Eurodollars." The sterling crisis erupted in the middle of this situation.[48] The sterling crisis demonstrated a subtle rela-tionship to Eurocurrency markets and became an impetus prompting changes in the ways international markets were managed and supervised. First, let's sum-marize the international responses to the sterling crisis, focusing on their relation to the BIS.

Since World War II the pound sterling had undergone occasional crises, and in the 1960s international support frameworks had been developed from time to time. Already since the start of the 1960, 15 central banks participating in the European Monetary Agreement (EMA), the successor organization to the EPU, had concluded support arrangements to support the pound and these had been extended several times.[49] Separately from these, in March 1963 and in October 1964 France, West Germany, Italy and Switzerland established a *bilateral con-certé* framework in an amount equivalent to $250 million for bilateral intervention to support the pound.[50] It should be noted here that in all of the various frameworks above to support the pound – from informal central-bank cooperation such as the *bilateral concerté* to EMA support – the BIS played the role of secretariat. From these developments, it can be seen that at the same time it played a behind-the-scenes role in the Eurocurrency markets, the BIS also stepped forward to play a coordinating role in international responses to the sterling crisis.

On the subject of the BIS's own role in supporting the pound, a letter from Frederik Conolly of the BIS Monetary and Economic Department to the vice president of the Federal Reserve Bank of New York, Charles Coombs, showed foresight. Conolly wrote his letter in March 1963 – at the time when the *bilateral concerté* was being established to support the pound. There Conolly introduced the method of this intervention as "modeled fairly closely on what the federal reserve bank of New York is now doing" and says "the inspiration for all this comes rather obviously from the Basel arrangements of 1961." According to Conolly, the *bilateral concerté*, which was centered on swap arrangements, had the advantages of a high level of confidentiality among participating nations and also enabling dynamic intervention, since it did not go through the decision-making processes of the OECD or the EMA. He described the roles performed by the BIS within this framework as (1) serving as a depository for letters from each central bank taking part in the framework, (2) acting as a center for information exchange among participants, and furthermore, (3) reporting to the EMA board. Conolly stated in his letter, "you will, I think, agree that the scheme is tailored to your fashion," urging the Fed to participate in this framework "in any way they may choose, formally of informally."[51]

The BIS strategy as described by Conolly was one of consolidating informal bilateral swap arrangements into the formal EMA framework, through having the BIS arrange them. As mentioned hereinafter, how the United States would respond to this framework was a point that would have a significant impact on the development of the Eurocurrency markets and, furthermore, on the outcomes of sterling and dollar crises.

Beginning in 1965, the BIS took a step beyond this backstage role, starting to conduct swap business on its own account. First of all, on January 10, 1965 Maurice Parsons of the Bank of England met with BIS Banking Department Deputy Head MacDonald, who had formerly worked at the Bank of England. In this meeting, MacDonald of the Banking Department introduced a proposal under which the BIS prepared to act as an "agent" of the Bank of England. MacDonald's proposal called for (1) sale, with the approval of the US Treasury Department, of $100 million in US treasuries held by the BIS to the Bank of England, and (2) resale of those treasuries by the Bank of England to the BIS with two days' notice.[52] This was a typical swap arrangement.

The day after this meeting, on January 11, 1965, MacDonald telephoned Bank of England Deputy Governor Roy Bridge, confirming the BIS proposal. Bridge responded with gratitude for the proposal and stated that the BIS's recommendation would be considered.[53] Furthermore, on the next day, January 12, Bridge and MacDonald conferred by telephone again, indicating agreement to entering into a swap of $100 million held by the BIS to the Bank of England in exchange for pounds sterling. The maturity date of the swap arrangement was agreed to be March 8.[54] The dollar–pound swap arrangement concluded between the BIS and the Bank of England through the above three days of negotiations would be renewed upon its maturity in March 1965.[55]

Bilateral concerté *and multilateral surveillance*

While this swap arrangement would be an important method of managing the Eurocurrency markets, so its relationship to multilateral surveillance emerged as an issue. Let's summarize the arguments on this point.

Multilateral surveillance refers to an arrangement established within the OECD WP3 frameworks. As its name implies, it was intended to manage multilaterally information on swap arrangements, which at the time were being conducted actively on a bilateral basis. A typical example of multilateral surveillance was the meeting held in May 1964, which clarified the relationship between the IMF and the G10 and decided that participant countries would "report promptly, regularly and confidentially, to a designated center, statistical data to show as far as possible the various means utilized to finance surpluses or deficits on their external account."[56] "Center" as used here refers to the BIS. Next, on November 8, 1964, in a meeting of central-bank governors hosted by the BIS methods of implementing multilateral surveillance for multilateral monitoring of market trends were discussed. This multilateral surveillance was based on statistics on the markets of each country collected and distributed by the BIS, and these statistics would provide an overview of the means used by each country to finance its international balance of payments surpluses and deficits.[57]

Incidentally, regarding the relationship between this multilateral surveillance and the BIS, one problem was pointed out in connection with the bilateral swap arrangements – *bilateral concerté* – that developed in the 1960s. When the BIS concluded a swap arrangement in January 1965, MacDonald of the BIS Banking Department made clear that "the BIS did not report any transaction it concluded with a central bank to third parties." However, in a conference held on the same day MacDonald indicated the view that in swaps between the BIS and the Bank of England the latter would itself "wish to report to the Multilateral Surveillance group." As seen above, multilateral surveillance was intended to share information on bilateral arrangements. It would seem logical that the swap arrangements in which the BIS participated directly also should be reported to multilateral surveillance. Regarding this view of the BIS, Bridge of the Bank of England stated only that the bank "was fully aware of its obligations and would comply with them in the manner which was judged to be appropriate."[58] To the Banking Department, which represented the BIS in its role as a bank, individual trades should be confidential. However, to the Monetary and Economic Department, responsible for the BIS's aspects as a forum for cooperation between central banks, even trades conducted on the BIS's own accounts would need to be reported to multilateral surveillance. It cannot be confirmed from available materials which of these two arguments prevailed, or how the swap arrangement between the BIS and the Bank of England was reported. However, a report circulated in the BIS Monetary and Economic Department in April 1965 – titled "Bilateral Concerté and Multilateral Surveillance" – explained in summary that *bilateral concerté* arranged bilaterally was reported to multilateral surveillance "in a satisfactory way" and emphasized that not just the previous participants of

European nations but also the United States and Japan were participating in the multilateral surveillance framework.[59] This meant that in the BIS the aspect of the banking business, of which the Banking Department was in charge, had been consolidated into multilateral cooperation among central banks.

In June 1965, the tightness in Eurodollars disappeared, albeit temporarily. The next year in 1966 the Eurocurrency markets again began moving toward tightening, which raised the issue of the connection between tightening of euro markets and the sterling crisis.

Eurodollar markets and the sterling crisis

Recognition of the crisis first came to be discussed in a meeting of specialists regarding gold, which was held on January 8, 1966 at the BIS. In this meeting, Deputy Governor Bridge of the Bank of England began by stating the following: While US investment restrictions were effective in improving the US international balance of payments, Eurodollar markets had tightened. Johannes Tungeler, representing the Bundesbank, added that West Germany's balance of payments deficit in 1965 had risen to $1.5 billion, of which only $370 million was financed from foreign reserves. The remainder appeared to have been covered by short-term borrowing by West German firms, and this could have led to contraction in short-term funds in Europe. MacDonald of the BIS Banking Department also expressed the recognition that not only Eurodollar markets but European short-term financial markets as a whole had tightened.[60]

But what happened with the sterling crisis at that same time? After rising to £4,472,000,000 in April 1966, Great Britain's sterling balance began to fall, decreasing to £4,020,000,000 in September of that year. To respond to these circumstances, on the morning of Sunday, May 8, 1966 the BIS convened a meeting of specialists on support for the pound. In the evening of that same day, this meeting continued in the form of a meeting of central-bank governors.[61] In June 1966, a BIS agreement was concluded to support the pound. Analysis in a meeting on the operation of this agreement determined that the sterling balance had begun decreasing in February 1966.[62]

On this aspect, the greatest issue was that of whether or not the sterling crisis was a result of the tightening of Eurodollar markets. In the Meeting of Experts on the Eurocurrency Market held at the BIS on July 11–12, 1966, Bridge, representing the Bank of England, brought up this issue. Bridge acknowledged that on one hand funds in London's Eurocurrency markets had undergone an outflow to the United States and Canada while on the other hand there also had been large outflows to countries such as West Germany that had recently had high interest rates. However, emphasizing that these fund movements were due to US policies of international balance of payments and rising US interest rates and that they would occur "mechanically and automatically" in an international market such as London, Bridge argued against the view that a lack of confidence in the pound was the main cause of the situation.[63] As information for this meeting, Bridge also pointed out that the share of US-affiliated banks in the London Eurocurrency markets had risen to roughly 40 percent and that these banks were acquiring Eurodollars and remitting funds to the United States.[64]

In response to Bridge's statement, Gilbert, the BIS Monetary and Economic Department head, opposed. According to Gilbert, the cause of the flight of capital from Britain consisted of not just the external factors cited by Bridge but domestic ones as well. As long as the Bank of England's bank rate was kept low, it was natural that investment funds would turn overseas. In response, Bridge explained that while theoretically it would be possible to raise the bank rate, under current conditions that would be infeasible.[65] In September 1966 conditions worsened further, and at the end of July the deficit in the sterling balance rose by £129 million. It is said that upon seeing this figure participants in the meeting uniformly expressed surprise, and that they had the impression that it was too late to begin measures to counter the deficit. The Meeting of Experts on the same day demonstrated a uniformity of opinion that central-bank cooperation would be needed in the future in order to overcome this difficulty.[66] The current of the debate had shifted even among the BIS and related parties, among whom the argument for a laissez-faire approach had dominated during the formative stages of Eurocurrency markets.

Eurocurrency markets had grown. The BIS and central banks had, despite criticism from France and others, left these markets alone. Nevertheless, as the United States took measures to improve its international balance of payments, market mechanisms functioned to tighten Eurodollar markets. This led to a sterling crisis. Here, we return once again to starting point – regulation or laissez-faire? Next, we will look at the process by which this issue developed into an even more structural-level crisis, in the form of a dollar crisis.

A dollar-swap dispute between the FRB and the EEC

Toward the end of 1966, the BIS and central banks focused their attention on the Eurocurrency markets. The market trends at the end of the year impact the balance sheets of commercial banks for they settle the accounts at the end of the calendar year. They also affect each country's national economic statistics. In November 1966, FRB representative Coombs expressed the expectation that the Eurodollar markets were likely to tighten again towards the end of the year. According to Coombs, this was because during the year US commercial banks had raised $3.5 billion in dollar funds.[67] Meanwhile, during the same period the situation of pound sterling improved. From October through November 1966, Britain's foreign-reserve balance rebounded, and as a result the Bank of England was able to repay its foreign debts completely.[68] Although the situation in Britain had improved, at least temporarily, the tight conditions in Eurodollar markets remained unchanged. In this context, the focal point of debate inside and outside the BIS shifted away from the sterling issue toward the issue of how the dollar should be treated.

The issue of the dollar, or strictly speaking, the issue of the responsibility of US authorities which let the dollar fall in value had arisen in February 1966. The debate began with a conflict between Western European states and the United States. In a meeting on multilateral surveillance held that month, representatives of Western European states brought up the concept of "harmonization" of foreign reserves. This harmonization concept argued for cooperation between the United States and Europe to prop up gold markets as liquidity of foreign reserves decreased when European authorities attempted to release dollar reserves and buy gold in response to the dollar decreasing in value at the same time dollar reserves in the European official sector increased. The European plan called for harmonization of the ratio of gold to dollars in each country's foreign reserves, as an attempt to stabilize currencies. However, US authorities, represented by Coombs of the FRB, rejected this plan based on their argument that the responsibility was with countries holding surpluses.[69] The composition of this dispute was identical to that concerning the response to the dollar crisis in the 1970s.

As such differences between the United States and Europe on responding to the dollar's fall remained unresolved, in September 1966 the United States expanded its own swap network to $4.5 billion, as a response to the drop in the dollar.[70] Viewed from Europe, this US expansion of its swap network appeared to represent a loss of the United States' own currency discipline and to be an act that deviated from the multilateral surveillance framework that had been constructed through cooperation between central banks. Criticism of the United States from this point of view appeared in a December 1966 multilateral surveillance meeting. The European Economic Community (EEC), qualified to take part in this meeting, criticized the FRB's swap network as primarily permitting free drawing of funds by the United States and weakening US discipline in connection with managing its international balance of payments.[71]

In response, Coombs argued that the swap arrangements were bilateral agreements and that liquidity drawn from them was conditional – rarely exceeding nine months. He also stated that the US swap arrangements involved exchange of past dollar claims and did not introduce new obligations.[72] Debate in this meeting continued for two hours, but no consensus could be found. The impression of an authority with the Bank of Japan who attended the meeting was that while the swap network was beneficial, there were major changes in both its size and significance, and that concerning its management there was likely to be a need for discussion with the BIS in the future.[73]

This conflict between the United States and Europe was expressed in concentrated form in the issue of restrictions on the Eurocurrency markets. This refers to the conflicts between (1) the overall frameworks of regulation or laissez-faire, and (2) multilateralism and bilateralism, in the forms of multilateral surveillance or swap networks. Until the previous sterling crisis, with some exceptions and deviations the BIS and individual countries took the approaches of largely maintaining a posture of laissez-faire on the first point and maintaining a multilateral surveillance framework on the second. In fact, while it did not delve into the London market bank supervision and restrictions, through the good offices of the BIS a meeting on supporting the pound was held during the sterling crisis, arranging foreign currency through cooperation among central banks. However, in 1966, on what could be called the eve of the dollar crisis, on the points regarding maintaining a multilateral surveillance framework the United States expanded its swap network and advanced an approach giving priority to its own bilateral negotiations.

But in which direction did the Eurocurrency markets head after this? It was the neoliberal policy theory that comes to the surface at the front of the debate.

4 International financial markets and neoliberalism: where to regulate, and where to take a laissez-faire approach?

The ultimate fate of restrictions: Gilbert's view

When the above US–European dispute was firing up, behind the scenes in international currency diplomacy a consensus was being formed on the Eurocurrency markets. Central-bank governors almost unanimously supported the argument for maintaining the current state of the Eurocurrency markets and adopting a laissez-faire approach toward them. This consensus came into the open in the July 1966 Meeting of Experts on the Eurocurrency Market. In this meeting, the US representative, Fred Klopstock of the Federal Bank of New York, touched on "a number of changes that have recently developed in the Euro-dollar market." After noting the movement of funds from European nations with surpluses to the United States Klopstock stressed that the movement, "of course, is the sort of short-term capital flow called for by economic theory." He also noted "a substantial integration of international money markets during the last year."[74] In response, French representative Marcel Théron, director-general of Foreign Services of the Banque de France – veering from France's past argument for market regulation – noted that French private-sector banks were earning profits from the Eurodollar markets. France had eased restrictions on capital movements in futures markets, enabling French banks to purchase dollar futures through swaps with correspondent banks. These swap correspondents aimed to receive premiums on the dollar by the franc futures, so that they too, along with French banks seeking dollars, profited on the trades. French representative Théron concluded that "the French authorities try to influence the money market in general so as to make it profitable for the commercial banks to retain and to invest their dollar receipts from the start. No direct incentives are used."[75]

Thus, not just the United States but even France, which had been on the vanguard of the argument for regulation, had advanced domestic deregulation and shifted to an argument that regulations were unnecessary internationally as well.

However, it was only the BIS authorities who continued advocating for restrictions on Eurocurrency markets at this time. This argument was proposed by the BIS Monetary and Economic Department head, Gilbert, in a July 1967 Meeting of Experts on the Eurocurrency Market. Gilbert reported on the development of the Eurocurrency markets since 1965, and presented a discussion on the necessity of regulating the size of the market, in cooperation with the central banks.

However, most meeting participants were opposed to restrictions and management of the markets. These opposition were – according to the records of a Japanese representative in attendance – due to the following reasons: (1) they made credit available at low cost for foreign-exchange settlement, (2) countries running deficits could use them to obtain financing for their international balance of payments deficits quickly from other countries' surpluses, and (3) countries running surpluses could use them to avoid excess domestic liquidity resulting from their external surpluses.[76] In fact, according to McClam of the BIS the restrictive measures taken by each country took two forms. The first consisted of restrictions on direct inflows and outflows of short-term funds through intervention in or restrictions on foreign-exchange trading (such as foreign-exchange controls, use of swaps, and position restrictions), and the second consisted of measures directly impacting domestic finance but also indirectly affecting euromoney market trades (such as restrictions on reserve deposits and maximum limits on deposit interest rates). In the second half of the 1960s, even in France, the first type of restrictions disappeared and only the second type remained.

But what happened later – as the age of the dollar crisis arose – to the argument for restrictions that only the BIS authorities continued to advocate?

At the start of this chapter, we quoted the congressional testimony of Gilbert, who argued for readjustment of the US international balance of payments deficit. His argument was repeated at the end of the 1960s as well. Let's look at an example from primary documents. In March 1969, Gilbert and Ferras, the BIS general manager held a confidential meeting with Paul Volcker – at the time he had taken the post of undersecretary for international monetary affairs – of the US Treasury Department. In this meeting, the BIS informed the United States of Europe's concerns about tightening of the Eurodollar market and urged the US government to take more aggressive measures on the international balance of payments. In response, Volcker dismissed this argument, stating, "The US could not guarantee any particular payments balance." Also, when the BIS asked about the response of Congress and others concerning a floating exchange-rate system, which had started to be a topic of discussion in the United States, Volcker expressed the view that there was "very strong support in the academic community, some support in government, and some soft spots in the financial community." It is quite interesting that Gilbert of the BIS here indicated a view critical of a floating exchange-rate system. Keeping in mind the response to the sterling crisis, Gilbert noted, "Any changes or moves to greater flexibility would 'knock off sterling'."[77] Gilbert argued that, while clearly maintaining the Bretton Woods system of fixed exchange rates, nations running deficits such as the United States should take responsibility for international balance of payments adjustments, and that the restrictions needed for this purpose should be adopted internationally. This criticism of floating exchange rates and argument that deficit-running states should bear responsibility truly was a point of view rooted in the genealogy of neoliberalism.

A similar point of view was spoken of in the 1970s as well – in a speech given by a deeply troubled Gilbert upon resigning as head of the BIS Monetary and Economic Department:

When I look back now over fifteen years, I have to admit that in the main thing I tried to accomplish I failed. And that was to convince my own country to take the action necessary to maintain the status of the dollar, to correct the balance-of-payments deficit and to abide by the Bretton Woods system.... It's not only that they did not want to follow me; they were so caught up by the political difficulty in the United States, they couldn't clear their minds enough to even understand me.... You know, they came to treat me not only as wrong, but as a kind of a half-traitor, lined up with Rueff and de Gaulle. Why? Just because I argued that we didn't have to sit on our hands and lose billions of dollars every year – to a total of over sixty-five billions, about five Marshall Plans.[78]

The head of the BIS Monetary and Economic Department had been jeered at as "a half-traitor, lined up with Rueff and de Gaulle." What is interesting here from the perspective of this chapter is the positioning of French neoliberal Rueff.

Rueff's theory: an international neoliberal structure

In 1975, Rueff said of Eurocurrency markets, "It is unacceptable that in any country its banking system is available to access two systems that create currency." One of these two systems was "a unilateral system, that is, a system strictly and rigidly controlled by the issuing bank, which is the lender of last resort and the watchman over the national currency." The other was "the Eurocurrency markets, which are free from any intervention through restrictions and exceed the controls of domestic and international authorities." According to Rueff, these markets were "indirect, transformed system of the gold exchange standard based on identification of national currencies with a currency traditionally payable in gold, the dollar." But what was his expectation for the future? "If inflation in the Eurocurrency markets were to come to an end, then various interest rates likely would fall massively, encouraging massive investment." "At the same time, such situation would likely make strikes and demands for wage increases to correct for the inevitable results of inflationary pressure ineffective. This is likely to mean that only justifiable social movements seeking to distribute productivity improvements would remain. Such productivity itself is likely to increase rapidly through a rapid recovery in investment.[79] Here, a neoliberal who called for free markets was playing a part in opposing the Eurocurrency markets and arguing for restraining their growth. There the BIS point of view – differing from popular theories of deregulation – showed excellent correspondence to neoliberal policy theory calling for restrictions on the Eurocurrency markets.

On the subject of Eurocurrency markets, the response of BIS authorities shifted from the laissez-faire approach to the regulation approach. Even the neoliberal Rueff continued developing criticisms of Eurocurrency. While their arguments are difficult to grasp at a glance, in fact they show a strong continuity. A hint is found in a paper published by Rueff at the end of the 1960s. The argument is outlined below.

Rueff assessed the measures in defense of the dollar advanced in the 1960s by multiple countries in cooperation with each other as follows. The response of each government was "naturally based on the implicit belief that the smooth operation and durability of an international monetary system require that the balance of payments of participating countries be in equilibrium." Rueff himself argued for the exact opposite on this point: "I am convinced that an efficient international monetary system alone can secure lasting equilibrium for such balances of payments." Rueff aptly described this as a "the problem of the chicken and the egg." According to Rueff, measures from mercantilism through the Marshall Plan were based on the preceding argument, that is, those had attempted to achieve equilibrium in the international currency system through artificial creation of equilibrium in international balances of payments.[80] Thus, Rueff said, it was neoliberalism that would correct this wrong way around.

In fact, Gilbert's position – although the actual contact point between Gilbert and the ideas and movement of neoliberalism had not been confirmed with him – was the same as this position of Rueff. He believed the Eurocurrency markets themselves should be welcomed and allowed to grow because they functioned as part of a free international currency system. However, he was opposed to intervention for dollar defense and to methods of mobilizing funds raised in the Eurocurrency markets toward domestic growth for policy purpose. From these arguments, one can see the view that the international currency system should be liberalized first, followed by an automatic equilibrium in the international balances of payments. However, the idea of neoliberals or authorities with positions close to them was unable to escape an aporia. How would liberalization of the international currency system be achieved? How could cooperation among nations be realized for that purpose? And could a "free" system extend across national borders to begin with?

Neoliberal currency and credit theories developed among a variety of theoreticians and parties involved in practical currency operations on the stages of the Eurocurrency markets and the BIS revealed the differences between them as mentioned above. It probably could be said that these diverse theories were an expression of a "split" between the domestic and international systems of postwar capitalism, exposed as a result of international currency issues.

We will conclude this section with a quick look at Japan's response to the Eurocurrency markets, focusing on the Bank of Tokyo.

Eurocurrency markets and the Bank of Tokyo: negotiations with the BIS

It is well known that the Bank of Tokyo was a leading Japanese foreign-exchange bank during the period of the Bretton Woods system. As the successor to the Yokohama Specie Bank, which had a seat on the BIS board in the prewar years, it is not hard to imagine that visitors from the Bank of Tokyo were especially welcome at the BIS even after Japan left the BIS. Below, we will look at the details and background of how the Bank of Tokyo began trading with the BIS in the postwar years, based on primary materials.

According to BIS records, the first contact between Bank of Tokyo representatives and BIS authorities took place on June 9, 1954, when Goro Hara, of the Bank of Tokyo representative office for Europe, met with Konrad Thiersch and Monetary and Economic Department Head Jacobsson of the BIS. For this meeting, Hara had been introduced by Kojiro Kitamura, who had been a prewar BIS board member, and Kan Yoshimura, who similarly had been manager of the BIS foreign-exchange section – both Kitamura and Yoshimura formerly had been with the Yokohama Specie Bank – and following the meeting he was appointed Bank of Tokyo managing director and London representative.[81]

Actual trading between the BIS and the Bank of Tokyo appears to have begun, however, ten years after this meeting. According to BIS records, beginning in November 1963 the Paris branch of the Bank of Tokyo had often made inquiries to the BIS by telex, mainly seeking to purchase Swiss franc foreign exchange with maturities of one to three months. The BIS had declined these trade offers uniformly, and such exchanges continued through June 1965.[82]

It was from October through December 1965 that a new phase arose. Over this period, a succession of visitors from the Bank of Tokyo, including President Shigeo Horie as well as the managers of the branches and representative offices in London, Hamburg and Zurich, arrived at the BIS, where they began to gather information.[83] The objective of the Bank of Tokyo's approaches to the BIS was to have the BIS discount bankers' acceptances accepted by the Bank of Tokyo to obtain foreign currency for import finance purposes. While when the BIS received this request it merely promised to consider the matter without giving an immediate answer, it would become clear that the situation had expanded to an unexpected extent.

Originally, behind the Bank of Tokyo's requests was the tightening of Eurocurrency markets, which deeply involved the BIS as well. Let's look at a case provided as an example by the Bank of Tokyo. While in the past pounds sterling had been used in import settlement for imports of flax from Australia to Japan, at that point of time settlement was conducted in dollars. The Bank of Tokyo had been obtaining dollars by having American banks discount acceptances purchased in US markets, but it needed to find a new source of funds because these US banks were withdrawing from trilateral trade finance. While the Bundesbank had accepted such trades for the time being, the Bank of Tokyo hoped to expand trades to be conducted with the BIS as well.[84]

At the BIS, Banking Department Head Mandel was responsible for this matter. Four days after the details of the Bank of Tokyo's request had been made clear, Mandel met with Bank of Japan representative Haruo Maekawa and inquired concerning the case of the Bank of Tokyo. Although Maekawa said he had no objection to the BIS discounting Bank of Tokyo acceptances, he "seemed troubled" by the idea of the Bank of Japan rediscounting these bills to the BIS in an emergency. Reasons given by Maekawa included the fact that such measures, similar to guarantees, required the authorization of Japan's Ministry of Finance and that since current Japanese monetary policy was oriented toward promoting exports it would be difficult to obtain such authorization for import finance.[85] On this point, the relationship between the Bank of Japan, the Bank of Tokyo and the BIS resembled the prewar relationship between the Bank of Japan, the Yoko-hama Specie Bank and the BIS, and corresponded to the relationship between the central bank and private-sector banks in each country. That same day, Mandel spoke with Tungeler of the Bundesbank to confirm that it was trading with the Bank of Tokyo.[86]

While details are unclear concerning the outcome of these meetings, in November 1967 a discount in the amount of ten million Deutschmarks took place between the Dusseldorf branch of the Bank of Tokyo and the BIS. Since the Union Bank of Burma was designated as the beneficiary in remittance of set-tlement proceeds, this appears to have been an example of the import finance referred to above.[87]

In the 1970s, the Bank of Tokyo opened branches across Europe, increasing its presence in the European banking world. Bank of Tokyo representatives visited the BIS frequently, and the BIS too began researching the Bank of Tokyo and other Japanese banks. In 1972, the Bank of Tokyo indicated intentions to accept dollar deposits from the BIS.[88] Also at the end of that same year, a trading limit of $30 million was established between the BIS and Japanese banks, as preparations began for regular trading.[89]

Beginning in 1973, trading between the BIS and the Bank of Tokyo grew rapidly. First of all, the BIS sent the Banking Department head, R. Hall, and Banking Department officer R. Stevenson to various locations in Europe and North America and to Japan and Malaysia to start negotiations with Japanese banks' head offices and branches in each location. At the start of these research trips in London (January–February 1973), from start to finish the BIS explained, that they were unfamiliar with the trades in which they (Japanese banks) were interested, and the number of dealers was limited as well.[90] However, in the next location visited, the United States (May–June 1973), Japanese banks in the United States requested the BIS for Federal Fund transactions and in-depth discussions were held concerning yields. A BIS staff member on this trip reported that Japa-nese banks appeared to take the initiative on negotiations with the BIS, and that Bridge of the Banking Department had been alerted by telephone of this fact.[91] During this visit of the BIS study group to the United States, agreement was reached at the Bank of Tokyo's New York branch on the start of deposit transac-tions between the BIS and the Bank of Tokyo.[92] During 1973, the limits on trading with Japanese banks were increased one after the other, so that in October of that year Daiichi, Fuji and Mitsubishi banks each had the highest limits of $85 million and the Bank of Tokyo had a limit of $35 million.[93] As can be seen here, the start of the 1970s was a period in which Japanese banks increased their over-seas presences and each bank was moving to secure dollar deposits.

After this, trading between the BIS and the Bank of Tokyo expanded at the London and New York branches. The euro–yen trades in which the London branch took part appeared to have interested the BIS particularly. Stevenson of the BIS, who visited the Bank of Tokyo's London branch in 1976, after ascertaining that the Bank of Tokyo had accepted yen deposits from Iraq and other Middle Eastern states, reported that the BIS "should keep this in mind" in connection with their own outlet in Japanese Government bonds.[94] Stevenson, who later visited the Bank of Tokyo's head office, paid close attention to the euro–yen transactions of the bank of Tokyo's London branch – which in the preceding fiscal year had accepted from central banks an amount totaling the equivalent of $200 million. While the BIS had purchased yen from the Bank of Tokyo for the purpose of these central banks' transactions, Stevenson and the Bank of Tokyo both assessed these yen trades to have been analogous in purpose. He also mentioned the fact of the Bank of Tokyo being the successor to the Yokohama Specie Bank, noting that as long as euro–yen markets exist the bulk is likely to be in the hands of the Bank of Tokyo.[95] From this report, one sees that the relationship between the Bank of Tokyo and the BIS was deepening as well as an aspect of the euro–yen markets in the 1970s – the fact that central banks deposited euro–yen with the Bank of Tokyo and the BIS provided yen accommodations for that purpose.

5 The banking business and distribution of profits

This section covers the financial statements for the fiscal years 1958 (settlement of accounts conducted March 31, 1959) through 1970 (settlement of accounts conducted March 31, 1971). Counted from the start of BIS operations, these correspond to the twenty-ninth through the forty-first fiscal years.

During this period, the activities of the BIS grew dramatically, and the total amounts on its balance sheet increased rapidly. At the same time, the issue of German reparations, which had been a subject of concern since the BIS's founding, appeared to have been resolved in terms of international agreements as well. Already in 1953, an agreement had been concluded between the Federal Republic of Germany, which succeeded the reparations obligations from World War I, and the BIS, ending payment of annual installments on reparations from postwar West Germany. In addition, in 1965 a separate agreement was concluded under which reparations-related deposit accounts maintained in the names of reparations payee states would be closed at the start of the 1966 fiscal year.[96] An internal document for the board of directors written in May 1966 states the following:

> The question of the Bank's assets and liabilities appertaining to the Hague Agreements of 1930 has been finally settled. The two parts of the balance sheet have been combined and the loss sustained by the Bank has been covered to the extent of 13,300,000 gold francs by drawing on the provision for contingencies and to the extent of 4,000,000 gold francs by utilizing the last annuity paid to the Bank in implementation of the Arrangement concluded on 9th January 1953 with the Federal Republic of Germany.[97]

However, resolution of this issue that had continued since World War I forced the BIS to face a management issue difficult to handle. The subject of this section is to make clear an overview of this situation through examination of BIS financial statements.

Trends in the financial statements (1): collection of deposits

First, let's check the movement of the total amounts on the balance sheet (Figure 5.1). The total amount on the BIS balance sheet increased more than sixfold from 3,528,240,000 Gold Swiss francs in fiscal 1958 to a level of 23,856,470,000 Gold Swiss francs in fiscal 1970. The second half of the 1960s in particular saw marked growth. While the total amount on the balance sheet had grown by 111 percent over the five-year period beginning with fiscal 1958, it rose by 190 percent over the five years starting with the 1966 fiscal year.

Next, let's look at the key factors in liabilities (on the debit side) that led to this growth (Figure 5.1).

First of all, paid-up capital is an account that requires a somewhat in-depth explanation. An extraordinary general meeting of shareholders was convened on

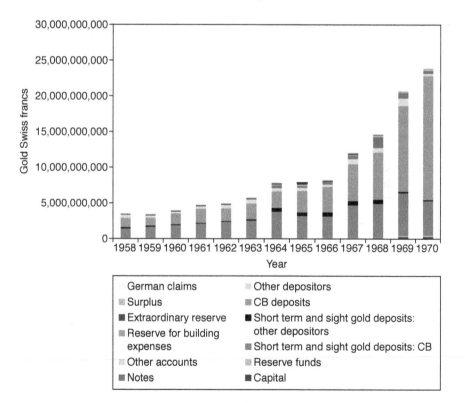

Figure 5.1 BIS balance sheet: major items on liabilities (fiscal years 1958–1970), in Gold Swiss francs (source: *BIS Twenty-ninth–Forty-first Annual Reports*).

June 9, 1969, in which an increase in capital and amendment of the BIS statutes were proposed and approved. These can be outlined as follows: (1) BIS authorized capital would be raised from 500 million to 1.5 billion Gold Swiss francs; (2) 200,000 new shares (for the second tranche) would be issued and offered to its present shareholders; (3) the board of directors would be authorized to issue a further 200,000 new shares (for the third tranche); and, (4) the BIS statutes would be amended in accordance with the above capital increase and the actual conditions of reserves. Put simply, the reason for the increase in capital was to create a "more appropriate relationship" between the swollen total amount on the balance sheet and capital accounts. The rapid increase in the total amount on the balance sheet in the mid-1960s led to a situation that "appropriations to the Bank's provisions and reserves would not be able to keep up with this movement." At the same time, the board of directors saw this increase in capital as having the effect of indicating to "the institutions that entrust deposits," and "more particularly the central banks" that "the BIS, although enjoying a special status, intends to adjust its resources to its commitments."[98]

These amendments appeared on liabilities accounts as an increase in paid-up capital beginning in fiscal 1969 and a corresponding buildup of various reserves. At the same time, the provisions for contingencies item was liquidated in accordance with these amendments to the statutes. This issue will be referred to later in the context of the BIS's policies on distribution of earnings.

How about various deposit items? As noted above, long-term deposits related to the Hague Convention already had been moved off the balance sheet, so that during this period short-term and sight deposits played a central role in deposit accounts. Also during this period, all liabilities accounts other than capital accounts and various reserves consisted of deposits. Here once again one's attention is drawn to the relationship between deposits and gold. Basically, this is the relationship between central banks' sight "deposits in gold" on one hand and central banks' "deposits in currencies" with terms not exceeding three months on the other – a negative correlation. A look at the former gold deposits shows that they began growing in fiscal 1959 and grew to account for nearly 40 percent of the balance sheet in the 1962 fiscal year. However, later the growth in these deposits dulled, and beginning at the end of the 1960s they once again accounted for a percentage of the balance sheet in the 10 percent range, although they did maintain a certain level in terms of monetary amount. Trends seen in the latter deposits – that is, deposits made with the BIS by each central bank, denominated in its own currency, with maturities not exceeding three months – contrasted with these. This item, which accounted for about 40 percent of the balance sheet in fiscal 1957, saw this percentage fall with the above growth in gold deposits, dropping to a level in fiscal 1962 of roughly 22 percent. However, these deposits with terms not exceeding three months rebounded later, reaching more than 52 percent of the balance sheet in fiscal 1969 and nearly 70 percent in the 1970 fiscal year (Figure 5.1).

A look at composition by currency shows that at the start of the 1960s national currencies and gold each accounted for about one-half of deposits, with the dollar being the most common currency while deposits were held in other currencies such as Swiss francs and Deutschmarks as well. However, this composition changed massively as the 1970s approached. In the second half of the 1960s, the percentage of deposits in gold fell dramatically and the percentage in national currencies, particularly those in the dollar, grew (Figure 5.2a). This corresponds to the negative correlation between "deposits in gold" and "deposits in currencies" seen above.

Also, a look at depositors shows that in the 1960s the largest depositor was the Bank of Italy, which alone accounted for 38.7 percent of central-bank deposits (central banks' own accounts), followed by West Germany, Belgium, France and Austria. At least 90 percent of the Bank of Italy's deposits were gold deposits.[99] While the rankings by country would change, there was no change in the lineup of the leading depositor nations. These central-bank deposits accounted for 80–90 percent of BIS deposits (Table 5.1).

As seen in Table 5.1, non-central bank depositors were the EMA fund of the OEEC followed by regional and private-sector Swiss banks such as Zürcher Kantonalbank and Basler Kantonalbank. No major change in these depositors took place over later years although some minor shifts in rank occurred.

But what about earmarked gold, which was not shown on BIS financial statements (Table 5.2)? Here too the leading depositor states of Italy and Switzerland are numbered among the top. However, one's attention is drawn to the fact that unlike in the case of gold deposits, the nations of South Africa, Morocco and

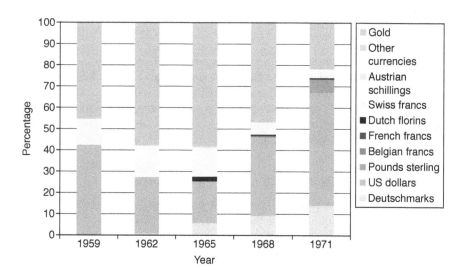

Figure 5.2a Currency composition of the BIS deposits (in Gold Swiss franc value) (source: Banking Department, Etat mensuel comptabilité – mars 1968, mars 1971, mars 1974).

Note
Data before 1965 represents the "resource" of the BIS before swap arrangements.

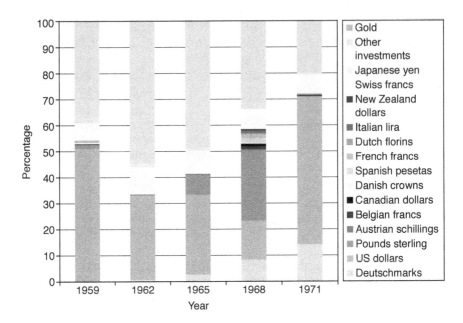

Figure 5.2b Currency composition of the BIS investments (in Gold Swiss franc value) (source: Banking Department, Rapport sur les opérations de la Banque pendant le mois d'avril 1965, annexe 275/C; Etat mensuel comptabilité – mars 1968, mars 1971, mars 1974).

Vietnam also placed gold in Bern (with the Swiss National Bank) and London (with the Bank of England). The entire amount of Italy's earmarked gold was placed in New York (with the Federal Bank of New York), and that amount alone gave the New York market the top position among destinations of earmarked gold, but with this exception one could say that London and Bern maintained their traditional positions as earmarking markets.

Trends in the financial statements (2): investment of funds

Investment of funds during this period took place mostly in investment targets with high levels of liquidity. For this reason, in considering asset accounts the focus is on selection of investment targets such as national currencies, gold and Treasury bills (Figure 5.3 and Figure 5.4).

First of all, as regards to the items cash and gold in bars (gold in bars and coins), it was gold in bars and coins that accounted for a major percentage of the balance sheet. While gold in bars and coins had accounted for 25 percent of total assets in fiscal 1957, this figure had risen to more than 50 percent in the 1961 fiscal year. This, while a succession of gold-related measures such as the Gold Pool Agreement was being announced, the BIS itself also was advancing active

Table 5.1 Depositors to the BIS (in 1,000 Gold Swiss francs)

March 1959

(Central banks)	No.	%
Gold	1,268,000	39.8
Currencies	1,305,000	40.9
Central banks	2,573,000	80.7
(Other depositors)		
Gold	172,000	5.4
Currencies	443,000	13.9
Other depositors	615,000	19.3
Bills	0	0.0
Total	3,188,000	100.0

March 1962

(Central banks)	No.	%
Gold	1,998,000	45.9
Currencies	1,988,000	45.7
Central banks	3,986,000	91.6
(Other depositors)		
Gold	62,000	1.4
Currencies	305,000	7.0
Other depositors	367,000	8.4
Bills	0	0.0
Total	4,353,000	100.0

March 1965

(Central banks)	No.	%
Gold	3,650,000	49.2
Currencies	2,384,000	32.1
Central banks	6,034,000	81.4
(Other depositors)		
Gold	483,000	6.5
Currencies	436,000	5.9
Other depositors	919,000	12.4
Bills	464,000	6.3
Total	7,417,000	100.0

March 1968

(Central banks)	No.	%
Banca d'Italia	1,646,268	14.9
Bank of England	1,461,349	13.3
Deutsche Bundesbank	1,206,704	11.0
Banque de France	914,029	8.3
Banco de Portugal	870,361	7.9
Other central banks	3,611,602	32.8
Central banks	9,710,313	88.1
(Other depositors)		
Instit. Espanol de Moneda Extranjera	485,000	4.4
Credit Suisse	149,392	1.4
Zürcher Kantonalbank	138,141	1.3
OECD-EMA	129,841	1.2
Société Générale	122,601	1.1
Other depositors	1,305,460	11.9
Total	11,015,773	100.0

March 1971

(Central banks)	No.	%
Bank of England	5,156,943	22.8
Banca d'Italia	3,441,620	15.2
Deutsche Bundesbank	2,479,798	11.0
Banque de France	1,491,056	6.6
Banco de Portugal	1,439,247	6.4
Other central banks	8,096,323	35.8
Central banks	22,104,987	97.7
(Other depositors)		
OECD-EMA	226,835	1.0
Zürcher Kantonalbank	97,136	0.4
Luxembourg finance ministry	33,024	0.1
Basler Kantonalbank	31,516	0.1
St.Gallen Municipal Credit	24,250	0.1
Other depositors	514,756	2.3
Total	22,619,743	100.0

Source: Rapport sur les operations de la Banque pendant le mois de mars 1959, annexe 214/C; mois d'avril 1962, annexe 245/C; mois d'avril 1965, annexe 275/C.

Table 5.2 BIS investments (in 1,000 Gold Swiss francs)

March 1959		*March 1962*		*March 1965*		*March 1968*		*March 1971*	
Gold Markets	1,088,000	Gold Markets	2,425,000	Gold Markets	3,398,000	Gold Markets	3,666,000	Gold Markets	4,202,000
USA	1,710,000	USA	616,000	UK	1,138,000	UK	4,385,000	UK	4,935,000
Belgium	245,000	France	279,000	USA	811,000	USA	1,089,000	West Germany	2,697,000
UK	95,000	UK	274,000	Belgium	556,000	Belgium	619,000	France	2,416,000
Turkey	67,000	Italy	243,000	Italy	422,000	France	486,000	USA	2,307,000
France	43,000	Belgium	217,000	Canada	299,000	West Germany	348,000	Italy	1,562,000
Other countries	2,160,000	Other countries	1,629,000	Other countries	3,226,000	Other countries	6,927,000	Other countries	13,917,000
	1,290,000		3,011,000		4,529,000		5,039,000		9,763,000
International organizations, etc.	77,000	International organizations, etc.	91,000	International organizations, etc.	94,000	International organizations, etc.	74,000	International organizations, etc.	175,000
Total	3,527,000	Total	4,731,000	Total	7,849,000	Total	12,040,000	Total	23,855,000

Source : Rapport sur les opérations de la Banque pendant le mois de mars 1959, annexe 214/C; mois d'avril 1962, annexe 245/C; mois d'avril 1965, annexe 275/C.

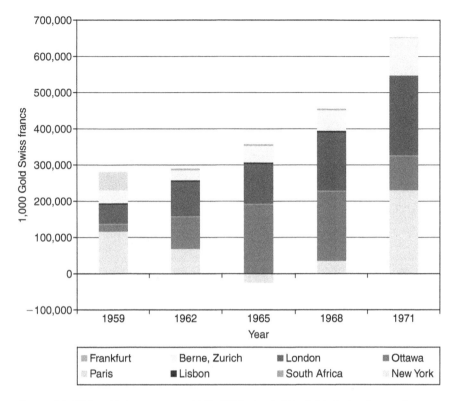

Figure 5.3 BIS gold investments, 1959–1971, in 1,000 Gold Swiss francs (source: Banking Department, Rapport sur les opérations de la Banque pendant le mois de mars 1959, annexe 214/C; mois d'avril 1962, annexe 245/C, mois d'avril 1965, annexe 275/C; Etat mensuel comptable, mars 1968, schedule E; mars 1971, schedule).

investment in gold. Later, the percentage accounted for by the item gold in bars and coins would decrease, falling to 17.6 percent in the 1970 fiscal year. While investment in gold in bars and coins maintained an increasing trend, a graph of the total amount indicated in Gold Swiss francs as a percentage of the balance sheet shows increases until fiscal 1961 and then decreases in fiscal 1961 and later years.

The item other bills and securities in currencies (with terms not exceeding three months) showed trends contrasting with these trends in gold in bars and coins. While this account had accounted for 16.9 percent of total assets in fiscal 1957, this percentage later fell as gold investment increased. In fiscal 1962 it fell to 3.8 percent, and the amount shown in Gold Swiss francs also reached its lowest level of this period. However, this account later revived, reaching a share of more than 25 percent in the 1969 fiscal year. Thus other bills and securities in currencies, which showed a negative correlation to the ups and downs in

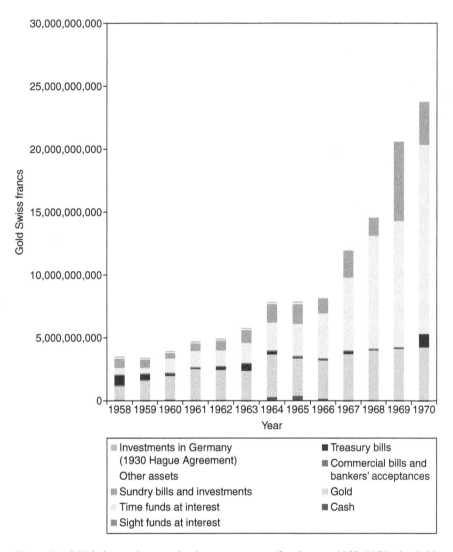

Figure 5.4 BIS balance sheet: major items on assets (fiscal years 1958–1970), in Gold
Swiss francs (source: *BIS Twenty-ninth–Forty-first Annual Reports*).

investment in gold, trended in a manner perfectly resembling a succession of
peaks and valleys.

If we look at the above two accounts as having crossed each other at the start
of the 1960s, then the item Treasury bills showed a constant decrease over this
period while the item time deposits and advances in currencies showed a constant increase. These show trends that together resemble a pair of scissors in
shape. While Treasury bills accounted for roughly 20 percent of the total amount
of assets at the end of the 1950s, in the 1960s this percentage fell rapidly, so that

in the second half of the 1960s this had become a truly minor account. While this account showed a slight increase in fiscal 1970, it accounted for no more than a truly small percentage of the total amount. At the same time, time deposits and advances in currencies, which had accounted for only about 10 percent of total assets at the end of the 1950s, grew to a share of more than 20 percent after the start of the 1960s and accounted for 40 percent of assets in the second half of the 1960s, truly emerging as the largest item on the debit side of the ledger.

Needless to say, the above ratios merely compare increasing and decreasing trends in share of assets and are not proof of any direct transfer relationship between correlated accounts. However, since the share of assets made up of the above four accounts rose from roughly 70 percent (in fiscal 1957) to 90 percent or more (in fiscal 1970), it probably can be said that the ups and downs in and switches between these accounts for the most part faithfully reflect trends in BIS investment strategies during this period. That is, while investment in gold in bars and coins was increasing, other bills and securities in currencies decreased, while constantly over this period investment in Treasury bills decreased, and time deposits and advances in currencies increased. At the end of the 1960s and the start of the 1970s, there was a clear trend of shifting away from gold and Treasury bills and toward bonds and loans in individual currencies.

A look at composition by currency shows that, as with deposits, there was a trend toward a decrease in gold and concentration on dollars, Deutschmarks and Swiss francs, with priority on the dollar in particular (Table 5.2).

But what was the situation concerning markets invested in? During this period, the percentages accounted for by gold, national markets and international institutions etc. showed trends toward contraction in gold and an increase in national markets, corresponding to the above asset trends. A look at a breakdown of national markets invested in shows that Britain uniformly held the top position, followed by the United States, West Germany, France and others. Here it should be noted that national markets include the Eurocurrency markets seen in this chapter. For example, since in the trades between the BIS and the Bank of Tokyo mentioned above euro–yen deposits were placed with the London branch of the Bank of Tokyo in central banks' own accounts with the BIS, these were counted as investments in Britain rather than Japan. Examination of the investment destinations in Table 5.2 shows that these corresponded with the distribution of the Eurocurrency markets.

Incidentally, as touched on earlier in this chapter the US State Department had conducted its own survey of trends in the BIS's business during this period. Referring to monthly figures announced by the Swiss National Bank in addition to the BIS annual report, the report on this survey raises conjectures about the business of the BIS. The main views in the report were as follows:[100] (1) Of the BIS gold operations, "the most well-known" is its "year-end sales to the Swiss National Bank in order to absorb the large increase in dollar holding that normally takes place due to the year-end window dressing operations by the Swiss

Table 5.3 Depositors of the ear-marked gold, in million Gold Swiss francs

	New York	London	Paris	Lisbon	Berne	Total
March 1968 – central banks						
Estonia	8.8	3.5				12.3
Finland		14.9				14.9
Netherlands				6.9		6.9
Italy	689.1					689.1
Lithuania		2.0				2.0
Morocco					41.4	41.4
Poland		10.4			52.8	63.2
Romania					25.2	25.2
Switzerland		145.8	68.9			214.7
Turkey		0.2	0.7		0.4	1.3
Vietnam					19.8	19.8
Yugoslavia		24.0			18.3	42.3
March 1968 – Other institutions						
Caisse Commune of Austria-Hungary		5.0				5.0
Special Administration of St. Siege (Vatican)					10.4	10.4
European Investment Bank	3.3	2.1				5.4
OECD	49.4	15.2				64.6
March 1968 – total	750.6	223.1	69.6	6.9	168.3	1,218.5
March 1968 – percentage	61.6	18.3	5.7	0.6	13.8	100.0
March 1971 – central banks						
South Africa					65.9	65.9
Estonia	8.8	3.5				12.3
Netherlands				6.9		6.9
Italy	689.1					689.1
Kuwait					32.1	32.1
Lithuania		2.0				2.0
Morocco					41.4	41.4
Poland		27.5			5.5	33.0
Vietnam					19.8	19.8
Yugoslavia					7.0	7.0
March 1971 – other institutions						
Special Administration of St. Siege (Vatican)					10.4	10.4
European Investment Bank	3.3	2.1				5.4
OECD	17.1	15.2				32.3
March 1971 – total	718.3	50.3	0.0	6.9	182.1	957.6
March 1971 – percentage	75.0	5.3	0.0	0.7	19.0	100.0

Source: Banking Department, Etat mensuel comptabilité-mars 1968, mars 1971.

commercial banks." (2) There was "a good deal of sensitivity" between trends in central banks' sight deposits and operations to support the pound sterling. In fact, from May through July 1966, when pound support measures were undertaken, BIS demand deposits increased from \$25 million to \$440 million, later peaking in September and then gradually returning to their previous level through May 1967. (3) "Movements in time deposits appear to be more related to the BIS's activities in the Euro-dollar market." For example, from May through September 1966 time deposits were withdrawn, and in October transfers from demand deposits to time deposits took place to make up for these. As a result, it was "clearly evident" that investment in the Eurodollar markets had taken place in December using gold swaps between the Swiss National Bank and the BIS. The above analysis was nothing more than a type of cause-and-effect analysis on the movement of funds through correspondence of monthly changes in BIS deposit accounts and the trends such as those in support for the pound and investment in Eurodollars, based on the fact that these took place at the same time. However, this probably can be seen to demonstrate somewhat persuasively a part of the BIS swap operations conducted while collecting deposits. More than anything else, the fact that the US State Department took part in such a survey on its own can be said to be proof of the strengthening of the BIS's position in this business domain.

Profits and losses, and appropriation of net profit: capital increase and amendment of the statutes

Next, let's examine these trends in profits in comparison with the total amount on the balance sheet. Like the total amount on the balance sheet, official net profit (business net profit) increased sixfold or more during this period (Table 5.4). During the postwar reconstruction looked at in the preceding chapter, the BIS had made every effort to increase ordinary profits, to say nothing of dividends. However, it restored dividends beginning in fiscal 1957, part of the period covered in this chapter. Perhaps the BIS's businesses can be said to have been on a path of stable growth during the period of the gold and dollar standard. Beginning in April 1968, part of BIS monthly profit was exchanged for gold under contracts between central banks and the BIS, and payment of dividends to each country came to be conducted in part in gold.[101]

However, a look in greater detail shows a decrease in revenues over the period of three fiscal years from the 1959 through the 1961 fiscal years. The main causes of this decrease in revenues were an increase in administrative and personnel costs on the expenditures side and a decrease in net interest income etc. on the revenues side, with the latter having a greater impact. In May 1961, the Banking Department analyzed this point as follows:

> An appreciable falling-off of the Bank's gold operations following the events on the international gold market in the autumn of 1960, and the

Table 5.4 BIS profit and loss account and P/L appropriation account (fiscal years 1958–1970) in Gold Swiss francs

P/L account

	Net income	Commissions earned	Expenditures		Other costs	Expenditure on EMA	Net profit	Account for exceptional costs of administration	Provision for contingencies
			Board	Administration					
1958	26,776,157	634,065	228,453	4,352,617	850,093	571,835	22,550,894		13,000,000
1959	33,450,513	650,802	227,091	4,359,472	1,009,447	559,411	29,064,716	750,000	13,000,000
1960	31,648,626	676,286	225,071	4,305,353	1,025,082	554,699	27,324,105	350,000	12,000,000
1961	24,824,428	721,534	237,729	4,613,129	1,025,668	515,736	20,185,172		7,500,000
1962	26,648,003	728,755	241,881	5,332,401	970,911	378,706	21,210,271		7,500,000
1963	33,115,350	711,691	230,498	5,535,150	1,023,304	378,966	27,417,055	2,000,000	7,500,000
1964	41,328,706	705,958	301,786	6,151,635	1,438,320	376,221	34,519,144	1,500,000	10,500,000
1965	46,311,387	698,390	355,216	7,006,473	1,440,145	370,808	38,578,751	1,000,000	15,000,000
1966	55,949,014		141,428	7,101,620	1,631,479		47,074,487	200,000	3,800,000
1967	62,457,488		141,920	7,101,184	1,716,536		53,497,848	1,997,848	
1968	60,109,088		175,272	8,375,659	1,871,837		49,686,320	1,336,320	
1969	113,513,818		176,492	9,550,586	2,418,184		101,368,556	2,188,986	
1970	146,766,911		171,708	10,361,121	3,185,056		133,049,026	1,600,120	

Appropriation account

	Net balance published	Provision for depreciation on buildings	Balance carried from previous year	Dividend at 6%	Additional dividend	Legal reserve fund 5% of net profit	General reserve	Special dividend	Free reserve	Balance carried forward
1958	9,550,894		7,706,579	7,500,000		477,545				9,279,928
1959	15,314,716		9,279,928	16,000,000		765,736				7,828,908
1960	14,974,105		7,828,908	14,500,000		748,705				7,554,308
1961	12,685,172		7,554,308	12,000,000		634,259				7,605,221
1962	13,710,271		7,605,221	13,000,000		685,514				7,629,978
1963	17,517,055		7,629,978	16,000,000		402,141				8,744,892
1964	22,519,144	400,000	8,744,892	21,500,000						9,764,036
1965	22,578,751		9,764,936	22,500,000						9,842,787
1966	32,074,487	11,000,000	9,842,787	18,394,000	4,106,000		9,409,310	10,007,964		
1967	45,000,000	6,500,000		7,500,000	7,500,000		15,000,000		15,000,000	
1968	45,000,000	3,350,000		7,500,000	7,500,000		15,000,000		15,000,000	
1969	83,179,570	16,000,000		15,453,047	7,726,523		30,000,000	12,000,000	18,000,000	
1970	99,448,906	32,000,000		16,965,937	8,482,969		37,000,000	14,800,000	22,200,000	

Source: BIS Twenty-ninth–Forty-first Annual Reports.

downward trend of interest rates for various categories of investment, particularly US Treasury bills, led to a certain decline in the Bank's profits compared with the previous financial year. [102]

The decrease in income in the following fiscal year was observed in a similar way on the subject of the state of gold operations and interest rates. In comparison with the preceding fiscal year, that fiscal year's "relatively large reduction in the size of the surplus" was

> mainly due to the fact that the Bank, in harmony with the policy followed by the central banks, considerably reduced the volume of its operations on the gold market. Another factor in the reduction of the profits has been the narrower margins between the cost of deposits and the yields obtainable on investments. [103]

Just because "transactions involving purchase options in gold" were assessed in May 1960, before this phase of decreasing income was entered, to have "contributed substantially to the year's earnings,"[104] in May 1960, the fact that the decrease in gold transactions was a major cause of the decrease in revenues – this too was intended for purposes of cooperation "with the policies adopted by each central bank – is an important point. Put another way, to avoid disorder in the London gold market and ensure the gold pool functioned smoothly, the BIS purposely decreased gold operations, which had been a source of income. This can be said to be a phase in which the gold policies (central-bank cooperation) led by the Monetary and Economic Department took priority over the intentions of the Banking Department (the BIS as a "bank").

As the situation at the start of the 1960s was overcome, BIS profits – aside from a slight decrease in fiscal 1968 – grew rapidly toward the 1970 fiscal year.

But how were the profits appropriated? Let's take a look at appropriation of net profits. As touched on above, dividends were restored during this period, increasing quickly in fiscal 1959 after the minimum dividends under BIS statutes were paid in the 1957 and 1958 fiscal years. What should be noted here is the fact that even in the phase of decreasing profit at the start of the 1960s, mentioned above, high levels of dividends were maintained. In the fiscal years in which income decreased markedly, measures were taken such as decreasing contributions to reserve accounts – provision for exceptional costs of administration and provision for contingencies – prior to the finalization of the total amount available for allocation in the period, and profit allocation policies were taken of securing previous levels of the total amount available for allocation in the period. This appears to have been related to the issue of when and in what form to pay the cumulative statutory dividends left unpaid during the war. It appears that the BIS general secretary needed to maintain increased dividend levels to avoid demands from central banks, perhaps in light of their status as BIS shareholders.

In connection with this issue, on the subject of appropriation of net income the argument arose at the start of the 1960s among directors that hidden reserves

should be reconstructed. The following circumstances were behind this argument: (1) Full delivery of German reparations obligations was incomplete, and
the amounts of claims by countries with claims to reparations had not been finalized; (2) Regarding dividends that had been suspended or decreased in amounts,
including during the war, the need for repayment retroactive to past portions
arose with the recovery in profits, and there were concerns that this could result
in a massive burden on the BIS over a short period of time, depending on their
amounts and payment methods;[105] and, (3) At the same time, BIS profits were in
a strong trend. In fact, as seen in Table 5.4, in fiscal years 1959 and 1960 the
amounts carried over to the following fiscal year surpassed the amounts allocated to dividends – the maximum amount to be carried over to the following
fiscal year was 7.5 million Gold Swiss francs, roughly the same as the amount of
dividends in these years – so that the BIS faced a fork in the road on profit distribution policies: whether to increase dividends or resume hidden reserves.

In the end, this issue appears to have reached a conclusion through increasing
dividends. While the course of developments over this period is unclear, it is
likely that behind this was the fact mentioned above that matters related to West
Germany and the Young Plan were resolved one after the other in the 1960s.

In May 1967, a new account was established for provision for building purposes, and accumulation of reserves in this account began. At that time, the
BIS's offices were divided across six buildings, and the head office, operated
out of a remodeled hotel in front of Basel station, had been constructed more
than 50 years earlier. In response to its high earnings in the 1960s, the BIS had
decided to begin remodeling its head office.[106] Also, as with other provisions
such as those for contingent liabilities, funds were transferred to these provisions from income prior to finalization of the amount available for allocation in
the period.

On the subject of appropriation of net income, a later development, in 1969,
should be given attention. This was the move to break into provision for contingencies and allocate the resulting funds to payment for the new shares issued as
seen above. According to the board of directors' explanation, this provision "can
be utilized for any purpose strengthening the Bank's financial position within the
framework of the Statutes."[107] Thus in fiscal 1969 transfers from the provision,
which until then had totaled 220 million Gold Swiss francs, decreased the
amount of the provision to 95 million Gold Swiss francs. This balance was transferred to the legal reserve fund and provision for building purposes, and the provision was liquidated.

Through such transfers from provision, existing shareholders (central banks)
were allocated new shares without any pay-in of cash. For this reason, the board
of directors took the opportunity to amend Article 53 of the statutes, partially
restricting the rights of shareholders. Specifically, the proposal included the
measures of (1) reducing the maximum rate of the supplementary dividend from
6 percent to 3 percent, (2) abolishing the 6 percent preferential dividends, and
(3) in return, allowing a larger portion of the profits to be appropriated to the
special dividend reserve fund. The proposed amendments to the statutes were

approved in a June 1969 extraordinary general meeting. Following this approval, a BIS internal document was self-laudatory, reviewing the amendments as follows:

> While respecting the shareholders' interests, the new statutory provisions will enable the Bank to increase its support to central banks and will furnish it with the means to perform, on the most advantageous terms possible, such services compatible with its Statutes as are requested of it by central banks.[108]

The increase in capital was a response to the following conditions of the 1960s: enlivening of the BIS activities, completion of processing of the issue of German reparations, expansion of the total amount on the balance sheet, and earned surplus that no longer could be handled completely through transfers to provisions. However, these responses were realized through a variety of compromises, reflecting the subtle bargaining between the BIS authorities and central banks.

6 Conclusion

The Bretton Woods system of the 1960s was forced to become a kind of patch-work system that deviated from the initial ideals of the system. During this period, in which the contradictions that led to the dollar crisis deepened, international finance took pains to settle the situations by launching a variety of forums including G10 meetings. While the BIS remained active in a backstage role in such forums, this crisis provided an opportunity for the BIS, which originally had opposed the Bretton Woods Agreement, to expand its activities. In fact, the BIS, and particularly the Banking Department, was aware of its own role holding a "very special position in the field of gold," as it started on the path of attempting to secure operating income while providing benefits such as gold, dollar and options trading. The enlivening of the BIS's activities during this period, together with factors such as buildup of surpluses, led to a large-scale capital increase. Thus, while the crisis in the Bretton Woods system was deepening, the BIS proved its merits and was growing rapidly as an organization.

The BIS also indicated its own view of the new circumstances of the gold and dollar crisis or the development of the Eurocurrency markets. Calls for stabilization of gold prices and restricting the Eurocurrency markets drew a line against the Keynesian utopian views of Triffin and others and differed from the proposed reforms attempting to rebuild American hegemony, leading to criticism of a floating exchange rate system and the argument that nations running deficits bore responsibility for the situation.

But what was the thinking behind these developments? Toniolo's official history says the following about Monetary and Economic Department head Gilbert, who most keenly embodied an "neoliberalism as an alternative" during this period:

Everything in the BIS's history, intellectual tradition, and top-staff composition made the Bank naturally lean towards the position of the Continentals. However, the presence of Milton Gilbert – an American with a deep knowledge of Europe, especially France – exercised a moderating influence, both political and intellectual, within the Bank itself as well as in the G10 deputies' debates.

In this way, Toniolo points out that Gilbert took a "middle-of-the-road position" between the United States and Europe.[109] However, in this book we attempt to depict Gilbert – as well as the broader current of thought subsuming the BIS as a whole – as proponents of European neoliberalism – that is, as being in a direct line of descent from a line of economic thinking existing in Europe, rather than in such a "middle-of-the-road position" between the United States and Europe. Perhaps this neoliberal tradition handed down across organizations and time can itself be said to express a type of continuity that would be linked to international banking supervision in coming eras as well.

In May 1963, Jacobsson died in London. Pained at the death of a current managing director, the IMF provided courteous support for the funeral held at the Church of Sweden in London and even held a memorial in Washington, DC. Letters of condolence and bouquets were delivered to Jacobsson's bereaved family returning to Sweden with his body on the *Queen Elizabeth*. Jacobsson's wife, Violet Jacobsson, noted the following in a letter of thanks sent to related parties:

> I have tried to write to you repeatedly but found I could not continue. Please forgive.... As you know he lived for the Fund for the last six and a half years, and he gave his best to and for it.[110]

Jacobsson, who was born in Sweden, was educated by Wicksell, and eventually made a name for himself in the world of international finance as the theoretical leader of the BIS, was in a position to demonstrate his leadership as IMF managing director beginning in 1956, from the peak of the Bretton Woods system through its period of reconstruction. He had clear arguments, fearless negotiation abilities and outstanding language abilities – blessed with a good family life, he would appear at first glance to have been an individual who lived his entire life under blue skies. But now the answer to the question we would like to ask him in this book, on what the Wicksellian, neoliberal Jacobsson thought of the repairs to the Bretton Woods system made through means including general borrowing agreements and gold pooling, can only be sought through related documents.

6   Conclusions

Now, we will look at the conclusions of this book, following the four perspectives introduced at the start: the BIS as a "venue" for cooperation between central banks, the BIS as a "bank," the BIS as a crossroads in the history of twentieth-century economic thought, and the BIS as a stage for the "story of individuals."

1   The BIS as a "venue" for cooperation between central banks: various phases

Starting from the relatively well-known fact that the BIS was established as a "venue" for cooperation between central banks and continues to perform that function, it is thought that this book has introduced a number of points of dispute.

First, the establishment of the BIS coincided with the appearance of "central banks." In fact, for most countries – even those of Europe – it was during the period between the world wars that modern central banks first appeared, as "bank for banks," "government banks," and "caretakers of currency" modeled on the Bank of England.[1] The BIS too defined central banks in Article 58 of its statutes at the time of its foundation. Also, in the period the central banks of each nation formed a sort of club in the process of disputes between national governments. It was the BIS that would provide the venue for this club, particularly in its monthly meetings of central-bank governors.

Second, cooperation between central banks at the BIS was forced to go through a process of repeated advances and retreats. During the Depression, which greatly worsened soon after the founding of the BIS, while central-bank cooperation achieved its own results the effects of these as countermeasures against the Depression were limited simply to providing one alternative in the history of monetary policy. During World War II and the postwar reconstruction period, while threats to central-bank cooperation appeared, under such threats it also demonstrated just what close cooperation could achieve. The relation between the Bretton Woods system and central-bank cooperation was one that should be described as a relationship of antagonistic complementarity. The cooperation between central banks that worked to restore the IMF system would have been unlikely without the intense participation of the BIS. And today, central-bank cooperation in the BIS again is in the process of breaking new ground, this time in the new area of international bank supervision.

Third, while the BIS meetings of central-bank governors sometimes served a healing function through dialogue between central-bank governors from different countries who were well acquainted with feelings of isolation, they also were home to vigorous bargaining behind the scenes.[2] An example is the currency diplomacy that offered a glimpse of the grim realities of international politics, such as disputes with the BIS, interaction between national governments unwilling to give up on their national interests, and extracurricular information warfare as seen in the case of France and Japan mentioned in this book. The BIS was both a club uniting parties such as individual governments and the IMF and, inside, a venue hiding important antagonistic relations. The history of the BIS should be seen from both these aspects of cooperation and conflict.

Fourth, the leading actors who actually coordinated cooperation between central banks changed over time. While at the time of its founding veteran central-bank governors such as Norman and Schacht led the design of the BIS system, soon after its founding the Monetary and Economic Department, led by Jacobsson, demonstrated its role as a stagehand, and on a theoretical basis as well the BIS seemed to have the momentum to overwhelm each country's central bank. While initiatives on the part of the Monetary and Economic Department stood out during the period from World War II through the postwar reconstruction, as the restoration of the Bretton Woods system was brought up on the agenda central-bank representatives took the initiative on policy coordination in venues such as G10 meetings. Perhaps the image of the BIS (the Monetary and Economic Department in particular) as stagehands also should be seen to have changed over time.

2 The BIS as a "bank": its roles regarding gold

Since its founding the BIS has been both a joint-stock company and a bank. In this book, we have attempted to make clear the following points by shining light on these aspects.

The first concerns the independence of the BIS. The fact that it is a joint-stock company generating profits has secured the independence of the BIS. Funding its operations on its own without financial support from national governments has served as the organizational foundation for the BIS as a club of central banks. Distribution of dividends to member countries' central banks also has proved a benefit of joining the BIS, particularly for countries establishing new central banks. However, the organizational structure as a joint-stock company has not always been to the benefit of the BIS. In fact, as the IMF, as a foundation funded by contributions from each national government, entered a golden age following World War II prospects did not look good for the BIS, which was forced to act under operational restrictions. This was remedied by the central-bank cooperation discussed above, in particular the mechanisms of the swap network and the gold pool.

The second aspect concerns the BIS's unique roles concerning gold. The fact that from the start the BIS promoted a concept of gold settlement and took part in gold markets proactively alone can be considered a point that should be noted in the financial history of the twentieth century. The acceptance of earmarked gold and management of gold deposits are operations that the BIS has carried out since its founding. In various gold-related operations of the 1960s as well, the BIS did not hide its motive of securing steady profits while also giving consideration to central-bank cooperation. In regard to these gold-related operations, conceptual differences and at times serious disputes arose between the BIS and the IMF, between the Banking Department and the Monetary and Economic Department within the BIS, or within the Banking Department.

The third is the actual state of financial statements. Reflecting the policy issues the BIS faced from time to time, the structure of the balance sheet has varied greatly as it shifted from long-term items related to reparations to short-term items concerning the commercial banking business, or from deposits of each country's central banks denominated in each nation's currency to gold deposits. In distribution of earnings, the BIS processed exchange differences by building up hidden reserves and secured a solid foundation for its business operations even during World War II.[3] Incidentally, approximate calculation of return on assets (ROA) and return on equity (ROE) from the BIS's public income statements resulted in an ROA of 0.59 percent and an ROE of 10.84 percent in the year of its founding.[4] Later, ROA averaged 1.21 percent per year over the years 1931–1946, and ROE averaged 6.31 percent per year over the same period. Factors in the background of these circumstances include the fact that a certain degree of income was maintained during the depression despite contraction of assets, and the fact that paid-in capital was kept to 125 million Gold Swiss francs after capital increases made through 1932. In contrast, behind the fact that ROA averaged 0.55 percent and ROE averaged 7.62 percent over the period 1947–1958 was a rapid increase in lines of business and sluggish profits (however, these grew rapidly in the second half of the 1950s). Then, from 1959 through fiscal 1978, while the ROA averaged its lowest level since the founding of the BIS at 0.48 percent, the average of ROE swelled to 41.91 percent. ROE in particular grew rapidly despite two large-scale capital increases, reaching as high as 73.92 percent in 1978. This tells the story of a new relation between BIS lines of business and capital accounts.

3 The BIS as a crossroads in the history of twentieth-century economic thought: the relation to organization theory

The BIS followed the current of a wide range of courses of economic thought in the twentieth century, from the "financial utopianism" upheld at the time of its founding through Jacobsson's theory appearing in the 1930s and the neoliberalism and Wicksellian thought behind these, to neoliberalism in opposition to Keynesianism and a unique continuity of neoliberalism in the postwar period. This book has attempted to draw out the following views from the history of twentieth-century economic thought in connection with the BIS.

While these trends in economic thought included important turning points, one major point of commonality is their relation to Europe. In fact, the financial utopianism of Blum and Mendès-France, as well as the neoliberalism related to the Austrian school of economists, can be considered to be an economic thought within a European framework – that is, aiming for democratic social stability by restricting growth within certain limits while being oriented toward increasing productivity. This is linked to the BIS's concept that positions gold as a *numéraire* of growth and stability.

To restate these circumstances somewhat schematically, perhaps it could be said that when it was standing up to the Keynesians the economic thought advocated by the BIS was so-called right-liberalism. However, as the United States came to play a leading role in the global economy and an international currency system based on the dollar began, the position of the BIS can be seen as having shifted gradually toward the left. While these changes in leftward and rightward orientation over time are apparent, the theory advanced by the BIS has itself remained strongly uniform. Today's "BIS view" in contraposition to the "FRB view" also may be connected to this tradition of "European" economic thought.[5] Perhaps the fact that the neoliberalism of Jacobsson, who started as a young advocate of Sweden's Liberal Party, showed an indifferent intermediary phase between the United States and Europe when he served as managing director of the IMF for a long period also can be explained from this point of commonality. In addition, the trajectory of Gilbert, Jacobsson's successor as head of the Monetary and Economic Department – which despite the fact that he was an American advanced Jacobsson's approach even further – must be considered an expression of this immutable European economic theory.

At issue perhaps is how to evaluate the major turning point from neoliberalism when seeing BIS economic thought as a blend of the strains of neoliberalism and Wicksellian thought that were born in Europe. It is said that there are major differences in neoliberalism, which like Ordo-Liberalismus and the Austrian school of economists appears at a glance to be part of "German and Austrian" thought. However, in this book we have attempted to address this point under the logic of organizational history as follows. BIS authorities, such as Jacobsson and Gilbert, also were members of the organization. While at some times they joined with the Ordo-Liberalismus to praise wide-ranging economic zones, with the changing times they switched to the Austrian school of economists. In addition, at one time they professed Hayekian views in opposition to the United States when faced with an unavoidable crisis in the Bretton Woods system while allowing the growth of Eurocurrency markets. As a historical study, this book has attempted, while looking at the sharp conflict in economic thought in the twentieth century and the organizational culture of the BIS under the logic of an organization that combines these together flexibly, to focus in particular on the latter, organizational dynamism.

4 The BIS as a stage for the "story of individuals": utopianism and its alternatives

The people gathered together at the BIS, both the central-bank governors of each country and BIS authorities, were each talented human resources with high levels of individuality. These include leaders from each country's central bank, such as Schacht, Norman and Moreau, members of the new elite such as Addis and Tetsusaburo Tanaka, who played active roles in the meeting at Baden-Baden, and practitioners such as Quesnay, Jacobsson and Huelse, who managed the BIS at its start; Fraser, Auboin, van Zeeland and Kan Yoshimura, who devoted themselves to the BIS from the depression through World War II; Monick, Holtrop, Guindey and Ferras, who restored the BIS during the postwar reconstruction period and, over time, led the way to restoration of the Bretton Woods system; and Haruo Maekawa, who devoted himself to Japan's return to the BIS. These and others can be described as the people of the BIS.

Viewed from the standpoint of prosopography, these BIS people can be characterized first by generation. At the BIS's founding in 1930, Schacht was 55 years old, Norman 59 and Moreau 62. In contrast, Quesnay was 35, Jacobsson 36 and Auboin 39. A substantial difference is apparent between the so-called nineteenth-century generation and the après-guerre generation, separated by World War I, particularly in their sense of distance from the postwar utopian international structure. The generation of this latter group of practitioners reached their fifties in 1945 (with the exception of Quesnay, who died young), while at that time Guindey was 36, Ferras 32 and Maekawa 34. As argued by Toniolo, the ranks of core human resources at international institutions broadened rapidly beginning with the generation that was in their mid-thirties at the end of World War II.

These generational differences also are apparent in connection to national interest. At the time the BIS was founded, reparations were the most pressing issue, and the people of the BIS were bound strictly, through various means, to the intentions of their own nations and governments. During the period from the depression through World War II – while there was no change in the requirement to serve the national interest – international plans and international cooperation were sought, and theoretical activities intended to overcome national interests appeared. This tendency strengthened further after World War II, bearing fruit in cooperative action such as addressing Eurocurrency markets, support for sterling, and the gold pool. However, it can be considered that even within the lineage of these BIS people, with an abundance of international sensitivity, it would not be appropriate to depict the change in generations as a simple shift in focus from national interest to international cooperation. As can be seen in the discussions of the central bank governors, discussions in the forum of the BIS, which at a glance would appear to extol an international public nature, in some aspects skillfully reflected national interests. Thus, perhaps the people of the BIS should be seen to continue seeking out and struggling for the space between national interest and international cooperation.

At the same time, one could ask the question of what was the source of the capabilities of these BIS people. Matters such as the career paths and human-resources promotion systems that developed these capabilities also are likely to be points of dispute. However, in fact capability is a vague concept. In the realities of international finance, the BIS as an organization is expected to play a certain role. The individuals who play parts in responding to these expectations appear in certain phases in history. Perhaps this should be seen as a case in which persons of unusual ability such as Jacobsson or skillful currency diplomats such as Guindey demonstrated their own capabilities pushed by the will of their own as well as hidden intentions in each of these phases. Each had a foothold in neoliberalism and Wicksellian thought, or in the subtle differences between the United States and Europe. The deeply shaded utopianism and alternatives that these individuals embodied can be considered their greatest legacy characterizing the twentieth century of the BIS – and remaining in the international financial system of the twenty-first century.

In August 2007, the author met with an Icelandic gentleman at BIS headquarters Basel. He was Mar Gudmundsson, deputy head of the BIS Monetary and Economic Department. Meeting with the author in his office, which once would have been frequented by Jacobsson and Gilbert – although the BIS had since changed buildings – he began to speak about the role the BIS should play in Asia in the future. He said, "We are there, we facilitate, we build networks."[6] This is a strategy of planting the BIS's function as a venue for central-bank cooperation in Asia as well. However, at the same time Gudmundsson said, "The BIS wants to be global, not universal." Put another way, the BIS would not propose policies based on subsumption of the whole world to a single standard, like the IMF. In Gudmundsson's phrase "We are not crisis managers," the long tradition of the BIS still survives, calling for an approach different from that of the IMF.

Nevertheless, it probably would not be accurate to characterize BIS participation in Asia from its organizational culture and business traditions alone. The BIS Asia strategies would appear to have what could be called a layered nature, suited to a new era. Gudmundsson expresses the background for these as follows: "Regional integration is one response to globalization." This is the idea that regional integration as seen in Europe is unavoidable as a response to a globalization that has advanced with the United States as its starting point. The BIS would provide information and policies toward integration in the region if the region desires to move in that direction. This can be said to fit the above position of being "global, not universal," and to hint at the course of action for the BIS in the future.

But what specific measures would the BIS take to support this direction toward regional integration? Gudmundsson argues for support for integration of capital markets and financial integration. Starting from the recognition that "It is impossible for the capital markets in any single nation of Asia to stand up to US capital markets," he proposes an agenda of integration of capital markets – such as liberalization and harmonization of regulations and internationalization of transactions. He envisions financial integration – such as cross-border lending by banks and harmonization of banking regulations – as the next step. He says that while the BIS would not enforce such steps, it would support member nations taking such steps, through the accumulation of information and utilizing its business experiences. Even today, during a global recession, the hopes about which Gudmundsson spoke against a backdrop of the summer Swiss sunlight still survive. Gudmundsson's view appeared to express the alternatives that the BIS has offered against the major current of the international financial system since its founding. Those alternatives had the backing of various utopian theories and thinking over money and capitalism.

Notes

Foreword

1 Hereinafter, except in convention titles, chapter titles, etc., where there are no specific reasons to do otherwise the Bank for International Settlements will be referred to by its abbreviation BIS. Incidentally, the French and German abbreviations appearing in document titles and elsewhere are as follows: BRI refers to Banque des Règlements Internationaux and BIZ to Bank für Internationalen Zahlungsausgleich.

2 Piet Clement, "Between Banks and Governments: The Records of BIS," in Ton de Graaf, Joost Jonker and Jaap-Jan Mobron, eds., *European Banking Overseas, 19th–20th Century*, ABN AMRO Historical Archives, Amsterdam, 2002; m.a., "Central Bank Networking at the BIS, 1930s–1960s" (paper submitted to the conference "Networks in the Process of European Construction, 1930s–1960s," Brussels, October 16–18, 2002). Other important studies are mentioned in the corresponding sections of the book.

3 Paul Einzig, *The Bank for International Settlements*, Macmillan, London, 1930. This is a work of reportage written by the leading economic journalist of the time. Eleanor Lansing Dulles, *The Bank for International Settlements at Work*, Macmillan, New York, 1932. Dulles, the author of this book, is the younger sister of John Foster Dulles, who later became US secretary of state. Concerning Eleanor Lansing Dulles, also see Mariko Maeda, *Erenoa Ransingu Daresu: Amerika no seiki wo ikita josei gaikokan* [Eleanor Lansing Dulles: A Female Diplomat who Lived in the American Century], Yuhikaku, 2004.

4 BIS, *Témoignages et points de vue*, BIS, Bâle, 1980; BIS, *The Bank for International Settlements and the Basle Meetings, Published on the Occasion of the Fiftieth Anniversary, 1930–1980*, Basel, 1980.

5 Giuseppe Ugo Papi, *The First Twenty Years of the Bank for International Settlements*, Bancaria, Rome, 1951; Roger Auboin, *The Bank for International Settlements, 1930–1955*, Princeton University Press, Princeton, 1955. Auboin, the author of this book, was the BIS's second general manager. Henry Han Schloss, *The Bank for International Settlements, an Experiment in Central Bank Cooperation*, North-Holland Publishing Company, Amsterdam, 1958.

6 Paolo Baffi, *The Origins of Central Bank Cooperation: The Establishment of the Bank for International Settlements*, Editori Laterza, Bari/Rome, 2002.

7 James Baker, *The Bank for International Settlements: Evolution and Evaluation*, Quorum Books, Westport, 2002.

8 Gunter Baer, "Sixty-five Years of Central Bank Cooperation at the Bank for International Settlements," in Carl Holtfrerich, James Reis and Gianni Toniolo, eds., *The Emergence of Modern Central Banking from 1918 to the Present*, Ashgate, Aldershot, 1999.

9 Gianni Toniolo, with the assistance of Piet Clement, *Central Bank Cooperation at the*

Bank for International Settlements, 1930–1973, Cambridge University Press, Cambridge/New York, 2005. This book, which began as a project while the author was researching the BIS, is a full history of the bank published before the present work. Its author, Professor Toniolo, and his collaborator, Piet Clement, BIS head of library, archives and research support, were in close communication with the author Yago, who also cooperated in the preparation of their work. As described below, while the subjects and approaches of this official history and the present work differ, they rely on the same materials and took shape through mutual exchange of opinion between the authors. In this way, they should be understood as complementary to each other rather than in competition. In Japan, Shinichi Yoshikuni, who had spent his career involved in international finance operations at the Bank of Japan, published *Kokusai kinyu noto: BIS no mado kara* [International Finance Notes: From the Windows of the BIS] (Reitaku University Press, 2008). Yoshikuni's witness is highly valuable since he is very familiar with backstage happenings at the BIS, for example having chaired meetings of the BIS Committee on the Global Financial System, which was commonly known as the "Yoshikuni Committee."

10 Claudio Borio and Gianni Toniolo, "One Hundred and Thirty Years of Central Bank Cooperation: a BIS perspective," *BIS Working Papers*, no. 197, 2006 and Richard Cooper, "Almost a Century of Central Bank Cooperation," *BIS Working Papers*, no. 198, 2006. Those works have been made into a collection: Claudio Borio, Gianni Toniolo and Piet Clement, eds., *Past and Future of Central Bank Cooperation*, Cambridge University Press, Cambridge, 2008.

11 Toniolo, *Central Bank Cooperation*, op. cit., p. xii.

12 Works that should be noted here are Richard Sayers, *The Bank of England 1891–1944*, Cambridge University Press, Cambridge, 1986, which discusses the formation of the Bank of England as a central bank; Giannni Toniolo, ed., *Central Banks' Independence in Historical Perspective*, Walter De Gruyter, Berlin, 1989, with important international comparison on the subject; and Olivier Feiertag et Michel Margairaz, dirs., *Politiques et pratiques des banques d'émission en Europe (XVII ème–XXème siècle) – Le bicentenaire de la Banque de France dans la perspective de l'identité monétaire européenne*, Albin Michel, Paris, which refers to many member central banks of the BIS.

13 Toniolo's history of the BIS considers this subject to be early history of central-bank cooperation and devotes several pages to it. Toniolo, *Central Bank Cooperation*, op. cit., pp. 5–9, 13–16.

14 Barry Eichengreen, "Central Bank Co-operation and Exchange Rate Commitments: The Classical and Interwar Gold Standards Compared," *Financial History Review*, vol. 2, no. 2, 1995; M. Flandreau, "Central Bank Cooperation in Historical Perspective: A Sceptical View," *Economic History Review*, no. 50, 1997.

15 Cf. Louis Galambos and Joseph Pratt, *The Rise of the Corporate Commonwealth: US Business and Public Policy in the Twentieth Century*, Basic Books, New York, 1988; For a methodological survey, cf. Alfred D. Chandler, Jr., Stuart Bruchey, Louis Galambos, eds., *The Changing Economic Order: Readings in American Business and Economic History*, Harcourt, Brace & World, New York, 1968.

16 For a manifesto for organizational history in recent years, see Patrick Fridenson, "Un nouvel objet: l'organisation" in *Annales, Histoire, Sciences Sociales*, vol. 44, no. 6, novembre–décembre 1989.

17 The original connotations of organizational history included comparative institutional analysis, and the courses of its later development have varied among advocates. However, Eric Godelier *et al.*, who have expanded the research domain from organizational history to business culture theory in recent years, clearly have adopted an explicitly antagonistic approach toward comparative institutional analysis and economics in general. Cf. Eric Godelier, *La Culture d'entreprise*, Editions La Découverte, Paris, 2006.

18 Concerning the neoliberalism discussed here, see François Denord, Genèse et institutionalization du néo-liberalisme en France (années 1930–années 1950), thèse, EHESS, Paris, 2003; Yasuo Gonjo, ed., *Shinjiyushugi to sengo shihonshugi: Obei ni okeru rekishiteki keiken* [Neoliberalism and Postwar Capitalism: Historical Experiences in the West], Nihon Keizai Hyoronsha 2006.

19 As for a theoretical and biographical study on Wicksell, cf. Torsten Gårdlund, *The Life of Knut Wicksell*, Edward Elgar, Cheltenham/Northampton, 1996; Concerning the relation between Wicksellian economic thought and the BIS see Kazuhiko Yago, "Wicksellian Tradition at the Bank for International Settlements: Per Jacobsson on Money and Credit," *History of Economic Thought*, vol. 48, no. 2, December 2006.

1 The founding of the Bank for International Settlements: a "commercial bank," or a "bank for central banks"?

1 *Tanaka Tetsusaburo-shi kinyushidan sokkiroku* [Tetsusaburo Tanaka's Shorthand Notes on Financial History], Bank of Japan, *Nihon kinyushi shiryo* [Documents on Japanese Financial History], vol. 35, Bank of Japan, Tokyo, 1974, p. 43.

2 Roger Auboin, *The Bank for International Settlements, 1930–1955*, op. cit. The author, Auboin, was the second general manager of the BIS. Born in Paris in 1891, Auboin served in the military in World War I after graduating from l'Ecole Libre des Sciences Politiques. After the war, he worked in organizations including the Conseil d'Etat and the prime minister's cabinet office and then was sent to the National Bank of Romania as an advisor in support of currency stability from 1929 through 1934. In 1937 he became secretary general in the Ministry of the National Economy and a member of the General Council of the Banque de France, before serving as BIS general manager for 20 years from 1938 through 1958. Archives de la Banque de France, 1489200303/132, Roger Auboin.

3 BIS Historical Archives, B14 Royot 39, Documents Georges Royot, M.v.Z., "BIS Reconsidered," 1944. The author of this note, Marcel van Zeeland, worked in the BIS Banking Department from the bank's founding until 1962 (serving as head of the Banking Department from 1947 through 1962).

4 BIS Historical Archives, B14 Royot 39, Documents Georges Royot, Rt, "Les idées de banque internationale de 1919 à fin 1922." The author of this note, Georges Royot, was the first BIS general manager.

5 See the Royot note above concerning the content of this Blum and Auriol proposal and its impact. Ibid.

6 Léon Blum, *L'OEuvre de Léon Blum*, tome III-1, Albin Michel, Paris, 1972, pp. 163–169.

7 Ibid., p. 172. While the Royot note above describes Frankfurt as the site of the socialist and labor-movement conference, it is likely that Blum submitted his plan in Amsterdam.

8 Pierre Mendès-France, La Banque Internationale, contribution à l'étude du problème des Etats-Unis d'Europe, Librairie Valois, Paris, 1930, p. 8.

9 Ibid., p. 18.

10 Ibid., pp. 172–179.

11 Dulles, *The Bank for International Settlements at Work*, op. cit., p. 6.

12 Bank of Japan Archives.

13 The course of debate on this day is based on notes from Quesnay, who was in attendance at the meeting. BIS Historical Archives, 7.20, Central Banking Series, "Extrait de comptes-rendus de Pierre Quesnay sur les discussions au Comité des Experts (Paris, Comité Young) relatives à la future Banque des Règlements Internationaux," 6 mars 1929, "Faut-il un organisme central?"

14 Dulles, *The Bank for International Settlements at Work*, op. cit., pp. 10–11.

15 BIS Historical Archives, 7.20, Central Banking Series, "Extrait de comptes-rendus de Pierre Quesnay…," 8 mars 1929.

16 The text of this declaration is reproduced in the appendix to Einzig's work. Einzig, *The Bank for International Settlements*, op. cit., pp. 113–115.

17 Ibid., p. 32.

18 André Liesse, "Au Comité des Experts, un projet de banque internationale," *L'Economiste Français*, 16 mars 1929, pp. 321–323.

19 "The proposed International Bank – the Federal Reserve should not participate," *Commercial and Financial Chronicle*, no. 3326, March 23, 1929.

20 "The Proposed International Bank – the Federal Reserve Banks Committed to it," *Commercial and Financial Chronicle*, no. 3328, April 6, 1929.

21 "The Committee of Experts and the Proposal for a New International Bank," *Banker*, April 1929. In connection with this point, Bank of England historian Sayers, citing an essay published in the August 1929 issue of the *Banker*, says, "The welcome the British press was giving to the proposal of a BIS in 1929 was therefore decidedly cool." However, perhaps it should be noted that as seen here the drift of the argument in the *Banker* in April of that same year was closer to acceptance of the BIS than that of the argument in August. Richard Sayers, *The Bank of England, 1891–1944*, Cambridge University Press, Cambridge, 1986 (First paperback edition, reprinted with correction), p. 354.

22 Joseph Caillaux, "The International Bank Scheme," *Banker*, April 1929.

23 BIS Historical Archives, 7.20, Central Banking Series, "Extrait de comptes-rendus de Pierre Quesnay…," 11 mars 1929, "Capital de la Banque internationale."

24 Ibid.

25 Ibid.

26 BIS Historical Archives, 7.20, Central Banking Series, "Extrait de comptes-rendus de Pierre Quesnay…," March 13, 1929.

27 Concerning this process, see Juichi Tsushima, *Mori Kengo-san no koto* [About Kengo Mori], vol. II (Hoto Kankokai, 1963), p. 307. As seen in Chapter 2 of the present work, Mori was the head of the Japanese delegation sent to the Young Committee from the Ministry of Finance. The author of this note, Tsushima, was a colleague who accompanied Mori.

28 SOAS, Sir Charles Addis Collection, PP MS 14/441 box 39, Correspondence, Addis to Henderson, June 25, 1941.

29 The text of the Young Plan cited here, and Einzig's assessment, are both from Einzig, *The Bank for International Settlements*, op. cit., p. 37.

30 "The Proposed New Bank," *Bankers' Magazine*, no. 1023, June 1929.

31 "The Bank for International Settlements," *Banker*, July 1929.

32 André Liesse, "Sur le Plan Young: la Banque des Règlements Internationaux" in *L'Economiste Français*, 6 juillet 1929. Managed currency theory as referred to here is the open-market policy of the 1920s, as typified by Keynes' *A Tract on Monetary Reform*. For this reason, it did not have in mind the demand control of the Depression and later. At the time this essay was announced, such managed currency had been introduced in France too, and the press was bustling with opinion in favor of and against it. For a representative portion of this argument, cf. Bertrand Nogaro, *Finances et politique*, M. Giard, Paris, 1927.

33 "Reparations and the New Bank," *Bankers' Magazine*, no. 1024, July 1929.

34 André Liesse, "Du Rôle de la Banque des Règlements Internationaux sur l'exécution par l'Allemagne du Plan Young," *L'Economiste Français*, 14 septembre 1929.

35 BIS Historical Archives, 3/6 I, Granting of medium-term credits (from October 13, 1930 to March 31, 1931), "Comité d'Organisation de la Banque des Règlements Internationaux," séance du 17 octobre 1929, 10.5h. This note was attached to a letter sent on a later date by the Banque de France governor, Moret, to Gates McGarrah, appointed chairman of the board of the BIS, asking about interpretation of the statutes.

BIS Historical Archives, 3/6 I, correspondence, Clément Moret to Gates McGarrah, March 12, 1931.

36 Ibid.

37 Ibid.

38 Einzig, *The Bank for International Settlements*, op. cit., p. 56.

39 Dulles, *The Bank for International Settlements at Work*, op. cit., p. 29.

40 Per Jacobsson, "The Young Plan and the Bank for International Settlements," *Some Monetary Problems, International and National*, Oxford University Press/Basel Centre for Economic and Financial Research, Basel, 1958, p. 108. These recollections of Jacobsson were part of a presentation before the annual general meeting of the Swedish Bankers' Association on October 29, 1929 – eight days after the above debate with Layton *et al.* For this reason, this is important as a statement based on the most recent atmosphere in the middle of the Baden-Baden meeting.

41 Einzig, *The Bank for International Settlements*, op. cit., p. 53.

42 Dulles, *The Bank for International Settlements at Work*, op. cit., pp. 29–31; *Tanaka Tetsusaburo-shi kin-yu shidan sokkiroku* [Tetsusaburo Tanaka's Shorthand Notes on Financial History], op. cit., p. 32 Tetsusaburo Tanaka will be discussed in detail in Chapter 2.

43 Jacques Rueff, "Le Marché financier devant les problèmes internationaux du crédit," in Charles Farnier *et al.*, *Les Problèmes actuels du crédit, Conférences organisés par la Société des Ancien Elèves et Elèves de l'Ecole Libre des Sciences Politiques*, Librairie Félix Alcan, Paris, 1930, pp. 207–211.

44 Archives of the Minister of Finances (France), B54770, "Note au sujet du siège de la BRI," October 7, 1929.

45 Concerning the above course of events, see Sayers, *The Bank of England*, op. cit., pp. 355–356.

46 Ibid., p. 355. Behind the attempt to secure independence for the BIS from the League of Nations was a debate on the nature of the BIS that took place in the Second Assembly of the league. For the background on this debate, see Koji Fujise and Soo-I Lee, *Josho: Kokusai renmei to keizai kinyu mondai* [Introduction: The League of Nations and Economic and Financial Issues], (Koji Fujise, ed., *Sekai daifukyo to kokusai renmei* [The Great Depression and the League of Nations], University of Nagoya Press, 1994), pp. 10–11; see also Yann Decorzant, "Internationalism in Economic and Financial Organisation of the League of Nations," in Daniel Laqua, ed., *Internationalism Reconfigured, Transnational Ideas and Movements between the World Wars*, I.B. Tauris, London/New York, 2011.

47 "The Bank for International Settlements: A Commentary upon the Statutes," *Banker*, December 1929.

48 André Liesse, "La Naissance de la Banque des Règlements Internationaux et le premier emprunt du Plan Young," *L'Economiste Français*, 10 mai 1930.

49 Archives of the Minister of Finances (France), B54770, correspondence, Boissard, Organisation Committee for the Bank for International Settlements, Baden-Baden, October 10, 1929.

50 André Liesse, "Sur l'organisation de la Banque des Règlements Internationaux," *L'Economiste Français*, 26 octobre 1929.

51 Joseph Caillaux, "The International Bank," *Banker*, August 1929. In this essay, Caillaux argues that "it may well be asked whether it is really necessary that this new organization should be a bank above the central banks" and that "it is the State that holds the supreme power of regulating economic life."

52 Joseph Caillaux, "After the Hague," *Banker*, October 1929.

53 "The Bank for International Settlements: A Commentary upon the Statutes," *Banker*, December 1929, op. cit.

54 Gustav Cassel, "Is the International Bank Necessary?," *Bankers' Magazine*, no. 1028, November1929. Another anonymous essay carried in this same issue warned that the

notes discounting operations provided for in the BIS statutes were a cause of serious criticisms in the City of London in particular and that such operations would result in "international inflation."

55 Paul Einzig, "Co-operation and International Bank," *Banker*, June 1930.

56 ***, "La Banque des Règlements Internationaux et l'internationalisme monétaire," *Revue d'Economie Politique*, vol. 43, 1929, pp. 1050–1066.

57 Olivier Feiertag, "La Banque de France et les problèmes monétaires européens de la Conférence de Gênes à la création de la BRI (1922–1930), in Eric Bussière and Michel Dumoulin, dirs., *Milieux économiques et intégration européenne en Europe occidentale au XXe siècle*, Artois Presses Université, Arras, 1998, pp. 29–30. This essay, relying on Banque de France materials, demonstrates that at the time of the BIS's founding the Banque de France had intended to use it as "a Trojan horse for financial infiltration into Central Europe and the Balkans" but that this intention was frustrated by the impact of the Depression and a change in strategy by General Manager Quesnay himself. Ibid. pp. 32–34.

58 ***, "La Banque des Règlements Internationaux et l'internationalisme monétaire," op. cit.

59 Feliks Mlynarski, *Gold and Central Banks*, Macmillan, New York, 1929, pp. 142–155.

60 Feliks Mlynarski, *Credit and Peace, a Way out of the Crisis*, George Allen and Unwin, London, 1933, pp. 48–54.

61 "Questions monétaires de l'heure présente," *Revue d'Economie Politique*, vol. 46, 1932, no. 2, p. 312 et passim.

62 Addis's words are from an April 3, 1930 presentation to a bankers' conference conducted by the Hudson's Bay Company. This presentation was introduced in an anonymous essay in the *Banker's Magazine*. "The Bank for International Settlements," *Bankers' Magazine*, no. 1034, May 1930.

63 BIS, *The First Annual Report*.

64 Archives de Ministère de Finances, B54770, Note sur les Statuts de la Banque des Règlements Internationaux, s.d.

65 The National Bank of Belgium, the Bank of England, the Banque de France, the Reichsbank, and the Bank of Italy.

66 Instead of the Bank of Japan, subscription was handled by a group of banks represented by the Industrial Bank of Japan. The US FRB was represented by Morgan, First National Bank of New York and First National Bank of Chicago.

67 At the end of the BIS's inaugural fiscal year (March 31, 1931), the following countries (through their central banks or groups of banks) owned shares: Great Britain, France, Germany, Belgium, Italy, the United States, Japan (the above six countries, and groups of banks in the case of Japan and the United States, owned 16,000 shares each), Poland, Danzig, Greece, Bulgaria, Romania, the Netherlands, Finland, Hungary, Czechoslovakia, Denmark, Austria, Switzerland, Sweden (each of the above 13 countries owned 4,000 shares), Latvia, Lithuania (each of the above two countries owned 500 shares), and 100 shares owned by Estonia, for a total of 165,100 shares owned by 23 countries. BIS, *The First Annual Report*, Appendix, Table 1.

68 The operations that the bank "may in particular" carry out are: (1) buy and sell gold coin or bullion for its own account or for the account of central banks; (2) hold gold for its own account under earmark in central banks; (3) accept the custody of gold for the account of central banks; (4) make advances to or borrow from central banks against gold, bills of exchange and other short-term obligations of prime liquidity or other approved securities; (5) discount, rediscount, purchase or sell with or without its endorsement bills of exchange, cheques and other short-term obligations of prime liquidity, "including Treasury bills and other such government short-term securities as are currently marketable"; (6) buy and sell exchange for its own account or for the account of central banks; (7) buy and sell "negotiable securities other than shares" for

its own account or for the account of central banks; (8) discount for central banks bills taken from their portfolio and rediscount with central banks bills taken from its own portfolio; (9) open and maintain current or deposit accounts with central banks; (10) accept deposits from central banks on current or deposit account, deposits in connection with trustee agreements that may be made between the bank and governments in connection with international settlements, and other deposits as in approved by the board.

69 These three items are: act as agent or correspondent of any central bank; arrange with any central bank for the latter to act as its agent or correspondent, and enter into agreements to act as trustee or agent in connection with international settlements. In later years, the French finance ministry cautioned that these three items should not lead to demands by the Bank of England or others that the BIS establish branches. Archives de Ministère de Finances, B54770, Note sur les Statuts de la Banque des Règlements Internationaux, s.d.

70 In connection with these provisions, in November 1930, after the BIS had begun operation, a Belgian private bank and the Belgian branch of an American private bank directly demanded to the BIS that it accept deposits and discount bills. The BIS rejected both demands. These examples are interesting in that they hint of the market's expectations (even if based on a misunderstanding) for the BIS after it started operation. Rapport spécial sur certaines opérations effectuées par la Banque entre le 1er et le 30 novembre 1930, pp. 1–2. Also, while this draft note prepared by the Banking Department clearly indicates the names of the banks making this demand (including the Banque de Bruxelles), the official note distributed to the board of directors had these names removed. Rapport spécial sur certaines opérations de la Banque entre le 1er et le 30 novembre 1930, annexe VI/D, pp. 7–8.

71 FRBNY, Research memorandum, from M.A. Kritz to Mr. Knoke, "Federal Reserve Participation in the Bank for International Settlements," May 12, 1950.

72 For the course through which these provisions were amended to their current form, see *BIS 44th Annual Report*, p. 192.

73 Ibid.

74 Incidentally, the numbers of employees assigned to each department at the time of the BIS's founding were 12 to the secretary general, five to the Banking Department, and four to the Central Banking Department. In addition, there were two employees in the president's office and the general manager's office, for a total of 23 "staff-level personnel." In addition to these, there were 14 accountants, 13 bookkeepers, three interpreters, five mail clerks, seven secretaries and 22 speed typists, for a total of 64 "employee-level personnel." Since there also were seven members of upper-level management such as department heads, BIS execution sections at the time of its founding included a grand total of 94 personnel. *BIS 1st Annual Report*, Appendix, 2.

75 The 10.5-month fiscal year was an anomaly in this year only, with subsequent fiscal years consisting of 12 months.

76 At the time of the first annual report, the gold price on which the value of a Gold Swiss franc was calculated was the London gold market price. From the second year through March 31, 1936 settlement of accounts, it was the Paris gold market, and thereafter the value has been calculated in reference to the official quotation from the New York gold market. *BIS 7th Annual Report*.

77 Article 4 of this trust agreement stipulates the minimal amount that should be deposited by these claimant nations. Of the minimum of approximately 1.15 million Gold Swiss francs in total, more than 630,000 francs were contributed by France, followed by Britain, which contributed approximately 250,000 francs, and Italy at approximately 120,000 francs. Japan was stipulated to contribute the second smallest amount besides Poland, at 8,459 Gold Swiss francs. *BIS 1st Annual Report*, p. 3.

78 BIS Historical Archives, Etats Mensuels d'Opération, "Report on the Operation of the Bank," May 1930, annex D, personal and confidential.

79 BIS *1st Annual Report*, p. 5.
80 Ibid., p. 4.
81 Ibid., p. 4.
82 Ibid., p. 5.
83 Ibid., annex IV.
84 Yokohama Specie Bank materials, period 2 (mf04/w3/69), "Details of the Balance Sheet as at June 10, 1930 (for the Information of Directors)."
85 BIS Historical Archives, Etats Mensuels d'Opération, "Report on the Operation of the Bank," May 1930, annex D, personal and confidential. The foreign-exchange section of the Banking Department established a system to communicate daily over the phone with London, Berlin and Paris.
86 BIS Historical Archives, Etats Mensuels d'Opération, "Rapport sur les opérations de la banque du 11 juin 1930 au 11 juillet 1930," annexe III/F.
87 BIS Historical Archives, Etats Mensuels d'Opération, "Report on the Operation of the Bank," May 1930, annex D, personal and confidential.
88 BIS Historical Archives, Etats Mensuels d'Opération, May 1930, "Report on the Operation of the Bank," annex D, op. cit.
89 See BIS Historical Archives, file 7.5, 1/2, "Disposal of the Surplus on the Profit and Loss Account, 1949–50," March 28, 1950.
90 Ibid.
91 The figures indicated on page 22 of the Japanese translated version of *BIS Annual Report 1*, are different from those given here. This is due to a typographical error mistaking the number "8" for "3." However, the calculation result as given on page 22 of the Japanese translated version is identical to that given in this English version.
92 BIS Historical Archives, file 7.5, 1/8a, Note for the use of the President, "A Few Remarks on the Desirability of Hidden Reserves," February 6, 1960.
93 BIS Historical Archives, Banking Department, Rapport sur les operations de la BRI du 1er au octobre 1930, annexe V/C, p. 10. However, it is not clear from these materials why this reserve account was booked only in the hidden ledgers.
94 Toniolo, Central Bank Cooperation at the Bank for International Settlements, op. cit., pp. 66–67.
95 Roberta Allbert Dayer, *Finance and Empire, Sir Charles Addis, 1861–1945*, Macmillan, London/New York, 1988, pp. 208–209 et passim. This work is a full biography of Addis's life, with numerous mentions of the in-depth negotiations concerning the BIS, including the Baden-Baden meeting.
96 SOAS, PP MS 14/46–57 Box.5, Diary, September 25, 1930, p. 78.
97 SOAS, Sir Charles Addis Collection, PP MS 14/46–57 Box.5, Diary, May19, , 1931, p. 40.
98 SOAS, Sir Charles Addis Collection, PP MS 14/46–57 Box.5, Diary, April 11, 1932, p. 31.
99 Dayer, *Finance and Empire*, op. cit., pp. 280, 307–320 et passim.

2 The Bank for International Settlements and central banks during the 1930s: another anti-depression measure

1 Procès-verbal de la Commission de Surveillance de la Caisse des Dépôts et Consignations, le 17 avril 1931. Regarding the CDC and its connection to this business, see the author's doctoral thesis, Kazuhiko Yago, *Epargne populaire comme fonds de placement public: rôle de la Caisse des Dépôts et Consignations* (Université Paris X Nanterre, 1996) and Kazuhiko Yago, *Furansu ni okeru koteki kin'yu to taishu chochiku – Yokin Kyotaku Kinko to chochiku kinko, 1816–1944* [Public finance and popular savings in France: the Caisse des Dépôts et Consignations and savings banks, 1816–1944], University of Tokyo Press, 1999, pp. 151–157.
2 Various studies have addressed the historical conditions under which the concept of

"central bank independence" took shape. These include literature by Kenneth Mouré which in the context argues that central banks came to assert their independence in return for supporting government finances mired in the crisis of the time, an essay by Sylvain Schirmann on the resonance between the theory of central bank independence in the Financial Committee of the League of Nations and the BIS, and the works of Yasuo Gonjo on the prospects for materialization of modern credit policies. Kenneth Mouré, *La Politique du franc Poincaré, Perception de l'économie et contraintes politiques dans la stratégie monétaire de la France, 1926–1936*, Albin Michel, Paris, 1998; Sylvain Schirmann, "Le Comité financier de la SDN et les questions monétaires en Europe au cours des années trente," *Centre de Recherche Histoire et Civilisation de l'Université de Metz, Organisations internationales et architectures européennes, 1929–1939*, actes du colloque de Metz (31 mai-1er juin 2001), Metz, 2003, pp. 385–396; Yasuo Gonjo, *Furansu shihon shugi to chuo ginko–Furansu ginko kindaika no rekishi* [*French Capitalism and the Central Bank: The Modernization History of the Bank of France*], University of Tokyo Press, 1999.

3　Nachlass Per Jacobsson, s3/d2, Note for Dr. Beyen, "Reorganization of Monetary and Economic Department," 6 viii, 1935. Hereinafter in this passage, except as noted otherwise citations refer to this document.

4　As a typical Jacobsson thought of the time, see Per Jacobsson, "The Value of Gold and Fluctuation in the Level of Prices, with Special Reference to Post-War Conditions," *Ekonomisk Tidskrift*, no. 10, 1917.

5　At the time, the *Economist* ran a series of unsigned essays by Jacobsson. Anon. [Per Jacobsson], "The Rate of Interest – a Forecast," *Economist* March 7, 14, 21, 28, 1925. The article has been published later in the book by Per Jacobsson, *Some Monetary Problems, Some Monetary Problems, International and National*, Basel Centre for Economic and Financial Research, Series B, no. 4, Oxford University Press, 1958.

6　Ibid., p. 64.

7　In later years, Jacobsson's daughter Erin interviewed his old friends. Among the respondents, the editor of the *Göteborgs Posten*, Harald Hjörne, indicated that the banker Marcus Wallenburg Sr. was involved in Jacobsson's transfer to the BIS. However, she rejected this speculation as groundless. Nachlass Per Jacobsson, s5/d1, Notes on Per Jacobsson.

8　See the following literature concerning Wicksell and the currents in economics around him: Eli Heckscher, "A Survey of Economic Thought in Sweden, 1875–1950" in *Scandinavian Economic History Review*, vol. 1, no. 1, 1953; Axel Leijonhufvud, *On Keynesian Economics and the Economics of Keynes: A Study in Monetary Theory*, Oxford University Press, New York, 1966; Leijonhufvud, *Information and Coordination: Essays in Macroeconomic Theory*, Oxford University Press, New York, 1981; Lars Magnusson, *An Economic History of Sweden*, Routeledge, New York, 2000.

9　Jacobsson, *Some Monetary Problems*, op. cit., pp. 228–229.

10　Hoover Institution Archives, Hayek Papers, Mont Pèlerin Society, box 81, folder 3, "Contra-cyclical Measures, Full Employment, and Monetary Reform," Hoff (chair), Graham (report), April 7, 1947, pp. 2–9. Hereinafter, these papers are referred to as the Hayek Papers, showing box and folder numbers. Concerning the pedigree of the 100 percent currency theory in the United States, see Chapter 4.

11　Hayek Papers, box 81, folder 3, "Free Enterprise or Competitive Order," address on monetary stabilization, Rappard (chair), Director (report), April 1, 1947, p. 10.

12　Jacques Rueff, "L'Etat actuel du système des paiements internationaux," *Revue d'Economie Politique*, t. 59, 1949, pp. 145–165. This study is a tour de force incorporating the future of the IMF structure and criticism of the Marshall Plan, as well as touching on Keynes's theories. The Mont Pèlerin Society produced an English translation of this paper, so the paper might have had an impact on the ranks of neoliberals as well. Hayek Papers, box 81, folder 2, Rueff, "The Present Status of the System of International Payments." For an overview of Rueff's theories on money and credit, see Yasuo Gonjo, ed., *Shinjiyushugi to sengo shihonshugi* [Neoliberalism and Postwar Capitalism], op. cit.

13 Hayek Papers, box 81, folder 3, "Contra-cyclical Measures, Full Employment, and Monetary Reform," Hoff (chair), Stigler (report), p. 1.

14 Hayek Papers, box 81, folder 3, "Contra-cyclical Measures, Full Employment, and Monetary Reform," Hoff (chair), Robbins (report), April 7, 1947.

15 Hayek Papers, box 71, folder 7, " 'Free' enterprise and competitive order," Rappard (chair), Hayek (report), April 1, 1947, p. 10.

16 The allegories of the "jungle" and the "jail" were employed by F. Graham at a Mont Pèlerin Society symposium. These expressions were used by Graham, who positioned himself inbetween Mises and Robbins on the subject of government regulation of monopolies, in the following manner: "Complete freedom is found in the jungle, where there is no law." "Is it not the case that we have met here to find a path in between the jungle and the jail?" Hayek Papers, box 81, folder 3, "Free Enterprise or Competitive Order," discussion, Rappard (chair), April 1, 1947, p. 5.

17 Hayek Papers, "Contra-cyclical Measures, Full Employment, and Monetary Reform," op. cit., p. 10.

18 Hayek Papers, box 81, folder 3, "The Problems and Chances of European Federation," Allais (chair), April 3, 1947, passim.

19 This argument was developed in a study titled "The Economic Conditions of International Federalism" (first published in 1939; later reprinted in a book, Friedrich von Hayek, *Individualism and Economic Order*, Routledge, London, 1949).

20 Hereinafter, concerning BIS plans on the establishment of subcommittees, see the BIS internal documents brought back to Japan by the representative of the Yokohama Specie Bank. Yokohama Specie Bank materials, period 2 (mf04/w3/69), "Note on Meetings to be Held after the Annual General Meeting," s.d. At this time, the Monetary and Economic Department was known as the Central Banking Department, and Jacobsson had not yet joined the BIS. While it is unclear who led these meetings in terms of theory, from a look at personnel assignments the presence of General Manager Quesnay and Head of Banking Department Huelse stands out.

21 BIS Historical Archives, 1/20b, vol. 1, Second Committee, II. 2, Credit Problems, "The Creation of Credit," rapporteur Bachmann. Hereinafter, references to the Bachmann report are based on this document.

22 Auboin, *The Bank for International Settlements*, op. cit., pp. 10–11.

23 Olivier Feiertag, "Les Banques d'émission et la BRI face à la dislocation de l'étalon-or (1931–1933)," *Histoire, Economie, Société* octobre–décembre 1999. Related essays are Olivier Feiertag and Alain Plessis, "Conjoncture et structures monétaires internationales en Europe à la fin des années trente: dislocation et convergences," *Revue Economique*, vol. 51, no. 2, mars 2000; Toniolo, *Central Bank Cooperation at the Bank for International Settlements*, op. cit., pp. 106–114 et passim.

24 Nachlass Per Jacobsson, s1/d2, "Memorandum on Central Banking by Dr. Jacobsson, Commission of Inquiry into Banking, Currency and Credit," February 2, 1935.

25 For the structure and reports of this committee hereinafter, see BIS Historical Archives, 3/6, vol. 1, annexe VI/F, Rapport du Comité pour les crédits moyen-terme. This report was prepared based on the deliberations in the committee on October 13 and November 8, 1930 and submitted to the board of directors.

26 Rapport sur les opérations de la Banque du 12 juillet au 30 septembre 1930, annexe IV/E, pp. 12–13.

27 Marcel Netter, *Histoire de la Banque de France entre les deux guerres, 1918–1939*, édition privée, Pomponne, s.d., p. 345. While the formal title given to these bodies by the board of directors was "sub-committee," in their reports and letters

subcommittee members themselves shortened this to "committee." In this book, the term "committee" will be used hereinafter.

28 BIS Historical Archives, 3/6, vol. 1, annexe VI/F, Rapport du Comité pour les crédits moyen-terme, op. cit.

29 Ibid.

30 Ibid.

31 Institutions in each country ascertained by the BIS general manager as of October 1930 were two English firms providing mid-term credit, Belgium's Société Nationale de Crédit à l'Industrie, and a company in Yugoslavia specialized in mid-term credit. In November of the same year, inquiries were made to France's Banque Française d'Acceptation and Austria's Oesterrichischen Genossenschaften as well. BIS Historical Archives, 3/6, Granting of medium-term credits, I, correspondence, de Quesnay à Siepmann (Banque d'Angleterre), le 29 octobre 1930; de Quesnay à Paul van Zeeland (Directeur de la Banque Nationale de Belgique), le 30 octobre 1930; de Quesnay à Bailony (Gouverneur de la Banque Nationale de Yougoslavie).

32 BIS Historical Archives, Banking Department, Rapport spécial sur certaines opérations effectuées par la Banque du 1er au 31 décembre 1930, annexe VII/E, p. 2.

33 BIS Historical Archives, 3/6, Granting of medium-term credits, I, Report of the Committee on Middle-Term Credits, March 7, 1931. At this time, separately from the matter of extension of maturity this committee also discussed whether to accept under the conditions for provision of mid-term credit bills drawn by the Soviet trade representative in Berlin, brought to the BIS by the German bank Golddiskontbank. While the committee found that there were no problems in terms of the formal requirements of the notes, it submitted the matter to the board of directors with the comment "we must not close our eyes to the fact that this matter involves political points of dispute." Ibid.

34 Gates McGarrah, "A Balance Wheel of World Credit," *Nation's Business*, March 1931.

35 Major projects included the lending by the Paris private-sector bank Société Européenne de Crédit et de Banque of 160 million French francs in response to an application secured by Yugoslavian government bond to fund a railway in southern Macedonia, discounting of 9,780 pounds sterling mortgage securities on the building of two merchant vessels in Estonia applied for personally by a Belgian businessman and then-Belgian consul to Estonia Léon Moreau, and financing to set up a bank syndicate for the purpose of providing mid-term credit applied for by Dutch financial institution Nederlandsche Crediet en Financiering Maatschappij. After conducting a credit inquiry through a credit agency, the BIS rejected the Moreau's application for the reason of "the need to conduct it through a central bank." In July 1931, it postponed consideration of the transaction with the Dutch financial institution because of "fundamental changes in the international credit and currency situation." Concerning these projects, see BIS Historical Archives, 3/6, Granting of Medium-term Credits, II/1–2. In 1934, mid-term credit in the amount of 1.21 million French francs (equivalent to 200,000 Reichsmarks) was extended to a French trading company Societe pour l'importation des charbons et autres produits through the French commercial bank Banque de Paris et des Pays-Bas. BIS Historical Archives, 3/6d, Granting of Medium-Term Credits.

36 These companies were named Compagnie Centrale des Prêts Fonciers à Amsterdam and Banque Internationale de Crédit Foncier à Bâle. For an overview of both, see the postwar explanatory letter from Royot of the BIS to Jacobsson. BIS Historical Archives, 7. 18(8), Documents Georges Royot (ROY7), Note pour Mr. Jacobsson, le 3 avril 1954, re: lettre du 31 mars 1954 de M. Kitzinger.

37 This plan of Norman's is described in a confidential memo circulated to the head office of the Yokohama Specie Bank by its representative. Yokohama Specie Bank

materials, period 2 (mf04/w3/69), "Mr. Norman's Proposal, February 2, 1931, Private and Confidential."

38 Archives de la Banque de France, BRI, 1930–1931, Crédit à moyen et long terme, correspondence, Gouverneur de la Banque de France à Monsieur Gates MacGarrah, February 27, 1931.

39 Regarding France's currency doctrines, including "the plan to make Paris a financial center," and relations between British, American and French central banks, see Yasuo Gonjo, *Furansu shihon shugi to chuo ginko* [French Capitalism and the Central Bank,], op. cit., pp. 31–54, and Kenneth Mouré, *The Gold Standard Illusion, France, the Bank of France, and the International Gold Standard, 1914–1939*, Oxford University Press, Oxford/New York, 2002, pp. 200–220 et passim.

40 BIS Historical Archives, Banking Policy of the BIS, Gold Operations, 1/19b, vol. 1, Note on the Questions of Principle submitted to the Board, Annex IV/F, October 13, 1930.

41 BIS Historical Archives, Banking Policy of the BIS, Gold Operations, 1/19b, vol. 1, Operations sur or effectuees par la BRI, novembre 1932.

42 Ibid.

43 BIS Historical Archives, Banking Policy of the BIS, Gold Operations, 1/19b, vol. 1, Karl Blessing, "Gold Deposit Accounts," September 14, 1933. This is a handwritten memo by Blessing, who was on temporary assignment to the BIS at the time. The BIS explanation mentioned in the text was introduced in this memo in a critical context as responses often used for explanations by the BIS to central banks.

44 Ibid.

45 BIS Historical Archives, Banking Policy of the BIS, Gold Operations, 1/19b, vol. 1, Banking Deposits in Weight of Gold, a Possible Alternative for Pledge of Gold as Security for BIS Credits, September 1, 1933.

46 BIS Historical Archives, Banking Policy of the BIS, Gold Operations, 1/19b, vol. 1, FW [F. Weiser], Remarks on Monsieur van Zeeland's note of September 1, 1933 and September 9, 1933.

47 BIS Historical Archives, Banking Policy of the BIS, Gold Operations, 1/19b, vol. 1, Remarks on Dr. Weiser's Note of September 9, and September 14, 1933.

48 BIS Historical Archives, Banking Policy of the BIS, Gold Operations, 1/19b, vol. 1, FW [F. Weiser], Re M. van Zeeland's Additional Note of September 14, 1933 and September 20, 1933.

49 BIS Historical Archives, Rapport sur les opérations de la Banque du 1er au 30 avril 1931, Special Operations. At this time, this report was written by Royot, mentioned above. The following citations in this section are from this document.

50 While there is a considerable literature on France's monetary and fiscal policies at this time, here see the proceedings of a symposium surveying monetary policies beginning with the franc Poincaré: Comité pour l'Histoire Economique et Financière de la France, *Du franc Poincare à l'écu, colloque tenu à Bercy les 3 et 4 décembre 1992*, imprimerie Nationale, Paris, 1993.

51 The following six points were identified as the subjects of prior consultation: (1) appointment of French representatives at the BIS; (2) appointment of the BIS general manager; (3) pay-in of BIS capital; (4) business conducted on French markets at or above a certain amount; (5) amendment of the statutes; and (6) business that could impact diplomatic policy. Archives de Ministère de Finances, B54770, Note sur les Statuts de la Banque des Règlements Internationaux, s.d.

52 In 1937 the Banque de France put together an internal document titled "Memorandum on the Post of BIS General Manager" which included consideration of the distribution of nationalities in important BIS positions in light of France's contributions to the BIS, such as the amounts of deposits, arriving at the conclusions that "it cannot be denied that a tradition has formed of maintaining the distribution of nationalities that developed in 1930" and "the successor to Pierre Quesnay, the first

General Manger, should be French." Archives de la Banque de France, 1489200303/132, Aide mémoire relatif au poste de Directeur Général de la BRI, October 15, 1937.

53 Acceptance by the Banque de France of foreign securities for rediscounting was restricted under Article 4 of a November 11, 1911 agreement and the June 25, 1929 budget act. Also, while in order to get securities rediscounted the BIS needed to open an ordinary current account at the Banque de France, the BIS had not opened such accounts. However, the Swiss National Bank and others were involved in similar business. Archives de la Banque de France, BRI, coopération des banques centrales, 96, 1930–1955, MM, Questions de principe soumises à l'examen du Conseil, October 7, 1930.

54 Regarding Schacht's plan, see the confidential letter from the French consul in Basel: Archives de Ministère des Finances (France), B48889, correspondence, Le Consul de France à Bâle à M. le Ministre des Affaires Etrangères, "Service des dettes allemandes à long terme. Réunion des créanciers à Bâle, 7/11 avril 1934," le 16 avril 1934, confidentiel.

55 In April 1934, Governor Moret forwarded to the head of the funding bureau of the French finance ministry letters exchanged on this issue with BIS President Fraser, describing the strategy of behind-the-scenes negotiation focused on Swiss private-sector banks. Archives de Ministère des Finances (France), B48889, correspondence, Gouverneur de la Banque de France (Clément Moret) à Monsieur le Ministre des Finances (Direction du Mouvement Général des Fonds), Paris, le 4 avril 1934.

56 On June 14, 1934, the BIS announced this decision to claimant nation governments. Archives de la Banque de France, 7Q 657, Copie d'une lettre, en date du 14 juin 1934, adressée par la banque des Règlements Internationaux aux Gouvernements de Belgique, France.

57 Archives de la Banque de France, 7Q 657, RLG, Telephone conversation with M. Quesnay, March 28, 1934, 16h30. The Policy of applying pressure on Swiss private-sector banks came about through this telephone call from Quesnay, with the party receiving the call at the Banque de France – from the initials, it is thought that this was Roger Lacour-Gayet, head of the economic research bureau – supporting Quesnay's proposal.

58 Archives de la Banque de France, 7J273, Organisation de la liaison (1930–1931), Note sur la liaison à établir entre la Banque de France et la BRI, Bâle, le July 12, 1930. While the written proposal was unsigned, it appears to have been made by a staff member of high rank highly familiar with the situation at the Banque de France, other than the general manager, Quesnay, or persons involved in the economic research bureau. It is thought that it could have been Georges Royot, the deputy head of the BIS Banking Department, but there is no evidence backing up this assumption.

59 For example, when the Banque de France objected to Norman's plan mentioned in the preceding section for companies to handle mid-term mortgage credit, the Banque de France liaison was aware of this plan as well even before Norman proposed it to the BIS board. The liaison sent a report to the Banque de France on February 2, 1931 and Lacour-Gayet, head of the economic research bureau, submitted a memo to the governor two days later, suggesting the approach of putting this plan "on hold" while "continuing to provide moral support." Archives de la Banque de France, BRI, 1930–1931, Crédit à moyen et long terme, 7J273, personal and confidential correspondence, February 2, 1931; RLG, Observations on the project of Sir Robert Kindersley, February 4, 1931.

60 Hereinafter, concerning the dispute between France and the BIS in this section, refer to the letter sent by Hisaakira Kano of the Yokohama Specie Bank addressed to the bank's president at its head office. Yokohama Specie Bank materials, period 2 (mf04/w3/72), Letter from Hisaakira Kano to the President of the Yokohama Specie Bank, Minutes of the Fifty-fourth BIS Board Meeting, July 10, 1935.

61 Ibid.

62 Regarding Japan's handling of negotiations on the establishment of the BIS, see Ju'ichi Tsushima, *Mori Kengo-san no koto* [About Kengo Mori], (I), Boto Publishing, 1963; and *Tanaka Tetsusaburo-shi kinyushidan sokkiroku* [Tetsusaburo Tanaka's Shorthand Notes on Financial History], Bank of Japan ed., *Nihon kinyushi shiryo: Showa hen* [Japan Financial History Materials: Showa Era], vol. 35, Bank of Japan, 1975.

63 Concerning Japan's international finance officials at this time, see Toshihiko Saito, "Kokusai kinyu kanryo no jinji to seisaku [International finance official appointments and policies]," *Kindai Nihon no keizai kanryo* [Economic officials in modern Japan], Shoichi Namikata and Yoshiaki Horikoshi, eds., Nihon Keizai Hyouronsha, 2000. Concerning specie holdings abroad and the role of the Yokohama Specie Bank, see Kazuo Yamaguchi and Toshihiko Kato, *Ryotaisenkan no Yokohama Shokin Ginko* [The Yokohama Specie Bank Between World Wars], Japan Business History Institute, 1988; Kanji Ishii, "Japanese Foreign Trade and the Yokohama Specie Bank, 1880–1913" in *Pacific Banking, 1859–1959, East Meets West*, Olive Checkland, Shizuya Nishimura and Norio Tamaki, eds., St. Martin's Press, 1994.

64 Hereinafter, concerning legal issues with Japan's membership in the BIS, see Bank of Japan, ed., *Bank of Japan One Hundred-Year History*, vol. 3, Bank of Japan, 1983, pp. 357–359.

65 In the Baden-Baden Committee, the Japan representatives confirmed in detail with the secretariat of the committee the meaning of the phrasing concerning "ownership" of shares in the draft BIS statutes on sale or issue of deeds for shares "held" by central banks, asking about the meanings of the French word *détenir*, the English *own*, and the German *Eigentum*. Archives de la Banque de France, BRI, Origines et activité, Comité des Experts, 1928–1932, GR, "Précisions demandées par M. Saito au nom de la délégation japonaise, sur certains points des statuts de la Banque des Règlements Internationaux," December 18, 1929. As shown in this document, the French representatives analyzed in detail the questions from the Japanese representatives in the Baden-Baden Committee and reported on these to France.

66 The syndicate had the following structure: The Industrial Bank of Japan and Kenji Kodama (president of the Yokohama Specie Bank) each held 1,160 shares and the Daiichi, Mitsui, Mitsubishi, Yasuda, Kawasaki Daihyaku, Sanjushi, Sumitomo, Yamaguchi, Konoike, Nagoya, Aichi and Meiji banks each owned 1,140 shares. Yokohama Specie Bank materials, period 2 (mf04/w3/68), Japanese Bank Syndicate for Accepting BIS Shares, Contract, February 6, 1930. It should be noted here that the portion accepted by the Yokohama Specie Bank was accepted not in the name of the Yokohama Specie Bank as a corporation but in the name of its president Kodama as an individual.

67 See the following concerning Japan representative board members in the prewar BIS: Concerning Tetsusaburo Tanaka (Bank of Japan), see *Tanaka Tetsusaburo-shi kinyushidan sokkiroku*, op. cit; Concerning Shozo Shimai (Bank of Japan), *Shimai Shozo-shi kinyushidan sokkiroku*, ibid., and Jacobsson's journal entry on a meeting with Shimai, Nachlasse Per Jacobsson, Diaries, A20, vendredi le 10 novembre 1933, are highly interesting. Jacobsson also recorded a conversation with Yoneji Yamamoto (Bank of Japan) in which Yamamoto predicted war between Japan and the United States half a year before the Pearl Harbor attack (ibid., A32, May 19, 1941), and was impressed with the latter's level-headed judgment (ibid., A43, September 22, 1942); For the history of Daisuke Nohara (Yokohama Specie Bank), see Bank of Tokyo, *Yokohama Shokin Ginko zenshi* [Complete history of the Yokohama Specie Bank], vol. 6, 1984; Lord Cobbold of the Bank of England spoke of his impression of Hisaakira Kano (Yokohama Specie Bank) as "the most important figure" and "highly Europeanized" (BIS, *Personal Recollections and Opinions,*

Published on the Occasion of the Fiftieth anniversary, 1930–1980, Basel, 1980,
p. 55); Kojiro Kitamura (Yokohama Specie Bank) also left his own memoirs: Kojiro
Kitamura, *Kokusai budai ni shoshite* [On the international stage] (Shinji Arai, ed.,
Zoku: jiyu kawase no shogai – monogatari shokinshi [A life of free foreign exchange
– the story of specie history: Part 2], Institute of Foreign Exchange and Trade
Research, 1965, pp. 166–174).

68 Kei'ichi Takizawa of the Yokohama Specie Bank was first appointed to head this
department. In April 1938, he was succeeded by Kan Yoshimura, deputy head of the
Yokohama Specie Bank's Paris branch. Behind the appointment of Kei'ichi Taki-
zawa was the recommendation of choosing somebody from the Yokohama Specie
Bank based on the judgment that "there were no suitable prospects at the Bank of
Japan," even though ordinarily the positions at BIS were "to be filled through choos-
ing several individuals from each central bank." See Yokohama Specie Bank materi-
als, period 2 (mf04/w3/68), Saburo Sonoda, Letter to the President of Yokohama
Specie Bank, Postmarked February 7, 1930. Regarding Yoshimura, see Erin Juker-
Fleetwood, *Per Jacobsson Mediation*, op. cit.

69 *Bank of Japan One Hundred-Year History*, op. cit., pp. 153–154. Instructions were
sent to the Yokohama Specie Bank through Tetsusaburo Tanaka of the Bank of
Japan London representative office, and investment was executed through telegrams
exchanged between the Yokohama Specie Bank and the BIS assistant manager and
head of the Banking Department. Yokohama Specie Bank materials, period 2 (mf04/
w3/69), correspondence, Secretary's Department, Yokohama Specie Bank, to BIS,
September 16, 1930.

70 *Bank of Japan One Hundred-Year History*, op. cit., pp. 153–154. The bulk of the
targets of investment consisted of bills addressed to textile firms, such as Nikka
Boseki, Kurashiki Boseki, Fuji Gas Boseki, Nagoya Boseki and Kanegafuchi
Boseki. Yokohama Specie Bank materials, period 2 (mf04/w3/70), Balance Sheet of
Commercial Bills discounted and held for a/c of the Bank for International Settle-
ments, The Yokohama Specie Bank, Ltd., Osaka, January 31, 1931.

71 *Bank of Japan One Hundred-Year History*, op. cit., pp. 153–154.

72 Ibid., pp. 153–154. The *Bank of Japan One Hundred-Year History* expresses the
viewpoint that this demand from the BIS was ungrounded in light of interest-rate
conditions and its true intent was to force the Yokohama Specie Bank to lower its
fees.

73 Ibid., p. 158.

74 BIS Historical Archives, file 2/7, vol. 1, "Japanese Market," February 2, 1932, annex
18/H.

75 *Bank of Japan One Hundred-Year History*, op. cit., p. 159.

76 BIS Historical Archives, file 2/7, vol. 1, "Japanese Market," op. cit.

77 Ibid. In BIS materials it is stated that in addition to gold value guarantees the BIS
also proposed earmarking gold to the Bank of Japan. The BIS understanding was
that the Bank of Japan rejected this proposal due to the lack of rules on earmarking.
Rapport sur les opérations de la BRI du 1er au 31 décembre 1931, annexe XVII/F,
pp. 8–9.

78 *Bank of Japan One Hundred-Year History*, op. cit., p. 159.

79 BIS Historical Archives, file 2/7, vol. 1, "Japanese Market," op. cit. In the original
document, the term "at present" is underlined.

80 For the background on this matter, see BIS Historical Archives, file 2/7, vol. 1, cor-
respondence, Leon Fraser, Alternate of the President of the BIS, to Hisaakira
Hijikata, Governor of the Bank of Japan, Basel, February 18, 1932; correspondence,
Hisaakira Hijikata to Leon Fraser, Tokyo, April 14, 1932; Extract from the Minutes
of the Twenty-first Meeting of the Board of the BIS, held May 9, 1932; *Bank of
Japan One Hundred-Year History*, op. cit., p. 161.

81 BIS Historical Archives, file 2/7, vol. 1, correspondence, personal, from Leon Fraser

to Tetsusaburou Tanaka, Representative in London of the Bank of Japan, July 6, 1932.

82 Since for most of fiscal 1939 World War II already had begun in Europe, and the fiscal year ended in March 1940, for our purposes that year is counted as part of the war years. In fiscal 1939, the total amount decreased further to 469 million Gold Swiss francs.

83 *BIS Third Annual Report.*

84 On this point, we refer to a postwar internal BIS document summarizing its business to that point in time. BIS Historical Archives, Banking Policy of the BIS, Gold Operations, 1. 19b, vol. 1, M.v.Z. [Marcel van Zeeland], "Problèmes actuels BRI," October 27, 1947.

85 *BIS Second Annual Report.*

86 Ibid.

87 *BIS Fourth Annual Report.*

88 Ibid.

89 More precisely, BIS's "stock of gold for its own account" corresponds to "the excess of assets in gold bars over deposits with the Bank expressed in a weight of gold." *BIS Ninth Annual Report.*

90 Concerning rules and practices relating to gold earmarks, see BIS Historical Archives, 1/19b, Banking Policy of the BIS, vol. 1, Note pour le Président de la Banque, 11 juin 1939.

91 *BIS Sixth Annual Report.*

92 Ibid.

93 *BIS Second Annual Report.*

94 Central banks: 85 percent; banking institutions selected by the central banks: 11 percent; other related institutions and other bodies: 4 percent. *BIS Third Annual Report.*

95 Rapport sur les opérations de la Banque du 1er au 31 mars 1932, annexe 20/D, p. 3.

96 Ibid., p. 5. The total amount of investment was US$69,767,000.

97 *BIS Eighth Annual Report.*

98 *BIS Ninth Annual Report.*

99 Toniolo, *Central Bank Cooperation at the Bank for International Settlements*, op. cit., pp. 106–114. Here, Toniolo assesses from a variety of perspectives the BIS's functioning as a crisis manager, on the assumption that in the midst of the crisis stemming originally from the Versailles system it would be impossible for the actions of central banks alone to resolve the situation.

100 Quesnay's personal history is according to Archives de la Banque de France, Dossier de personnel de Pierre Quesnay and Olivier Feiertag, "Pierre Quesnay et les réseaux de l'internationalisme monétaire en Europe (1919–1937)," *Réseaux économiques et construction européenne*, Michel Dumoulin, ed., PIE-Peter Lang, Bruxelles.

101 For the testimony of his contemporaries see Jacques Rueff, "Préface," in Emile Moreau, *Souvenirs d'un Gouverneur de la Banque de France, histoire de la stabilisation du franc (1926–1928)*, Editions M. Th. Génin, Paris, 1954; for a historical study, see Mouré, *La Politique du franc Poincaré*, op. cit., pp. 58–91.

3 On the eve of Bretton Woods: the BIS during World War II

1 Charles Kindleberger, *The Life of an Economist, an Autobiography*, Basil Blackwell, Cambridge, MA, 1991, pp. 57–60.

2 Concerning the above developments, see Piet Clement, "The Bank for International Settlements during the Second World War," conference paper submitted to the Nazi Gold, the London Conference, December 2–4, 1997, Foreign Commonwealth Office, London; m.a., "The Touchstone of German Credit: Nazi Germany and the Service of the Dawes and Young Loans," *Financial History Review*, vol. 11, no. 1, 2004,

pp. 35–50; and Gian Trepp, *Bank- geschäfte mit dem Feind: Die Bank für Internationalen Zahlungsausgleich im Zweiten Weltkrieg, von Hitlers Eurobank zum Instrument des Marshallplans*, Rotpunkt Verlag, Zürich, 1993.

3 Hereinafter the background of this evacuation is based on BIS Historical Archives, 7. 18(6), AUB 4, Comptes-rendus adressés à Mr. Fournier, Auboin, "Mémorandum sur les circonstances qui ont conduit au transfert de la Banque des Règlements Internationaux à Château d'Oex," 22 mai 1940.

4 Here we will provide one example related to the gold issue. Just after the outbreak of World War II, in a letter to Governor Fournier of the Banque de France, Auboin reported having witnessed a director of the Banque de Boheme et de Moravie named Malik vacationing in Switzerland with his wife. Auboin ascertained information to the effect that Malik was in communication with a group of exiles in London and urged intelligence authorities to act to investigate Malik's true intentions. The Banque de Boheme et de Moravie was an institution that had been established through a restructuring of the existing central bank under the auspices of the Germans, and gold of the restructured central bank had been blocked there. Auboin commented that if the true intention of Malik's self-exile to London could be confirmed, "Malik could be used to act to block the Banque de Boheme et de Moravie." BIS Historical Archives, 7. 18(6), AUB 4, Comptes-rendus adressés à Mr. Fournier, correspondence, d'Auboin à Fournier, le 5 septembre 1939, personnel.

5 This memo advised measures such as (1) revision of the method of determining dividends to shareholders from a fixed rate to fluctuating rate and (2) reconfirmation of payment of German reparations and guarantee by BIS assets as a whole of the minimum amount of BIS deposits paid in by the French government. This also could be read as a scenario for advancing the handling of BIS concerns by compromises while professing they are in the interest of France. At this time, French BIS shareholders consisted of the Banque de France (6,828 shares) and private-sector shareholders (12,944 shares, 1,163 of which were held by the Caisse des Dépôts et Consignations). BIS Historical Archives, 7. 18(6), AUB 4, Dossiers du début de la guerre, R.A., "Note sur la BRI du point de vue des intérêts français," August 17, 1939.

6 BIS Historical Archives, 7. 18(6), AUB 4, Rapports et lettres, Roger Auboin, "Mesures à prendre dans l'intérêt français concernant la BRI pendant la durée des hostilités," September 21, 1939.

7 Yokohama Specie Bank materials, period 2 (mf04/w3/74), letter from Kan Yoshimura to Yanagida, August 22, 1940.

8 The following testimony is from Yokohama Specie Bank materials, period 2 (mf04/w3/74), letter from Kan Yoshimura to Yanagida, August 22, 1940.

9 Yokohama Specie Bank materials, period 2 (mf04/w3/74), letter from Kan Yoshimura to Yanagida, September 24, 1940. Ibid., letter from Kan Yoshimura to Yokohama Specie Bank Berlin Branch Manager Kunitake Kume, October 25, 1940.

10 BIS Historical Archives, file 2/7, vol. 1, Marcel van Zeeland, "Comptes de dépôts eventuels au nom de la Yokohama Specie Bank dans les livres de la BRI," October 23, 1940.

11 BIS Historical Archives, file 2/7, vol. 1, Yoshimura, "Note," August 5, 1941; Georges Royot, "Banque du Japon," August 12, 1940.

12 BIS Historical Archives, file 2/7, vol. 1, Marcel van Zeeland, "Redaction envoyee a M. Yamamoto," May 16, 1941.

13 Concerning these maneuvers to end the war, see Shuji Takeuchi, *Maboroshi no shusen kosaku: pisu firazu 1945 natsu* [Phantom Maneuvers to End World War II: Peace Feelers in the Summer of 1945], Bunshun Shinsho, 2005. This work is a detailed study elucidating a full view of these maneuvers using primary materials such as Dulles's documents. Another material that should be mentioned is Erin Juker-Fleetwood, *Per Jacobsson Mediation*, Basel, s.d. This document is edited from Jacobsson's journals, notes and other writings of the time.

14 BIS Historical Archives, Board of Directors, Banking Policy during War Time (1939–1945), file 1/3(5), vol. 1, correspondence, Beyen to Cochran, Treasury Department, Washington, DC, November 2, 1939, personal.

15 In 1940, a gold transaction between the BIS and a private-sector American bank took place in Genoa based on this request. BIS Historical Archives, Report on BIS Operations, file 1/3(4), Rapport sur les opérations de la Banque du 1er au 31 mars 1940.

16 The planned procedures for this transaction were as follows: Japan would send gold to Cape Town and sell it to the BIS; the BIS would sell the gold to the Swiss National Bank, and the gold received would be placed in Cape Town as intended by the Swiss National Bank; the BIS would convert the proceeds from the sale of gold to the Swiss National Bank (in Swiss francs) to escudo and then receive gold from the Banco de Portugal in exchange for the escudo; and the gold received would be delivered to Japan in Lisbon. The transaction was brokered by Kan Yoshimura, manager of the BIS foreign-exchange section. BIS Historical Archives, Banking Policy of the BIS, Gold Operations, file 1/19(b), vol. 1, Reference Note dated September 27, of Mr. Yoshimura on Gold of Japanese Origin to be Sent in the Course of November from Japan to Lisboa through the Cape, September 29, 1941.

17 Beyen sent the same letter to each central bank. The letter addressed to the Bank of Japan is cited here. BIS Historical Archives, Board of Directors, Banking Policy during the War, file 1/3(5), vol. 1, correspondence, Beyen to K. Futami, Bank of Japan, December 2, 1939.

18 On this point, in his reply to Beyen, Governor Fournier, while agreeing with the BIS policy, expresses his concern that those principles cover only the financial markets of belligerent countries and gold earmarked by those countries. BIS Historical Archives, Board of Directors, Banking Policy during the War, file 1/3(5), vol. 1, correspondence, Le Gouverneur de la Banque de France (Fournier) à Beyen, le 18 décembre 1939. This concern later proved to be on the mark.

19 BIS Historical Archives, Board of Directors, Banking Policy during Wartime, file 1/3(5), vol. 1, MvZ [Marcel van Zeeland], Opérations BRI sur or pendant la guerre, 2ème projet, December 10, 1945.

20 BIS Historical Archives, Board of Directors, Banking Policy during Wartime, file 1/3(5), vol. 1, T.H. McK [McKittrick], Memorandum of conversations with M. Yves Bréart de Boisanger on August 11 and 12, 1943.

21 BIS Historical Archives, Board of Directors, Banking Policy during Wartime, file 1/3(5), vol. 1, MvZ [Marcel van Zeeland], Opérations BRI sur or pendant la guerre, op. cit.

22 BIS Historical Archives, Banking Policy of the BIS, 1/19b, M.v.Z. [Marcel van Zeeland], "Problèmes actuels BRI," le BRI," October 27, 1947.

23 BIS Historical Archives, Roger Auboin file, series 2, carton 7, folder 24, Copy of telegram (decode), from Federal Reserve Bank of New York, New York, to Bank for International Settlements, Basel, dated June 25, 1940; Copy of telegram (dispatched in code), from Bank for International Settlements, Basel, to Federal Reserve Bank of New York, New York, dated July 19, 1940.

24 BIS Historical Archives, file 2/7, vol. 1, Extract from Minutes of the 119th Meeting of the Board of Directors held in Basel on November 14, 1949, "Dollar Assets Deposited by the Bank of Japan with the Bank for International Settlements."

25 Japan's BIS accounts frozen at this time were not included in the release. BIS Historical Archives, file 2/7, vol. 1, "Chronological Summary of Events Relating to Two Dollar Accounts of the Bank of Japan," March 21, 1951.

26 *Testimony of Leon Fraser on the Bretton Woods Agreements Act*, Thursday, March 22, 1945, House of Representatives, Committee on Banking and Currency (Printed for the First National Bank, New York).

27 Ibid., p. 15.

28 Nachlass Per Jacobsson, s1/d2, PJ "Work for the BIS after the Agreement in Munich," October 1, 1938.

29 Jacobsson added his own notes by hand in the margins of this memo, listing "construction of new rail lines" and "establishment of customs offices" as expenditures that would be required after conclusion of the agreement. Ibid.

30 Hereinafter, concerning this lecture see Jacobsson, *Some Monetary Problems*, op. cit., chapter 6, "Gold and Monetary Problems," pp. 135–152.

31 Ibid., p. 143.

32 *BIS Tenth Annual Report.*

33 *BIS Eleventh Annual Report.* The annual report for this fiscal year listed as means of neutralizing inflation voluntary savings, depreciation, and use of foreign assets.

34 *BIS Twelfth Annual Report.*

35 *BIS Thirteenth Annual Report.*

36 *BIS Twelfth Annual Report.*

37 BIS Historical Archives, Roger Auboin file, series 2, carton 7, folder 24, "Some Notes on the Annual Report," confidential, October 15, 1942.

38 Nachlass Per Jacobsson, Diaries, February 18, 1941.

39 Kindleberger, *The Life of an Economist*, op. cit., p. 55.

40 Hereinafter, concerning this lecture see Jacobsson, *Some Monetary Problems*, op. cit., chapter 7, "Small Countries and World Economic Reconstruction," pp. 153–174.

41 Nachlass Per Jacobsson, s1/d3, PJ, "Some Monetary Problems and the BIS," October 17, 1940. Two weeks after writing this memo, Jacobsson wrote a letter to the BIS secretary general, Rafaelle Pilotti, an Italian, expressing regret at the content of the memo as having been somewhat rash in light of the BIS duty of neutrality. However, in the letter he also developed the above concept in greater depth, repeating the view that the gold standard itself could restrain dominance by multiple large countries. Nachlass Per Jacobsson, s1/d3, correspondence, Per Jacobsson to R. Pilotti, November 4, 1940.

42 According to internal BIS documents, the impetuses behind the BIS change of position here were Japan's attack on Pearl Harbor and the US entry into World War II that followed. BIS Historical Archives, Roger Auboin file, series 2, carton 7, folder 24, "Post-war Position of the BIS," s.d. Jacobsson's journal can be seen to offer a similar view.

43 *BIS Twelfth Annual Report.* Harrod published a review of this year's Annual report in which he expressed doubts concerning the form of postwar currency exchange adjustments discussed in the annual report. Roy Harrod, "The Bank for International Settlements, Twelfth Annual Report," *Economic Journal*, vol. 53, April 1943, pp. 112–113. This can be seen as a foreshadowing of the later dispute between Jacobsson and the Keynesians.

44 *BIS Fourteenth Annual Report.*

45 There have been an enormous number of studies on the Bretton Woods Conference and the Bretton Woods system. Here we will cite only Richard Gardner, *Sterling-dollar Diplomacy: Anglo-American Collaboration in the Reconstruction of Multilateral Trade*, Clarendon Press, Oxford, 1956, which discusses in detail the history of British–American relations at the time, and Michael Bordo and Barry Eichengreen, eds., *A Retrospective on the Bretton Woods System, Lessons for International Monetary Reform*, University of Chicago press, Chicago and London, 1993, which summarized the Bretton Woods system theoretically as of that time. For a recent study, see David Andrews, ed., *Orderly Change, International Monetary Relations since Bretton Woods*, Cornell University Press, Ithaca, 2008. This study proposes ascertaining the "Bretton Woods Order" more broadly as a regime that supported postwar growth instead of the view of the Bretton Woods system that had tended toward currency system theory. The concept of this book also is closer to this latter approach.

46 Concerning Jacobsson's relation to the Bretton Woods Conference, see the following study by Jacobsson's daughter Erin: Erin Juker-Fleetwood, "Per Jacobsson on Bretton Woods," *Banker*, September 1970, vol. 120, no. 535, pp. 964–971.

47 Ibid., p. 965.

48 *BIS Thirteenth Annual Report.*

49 Concerning this meeting, see Nachlass Per Jacobsson, Diaries, A61, February 28, 1942.

50 Livingston, Kaldor and Myrdal each developed the theory of a postwar depression in US Department of Commerce economic forecasts, an appendix to the *Beveridge Report*, and a work published in 1944, respectively. In response, Jacobsson included a section entitled "Postwar Problems" in the introduction to the BIS annual report, in which he stated his own theory. *BIS Fourteenth Annual Report.* For the background of this dispute, see Erin Jacobsson, *A Life for Sound Money*, op. cit., pp. 167–168.

51 On the interaction between Keynes and Jacobsson see Yago, "Wicksellian Tradition," op. cit.

52 See Jacobsson, *Some Monetary Problems*, op. cit., chapter 17, "Keynes – Costs and Controls," pp. 334–335.

53 John Maynard Keynes, "The Balance of Payments of the United States," *Economic Journal*, June 1946, pp. 172–187.

54 Ibid., p. 186.

55 Jacobsson, *Some Monetary Problems*, op. cit., chapter 17, "Keynes – Costs and Controls," p. 339.

56 BIS Archives, HS 279, Address by Per Jacobsson on "Credit Policy: Recent European Experience" at a luncheon arranged on January 23, 1952 by the National Industrial Conference Board, Waldorf-Astoria, New York, NY. The text of this lecture later would be republished in a collection of Jacobsson's papers. Jacobsson, *Some Monetary Problems*, op. cit., chapter 14, "Credit Policy," p. 257.

57 Roy Harrod, "Keynes, Keynesians, and Mr. Jacobsson: a note," *Kyklos*, vol. xii, 1959, Fasc. 2, pp. 196–199.

58 *BIS Tenth Annual Report.*

59 *BIS Fifteenth Annual Report.*

60 Among the accounts constituting long-term deposits, the French Government Guaranteed Fund was repaid during September 1939, since there was no further need to maintain it under the terms of Article 199 of the Annexes to the Young Plan. Also, the item of "Guaranty on commercial bills sold," which was entered as credits on the balance sheet in the 1930s, disappeared because "certain institutions on the continent of America" "cut down their commitments and holdings in Europe as far as possible." *BIS Tenth Annual Report.*

61 *BIS Tenth Annual Report.*

62 *BIS Eleventh Annual Report.*

63 *BIS Twelfth Annual Report.*

64 *BIS Fifteenth Annual Report.*

65 *BIS Eleventh Annual Report, BIS Twelfth Annual Report, BIS Thirteenth Annual Report, BIS Fourteenth Annual Report, BIS Fifteenth Annual Report.*

66 BIS Historical Archives, 7. 18(6), AUB 3, Situation Genetale de la BRI, Repartition par pays des actifs et des passifs de la BRI, Situation a fin août 1944.

67 *BIS Fifteenth Annual Report.*

68 *BIS Thirteenth Annual Report.*

69 According to the BIS annual report for fiscal 1940, "of the total of gold deposits all except 1.6 million Gold Swiss francs were at sight on March 31, 1941." The BIS assessed that this "seems to prove that the clients of the Bank recognise the advantages which these particular facilities afford." *BIS Eleventh Annual Report*, p. 304.

70 *BIS Fourteenth Annual Report.*

71 *BIS Tenth Annual Report.*

72 *BIS Eleventh Annual Report.*

73 *BIS Fourteenth Annual Report.*

74 *BIS Twelfth Annual Report.*

75 *BIS Thirteenth Annual Report.*
76 *BIS Fifteenth Annual Report.*
77 *BIS Fifteenth Annual Report.*
78 Rapport sur les opérations de la Banque du 1er juillet au 30 septembre 1939, annexe 95/D(1), p. 4.
79 Rapport sur les opérations de la Banque pendant le mois de décembre 1949, annexe 121/C, p. 3.
80 Toniolo, *Central Bank Cooperation at the Bank for International Settlements*, op. cit., p. 257.
81 For the background of this matter, see BIS Historical Archives, file 7. 5, box1/3a, "Observations concernant la note qui figure au bas du bilan annuel de la BRI et qui se rapporte au dividende cumulatif," texte annulé, March 6, 1954.
82 For background see BIS Historical Archives, file 7.5, box 1/2, "Disposal of the Surplus on the Profit and Loss Account, 1949–50," March 28, 1950.
83 Toniolo, *Central Bank Cooperation at the Bank for International Settlements*, op. cit., pp. 201, 259.
84 Per Jacobsson Diaries, A63, April 22, 1946.
85 On the relationship between Keynes and Jacobsson, see Yago, "Wicksellian Tradition at the Bank for International Settlements," op. cit.

4 The road to a gold–dollar standard: the BIS in the postwar reconstruction period

1 Olivier Feiertag, *Wilfrid Baumgartner, un grand commis des finances à la croisée des pouvoirs (1902–1978)*, CHEFF, Paris, 2006, pp. 536–540.
2 This point is based on a postwar *New York Times* story. This story, which dismissed White's attacks on the BIS as unfounded, is colored with a tone supportive of the continued existence of the BIS. It also berates the argument in the Bretton Woods Conference to liquidate the BIS as a "lynching party that failed." Edward Collins, "A Lynching Party that Failed," *New York Times*, January 4, 1954.
3 An example is Herbert Bratter, "Clarification of International Settlements Bank," *Commercial and Financial Chronicle*, July 10, 1947. This article reports that the FRB was secretly investigating the business of the BIS on its own, to avoid liquidation of the BIS which was looked on with suspicion. Shaken by this article, the FRB apologized to the BIS and promised that it would disclose to the BIS its informants in the organization. BIS Historical Archives, 1/26d(1), Annual Meetings, Correspondence, O. Ernest Moore, Manager of Research Department of the Federal Reserve Bank of New York, to Roger Auboin, General Manager of the BIS, July 18, 1947. From these developments, one can sense the circumstances under which suspicion about the BIS's actions during the war were related to the argument to liquidate it, an argument that involved the US Congress. Bratter, the author of this article, continued relentlessly investigating the BIS's wartime behavior, publishing a public letter questioning the BIS in 1948. The BIS prepared a careful response to this letter internally. The above developments are from BIS Historical Archives, 1/6(2), Relations with the Press, Articles written by Members of BIS Management, October 1, 1937–September 30, 1964, "Monsieur Maurice Frere's Reply of June 14, 1948 to Mr. Bratter's Questionnaire (for publication in the *Commercial and Financial Journal*)."
4 Ernst Weinwurm, "The Future of the Bank for International Settlements and the Marshall Plan," *Commercial and Financial Chronicle*, September 4, 1947.
5 BIS Historical Archives, Roger Auboin file, 7/15.1(6), 24 "Past and Future of BIS."
6 Banque des Règlements Internationaux, *Témoignages et points de vue, publication du cinquantenaire*, op. cit., p. 29. Holtrop was involved in the BIS board beginning in 1946, as governor of the Nederlandsche Bank, and he served as president of the BIS from 1958 through 1967.

7 Nachlass Per Jacobsson, s2/d3, Bretton Woods' Decision to Dissolve BIS (1945–1948), "Present Functions and Organization of the United States and International Agencies Related to a Program of Foreign Aid and Recovery," Preliminary Report 22 of the House Select Committee on Foreign Aid, March 12, 1948.

8 Yokohama Specie Bank materials, period 2 (mf04/w3/74), "On the Decision to Dissolve the BIS" (19, 7, 23).

9 IMF Archives, Documents issued by United Nations Monetary and Financial Conference, July 1–22, 1944, Arranged by Document Number, vol. II, Documents 170–280 inclusive, Report Submitted to Commission III by the Agenda Committee Appointed to Receive and Consider Proposals Submitted for Consideration in Commission III (to be presented at meeting of Commission III, July 10), Bretton Woods, July 10, 1944; IMF Archives, Documents issued by United Nations Monetary and Financial Conference, July 1–22, 1944, Arranged by Document Number, vol. V, Documents 481–547 inclusive, Report Submitted to Commission III by Committee 2 on Enemy Assets, Looted Property, and Related Matters (to be presented at the meeting of Commission III) July 20, 1944.

10 Information on this unofficial meeting is from BIS Historical Archives, Board of Directors, Banking Policy during Wartime, 1/3(5), R.A.[Roger Auboin], Note pour Monsieur Monick, le 27 mai 1946.

11 Bank for International Settlements, *Personal Recollections and Opinions, [Témoignages et points de vue] Published on the Occasion of the Fiftieth Anniversary, 1930–1980*, Basel, 1980, pp. 44–46. Monick served as governor of the Banque de France from 1944 through 1949. Cobbold, governor of the Bank of England at this time, testified in a response to an interviewer's question in 1979, "Yes, but frankly it was the influence of the British Government on Snyder [Vinson's successor as US Treasury Secretary] that was crucial." If we believe this testimony from Cobbold, then the phase in which Snyder took office as Treasury secretary was very important to avoidance of BIS liquidation. Ibid., pp. 61–62.

12 Archives de la Banque de France, BRI, Conseil d'administration, ordre du jour de la 95ème séance qui se tiendra le 9 décembre 1946, Liste des membres de la Direction et des Fonctionnaires de la Banque des Règlements Internationaux.

13 BIS Historical Archives, Roger Auboin file, series 2, carton 7, folder 11, correspondence, Auboin à McKittrick, August 14, 1945.

14 BIS Historical Archives, Board of Directors, Banking Policy during Wartime, file 1/3(5),vol. 1, MvZ [Marcel van Zeeland], "Avertissement," December 10, 1945.

15 BIS Historical Archives, Roger Auboin file, series 2, carton 7, folder 11, correspondence, Auboin à McKittrick, October 19, 1945.

16 BIS Historical Archives, 7.18(6), AUB 1, List of documents relating to gold looted or called in question as possibly looted and to gold delivered to the BIS at Constance, "Statement of Total Gold Received from the Reichsbank during the War which has been Identified as Looted or Called in Question as Possibly Looted."

17 NARA, 450.81.12.01, box 169, "Looted Gold," correspondence, Elting Arnold to Frank Southard, May 11, 1948.

18 BIS Historical Archives, Roger Auboin file, series 2, carton 7, folder 11, Résumé d'un télégramme de l'US Trésorerie et du Département d'Etat à la Légation des E.U. à Berne, décembre 1945.

19 BIS Historical Archives, Roger Auboin file, series 2, carton 7, folder 11, correspondence, McKittrick à Auboin, January 22, 1946.

20 *BIS Nineteenth Annual Report*, pp. 216–217.

21 BIS Historical Archives, 7.18(6), AUB 1, Avoirs BRI aux E.U., correspondence, de Roger Auboin a Maurice Frère, October 27, 1947.

22 For the background on these developments, see BIS Historical Archives, 7/18(6), AUB1/5, correspondence, Maurice Frere to John Snyder, Secretary of the Treasury, February 16, 1948.

23 BIS Historical Archives, 7.18(6), AUB 1, Avoirs BRI aux E.U., correspondence, de Roger Auboin à Maurice Frère, October 27, 1947.

24 BIS Historical Archives, 7.18(6), AUB 1, Avoirs BRI aux E.U., HG, Certification des avoirs de la B.R.I. bloqués aux Etats-Unis, November 7, 1947.

25 BIS Historical Archives, 7.18(6), AUB 1/5, Assets and Liabilities Connected with the Application of the Hague Agreement of 1930, March 1, 1947.

26 BIS Historical Archives, 7.18(6), AUB 1/5, HG [Henri Guisan], Certification des avoirs de la B.R.I. bloquée aus Etats-Unis.

27 BIS Historical Archives, 7.18(6), AUB 1, Avoirs BRI aux E.U., correspondence, Snyder to Arthur H. Vandenberg, Chairman, Senate Foreign Relations Committee, February 2, 1948. This letter, which originally should have been sent from Snyder to Vandenberg as private correspondence, was delivered to Frère via BIS General Manager Auboin, leading one to suspect that these congressional maneuverings too were coordinated with the BIS.

28 BIS Historical Archives, 7.18(6), AUB 1, Avoirs BRI aux E.U., correspondence, Maurice Frere, Chairman of the BIS, to Snyder, Secretary of Treasury, May 13, 1948.

29 The Swiss National Bank was opposed to the BIS decision to return the looted gold. Also, the looted gold returned at this time involved the central-bank gold reserves of each region and did not include the so-called gold of the dead (such as gold taken from Holocaust victims). This issue was resolved in the 1990s. Trepp, *Bankgeschäfte mit dem Feind*, op. cit.

30 While Toniolo's official history depicts the process of rehabilitation of the BIS in detail along with developments on the issue of looted gold, it does not appear interested in the issues of looted gold or the asset freeze. Toniolo, *Central Bank Cooperation at the Bank for International Settlements*, op. cit., pp. 267–282.

31 BIS Historical Archives, 7.18(6), AUB 1, Avoirs BRI aux E.U., HG, "Avoirs de la B.R.I. situés aux Etats-Unis d'Amérique," May 7, 1949.

32 Concerning the international diplomatic and political processes from proposal of the Marshall Plan through its implementation, see CHEFF, *Le Plan Marshall et le relèvement économique de l'Europe*, Paris, imprimerie Nationale, 1993.

33 For international currency system plans and the position of the pound around the time of the Marshall Plan, in addition to the literature cited above see Harold James, "The IMF and the Creation of the Bretton Woods System, 1944–58," in Barry Eichengreen, ed., *Europe's Post-War Recovery*, Cambridge University Press, Cambridge, 1995, pp. 105–111.

34 Anon., "Inconvertible Again," *Economist*, August 23, 1947.

35 NARA, 450.81.12.01, box 169, "Liquidation," Office Memorandum, from J.S. Friedman, to Frank A. Southard, December 10, 1947.

36 Kaplan and Schleiminger, *The European Payments Union*, op. cit., pp. 23–27.

37 To use France as an example, over the single year from July 1, 1948 through June 30, 1949, drawing rights established for counterpart countries in deficit with whom France was running a surplus totaled $9.7 million, while drawing rights from counterpart countries in surplus with whom France was running a deficit totaled $333 million. In addition to this net balance of $323.3 million in drawing rights, France was delivered during this period $981 million in Marshall Plan aid for that fiscal year. BIS Historical Archives, Monetary and Economic Department, CB 210, "The Post-war Economic and Financial Position of France from the Liberation to the Beginning of 1949," Basel, Second impression, March 1949, pp. E14-E18.

38 Nachlass Per Jacobsson, s1/d3, R.A., "Rôle de la Banque des Règlements Internationaux dans l'application des Accords monétaires projetés," 9 décembre 1949.

39 NARA, 450.81.12.01, box 169, "Liquidation," Andrew M. Kamarck, Memorandum for the Files, January 8, 1948.

40 BIS Historical Archives, 7.18(6), AUB 1, Avoirs BRI aux E.U., Statement of Mr.

A.N. Overby, US Executive Director, to the Executive Board Meeting of the International Monetary Fund on April 22, 1948; Statement of Mr. John S. Hooker, US Alternate Executive Director, to the Executive Board Meeting of the International Bank for Reconstruction and Development on April 28, 1948.

41 The study group established by General Manager Auboin prepared in October 1947 a memo entitled, "Possible Functions of the Bank for International Settlements." This memo identified as reasons for the continued existence of the BIS: (1) the organizational "flexibility and adaptability" called for in the BIS Statues, (2) its "lengthy experience" in European finance, (3) its "complementary, not competitive" relations with the newly established IMF and BIRD, and (4) the "close relations" built on trust with European central banks. BIS Historical Archives, 7.18(6), AUB 3, Documents remis à la Trésorerie américaine, avril 1947, "Possible Functions of the Bank for International Settlements," Note October 6–13, 1947. As implied by its title, this memo was sent to the US Treasury Department.

42 Nachlass Per Jacobsson, s2/d3, Bretton Woods' Decision to Dissolve BIS (1945–1948), "Present Functions and Organization of the United States and International Agencies…," op. cit.

43 BIS, *The Seventeenth Annual Report.*

44 Contact between the two was realized in a meeting in London between BIS chairman of the board Maurice Frère and Gutt, first managing director of the IMF. In this meeting, both leaders confirmed their intention to build a sufficient foundation for cooperation. BIS Historical Archives, 1/26d(1), Annual Meetings, Extracts from Minutes of the Ninety-seventh Meeting of the Board of Directors, May 12, 1947. Both Frère and Gutt were Belgians.

45 BIS Historical Archives, Banking Policy of the BIS, Gold Operations, 1/19b, vol. 1, M.v.Z.[Marcel van Zeeland], "Problèmes actuels B.R.I.," October 27, 1947. The meeting with the Export–import Bank of the United States took place on October 22, 1947.

46 Erin Jacobsson, *A Life for Sound Money*, op. cit., p. 188.

47 BIS Historical Archives, file 7.18(6), AUB 1/5, correspondence, Auboin to Eugene Black, United States Executive Director, IBRD, April 14, 1948.

48 Gardner, *Sterling–Dollar Diplomacy*, op. cit., pp. 293–303.

49 Nachlass Per Jacobsson, s1/d3, R.A., "Rôle de la Banque des Règlements Internationaux dans l'application des Accords monétaires projetés," 9 décembre 1949, op. cit.

50 Kaplan and Schleiminger, *The European Payments Union*, op. cit., pp. 28–47.

51 Ibid., pp. 31–40. Incidentally, Ansiaux held the posts of director of the National Bank of Belgium and executive director of the IMF, as well as alternate member on the BIS board of directors.

52 In a memo delivered to the Banque de France, Auboin insisted that the EPU plans should be based on a "transitory character [*un caractere transitoire*]" until convertibility of European currencies was restored. Archives de la Banque de France, U.E.P., Travaux preparatoires, 1949–1950, no. 55, R.A. [Roger Aubion] 69, Questions relatives au projet d'Union Europeenne de paiements interessant particulierement les banques centrales europeennes; Kaplan and Schleiminger, *The European Payments Union*, op. cit., pp. 64–65.

53 Ibid., pp. 38, 64–65.

54 Per Jacobsson, "The problem of the Dollar Shortage," *Skandinaviska Banken Aktibolag*, vol. 30, no. 1, January 1949.

55 Per Jacobsson, "European Payments," *Skandinaviska Banken Aktibolag*, vol. 31, no. 3, July 1950.

56 Nachlass Per Jacobsson, s2/d1, "After the Marshall Plan," manuscript (beginning of 1950).

57 Hereinafter, references to this meeting are from Nachlass Per Jacobsson, s3/d1, PJ,

"Note on conversations with Mr. John W. Snyder, Secretary to the US Treasury and Mr. William McChesney Martin, Jr., at the Hôtel des Bergues in Geneva on July 14, 1949," July 18, 1949.

58 Concerning this devaluation of the franc and establishment of free markets, see BIS Historical Archives, H.S.176, "La réforme monétaire en France," 29 janvier 1948. The main reasons Britain opposed this French decision were based on its concerns about high dollar rates recorded in trades on French free markets and the possibility that sterling would fall further as a result. Anon., "The Franc Devalued," *The Economist*, January 31, 1948. Incidentally, Britain's concerns would prove unfounded at the time when the franc again fell rapidly in October 1948. Anon., "The Sliding Franc," *The Economist*, October 23, 1948. Regarding the devaluation of the franc, also see Gérard Bossuat, "La France et le FMI au lendemain de la seconde guerre mondiale," Comité pour l'Histoire Economique et Financière de la France, *La France et les institutions de Bretton Woods*, op. cit., pp. 28–31.

59 Nachlass Per Jacobsson, s3/d2, Special Report of the National Advisory Council on International Monetary and Financial Problems on the Operations and Policies of the IBRD and the IMF, s.d. [1948]. This report was signed by six signatories including Snyder and McChesney Martin, who later would attend the secret meeting in 1949, and Secretary of State Marshall.

60 Weinburm, "The Future of the Bank for International Settlements…," op. cit. It goes without saying that deceasing trend was due in great part to the April 5, 1948 IMF board decision not to execute loans to countries receiving Marshall Plan aid – the so-called ERP decision. James, *International Monetary Cooperation…*, op. cit., pp. 78–79. The British journal the *Economist* saw this decision as follows: Automatic access by member countries to accommodations provided by the IMF was the concept "subject to the rules agreed at Bretton Woods." Nevertheless, this ERP decision was "a diktat" which cut right across this concept. Anon, "Bretton Woods Twins," *Economist*, September 25, 1948.

61 Gutt's speech is from BIS Historical Archives, 1/26c, vol. 1, International Monetary Fund, "Notes for the Statement made by the Managing Director, M. Camille Gutt, to the Executive Board of the IMF at Meeting 652 (off the record)," March 19, 1951.

62 These figures are from a table distributed to the IMF board on May 22, 1956. Nachlass Per Jacobsson, s3/d2, "Agenda to Members of the Executive Board from the Acting Secretary, IMF," May 22, 1956.

63 Anon., "IMF Wins over the Skeptics." in *Business Week*, March 30, 1957.

64 Anon., "Bretton Woods Triplets," *The Economist*, September 29, 1956.

65 Per Jacobsson, "European Payments Union, a Means – Not and End," *Quarterly Review, Skandinaviska Banken*, July 1950. This is a supplement to the journal *Skandinaviska Banken Aktibolag* cited above; "and End" in the subtitled appears to be a misprint for "an End."

66 Nachlass Per Jacobsson, s2/d1, "European Monetary Problems," outline of address to be delivered on September 4, 1950, the Third International Banking Summer School.

67 Regarding this crisis, which was highly significant to both German financial history and Jacobsson himself, see Kaplan and Schleiminger, *European Payments Union*, op. cit., pp. 97–118; Erin Jacobsson, *A Life for Sound Money*, op. cit., pp. 236–245; and Ishizaka, *Fukkoki doitsu renda banku no kinyu seisaku* [Financial Policies of German Lender Banks during Reconstruction], op. cit.

68 Nachlass Per Jacobson, s2/d3, Stockholm Lectures, F.G.C., "Foreign Exchange Arbitrages in Europe since 18th May 1953," confidential, first draft, September 17, 1953.

69 The memo cited in the preceding note was prepared prior to the meeting of the EPU board on September 21 of that year. From the initials on the memo, it can be inferred that it was prepared by Frederik G. Conolly – the BIS representative to the EPU. In

the margins of the memo, its author had written by hand, "Mr. Jacobsson: comments please," implying that Jacobsson had seen the memo from the drafting stage.

70 Per Jacobsson, "The Market Mechanism of Adjustment," *Skandinaviska Banken Aktibolag*, vol. 34, no. 2, April 1953.

71 Per Jacobsson, "Investment without Inflation," *Skandinaviska Banken Aktibolag*, vol. 34, no. 3, July 1953.

72 Nachlass Per Jacobsson, s2/d3, "The Immediate Problems of EPU," November 3, 1953. Here, the logic of the policies of surplus countries was to increase the percentage of gold settlement conducted in settlement within the EPU region, while deficit countries needed to raise, in their own capital markets, the funds needed to repay EPU obligations. For this reason, each country would shift to policies of high interest rates, developing an environment that would lead toward restoration of convertibility.

73 Roger Auboin, "La Banque des Règlements Internationaux et l'Union Européenne de Paiements," *Kyklos*, vol. 7, 1954, fasc.1/2, p. 51.

74 This commission would be succeeded by the Lewis Douglas Mission established after the start of the Republican administration of Dwight D. Eisenhower. The objective of the Douglas Mission was to examine the relationship between the dollar and sterling and its impact on US international economic policy. Regarding the state of affairs around the time of the establishment of the Randall Commission, see Per Jacobsson, "The Problem of Convertibility for Western Europe," *International Affairs*, vol. 30, no. 2, April 1954, pp. 137–147.

75 Hereinafter, information on this meeting is from BIS Historical Archives, H.S.324, Communication to the Randall Commission by Per Jacobsson, "Corrected Transcript of Statement by Per Jacobsson in Hearings before the Commission on Foreign Economic Policy at the US Embassy in Paris on November 12, 1953."

76 Around the time of the Bretton Woods Agreement Williams, known as an advocate of the key-currency approach, was a strong critic of this system. John Williams, *Post War Plans, and Other Essays*, A.A. Knopf, New York, 1947. However, in an essay published in July 1952, prior to his meeting with Jacobsson, he revised his own past arguments, expressing the view that IMF funds should be utilized effectively. m.a., *Economic Stability in a Changing World*, Oxford University Press, New York, 1953. Senator Bush, who also attended this meeting, was the father and grandfather, respectively, of later US presidents George H.W. Bush and George W. Bush.

77 Regarding Jacobsson's appointment as IMF managing director, his daughter Erin recalls that the US Undersecretary of the Treasury, Burgess, and the Bank of England governor, Cobbold, played leading roles in this appointment. Erin Jacobsson, *A Life for Sound Money*, op. cit., pp. 283–284.

78 Lombard, "The Sisters don't Quite Agree," *Financial Times*, August 31, 1959.

79 BIS Historical Archives, Banking Policy of the BIS, Gold Operations, file 1/19b, M.v.Z. [Marcel van Zeeland], "Problèmes actuels BRI," le 27 octobre 1947.

80 BIS Historical Archives, Banking Policy of the BIS, Gold Operations, file 1/19b, RA/MvZ [Roger Auboin, Marcel van Zeeland], Note pour la Banque de France, February 23, 1951. This memo originally was delivered personally by General Manager Auboin to Bolgert of the Banque de France.

81 Ibid. This rate of profit concerned business conducted in 1950 in countries other than France. At the time, this business was not yet conducted in France, and the memo sited recommended that French banks enter this business.

82 Archives de la Banque de France, BRI, Origines et activités, historique (1929–1955), correspondence, Ministre des Finances et des Affaires Ecnomiques à Monsieur le Gouverneur de la Banque de France, le 21 juillet 1949; Le Gouverneur de la Banque de France à Ministre des Finances et des Affaires Economiques, le 12 août 1949.

83 Ibid. Concerning French currency diplomacy during this period, see CHEFF, *La France et les institutions de Bretton Woods*, op. cit.

84 A graduate of a school of science and engineering, de Largentaye was a theorist who, as a high-ranking official in the finance ministry in the post of inspector of finance, translated Keynes's *General Theory* into French. He served in the IMF as France's first representative director from 1946 through 1964. Solenne Lepage, "Chronique d'un malentendu: la Direction des Finances Extérieres et le Fonds Monétaire International, 1944–1958," in CHEFF, *La France et les institutions de Bretton Woods, 1944–1994, Colloque tenu à Bercy le 30 juin et 1er juillet 1994*, CHEFF, imprimerie nationale, Paris, 1998, p. 37.

85 Guindey held the position of BIS general manager until 1963, later served in important positions in economic organizations both inside and outside France, and passed away in 1989. He himself introduced an overview of the BIS in the following journal article: Guillaume Guiney, "La Banque des Règlements Internationaux hier et aujourd'hui," *Revue d'Economie Politique*, 70e année, no. 6, novembre–décembre 1960, pp. 37–57. According to the recollections of André de Lattre, a difference in policy direction between Guindey and French then-Prime Minister Antoine Pinay was behind Guindey's appointment to the BIS, with Pinay "exiling" Guindey to the BIS. Andre de Lattre, *Servir aux Finances, mémoire*, CHEFF, Paris, 1999, p. 73. After serving, like Guindey, as director of the international finance bureau in the finance ministry, de Lattre served as deputy governor of the Banque de France, governor of a government financial agency *Crédit National*, and chairman of the board of the Institute of International Finance. As such, he was a major figure in the world of international finance in France. It is said that twice during his life he was approached about the position of BIS general manager but turned it down. Ibid., pp. 175–177.

86 Archives de Ministere des Finances (France), B48885, correspondence, J. de Largentaye a Guillaume Guindey, le 21 avril 1950.

87 Archives de la Banque de France, U.E.P., Travaux preparatoires, 1949–1950, no. 55, Note pour le Ministre, Guindey, objet: Union Europeenne de Paiements, le 12 juin 1950.

88 Archives de la Banque de France, U.E.P., Travaux préparatoires, 1949–1950, no. 55, R.A. [Roger Auboin] 66, Remarques sur le projet d'Union de Paiements Européenne, le 12 mars 1950.

89 Kaplan and Schleiminger, *The European Payments Union*, op. cit., pp. 64–65.

90 BIS Historical Archives, file 2/7, vol. 1, "Chronological summary of events relating to two dollar accounts of the Bank of Japan," March 21, 1951.

91 BIS Historical Archives, file 2/7, vol. 1, "Enclosure to letter to Bank of Japan, Tokio," August 8, 1952.

92 BIS Historical Archives, file 2/7, vol. 1, Extract from Minutes of the 119th Meeting of the Board of Directors held in Basel on November 14, 1949, "Dollar Assets Deposited by the Bank of Japan with the Bank for International Settlements."

93 Bank of Japan materials.

94 BIS Historical Archives, Thomas McKittrick Collection, Series 2, Carton 7, f22, 16-1-46, "Conversation with Mr. Kitamura at the Swiss National Bank, Zurich, January 15, 1946."

95 This meeting was held after Lord Cobbold of the Bank of England had raised the issue in a letter during the previous month of June. Attendees at the meeting included Vallat of the legal bureau in the British foreign ministry, Pridham of the Swiss bureau of the British foreign ministry, a representative of the Japan bureau of the British foreign ministry and Macdonald of the Bank of England. This background too implies that the Bank of England had played some role in pushing Japan out of the BIS. Archives of the Bank of England, OV4–110, Notes following Basel Meetings, Bank for International Settlements (Mr. Cobbold's letter to Markins (Foreign Office) of June 17, 1948 concerning the Japanese Connection with the BIS), Meeting at the Foreign Office, 11 a.m., July 19, 1948.

96 In an October 30, 1950 letter, the Bank of England proposed the seizure of BIS stock held by Japan, and an unsigned letter of November 7 of that year, addressed to Sir Roger Markins, recommended removing Japan since it was unrelated to the agent operations in the OEEC, which the BIS would be handling thenceforth. Archives of the Bank of England, OV4–110, Notes following Basel Meetings, Correspondence to Sir Roger Markins, October 30 and November 7, 1950.

97 Bank of Japan materials.

98 Bank of Japan materials.

99 Archives of the Bank of England, OV4–110, Notes following Basel Meetings, Personal Correspondence, H. Guisan, the Bank for International Settlements, to Kan Yoshimura, Economic Adviser, Foreign Exchange Department, Bank of Japan, July 25, 1951.

100 Information on the above developments is from *BIS Twenty-third Annual Report*, pp. 228–229.

101 BIS Historical Archives, file 2/7, vol. 1, Note "Visit to Basle of Mr. Kazuo Fukano of the London Branch," February 7, 1961.

102 Saburo Tanaka, *Ima to mukashi* [Then and Now], self-published, 1968, pp. 26–40.

103 Information on the above developments is from Takeshi Ohta, *Kokusai kinyu, genba kara no shogen: nichigin kara mita gekido no sanjunen* [Testimony from the Front Lines of International Finance: 30 Turbulent Years as Viewed from the Bank of Japan], Chuokoron-Shinsho, 1991, pp. 22–23.

104 *BIS Seventeenth Annual Report*.

105 *BIS Twentieth Annual Report*. These four countries accounted for 93 percent of the total amount of reparations claims against Germany. Also, under the 1953 London Debt Agreement the total amount of German obligations, including Young bonds, was finalized and a decision made to resume payment.

106 *BIS Eighteenth Annual Report*.

107 *BIS Eighteenth Annual Report*.

108 *BIS Nineteenth Annual Report*.

109 *BIS Twenty-fifth Annual Report*.

110 *BIS Nineteenth Annual Report*. Beginning in fiscal 1954, the item of "deposits of central banks for the account of others" was discontinued, instead booked under the item of "deposits of central banks" (combined with central banks' own accounts). This change took place because since fiscal 1952, central bank trust accounts had already become a very minor account. *BIS Twenty-fifth Annual Report*.

111 *BIS Seventeenth Annual Report*. Also, at the end of this fiscal year (March 1947), the composition of these deposits by currency, totaled together with gold, was as follows: 18 million in gold, eight million in Swiss francs, one million in dollars, and one million in other currencies, for a total of 28 million (all figures are denominated in Gold Swiss francs). Rapport sur les opérations de la Banque du 1er au 31 mars 1947, annexe 97/D(2), p. 2.

112 Rapport sur les opérations de la Banque pendant le mois de novembre 1947, annexe 100/C(2), p. 2.

113 Rapport sur les opérations de la Banque pendant le mois de février 1948, annexe 103/C, p. 2.

114 Rapport sur les opérations de la Banque pendant le mois d'avril 1948, annexe 105/C, p. 2.

115 *BIS Twenty-fourth Annual Report*. The earmarked gold referred to here does not include gold held for the EPU.

116 *BIS Nineteenth Annual Report*. However, this conversion did not go perfectly smoothly. In fiscal 1948, a state of affairs arose in which various "factors ... have tended to restrict the scope of these operations." In this way, restrictions on use of each country's currency under enactment of the Economic Recovery Program, related restrictions on shipments of gold, and the fact that the gold trades requested

of the BIS involved "movements … in the same direction" all acted in the direction of restraint. Ibid., p. 220.

117 *BIS Twenty-second Annual Report.*
118 *BIS Twenty-eighth Annual Report.*
119 *BIS Sixteenth Annual Report.*
120 *BIS Seventeenth Annual Report.*
121 *BIS Nineteenth Annual Report.*
122 *BIS Eighteenth Annual Report.*
123 *BIS Seventeenth Annual Report.*
124 *BIS Twenty-first Annual Report.*
125 *BIS Twenty-second Annual Report.*
126 *BIS Twenty-third Annual Report.*
127 *BIS Twenty-fourth Annual Report.*
128 *BIS Twenty-sixth Annual Report.*
129 *BIS Twenty-eighth Annual Report.*
130 *BIS Seventeenth Annual Report.*
131 *BIS Seventeenth Annual Report.*
132 *BIS Eighteenth Annual Report.*
133 Rapport sur les opérations de la Banque pendant le mois de mars 1949, annexe 114/D, p. 6, le mois de mars 1957, etc.
134 *BIS Sixteenth Annual Report.*
135 *BIS Nineteenth Annual Report.*
136 *BIS Seventeenth Annual Report.*
137 *BIS Eighteenth Annual Report*, p. 257.
138 *BIS Twenty-sixth Annual Report*, p. 309. The annual report for fiscal 1957 reports that three-quarters of the total are in US treasuries, with the bulk of the remainder being in British Treasury bills. *BIS Eighteenth Annual Report.*
139 Rapport sur les opérations de la Banque pendant le mois de mars 1949, annexe 114/D, p. 6.
140 *BIS Twentieth Annual Report.*
141 *BIS Twenty-second Annual Report.*
142 *BIS Nineteenth Annual Report.*
143 For the background on this, see BIS Historical Archives,file7.5, box 1/2, "Disposal of the Surplus on the Profit and Loss Account 1949–50," March 28, 1950.
144 *BIS Sixteenth Annual Report.*
145 *BIS Seventeenth Annual Report.*
146 BIS Historical Archives,file7.5, box 1/2, "Disposal of the Surplus on the Profit and Loss Account 1949–50," op. cit.
147 Ibid. This memo was a report on trends in distribution of profits prepared by the Banking Department annually. Regarding the third point, already in 1945 the BIS had received a telegram from the Bank of Greece (Greece's central bank) demanding payment of dividends unpaid during the war (under occupation). The BIS estimated that the portion payable to Greece alone had accrued in the amount of 2.26 million Gold Swiss francs, the equivalent of 658 kg of gold in bars. BIS Historical Archives, Banking Policy of the BIS, Gold Operations, MvZ [Marcel van Zeeland], Paiement aux Banques Centrales des dividends retenus pendant les hostilités, 2 juin 1945.
148 *BIS Sixteenth Annual Report.*
149 *BIS Seventeenth Annual Report.*
150 *BIS Eighteenth Annual Report.*
151 Estimated based on Table 4.1 In fiscal 1945, official income was in the red despite gains on exchange differences, and eventually in fiscal 1946 a profit was recorded as operating losses were supplemented by gains on exchange differences. Since exchange differences are unclear in fiscal year 1950 and later, those years are not included in the estimates.

152 Toniolo, *Central Bank Cooperation at the Bank for International Settlements*, op. cit., p. 288.

153 "Leon Fraser Dies from Suicide Shot on Summer Estate," *New York Times*, April 9, 1945.

154 Hereinafter, information on the meeting between Fraser and Kano is from Yokohama Specie Bank materials, period 2 (mf04/w3/72): Hisaakira Kano, "*Dai yonjukyu-kai kokusai kessai ginko rijikai kiroku* [Minutes of the Forty-ninth BIS board meeting]," and no. 3, "*BIS todori konin sentei mondai* [The Issue of Appointment of a Successor as BIS President]," February 18, 1935.

5 Neoliberalism as an alternative: international currency issues and the Bank for International Settlements in the 1950s and 1960s

1 BIS Library, NM1425, "Statement before the Subcommittee on International Exchange and Payments of the Joint Economic Committee, US Congress on June 22, 1971 by Dr. Milton Gilbert, Economic Adviser and Head of the Monetary and Economic Department, Bank for International Settlements."

2 Robert Triffin, *Gold and the Dollar Crisis: The Future of Convertibility*, New Haven, Yale University Press, 1961.

3 BIS Historical Archives, Banking Policy of the BIS, Gold Operations, file 1/19b, M.v.Z. [Marcel van Zeeland]/G.R.[Georges Royot], "Opérations sur or de la B.R.I.," August 16, 1951.

4 Ibid.

5 BIS, *The Twenty-fifth Annual Report*.

6 BIS Historical Archives, Banking Policy of the BIS, Gold Operations, file 1/19b, D.H.M. [Donald H. Macdonald], Note for the Banking Department, October 17, 1955.

7 BIS, *The Twenty-first Annual Report*.

8 Hereinafter, concerning this memo see BIS Historical Archives, 1/19b, Banking Policy of the BIS, Gold Operations, D.H.M. [Donald Macdonald], "Gold," November 13, 1956.

9 BIS Historical Archives, 1/19b, Banking Policy of the BIS, Gold Operations, Ma [Mandel], "Nouvelle étape de l'évolution de la BRI," April 2, 1959.

10 BIS Historical Archives, 1/19b, Banking Policy of the BIS, Gold Operations, Projet d'opérations sur or, June 18, 1959.

11 BIS Historical Archives, 1/19b, Banking Policy of the BIS, Gold Operations, D.H.M.[Donald Macdonald], "Gold," June 19, 1959.

12 BIS Historical Archives, 1/19b, Banking Policy of the BIS, Gold Operations, D.H.M.[Donald Macdonald], "Some Comments on the Note of Baron Van Zeeland of October 28 Concerning New Techniques Designed to Enable Us to Live with Regulation Q," October 30, 1959.

13 Triffin, *Gold and the Dollar Crisis*, op.cit, pp. 87–93 et passim.

14 Regarding the connection of the Basel Agreement and the Gold Pool Agreement with the BIS, see Toniolo, *Central Bank Cooperation at the Bank for International Settlements*, op. cit., pp. 375–381, 410–423. As the testimony of a person involved, see Charles Coombs, *The Arena of International Finance*, John Wiley and Sons, New York, 1976, pp. 24–67 et passim: in this book, the author, Coombs, (at the time deputy president of the Federal Bank of New York responsible for international business) recalls the interactions between central banks on the gold pool, assessing the contributions of the central banks of Switzerland and Italy in particular. At the same time, his assessment of the BIS was limited to its behind-the-scenes role.

15 BIS, *The Thirty-third Annual Report*.

16 Ibid.

17 While Ferras was from France, unlike the previous three general managers who while also from France had been sent directly from the French finance ministry or the Banque de France, he had been called back to Europe while on assignment at the IMF. Toniolo's official history says of the background behind this appointment, "The coming of age of the new international financial institutions was at the time creating a large pool of competent international civil servants in a job market that had already existed before the war but hitherto been quite thin." Toniolo, *Central Bank Cooperation at the Bank for International Settlements*, op. cit., p. 358.

18 BIS, *The Thirty-third Annual Report*.

19 LSE Per Jacobsson Diaries, mid-February [s.d.] 1962.

20 Triffin, *Gold and the dollar crisis*, op.cit, p. 151.

21 Matsumura, Kentaro, *Kokusai tsuka doru no kenkyu* [Study of the International Currency the Dollar], Diamond, 1964, pp. 274–275. After working at Mitsubishi Bank before the war, Matsumura taught at Wakayama University and Osaka Prefecture University. A work of his that relates closely to this chapter is *Kin to SDR* [Gold and SDRs], Nihon Keizai Shimbun, 1969. The citation being translated into Japanese, no English original was available.

22 BIS Historical Archives, Gabriel Ferras File, 7.18(10), FER2, note, s.a., "Eurodollars (Some First Thoughts)," August 24, 1962.

23 BIS Historical Archives, Confidential Paper for the Group of Ten, "The Eurocurrency Market and the International Payments System," January 20, 1964, 7.18(12), DEA14.

24 As a typical study, see Catherine Schenk, "The Origins of the Eurodollar Market in London: 1955–1963," *Explorations in Economic History*, no. 35, 1998. Historical studies in recent years are making clear the structure of the Eurocurrency markets, particularly focusing on the actions of private-sector banks – by looking at the state of competition and cooperation between banks. In addition to the above study by Schenk, see Stefano Battilossi, "The Eurodollar Market and Structural Innovation in Western Banking, 1960–1985," paper read at the European Association for Banking History Conference, Warsaw, May 19–20, 2000; Stefano Battilossi and Youssef Cassis, eds., *European Banks and the American Challenge, Competition and Cooperation in International Banking under Bretton Woods*, Oxford University Press, Oxford, 2002.

25 BIS Historical Archives, 1/3a(3), Meeting of Experts [euro-currency market], "Suggested Questions for Discussion at the Meeting on the Eurodollar Market, Basel, October 6–8, 1962."

26 BIS Historical Archives, 1/3a(3), Meeting of Experts [euro-currency market], "Meeting of Experts [euro-currency market], note, s.a., "Proposal for a Meeting of Central-bank Officials at the BIS to Discuss the Eurodollar Market," June 14, 1962.

27 BIS Historical Archives, 1/3a(3), Meeting of Experts [euro-currency market], "Suggested Questions for Discussion at the Meeting on the Eurodollar Market, Basel, October 6–8, 1962."

28 BIS Historical Archives, Gabriel Ferras file, 7.18(10), FER 7, Note re: Conversation with Undersecretary Roosa on Friday, October 4, Washington DC, October 9, 1963 [Marius Holtrop]. One work on the subject of the WP3 is the autobiography of Emile Van Lennep, the Dutch finance minister who chaired the WP3: Emile Van Lennep with Evert Schoorl, *Working for the World Economy*, Nederlands Instituut voor het Banken Effectenbedrief, Amsterdam, 1998. BIS participation in the WP3 was considered a "good idea" at the time, with the participation of Robert Roosa, the US undersecretary of the treasury. On October 4, 1963 Roosa met with BIS President Holtrop in Washington and recommended BIS participation in the WP3. Holtrop pledged to make this proposal in the meeting of central-bank governors planned for ten days after this meeting. BIS Historical Archives, Gabriel Ferras file, 7.18(10), FER 7/10, Meeting of the Esteva Working Party, October 22–23, 1964; 7.18(10),

FER 7, Note re: Conversation with Undersecretary Roosa, op. cit. The WP3 will be considered in the next chapter.

29 Cf. Jacob Kaplan and Günter Schleiminger, *The European Payments Union*, op. cit.
30 Van Lennep, *Working for the World Economy*, op. cit.
31 Regarding the starting point of swaps, see Harold James, *International Monetary Cooperation since Bretton Woods*, IMF/Oxford University Press, London/New York, 1996, p. 160. In this work, James' assessment is that "Already in the 1950s, the BIS had organized within the European payments union what amounted to a swap system for European central bankers."
32 Archives de la Banque de France, 1489200303/132, Banque des Règlements Internationaux, "Proposition de Swap faite par la BRI," le 10 août 1949. This memo reports on a proposal for swap arrangements submitted to the Banque de France by the BIS Banking Department head, van Zeeland. In accordance with this proposal, the Banque de France entered into a swap arrangement with the BIS that same month, swapping US$7,385,000 for 20 million Swiss francs (French francs equivalent). Archives de la Banque de France, 1489200303/132, Banque des Règlements Internationaux, "Entretien téléphonique du 22 août 1949 avec MM. Van Zeeland et Royot de la BRI."
33 BIS Historical Archives, 2.2, vols. 3 and 4, "Conversation téléphonique avec la Banque d'Angleterre, Londres (MM. Preston, Bridge-O.Berntsen)," June 16, 1954, 16.00h.
34 According to confidential BIS documents, some opinion within the BIS was opposed to investment in British Treasury bills. BIS Historical Archives, 2.2, vols. 3 and 4, DHM, "BIS Investments in UK Treasury Bills," July 5, 1956.
35 BIS Historical Archives, 2.2, vols. 3 and 4, Aide Memoire for Monsieur Guindey, February 26, 1959, Confidential.
36 BIS, *The Thirty-fourth Annual Report*, pp. 131–132.
37 NARA 450.81.12.01. box 169, General, vol. 1, F. Lisle Widman and Jerry H. Nisenson, "Transactions of the Bank for International Settlements," September 1, 1967. This report also drew attention to the fact that BIS gold deposits had increased by $200 million when emergency aid measures for sterling were implemented in June and July 1966 and then fell by $100 million, surmising that the majority of this gold or hard currency had been used to support sterling.
38 The proposal from Mandel was stated in a letter to the Swedish central bank's BIS representative director. BIS Historical Archives, 1/3a(3), Meeting of Experts [euro-currency market], correspondence, H.H. Mandel to Gunnar Akermalm, Manager, Sverigs Riksbank, December 3, 1963, personal and confidential.
39 BIS Historical Archives, 1/3a(3), Meeting of Experts [euro-currency market], correspondence, Banque de France, Direction Générale des Services Etrangers, Paris, le 19 décembre 1963, à Mr. Milton Gilbert.
40 BIS Historical Archives, Gabriel Ferras file, 7.18(10), FER 7, correspondence, Milton Gilbert to André de Lattre, Directeur des Finances Extérieures, Ministère des Finances, December 20, 1963.
41 BIS Historical Archives, 1/3a(3), Meeting of Experts [euro-currency market], correspondence, Gabriel Ferras to Yamagiwa Masamichi, Governor, Bank of Japan, January 23, 1964.
42 Ibid. Regarding the course of credit reforms underway in France at that time and the roles of neoliberal policy theory and Brunet in that process, see Yasuo Gonjo, "*Furansu ni okeru shinjiyushugi to shinyo kaikaki (1961–1973-nen)* [Neoliberalism and credit reforms in France (1961–1973)]," *Economia*, vol. 54, no. 2, 2003.
43 BIS Historical Archives, 1/3a(3), Meeting of Experts [euro-currency market], correspondence, Gabriel Ferras to Yamagiwa Masamichi, op. cit.
44 Archives of the Bank of England, c20–5, R.A.O.Bridge Papers, "Eurodollars," Confidential, May 1, 1963.

45 Archives of the Bank of England, c20–5, R.A.O.Bridge Papers, Extract from "International Reports" (Guenter Reimann) dated December 6, 1963; "Telephone Conversation with Mr. Magruder, First NCB re Ira Haupt," December 6, 1963.

46 BIS Historical Archives, Gabriel Ferras file, 7.18(19), FER 8, February 1, 1965, H.M., "Recent Eurodollar Development." Reporting countries referred to here were Belgium, Canada, France, West Germany, Italy, Japan, the Netherlands, Sweden, Switzerland and Great Britain.

47 Regarding measures to defend the dollar at this time, see Eiji Yamamoto, *Kijiku Tsuka no Kokan to Doru* [The Dollar and the Change In Base Currency], (Yuhikaku, 1988), and Ikuya Fukamachi, *Doru Hon'isei no Kenkyu* [Studying the Dollar Standard] (Nihon Keizai Hyoronsha, 1993).

48 Concerning the preconditions of the pound crisis, see Catherine Schenk, *Britain and the Sterling Area, From Devaluation to Convertibility in the 1950s*, Routledge, London, 1994.

49 BIS Historical Archives, 7.18(23), GILB 9, Organization for Economic Co-operation and Development, Council, Continuation of the European Monetary Agreement until the End of 1963, Final Report by the Board of Management of the E.M.A., restricted, Paris, January 21, 1963.

50 BIS Historical Archives, 7.18(23), GILB 9, Support arrangements (March/June 1963), £200 million deposited with the Bank of England on March 29, 1963 by the central banks of France, Germany, Italy and Switzerland, confidential (for internal use only); BIS Historical Archives, 2.2, vols. 3 and 4, "Bank of England, Conversation in Basel, MM.Bridge/Macdonald," October 11, 1964.

51 BIS Historical Archives, 7.18(23), GILB 9, Correspondence, F.G. Conolly to Charles Coombs, Personal, March 13, 1963.

52 BIS Historical Archives, 2.2, vols. 3 and 4, DHM, "Bank of England, Conversation in Basel, MM. Parsons/Macdonald" January 10, 1965. Parsons of the Bank of England recalled MacDonald in this conversation "did not seem to be greatly interested by it."

53 BIS Historical Archives, 2.2, vols. 3 and 4, DHM, "Bank of England, Telephone Conversation, MM. Bridge/Macdonald," January 11, 1965, 10.40 a.m.

54 BIS Historical Archives, 2.2, vols. 3 and 4, DHM, "Bank of England, Telephone Conversation, MM. Bridge/Macdonald," January 12, 1965, 5.05 p.m.

55 BIS Historical Archives, 2.2, vols. 3 and 4, DHM, "Bank of England, Conversation in Basel, MM. Bridge/Macdonald," March 7, 1965.

56 BIS Historical Archives, 7.18(23), GILB 9, Extract from the Report to Ministers and Governors by the Group of Deputies dated May 30, 1964 (pp. 15–17).

57 BIS Historical Archives, Gabriel Ferras file, 7.18(10) FER 8, Note, "Procedure for Multilateral Surveillance agreed by the Governors," November 8, 1964.

58 BIS Historical Archives, 2.2, vols. 3 and 4, DHM, "Bank of England, Telephone Conversation, MM. Bridge/Macdonald," January 12, 1965, 5.05 p.m., op. cit.

59 BIS Historical Archives, 7.18(23), GILB 9, Bilateral Concerté and Multilateral Surveillance, Dr. Gilbert, Dott. Rainoni, Dott. D'Aroma/Mr.Knapp, Confidential, April 14, 1965. This report featured a table on arrangements that had been ascertained under multilateral surveillance as of April 1, 1965, listing amounts of arrangements of each country with Britain and the United States. While the table covered BIS swaps with the United States, it did not cover the swaps with Britain touched on here.

60 Bank of Japan materials. The above statement by Bridge is recorded in English by the Bank of Japan staff member who prepared the document. MacDonald's impressions are based on information from a personal conversation with Bank of Japan representative Daisuke Hoshino following the meeting.

61 Bank of Japan materials.

62 Bank of Japan materials. Under the framework for support for sterling at this time, it

was planned that the BIS and each central bank taking part in the support would provide a credit line of $700 million over one year. NARA 450.81.12.01, box 169, General, vol. 1, Correspondence, Gabriel Ferras to Alfred Hayes, January 28, 1966, Confidential.

63 Bank of Japan materials. The BIS has kept the following records of the meeting held that same day: BIS Historical Archives, Gabriel Ferras file, 7.18 (10) FER 8, Note "Meeting of Experts on the Euro-Currency Market at the BIS," July 11–12, 1966, Confidential. The impressions described by Japan's representatives differ slightly from what is written in the BIS materials.

64 BIS Historical Archives, Gabriel Ferras file, 7.18 (10) FER 8, Note "Meeting of Experts on the Euro-Currency Market at the BIS," ibid.

65 Bank of Japan materials.

66 Bank of Japan materials.

67 Bank of Japan materials. Daisuke Hoshino, who took part in this meeting as a representative of Japan, noted in these materials his impression that "From speaking with MacDonald and Tungeler personally, they did not seem to be worried about the Eurocurrency markets at the end of the year."

68 Bank of Japan materials.

69 Bank of Japan materials. The Bank of Japan staff member who wrote this memo was Haruo Maekawa, who was later promoted to the position of Bank of Japan governor.

70 Bank of Japan materials.

71 Bank of Japan materials.

72 Bank of Japan materials.

73 Bank of Japan materials.

74 BIS Historical Archives, Gabriel Ferras file, 7.18 (10) FER 8, Note "Meeting of Experts on the Euro-Currency Market at the BIS," July 11–12, 1966, Confidential.

75 Ibid.

76 Bank of Japan materials.

77 NARA, 450.81.12.01, box 169, Letters to Finance Ministers, "Memorandum of Conversation," March 21, 1969. As of 1965, Gilbert did not see the US international balance of payments as being that much of a problem, and the BIS annual reports of which he was in charge also expressed optimistic outlooks concerning the US international balance of payments. NARA, 450.81.12.01, box 169, General, vol. 1, "Conversations with BIS Officials," May 14, 1965. For this reason, the severe criticism of the United States seen in this chapter began in the second half of the 1960s.

78 Milton Gilbert, *Quest for World Monetary Order: the Gold–dollar System and its Aftermath*, Twentieth Century Fund Study, New York, 1980, p. xiii.

79 Jacques Rueff, "Les Euromonnaies et la création monétaire," *Le Monde*, le 8 avril 1975, cité in Rueff, *OEuvres Complètes, III, Politique Economique 2*, Plon, Paris, 1980, pp. 315–325.

80 Jacques Rueff, *Balance of Payments, Proposals for Resolving the Critical World Economic Problem of Our Time*, McMillan, New York, 1967, p. xii.

81 BIS Historical Archives, 2/402, Policy, Bank of Tokyo, Visit of Mr. Goro Hara, June 9, 1954; Correspondence, Goro Hara to Konrad Thiersche, June 28, 1954.

82 BIS Historical Archives, 2/402, Policy, Bank of Tokyo, Service telex, Tohbank, November 25, 1963; Reply November 25, 1963, Interbank, etc.

83 BIS Historical Archives, 2/402, Policy, Bank of Tokyo, Bank of Tokyo, October 31, 1965; December 8, 1965. Visitors from the Bank of Tokyo were President Horie, London branch head Yokoyama, Hamburg resident office head Ando, and Zurich resident office head Tanaka. They were met by Gilbert, the Monetary and Economic Department head; Mandel, the Banking Department head; and Rainoni, the BIS general-affairs manager. Horie recalled "being allowed to attend BIS board meetings from time to time" when he was stationed at the London branch of the Yokohama Specie Bank in the years 1935–1937, "accompanying branch manager Hisaakira

Kano." Horie said he came to know central-bank governors of that time, such as Norman and Schacht, as well as later Bundesbank governor Blessing and Monetary and Economic Department head Jacobsson through these BIS board meetings. Shigeo Horie, *Watashi no rirekisho* [My Resume], (*Watashi no rirekisho* no. 34, Nihon Keizai Shimbun, 1968), pp. 253–255.

84 BIS Historical Archives, 2/402, Policy, Bank of Tokyo, December 8, 1965.

85 BIS Historical Archives, 2/402, Policy, Bank of Tokyo, "Bank of Japan, Conversation MM. Mayekawa/Mandel," December 12, 1965.

86 BIS Historical Archives, 2/402, Policy, Bank of Tokyo, "Deutsche Bundesbank, Francfort a/M., Conversation MM. Tungeler/Mandel," December 12, 1965.

87 BIS Historical Archives, 2/402, Policy, Bank of Tokyo, Service telex, Tohbank, November 20, 1967; Reply November 20, 1967, Interbank.

88 BIS Historical Archives, 2/402, Policy, Bank of Tokyo, "The Bank of Tokyo, Ltd. London," May 4, 1972. At this time, the fording-exchange department head, Asakura, and the Zurich branch managing director, Nikishima, visited from the Bank of Tokyo. At the end of the year, the Bank of Tokyo London branch telephoned the BIS to make an offer to accept dollar deposits. "The Bank of Tokyo, London" (Telephone Call Messrs. Kanbayashi/Stevenson) December 27, 1972.

89 BIS Historical Archives, 2/402, Policy, Bank of Tokyo, "Japanese Banks," December 13, 1972.

90 BIS Historical Archives, 2/402, Policy, Bank of Tokyo, "Visit to London" from January 29 to February 5, 1973, by Mr. R.G. Stevenson, February 8, 1973.

91 BIS Historical Archives, 2/402, Policy, Bank of Tokyo, "Visit to USA and Canada" from May 16 to June 8, 1973, by Mr. R.T.P. Hall and R.G. Stevenson, June 18, 1973.

92 Ibid. The transaction conditions agreed here involved an initial transaction amount with the branch (local subsidiary) of $75 million and no need for a guarantee by the parent bank.

93 BIS Historical Archives, 2/402, Policy, Bank of Tokyo, "Japanese Commercial Banks-limits," August 3, 1973, etc.

94 BIS Historical Archives, 2/402, Policy, Bank of Tokyo, "Visit to London" from February 16–20, 1976, by Mr. R.G. Stevenson and Sig. G. Panizzutti, February 24, 1976.

95 BIS Historical Archives, 2/402, Policy, Bank of Tokyo, "Visit to Tokyo, Kobe, Singapore, Jakarta, Bangkok and Karachi" from April 12–30, 1976, by Mr. R.G. Stevenson, May 4, 1976.

96 Regarding resolution of the reparations issue in international agreements during this period, see BIS Historical Archives, file 7/5, box 2/4a, "The Suspension of the Execution of the Young Plan and its Effects as Regards the BIS," May 6, 1967.

97 BIS Historical Archives, file 7.5, box 2/1, "Memorandum Concerning the Financial Results of the Thirteenth Financial Year ended March 31, 1966," May 9, 1966, p. 1.

98 BIS Historical Archives, file 7.5, box 3/1, "Adjustment of the Capital of the BIS and Amendment of its Statutes," April 14, 1969.

99 Calculated based on BIS, Rapport sur les operations de la Banque pendant le mois de mars 1959, annexe 214/C.

100 NARA 450.81.12.01. box 169, General, vol. 1, F. Lisle Widman and Jerry H. Nisenson, "Transactions of the Bank for International Settlements," September 1, 1967, op. cit.

101 BIS Historical Archives, file 7.5, box 2/2b, Note for the Governors of the Participating Central Banks, "The Bank's Profits," May 9, 1968. This measure involved cooperation among central banks holding seats on the board of directors to sell gold to the BIS, in order to enable the BIS to convert some of its profits to gold as it had done in the past. Without going through foreign-exchange markets, each country's gold on the balance sheet was exchanged for the dollar amounts corresponding to

some of the BIS's monthly profits, and gold is used in payment of dividends to shareholders (i.e., central banks) as well. This memo estimated that the total amount of gold that should be sold in accordance with each country's percentage of shares held as 7,200 kg per year, assuming that one-half of 48 million Gold Swiss francs in income were exchanged for gold. Ibid.

102 BIS Historical Archives, file 7.5, box 2/1, Memorandum Concerning the Financial Results of the Thirty-first Financial Year ended March 31, 1961, May 8, 1961, p. 1.

103 BIS Historical Archives, file 7.5, box 2/1, Memorandum Concerning the Financial Results of the Thirty-second Financial Year ended March 31, 1962, May 7, 1962, p. 1.

104 BIS Historical Archives, file 7.5, box 2/1, Memorandum Concerning the Financial Results of the Thirtieth Financial Year ended March 31, 1960, May 9, 1960, p. 1.

105 BIS Historical Archives, file 7.5, 1/7a, "Ways of Settling the Unpaid Cumulative Dividend," Confidential, January 9, 1960; file 7.5, 1/8a, Note for the use of the President, "A Few Remarks on the Desirability of Hidden Reserves," February 6, 1960.

106 BIS Historical Archives, file 7.5, box 2/1, Memorandum Concerning the Financial Results of the Thirty-seventh Financial Year ended March 31, 1967, May 8, 1967, p. 1.

107 BIS Historical Archives, file 7.5, box 3/1, Adjustment of the Capital of the BIS and Amendment of its Statutes, April 14, 1969. Hereinafter, information on the capital increase and statutes amendments in this fiscal year is from this source.

108 BIS Historical Archives, file 7.5, box 3/2, Adjustment of the Capital of the BIS and Amendment of its Statutes, July 7, 1969.

109 Toniolo, *Central Bank Cooperation at the Bank for International Settlements*, op. cit., pp. 403–404.

110 IMF Archives, Secretary's Circular, no. 63/48, Correspondence, Violet Jacobsson to Frank Southard, Basel, July 21, 1963.

6 Conclusions

1 For details on this point, see Yasuo Gonjo, *Fransu shihon shugi to chuo ginko* [French Capitalism and the Central Bank], op. cit., Holtfrerich *et al.*, eds., *The Emergence of Modern Central Banking from 1918 to the Present*, op. cit., etc.

2 It was Louis Rasminsky, governor of the Bank of Canada, who described the meetings of central-bank governors as useful for recuperative purposes. Toniolo, *Central Bank Cooperation at the Bank for International Settlements*, op. cit., p. 365.

3 In his official history, Toniolo breaks BIS history into four periods, characterizing the balance sheet in each period as a strong start (1930–1931), a rapid retreat in activities (1931–1946), a gentle recovery (1947–1958), and a long period of strong, largely unceasing expansion (1958–2000). Ibid., p. 651.

4 For ROA, the total amount available for allocation for the period from the official income statement is used as the numerator and the total value of BIS assets as the denominator. For ROE, the paid-in capital of BIS is used as the denominator. The calculations here are only rough approximations, due to the presence of hidden reserves as mentioned in this text and to changes in presentation methods in the BIS financial statements.

5 The expressions "FRB view" and "BIS view" are from Masaaki Shirakawa, *Gendai no kinyu seisaku: riron to jissai* [Modern Monetary Policy in Theory and Practice] (Nihon Keizai Shimbun Shuppansha, 2008). In connection with this, see William White, "Is Price Stability enough?" in *BIS Working Papers*, no. 205, April 2006. The author of this paper, White, is the recently retired fifth head of the BIS Monetary and Economic Department and a theoretical leader of the "BIS view."

6 Stated in an interview of Gudmundsson conducted by the author on August 28, 2007. Quotes from Gudmundsson hereafter are from the same interview.

Index